D1563552

METAMORPHOSES OF THE CITY

METAMORPHOSES OF THE CITY

On the Western Dynamic

Pierre Manent

TRANSLATED BY MARC LEPAIN

Harvard University Press

Cambridge, Massachusetts

London, England

2013

Originally published in French as *Les métamorphoses de la cité* by Flammarion,
© Flammarion, 2010

Library of Congress Cataloging-in-Publication Data

Manent, Pierre.
[Métamorphoses de la cité. English]
Metamorphoses of the city : on the Western dynamic / [Pierre Manent].
pages cm
"Originally published in French as Metamorphoses de la Cite by Flammarion, 2010."
Includes bibliographical references and index.
ISBN 978-0-674-07294-7 (alk. paper)
1. Cities and towns—History.   2. Cities and towns—Political aspects—History.
3. Municipal government—History.   4. Civilization, Western.   I. Title.
HT113.M3613 2013
307.7609—dc23   2013006902

CONTENTS

III

EMPIRE, CHURCH, NATION

METAMORPHOSES OF THE CITY

INTRODUCTION
The Dynamic of the West

We have been modern now for several centuries. We are modern and we want to be modern. This is the orientation of the entire life of our societies in the West. There is frequent criticism of this or that aspect of modernization, and some even criticize "modernity" as such, but "conservative" efforts have succeeded only in slowing the movement at most, while "conservative" endeavors in general have ended up accelerating the movement. And so we want to be modern. We give ourselves an order to be modern. But the fact that the will to be modern has been at work for centuries means that we have not yet arrived at being truly modern. The goal of the march that at several turns we thought we had reached showed itself to be misleading, a sort of mirage; 1789, 1917, 1968, 1989 were only deceptive stages on a road that leads we know not where. The Hebrews were lucky—they only wandered forty years in the wilderness. What does it mean if this will, this command to be modern, does not cease to remodel the conditions of common life, to make revolutions follow revolutions, without ever arriving at its fulfillment, without ever arriving at a point where we could rest and say, "here at last is the goal of our undertaking," if this will or command never grasps its object? How could we have *willed* for so long and allowed ourselves to be so often deceived? Is it, perhaps, that we might not know what we truly want?

As familiar as the signs or criteria of the modern may be for us, whether it is a matter of architecture, art, science, or political organization, we do not know what unites these traits or criteria and justifies our designating them by the same term. We are faced with a fact that resists explanation.

We are under a command that we have given ourselves and we ask ourselves just what exactly and finally it consists of.

Some are willing to give up questioning. They suggest that we have left the modern era to enter the postmodern era and that we have given up the "great narrative" of Western progress. I am not aware that we have given up on the great narratives of science or democracy. It is true that we experience a certain fatigue after so many modern centuries, but the question remains intact and its urgency is not dependent on the dispositions of the one who asks it. The question needs to be asked anew again and again, if at least we care to understand ourselves. And if we do not presume to provide a truly new answer, let us at least be ambitious in giving the question new life.

How are we to proceed? When it is not clear just what something is, one asks when and how it began. When and how did modernity begin? What was the genesis of modernity? Such are the questions we raise willingly and with good reason.

This is a legitimate and even necessary undertaking, but it immediately gives rise to difficulties. Beginnings are by definition obscure. The first shoots are difficult to discern. It is easy to be mistaken. Thus we seek clarity in beginnings that are necessarily obscure or uncertain. Is this work, this idea, this literary or architectural style, ancient or is it modern? At what moment will we begin to seek the beginning of modernity? In the eighteenth century, at the time of the American and French revolutions? In the seventeenth century, when the notion of natural science was developed? In the sixteenth century, at the time of the religious Reformation? How is one to answer? These diverse hypotheses are not contradictory; the constituent elements of modernity certainly include the religious Reformation, science that is specifically modern, and democratic political revolutions. But what connection is there between Luther's faith and Galileo's science? Might there be a sort of primary disposition, an intellectual and moral disposition that would define modern man? Or must one be resigned to the elements of the modern being dispersed, to a patchwork held together by the magic of a word?

Let us start with a single unquestionable point in the series of perplexities I have just laid out. We have wanted and we do want to be modern.

We do not need to know exactly what we want in order to know that, in so willing, we form a *project*. Modernity is in the first place a project, a collective project formulated in Europe, implemented at first in Europe, but intended from the beginning for all of humanity. Now, what is a project? A project is no small thing. If we first identify a bit more precisely what is implied in such a project, we will learn some important things about the modern project.

Forming a great collective project intended in the end for all of humanity calls first of all for great faith, in the sense of confidence in one's own strength. It is said that the strongest rule among us, but the fact is that people or groups that have confidence in their own strength are rare. One thing that is striking in the beginnings of modern science is the extraordinary confidence of Bacon or Descartes, to name but two, in the new science's capacity to radically transform the conditions of human life. What faith they had, what blind faith, one is tempted to say. Indeed, at the time, modern science had not yet produced any—or had produced hardly any—of its effects. The famous "miracles of science" were yet to come. Descartes imagined medicine prolonging human life prodigiously when the medicine of his time was incapable of curing anything and he himself had strange ideas about the circulation of blood.

A project presupposes that we are capable of acting and that our action is capable of transforming our situation or the conditions of our life. Many analysts of modernity have insisted on the second point, on the transforming ambition or the fabricating or constructivist ambition of the modern project. The transformation of nature, the organization of production, the Plan, humans producing themselves, the engineers of souls even—all this is very important. But we must not pass over the first point too quickly. We are capable of acting. A whole world is contained in that statement. Humans have always acted in some fashion, but they have not always known that they were capable of acting. There is something terrifying in human action. What expresses human beings is also what exposes them, makes them come out of themselves, and at times lose themselves. In the beginning people gather, fish, hunt, even make war, which is a sort of hunt, but they act as little as possible. They leave the greatest room for the gods, and they hamper themselves as much as possible by all sorts of prohibitions, rites, and sacred constraints. That is why human action, action that is properly human, appears at first as a crime, a transgression. This is precisely, according to Hegel, what Greek tragedy reveals: innocently criminal action. Tragedy tells what cannot be told, the passage from what precedes action to properly human action. It tells of the passage to the city, the coming to be of the city. For the city enables one to act. The city is that ordering of the human world that makes action possible and meaningful.

If we want to understand the modern project, we must understand it beginning with the first complete implementation of human action, which was the city. The Greek city is not the outcome of a project, to be sure, but it is in the city that people can deliberate and form projects of action. It is in the city that people discover that they can govern themselves and that they learn to do so. They discover and learn politics, which is the great domain of action.

Thus, if modernity is characterized first of all as a project of collective action, and if politics is the implementation and ordering of action, the modern project must in the first place be understood as a political project. It must be situated anew in the history of European and Western political development. The ambition of this book is to propose an interpretation, or at least the elements for an interpretation, of the political development of the West.

What are the proper characteristics of the history of the West? What is its formula, so to speak?

I have insisted on the modern *movement,* on modernity's character as movement, a movement that never arrives at its term, its resting place. There are great civilizations apart from the West, and many things take place there, but they have not known movement, historical movement. They had chronicles but no history, at least not before the pressure or aggression of the West made them enter history. There is in the West a singular principle of movement and that is what characterizes it above all.

The principle of Western movement is politics, and therefore the city. The movement of the West begins with the movement of the city. It has been said that the Greeks did not know history, that they had a cyclical understanding of time and that the linear time of history began with Christianity, or with the modern philosophy of history. That does not hold. The Greeks knew very well the irreversible time of political history. Aristotle was just as capable as Tocqueville of observing that democracy was in his time the only regime that was still possible.

The Western movement begins with the movement of the Greek city, the internal and external movement of the Greek city, of class struggle within and foreign war without. The city is the shaping of human life that made the common thing appear, the government of the common thing, and the execution of the common thing in a plurality of cities hostile to each other and divided within. The Greek city was the first form of human life to produce political energy. It was a deployment of human energy of unprecedented intensity and quality. It was finally consumed by its own energy in the catastrophe of the Peloponnesian War. Later history appears, in sum, as the ever-renewed quest for the political form that would permit the gathering of the energies of the city while escaping the fate of the city, of the city that is free but subject to internal and external enmity.

The form that succeeded the city was empire. The Western empire, by contrast with the Eastern empire, is a type of continuation of the city. The city of Rome deployed such powerful energies that it broke all the limits that circumscribed cities, as it joined to itself ever more numerous and distant populations to the point of seeming on the verge of assembling the whole human race. The Western empire surrendered the freedom of the city but promised unity and peace. It is a promise that was not kept or not entirely kept, but, as in the case of the city, the political and spiritual energies partially survived the fall of the form, and the imperial idea marked the West not only by the enduring prestige of the Roman Empire but also under an absolutely unprecedented form that is also proper to Europe, which is the Church, the catholic, that is, the universal Church, that seeks to gather all men in a new communion, more intimate than the closest-knit city, more extended than the vastest empire. Of all the political forms of the West, the Church is the one most fraught with promises since it proposes, as I have just said, a community that is once city and empire, but it is also the most disappointing because it never succeeds, and falls far short, in bringing about this universal association for which it has awakened the desire.

I have just reviewed the history of premodern Europe with the speed and delicacy of Attila. But my plunder would make a barbarian king turn green with envy. For I have assembled the elements of the situation that will condition the elaboration of the modern project. How can this situation be characterized? I will say simply that the Europeans of that time were divided among the city, the empire, and the Church. They lived under the mixed and competing authorities of these three modes of human association. The cities that subsisted or revived were in competition with, often at war with, the Roman Empire that became the Holy Roman Empire of the German nation, and the Church was in competition with the cities and the empire, which were in competition with it. This is an awful disorder, a conflict of authorities and loyalties. It is out of this confusion that the modern project seeks to take us and will effectively take us. The quarrel has to do with institutions, to be sure, but also, more profoundly, with the human type that must inspire human life. Whom is one to imitate? Must one follow the life of humble sacrifice for which Christ provides the model? Or must one rather lead the active and proud life of the citizen warrior who produced Rome and was produced by it? And among the pagans themselves, will we admire Cato, or Caesar? The Europeans did not know which city they wanted to or could inhabit; they did not know which man they wanted to or could be. It is in this radical perplexity and in order to confront it, that, I repeat, the modern project was born.

Let us try to identify a bit more precisely what this perplexity consists of. Because of those conflicting and competing authorities, the Europeans were assailed by prestigious and contradictory words—the words of the Bible, the words of the Greek philosophers, the words of Roman orators and historians—and they did not know which to retain and which to discard. Thus they did not know how to act, how to answer the question of what is to be done. Words and actions were disjointed or badly linked. The modern moment crystallized when the effort was engaged to join word to action and action to word more vigorously and more rigorously. This is just what the Reformation sought to do. The authority of the Word of God was divided between the Scriptures and the Tradition of the Church, but the Scriptures themselves were accessible only through the mediation of the Church, and in the first instance in the language of the Church, Latin. Luther wanted to attach the faith of the Christian to the Word of God immediately as it was found in the Scriptures by resolutely jettisoning the mediation of ecclesiastical authority and to do that by translating the sacred text into the language spoken and understood by the faithful. *Sola Scriptura,* Scripture alone.

But it was Machiavelli, at exactly the same time as Luther, who would formulate in the most general terms what goes to the heart of the problem and will be the principle of the solution, the *political* solution. The problem and the solution are contained in a few lines of chapter 15 of *The Prince:* "But since my intent is to write something useful to whoever understands it, it has appeared to me more fitting to go directly to the effectual truth of the thing than to the imagination of it. And many have imagined republics and principalities that have never been seen or known to exist in truth; for it is so far from how one lives to how one should that he who lets go of what is done for what should be done learns his ruin rather than his preservation."[1]

As can be seen, Machiavelli proposes to side with the way humans live effectively by discarding their imaginary republics and principalities because there is *tanto discosto,* such disparity, between what humans do and what they say. Now the greatest disparity between words and actions is introduced by the Christian Word, which asks humans to love what they hate naturally—their enemies—and to hate what they love naturally—themselves. Christianity introduced an unprecedented disparity between what humans do and what they say. Thus the modern political project, which Machiavelli was the first to formulate, was a response, in any case was in the first instance a response to a situation, the "Christian situation," marked by the competition of authorities, the disorder of reference points, the anarchy of words, and, above all, the demoralizing contrast between what humans say and what they do.

What then does it mean for Machiavelli to consider or follow "the effectual truth of the thing"? It is in any case a question of preparing the way for an action entirely liberated from the words that praise and blame, be they religious or other, for an action that cannot be hindered by any word, whether the external word of the institution or of opinion, or the internal word of conscience. The word that carries the greatest weight, and for that reason constitutes the greatest hindrance to action, is the word that says, "This is good; this is evil." It is the word that distinguishes good from evil. Machiavelli does not seek to annul this distinction. He does not confuse good and evil. But he endeavors to encourage humans to be prepared to do evil, to "be able not to be good," as he says, when it is necessary. Machiavelli endeavors to break the grip of these words that tell us what we should do, words that do not guide us since, in any event, we follow our nature and not our words, but that hinder our freedom to act by limiting for us the field of possible or contemplated actions. It is difficult to say what new political order Machiavelli envisaged concretely. Let us say that by delivering humans from all respect for any opinion, for any word, he was preparing them for every possible action, that he opened the way for every possible action, including the most daring and the most ambitious, and even the most terrible.

Of all the daring and ambitious actions that Europe witnessed, the one engaged in by the modern State is without doubt the most decisive. As I have said, Christianity renders uncertain the motives of action and doubtful the words that ought to be authoritative in the city. The "Christian situation" is characterized by the conflict of authorities. But the modern State—and this is how it becomes sovereign—resolves or overcomes this conflict by monopolizing the word that commands, more precisely and more boldly, by producing a command that is independent of every opinion, including and above all religious opinion, a command that authorizes and prohibits opinions according to its sovereign decision. The modern State, still uncertain of its strength, at first joined to itself a religious opinion or word, which was the State religion. Once it had attained its full strength, it raised itself above every word; it was truly without a word of its own. It became the "neutral," "agnostic," "secular" State that we know.

The State thus constitutes the first half of the solution to the problem of the disparity between word and action that is proper to the Christian world. The State has the right to prohibit and to authorize every word, and will prohibit less and less and authorize more and more. But the State is only half of the solution, precisely since—and this is the condition of its effectiveness—it has no word of its own. Human life cannot be without a word that is authoritative. Where will the modern State find this word? It will find the word, the pertinent word, the political word, in society, by becoming "representative" of society. The invention and the problem of modern politics, as is well known, is representation. Representation articulates the word of society to the action of the State that is without a word, or that has no word of its own.

That, then, is how the problem of Christian times was solved, the problem of the anarchy of authorities, of the disjunction and disparity between words and actions. It was solved by the sovereign State and the representative government of society. It is our political regime considered in its entirety that is the solution to the problem. It is not my concern here to describe the structure of the representative regime or simply to sketch its history. One point, however, needs to be underlined. The decisive factor of the junction or reconciliation between actions and words is the formation of a common word by the development, the refinement, and the diffusion of a national language. Luther's Reformation was a spiritual upheaval, but it was also and inseparably a political revolution, a national insurrection. This is what is so often forgotten: even before the modern State was consolidated and capable of effectively authorizing and prohibiting, the nation appeared in Europe as the framework for appropriating the Christian Word that the universal Church showed itself incapable of teaching effectively. The different European nations chose the Christian confession in which they wanted to live, and in sum imposed it, after a good many (often chaotic) turns of events, on their respective "sovereigns." With the "confessional nation," soon crowned with its absolute sovereign who would later be the operator of "secularism," Europe took its "classical" form in which it organized itself in the most stable and enduring manner, "solving" the problem posed by the "Christian situation" as much as a human problem can be solved. It is henceforth in the framework of a national civic conversation that Europeans essentially sought to join their words to their actions and their actions to their words. The national form preceded and conditioned the representative regime.

Such is the history that this book proposes to recount or rather to disentangle. Its concern is to lay bare the illuminating power of a carefully considered history of political forms. The history of the West unfolds in the tension between the civic operation, such as the Greek city gave birth to and that the republican or "Roman" tradition endeavored to preserve and to spread, and the Christian Word that, in proposing a new city where actions and words would attain an unprecedented unity and where one would live *in conformity with the Word,* opened a disparity between actions and words in political society that was impossible to master. In promising a perfect equation between action and word in the city of God, the Christian proposition opened an insurmountable disparity between actions and words in human cities. As I have stated, the practical solution of a confessional stamp was found in the nation, administered by a secular State, and governed by a representative government. But this solution had neither the energetic simplicity of the civic form nor the ambitious exactitude of the ecclesial form, and the West would not cease to search for a "solution" that would at last be complete and that would unite the energy of the civic operation and the exactitude of the religious proposition. Do not the regimes that are called "totalitarian," which are capable of joining the most chaotic and terrible action to the most pedantic ideological and linguistic orthodoxy, offer the monstrous but very recognizable expression of this ambition?

In Europe today, the civic operation is feeble and the religious Word almost inaudible. The two poles between which the Western arc was bent for so long have lost their force. As I said at the beginning, the modern project nonetheless continues to drift along. Does it obey only its own inertia, or is the European political structure I have just reviewed always in operation? It is without doubt not useless, in order to confirm the relevance of the viewpoint developed in these pages, to sketch a description of the present situation in Europe inasmuch as the rapport between word and action is concerned.

I have insisted on the importance of the national framework for the solution of the European or Christian problem. I have not yet mentioned a humbler but very important element of our regimes, which is the articulation of the word on action by majority decision. It was a common critique of representative democracy or the parliamentary regime that it multiplied words but was incapable of action. Lenin spoke of "parliamentary idiocy." Carl Schmitt willingly cited the sarcastic remarks of Donoso Cortès against the bourgeoisie, *clase discutidora*. In reality, a representative democracy, a parliamentary regime that functions, constitutes an admirable articulation of actions on words. In an election campaign, everyone proposes every imaginable action, whether possible or impossible. As soon as the election is won, those who obtained the majority undertake to act according to their words, while the minority, abstaining from any action, is content to speak in preparation for the next election. Alternation, or the effective possibility of alternation, is the heart of the mechanism.

Where are we? How do things stand with the political structure in which the modern project found its most satisfactory instrument? It seems to me that today in Europe this structure is considerably weakened and almost unrecognizable.

We congratulate ourselves on the attenuation of oppositions all the while we worry about the crisis of alternation. This is to congratulate and to worry ourselves over the same things. The political landscape has been leveled. The bonds of affects, opinions, words that shaped political convictions have been dissolved or are frayed. Henceforth one can no longer have access to the political terrain by occupying a position. That is why all the political actors speak all the words.

In recent times political speech has been progressively severed from any essential connection to a possible action. The notion of a program, reduced to "promises," has been discredited. The conviction has spread, whether explicit or tacit, that in any event one has no choice. What will be done will be dictated by circumstances over which one has no control. From then on political speech has no longer had the purpose of preparing a possible action but simply has conscientiously covered the field of political speech. Everyone or nearly everyone acknowledges that the final meeting of action and word will in sum be the meeting of independent causal chains.

This divorce between action and word contributes to explaining the novel role of "political correctness." Political correctness is a particularly significant aspect of the contemporary emancipation of speech. One no longer expects that speech will be linked to a possible action; thus it is taken seriously as though it was itself an action. Not being linked to a possible and plausible action that measures its purport, speech is willingly considered, if it is unpleasant, as the equivalent of the worst action imaginable. Thus one tracks those infamous words that are designated as "phobias" in clinical language. The progress of freedom in the West consisted of measuring words by the yardstick of visible actions. "Political correctness" consists of measuring words by the yardstick of invisible intentions.

The characteristics of the political situation in our countries that I have just recalled are to be found in an accentuated form in the European framework. What characterizes the European situation is that what we say as citizens has no importance whatsoever, since political actions will be decided in an indeterminate place, a place that we cannot situate in relation to the place from which we speak. The only thing that we might know is that these actions will be necessary. The actions that *appear* necessary are those that are not accompanied by any properly political word or over which the most solemn political words, such as a referendum, have no control. Everyone in Europe knows well that the most solemn word that a people can formulate, which is a referendum vote, is considered in advance with indifference by the European political class that deems itself charged with guiding the necessary process of European "construction." The supposed necessity of the process discredits and invalidates in advance any political word.

If the process continues, we will soon leave behind the representative regime to return to a command without word. This command will no longer be that of the State, which at least occupied an elevated place, but that of the *rule,* the rule of indeterminate origin. One does not know where the rule comes from, only that one must obey it. Thus the structure or process that imposes itself more and more in Europe is the following: actions on principle in conformity with a rule without word, words without relation to a possible action.

With the end or weakening of the representative regime that articulated actions and words in the national framework, the modern political order nears the end of its course. The sciences and technologies continue to run in their sphere, but they are more and more detached from the framework in which they found their meaning and their usefulness, when the modernization of national life in all its aspects was the evident and common task. We are witnessing a more and more profound divorce between the process of civilization and the political structure. The ever more complex and constraining order of ordinary life, the ever-tighter network of the rules we obey with ever-greater docility, must not blind us to the growing uncertainty, that is to say, the growing disorder of the form of common life. We are evolving, if I may say so, on thinner and thinner ice.

It seems that we are on the way to returning to a situation of political indetermination comparable in one sense to the one that preceded the construction of modern politics. But with a great difference, however. During the premodern period, there were too many competing political forms that hampered one another—I have mentioned the city, the empire, the Church—and so the new political form of the nation had to be invented. Today, it is in short the reverse. We observe not the excess but the dearth of political forms. At least in Europe, its native land, the form of the nation is discredited, delegitimized, without there being any other form in the process of being elaborated. Not only that, but the authoritative, if not unique, opinion has been hammering at us for twenty years that the future belongs to a delocalized or global process of civilization and that we have no need of a political form. Thus the necessity to articulate words and actions politically has been lost from view. The technological norm and juridical rule are supposed to be enough for organizing common life.

Europe produced modernity. For a long period of time Europe was its master and owner, putting it in the almost exclusive service of its power. But the transformative project in itself was intended for the whole of humanity. Today Bacon and Descartes reign in Shanghai and Bangalore at least as much as in Paris and London. Europe finds itself militarily, politically, and spiritually disarmed in a world that it has armed with the instruments of modern civilization. It soon will be wholly incapable of defending itself. It has for a long time been incapable of defining itself, since in the common European opinion it is confused with humanity itself on the way to pacification and unification. By renouncing the political form that was its own, and in which it had tried not without success to solve the European problem, Europe deprived itself of the association in which European life had found its richest meaning, diffracted in a plurality of national languages vying with one another for strength and grace.

For over three centuries "moderns" and "antimoderns" have made the European scene echo their disputes. In previous works I have given great attention to these disputes, elaborating an interpretation that made "modern democracy" the goal and heart of European development. The search for which I here provide the elements distances itself from this perspective that was "Tocquevillean" in more than one sense. The defect that I see in this procedure today, a defect from which Tocqueville himself is not immune, is to exaggerate the political and human transformation, the "anthropological" transformation that the progress of modern democracy brings with it. It appeared to me more and more clearly that the formation of the Greek city represented a much more substantial anthropological transformation, if one can use the term, than the modern democratic revolution, which moreover was in some sense built upon the Greek one. Instead of seeing history as facilely running toward us, toward the grandeur and miseries of our democracy, I saw it more and more clearly unfolding starting from the prodigious innovation that was the first *production of the common,* something much more substantial and moreover much more interesting than the virtues and vices of our too-famous equality. I saw more and more clearly the forms of our common life unfolding from the first and master form as so many reverberations of this original conflagration, as so many metamorphoses of this primordial form.

I

THE ORIGINAL EXPERIENCE OF THE CITY

1

WHAT SCIENCE FOR THE CITY?

Greek Science and Greek Experience

As we take up the great question of the political development of the West, it is necessary to briefly take stock of our tools of knowledge. To sum up the resources of our workshop, we have at our disposal two political sciences, the ancient and the new, namely, Greek political science and modern political science. The latter could be called European since it was elaborated from the sixteenth to the eighteenth centuries, principally by the Italians, the British, and the French.

In Greek political science, politics and the science of politics came to light together, and for the first time. This conjoining is what defines its founding character. "Together" here does not mean "simultaneously." The development of Greek political science was posterior to the beginnings of Greek civic or political experience, and was even contemporaneous with the decline of this experience. "Together" means that politics and the science of politics appeared in the framework of one and the same experience that in this way came to know itself. The Greek experience was that of self-government, and therein lay its political character. This unprecedented experience attained self-knowledge in a new science, *political science,* as it was elaborated in the works of Thucydides, Plato, and Aristotle. The twofold Greek foundation brings out in a particularly instructive manner the circle within which we will not cease to struggle: political science is science of political experience, but science and experience are distinct and at the same time inseparable. Whence the question: in what measure does science complete experience, which without it would remain mutilated or confused? Or on the contrary does it falsify experience by illuminating it with a light that is no longer that of political experience, properly speaking?

In any case the Greek experience unfolded in a definite framework, which was that of the city. This framework was the condition for the possibility of the experience. Self-government presupposes the city; politics in its full and original sense presupposes the *polis*. This is the meaning of Aristotle's sentence that sums up Greek political science: "Man is a political animal." Since the city was, according to the Greeks, the political form most in conformity with the nature of humanity, or even the only truly natural one, the Greek analysis not only of political life properly speaking but of moral life and in general of human life is an analysis of the life of humans in the city. In the eyes of Greek thinkers, the human phenomenon reveals itself first of all and most eminently in the city. We could say that the *things in themselves* are the political things.

We must take stock of what this means for us who have long since ceased to live in cities. This means that in the eyes of Europe's first political science, our moral life is necessarily mutilated, for, since the end of the city we no longer achieve the highest possibility inscribed in our nature; we fall short of our potential. The original political experience that ushered in the series of our political experiences, the one that continues to inspire them, has become strangely inaccessible. In a great variety of forms, this feeling of shortcoming or loss has been with us for centuries. In any case, the effort to know ourselves requires the most rigorous examination possible of our relationship to this original experience, and so first of all the most rigorous examination possible of this experience itself.

The city, the *polis*, is the first *political form*. It is the condition for the production or the matrix of a new form of life, political life, in which men govern themselves and know that they govern themselves. This form of life can take diverse forms, for there are different ways of self-government. The city opens the possibility of a self-government that actualizes or concretizes itself according to a particular mode, according to a particular *regime*. Greek political science, the science of the city, came to light as the *science of regimes*, the science of the different ways of self-government in the city. As we shall see in detail, the regimes are distinguished according to the *number* of those who govern. Governors can be *one,* or *few,* or *many.*[1] From this arises the interest of Greek political science in classifying regimes as monarchy, oligarchy, democracy, and so on. Indeed, Greek political science manifests a subtlety in analyzing political regimes that has not been equaled.

Yet, as we know well and I have just recalled, the form of the city eventually disappeared. The primary framework of Greek political analysis ended by disappearing. What will become of the science of regimes when the framework for the deployment of the diversity of regimes is no longer available? Human association in fact took other forms than that of the city, other forms that must be taken into account. Greek political science is the science of the first experience of politics, thus the first political science. It has little to say about political forms other than the city since those other forms, at least those that interest us most, appeared after the decline or the end of the city and in some way as successors to it. The inquiry I am undertaking deals principally with *political forms,* those modes of human association that no science has taken as its specific object but whose succession orders the movement of European history.

The Greek authors were not unaware that political forms other than the city existed, even if they showed little interest in them. They knew very well at least two other political forms, namely, the tribe—*ethnos*—and the empire (in particular the Persian Empire, which more than once imposed itself on their attention). A fourth form could be added, that of the tribal monarchies such as those in Epirus and Macedonia.[2] This is enough for instructive comparisons, but the Greek thinkers assumed them more than they developed them, or only very expeditiously. The most significant text on this score without doubt is found in the *Politics* of Aristotle:

> The nations in cold locations, particularly in Europe, are filled with spiritedness, but relatively lacking in thought and art; hence they remain freer, but lack [political] governance and are incapable of ruling their neighbors. Those in Asia, on the other hand, have souls endowed with thought and art, but are lacking in spiritedness; hence they remain ruled and enslaved. But the stock of the Greeks shares in both—just as it holds the middle in terms of location. For it is both spirited and endowed with thought, and hence both remains free and governs itself in the best manner and at the same time is capable of ruling all, should it obtain a single regime.[3]

Thus, the city is the best political form, because Greek civic life combines the freedom of the tribes of the North and the civilization of the Asiatic empires. It is the political form that unites the two great qualities of humans in society, qualities that are otherwise distributed between two distinct and so to speak opposed political forms. It is worth noting that Aristotle makes a necessary link between the internal freedom of the city and its domination over its neighbors. Civic freedom, no doubt because it encourages the deployment of human powers (but Aristotle does not explain this point here), naturally produces domination over neighboring populations whose capacities are constrained in their development by the defects of collective organization. Herein appears a very marked difference between the Ancients and ourselves. We always presuppose and affirm that freedom, in order to be authentic, must be equal and so to speak reciprocal, that a people that oppresses another people cannot be free. The Greeks thought, on the contrary, that the more a city is free, the more it naturally rules those that are less free. Athens was, without excessive qualms of conscience, the imperialist city par excellence. At the end of the passage, Aristotle seems to envisage a sort of general domination of the Greeks, a domination over "all," if only they would achieve a unified political organization—*mia politeia*. These two words are not enough to allow us to give even a modest interpretation of Aristotle's thinking. Does Aristotle envisage a federation of Greek cities? In that case the term *politeia* (which designates the regime, the constitution of the city) does not seem appropriate. Does he envisage a fusion of Greek cities in a new body politic bound by one regime or one constitution? In that case the term *politeia* could be appropriate, but it would mean that Aristotle abjured so to speak his entire political science as he deployed it in the *Politics* where the city, with its limited dimensions, is the only political form that allows, as we have just seen, the marriage of freedom and civilization. In truth, we do not know what "construction of Greece"—as we speak of a "construction of Europe"—Aristotle envisages here, or even if he envisages anything of the kind. Some have seen in these two words an allusion to the empire of Alexander, but this suggestion is the more arbitrary in that this empire never had a consistency approaching that of a *politeia*. Thus, this passage that, in the *Politics,* comes the closest to a comparison of political forms shows us instead how Aristotle glosses over the matter, how he insists on the unique excellence of the city to the point of passing over in silence the action of his former student Alexander, who was in the process of shattering the conditions of Greek life. One could say, to conclude these remarks, that Greek political science, which was very well aware of political forms other than the city, "wanted to see" only the city, not by "conservative reflex," an arbitrary attachment to the accustomed form, but because it was only in the city, in the mirror of the city, that it could see, and allow us to see, the human phenomenon in all its breadth and wholeness.

Modern Political Science

I emphasized the importance of the fact that in Greece politics and the science of politics, experience and the interpretation of experience came to light together, or at least in a proximity and intimacy that were never to be found again. Modern political science—the one that is not Greek[4]— will on the contrary always find itself confronted with the necessity of *deliberately* joining these two aspects that in Greece were joined *naturally*. It must be elaborated in a world where *there already is* an authoritative political science, that of the Greeks, especially Aristotle's. Modern political science will thus necessarily have a very deliberate and "constructed" character. I seek in vain for the proper adjective to give an idea of this specific effort that modern political science must make to bring together science and political experience. In any case, this effort necessarily encounters the alternative of whether to bear more (or first of all) upon science or more (or first of all) upon experience. Of course, the choice between the two ways is not arbitrary. It is conditioned in every epoch by the relative situation of science and experience.

Two great versions of modern political science can be distinguished accordingly, one that emphasizes science and one that emphasizes experience.

It is not difficult to surmise what style of political science, which doctrines, which authors fall into the first category. Modern natural right, the political science of Hobbes, Spinoza, and Locke, is insistently and even emphatically presented as demonstrative. These philosophers propose a political science that is as or even more demonstrative than mathematics, more precisely geometry. They oppose this rigorous science to the empirical and inaccurate science of the Ancients, encumbered with prejudices, that does not deserve to be called science. This global rejection of ancient science does not exclude distinctions made within this science. One can say that the founders of modern political science prefer Plato to Aristotle, or are less harsh toward the one than the other. One reason is surely that the doctrine of the Church, which they wish to dismantle, was built with elements borrowed from Aristotle rather than Plato; but the other reason, as Hobbes makes explicit, has to do with the emphasis Plato places on science, or pure science as distinct from experience, because it resides, so to speak, entirely in the mind of the knower.[5] Plato's noetic effort, with its wrenching force and its upward thrust, provides an anticipation or a sketch of the inaugural act of modern political science, which, through eliminating all real communities as so many insubstantial appearances, fixes its gaze on a purely abstract being, the individual out of which—out of whose rights and power—a political order that at last is rational can be constructed.

The preference for science and the emphasis on science to the detriment of experience were conditioned, although not determined, by the actual political experience of the historical period that we are considering, chiefly the seventeenth century. If our philosophers elaborated a pure, "geometric" science, if they reconstructed the edifice of political science from the starting point of science and not from contemporary political experience, it was because this experience presented to them characteristics that ruled it out as a foundation. We know what renders modern political experience useless for modern political science. It is that it is not a political experience or rather that modern political experience is so mixed with another experience, an apolitical or even antipolitical experience, that one can no longer speak properly of political order among the moderns. This apolitical or antipolitical experience is obviously the Christian experience. The human phenomenon is no longer to be seen wholly in the mirror of the city; behind the political city looms another city, filled with mysteries but also with power, and the two cities intermingle—that is, they are one and two at the same time—to such a point that citizens have the feeling of "seeing double." What solid science can one construct on such a split experience, or on the experience of a life so split in two or divided? One must then wrench oneself away from this irremediably confused experience and begin by elaborating a radically new political order in the pure realm of science.

But it will be said that these authors—Hobbes, Spinoza, and Locke—are the architects of the modern State, the guiding spirits of modern politics. If they have been so influential, it is because their science has some relation to the experience of modern man. It was not so pure as that. To be sure, their science would have been neither valid nor effective if it had not been grounded in experience, if it had not been in some fashion science of experience. But of what experience? Of a human experience certainly, but not a political experience. It was more precisely the experience humans have when they are deprived of political order, or when this order is greatly disturbed. Modern political science, in its founding movement, overcomes the grave deficiencies of modern political experience, the absence so to speak of an authentic political experience in the Christian world, by forging access to a prepolitical human experience on the basis of which it will be possible to construct a new political order. In fact, on the basis of the state of nature, of the human experience of the state of nature—that is, of the terrible vulnerability of the individual reduced to his or her own forces—there were constructed first of all the theory or science, and then the reality or practice of the modern State. Such was the first version of modern political science with its impressive fruitfulness.

This political science is thus first of all the science of a pre- or apolitical experience. To be fully science, science certain of itself, it must first of all assure itself of this experience, verify and warrant it. The only way to do this is finally to produce it. In order to firmly grasp its object, modern political science, at least in this version, must begin by producing the apolitical or prepolitical experience of the individual placed in the apolitical or prepolitical condition of the state of nature. Thus it posits this individual, defines it as the source of all political legitimacy, and produces it as follows: on the one hand, as a member of a State ruled by law, in which all individuals are equal in rights, that is, all equidistant from the State; on the other hand, as a member of civil society, in which all individuals are equal in rights; that is, they are all equally authorized to assert their independence as they see fit in that society. Thus, by means of a State that protects equal rights, modern political science in this version transforms the state of nature, that is, the state where the risks are equal, into the society of the equality of opportunity.

I have said enough about this first version of modern political science, the one that emphasizes science, the one that constructs the modern

State in such a way that it produces the free individual as a replacement for the citizen of the ancient city who was alternatively the one commanding and the one commanded. Let us now come to the second version, the one that criticizes ancient political science because of the limits of the Greek experience, thus in the name of a larger and more complex political experience.

The most characteristic and most eminent representative of *this* modern political science is without any doubt Montesquieu. Since I do not have the leisure to present his doctrine, I limit myself to three remarks:

1. In *The Spirit of the Laws,* Montesquieu directly takes to task ancient political science, naming and shaming Aristotle in particular. According to Montesquieu, Aristotle and ancient political science "had no clear idea of monarchy" (11.8) or "could not achieve a correct idea of monarchy" (11.9). In the narrow space of the city, where the people were "enclosed" (11.11), the monarchy could not deploy its true nature. It was only with the dispersion of the Germanic tribes across the Roman Empire that they had conquered (11.8) that the monarchy was able to deploy all of its possibilities, in particular its ability to accommodate "the true distribution of the three powers in the government of one alone" (11.9). Thus the political regime called monarchy only fulfills its nature— its "idea"—in the framework of a political form the Ancients did not know. Ancient political science, which culminates in the classification of regimes, must be carefully corrected if one wants it to embrace modern political experience. The new classification will be a classification of political forms at least as much as political regimes.[6]

2. Modern political experience comprehends not only the development of national monarchies and of "Gothic government" after the collapse of the Roman Empire. It also encompasses the development of a process whose causes are obscure, but whose political *effects* are beyond questioning: commerce, which softens mores. It suffices for our purpose to underline that commerce can make people communicate who have nothing in common, in particular who do not belong to the same political community. The principle of commerce being the independence and self-interest of each, this princi-

ple is in brief contrary to that of the city, which lies "in living with others, and in sharing words and deeds."[7] Thus, observing the mechanism and the effects of commerce brings out the limits of ancient experience, and even more, of the ancient science of politics that is so preoccupied with self-sufficiency.

3. One could say that the ancient city, because of its size and more generally its form, produced the compression and almost the fusion—through "politicization" in the proper meaning of the term—of elements of human life that, in other political forms, find themselves distinguished and even separated. In those forms it seems that politics ceases to be the determining and synthetic authority to become one parameter among others of social life. As a consequence, the science of human things is no longer found in the synthetic science of the government of humans—the political science of the Ancients—but rather in the analytical science of the diverse parameters of the human or social world, or in the plurality of the analytical sciences—the "human" or "social" sciences—charged with exploring the diverse parameters separately. *The Spirit of the Laws* is the document that testifies to this "epistemological revolution" and that argues for it. At the same time, Montesquieu is more concerned than his sociological or anthropological successors will be to maintain or to retrieve on new foundations the primacy of the political order.

The remarks I have just made concern more than the history of political science. It is easy to recognize the two versions of modern political science in the theory of democracy on the one hand, and in the social sciences on the other, namely, in the two great genres of contemporary reflection concerning our common life.

The theory of democracy accepts as axioms the basic propositions of the science elaborated by Hobbes and Locke, and to a certain extent Rousseau. Technically, it is a reprise, a refinement, if one wishes, of the contractualist doctrines. It suffices to mention the name of John Rawls. Concerning the foundation, as I have just suggested in my use of the term "axiom," the theory of democracy, unlike the original contractualist doctrines, does not seek to justify its principal theses against other possible theses. Rather, it receives or accepts them as evidences—not philosophical evidences in the Cartesian sense of the term, but as political evidences: who would dare to seriously challenge the principles of modern democracy? Hobbes, Locke, and Rousseau justified their theses, founded them on a certain interpretation of the state of nature, that is, ultimately of human nature. There is nothing of this among the theoreticians of democracy who reject any kind of "foundationalism." As it has been remarked, the "original situation" of Rawls is the state of nature *without* nature. Indeed, the proponents of the theory of democracy rely with confidence on our experience of democracy, on the general satisfaction that accompanies it and that renders a serious attempt at justification superfluous. The surprise then is that the version of political science that emphasizes science in relation to experience, the one that places its demonstrative rigor in the forefront even if it means devaluing experience and setting aside all facts, has today come to draw most of its strength from our contemporary experience, not to say our prejudices.

As for the second version, if it is less unfaithful to its origins, if the contemporary human sciences are less unfaithful to Montesquieu than the theory of democracy is unfaithful to Hobbes or Rousseau, it nonetheless remains that they have abandoned the primacy of the political that Montesquieu had maintained. Montesquieu, it is true, had in some way given them carte blanche when he had written in *The Spirit of the Laws* that "many things govern men" (19.4), thus making government, properly speaking, one government among other governments, one thing or one cause among others. (For Greek political science, only humans, properly speaking, govern humans.)

Thus, the two great versions of modern political science, so impressive and convincing in their founding moment, have ended up today as their contraries. Rigorous science lives only from the unofficial support of experience and is no longer science; the sciences that deliberately take their bearings from the breadth and diversity of human experience have abandoned politics, or have reduced it to one parameter among others, and are no longer political. Thus, on today's menu we have only a choice between a political science—the theory of democracy—that is not scientific, and a political science—the human sciences as a whole—that is not political. It is natural to desire to escape these alternatives.

The Three Natures of the City

How shall we proceed? Since in the end we find ourselves before two alternatives, neither of which we can choose, we need to return to the point of departure. We need to boldly go back to the first and founding polarity and pitch our base camp in that uncertain and decisive zone where the ancient experience and the ancient science of politics, that is, the experience and science of the city, are articulated, so as to attempt to extract the constitutive elements of our political condition. It will soon appear that the ancient science of politics is pluralistic.

To the question, what is a city? it is tempting to reply equally or indifferently that it is a "big family" or a "little world." These are the illusions that are inseparable from the city. In reality, the city cruelly or imperiously subordinates the family and the world. It takes young men from their families living, and brings them back dead. It declares the world, the unknown beyond the walls of the city, enemy territory where one does not venture unarmed.

These very simple remarks allow us to extract three elements, not three "perspectives" or "viewpoints" on the city, but in truth the three "natures" of the city:

- Its *tragic* nature, as it appears in its conflicting rapport with the family, the families from which it issues. This is the city according to its birth, the city inasmuch as it is born and as it signifies a second birth for its members. *Birth* is one of the meanings of the notion of nature.
- Its *philosophic* nature, in the measure that it arouses and constrains the desire to accede to the world without borders, the pure world that is beyond the city. This is the city according to its ultimate end, or the end that is beyond it. *Finality* is one of the meanings of the notion of nature.
- Between birth and end, there is the city according to its own life, forgetful of its prepolitical birth as well as of its metapolitical end, the city according to its *political* life, according to the *movement* of its political life—of internal struggle and external war—the movement of its life that leads it naturally to death. What has in itself the principle of its *movement* is natural.

The first nature is explored by Sophocles and the other Greek tragedians; the second by Plato and Aristotle; the third by Thucydides, and also by Plato and Aristotle. The three Greek approaches to politics thus define not a plurality of "perspectives" or "viewpoints" but much more the very articulations of the human world once this world is grasped and determined by the political form, the form of the city.

We can now return to the question of political science and conclude this lengthy introduction. I have just suggested that the Greek sciences of the city are also, and perhaps above all, sciences of the limits of the city: its birth, its finality, its life in its movement toward death. Where Montesquieu saw the limits of Greek political science, perhaps one should rather see the science of the limits of the city. But that means that we can do justice, more easily than we thought, to Montesquieu's legitimate demand, and more generally that of the modern social or human sciences. If we understand the city according to its limits, we place ourselves in a position to understand the possibility, perhaps the necessity, of the other political forms. More precisely, by keeping before us both the ancient science of the city and its limits as well as the later experience of other political forms, we open for ourselves the possibility of a more complete science. We then consider the city in the perspective of its death and metamorphosis into other political forms and we consider the succession of political forms as a commentary on and an illustration of not only the potentialities of the city but its limits as well.

I am not here proposing a third political science that would be the sum or synthesis of the ancient and the modern. The approach I will attempt to develop belongs, I hope, to ancient political science, not because it is ancient but because it is political and it alone is wholly political; that is, it is wholly science of the government of humans by humans. According to this science, the state of human things results principally from the deliberations and actions of humans, whereas modern political science, even in the most "liberal" authors, such as Montesquieu, tends to make us the playthings of "causes" that "govern" us. The human world is formed by the way people govern themselves: it is in the city, in the city-form, that people came to know this.

2

THE POETIC BIRTH OF THE CITY

Homer and Philosophy

After what we have said of the three "natures" of the city, it is natural to begin with its first nature, with its poetic "birth," or with its birth as displayed and analyzed by poetry. Poetry here is meant to include epic and tragedy, since comedy does not give us the birth of the city but an image of its life and perhaps of its decline.

Epic and tragedy have in common that they "imitate noble actions" (*Poetics*, 1448b25), that they are "an imitation of people who are to be taken seriously" (1449b10), whereas comedy is "an imitation of persons who are inferior" (1449a31–32).[1] In effect, epic is the matrix of tragedy in that Homer is the father of "serious" poetry (1448b34), the author of two epic poems that not only furnished the matter or inspiration of numerous tragedies, but that moreover are in themselves "dramatic imitations" (1448b35–36). In the tenth book of the *Republic* Plato deliberately joins Homer with the other "tragic poets" (605c11) and states precisely that Homer was "the most poetic and the first of the tragic poets" (607a2–3).[2]

The difference between epic and tragedy lies in epic "having its verse unmixed with any other and being narrative in character" (1449b11), whereas tragedy presents characters actually engaged in "action" (1449b26). Tragedy's principal superiority, according to Aristotle, is that the tragic fable is more unified and visible; thus it is more "concentrated" than the epic narrative. In matters of art as in those of nature, there is a certain "dimension" that makes them susceptible of being encompassed "in a single view [eusunopton einai]" (1451a4 and also 1459a33). Now, Homeric epic is, so to speak, as concentrated, as "synoptic," as a tragedy. The *Odyssey* and the *Iliad* are constructed around "a unified action [peri mian praxin]" (1451a28).

We could go on with the list of praises that Aristotle showers on Homer. We have said enough to justify starting our inquiry into the poetic birth of the city, the birth of the city as poetry gives us access to it, with Homer, or more precisely with some reflections on the *Iliad*.

But how could Homer give us access to the birth of the Greek city? In gathering oral traditions around the year 725 B.C., he gives voice to a state of Greek life that is, however one situates it in time and place, clearly prior to or different from civic life as such. The first to hear the Homeric poems as we know them were probably citizens of the Greek cities of Ionia, but the narrative that enchanted them spoke of a life very different from their own. How in these conditions could Homer be considered by the enlightened opinion of the cities as the educator of Greece, not in a general and so to speak decorative sense, but in the precise and rigorous sense of a master to whose teaching one should conform all the actions of one's life?[3]

Whatever the uncertainties weighing on Homeric chronology and the history of Greece before the development of the cities or at their beginnings, there is no doubt that the *Iliad* and the *Odyssey* constitute the spiritual base of their development. I have many times emphasized how Greek civic experience formed the original experience of Europe, or at least one of the two great constitutive experiences of the European spirit; it is in any case the original *political* experience of Europe, which incudes reflection on this experience itself. To speak of Homer as educator of the city means that there was an experience prior to the experience, an origin prior to the origin. Before there was the city there was the educator of the city.

But what does "educator of the city" mean? What does "educator" mean? The answer to be sure is elusive, since in short all of Greek life is an immense and complex endeavor to provide this answer, to attain clarity regarding what *paideia* truly is. We recall, however, that in book 2 of the *Republic*, when Socrates and his companions begin to examine the question of the education of the guardians of the just city, when they order themselves to "educate these men in speech [logô païdeuômen tous andras]" (376d10), and somewhat solemnly raise the question, "what then will be their education? [tis oûn è païdeia]" (376e2), their first step is to call into question the stories that mothers and nurses tell children and that "are, as whole, false" (377a5). Now, these nurses' stories are not invented separately in each family but are tales common to the households of Greece that were elaborated by Hesiod, Homer, and the other poets (377d). The greatest falsehood in these stories is obviously the one that bears on the most important beings, namely the gods (377e6–7). Socrates gives some examples of the inadmissible things that Hesiod and Homer, or other poets, said about the gods. We will be following Plato's suggestion if we say that Homer as well as Hesiod established "models for speech about the gods [oï tupoï peri theologias]" (379a5–6), models that are false or distorted and that ought to be corrected. It is first of all as a "theologian," then, or as a poet of "theologies" that Homer was the educator of Greece.[4]

It is difficult for us to take these passages of the *Republic* altogether seriously, for two opposed reasons. On the one hand, we are shocked that Socrates should presume to correct Homer (we will be even more shocked when in book 10 he will want to expel him from the city), since this seems to us to impugn the high idea we have of poetry, to imply a lowering of its lofty status. On the other hand we find it hard to believe that Homer and Hesiod were really the authors of Greek religion, since this seems to us beyond their power and beyond the power of poetry. Spontaneously sociological as we are, we think that the religion of all can have no other author but "all." For these two contrary motives, our too lofty or rather too delicate idea, and our too modest estimate of poetry, we are inclined to deplore or simply to neglect Plato's "polemic." Yet, it seems here that Plato hangs his critique on an appeal to what in the eyes of informed Greeks was a historical fact that was at least probable. Herodotus instructs us very clearly in this matter:

> But whence these gods came into existence, or whether they were for ever, and what kind of shape they had were not known until the day before yesterday, if I may use the expression; for I believe that Homer and Hesiod were four hundred years before my time—and no more than that. It is they who created for the Greeks their theogony; it is they who gave to the gods the special names for their descent from their ancestors and divided among

them their honors, their arts, and their shapes. Those who are spoken of as poets before Homer and Hesiod were, in my opinion, later born. The first part of this that I have said is what the priestesses at Dodona say, but the latter, as concerns Homer and Hesiod, is my own statement.[5]

Eric Voegelin comments on this passage as follows: "From this text two pieces of information can be extracted. In the first place, the Hellenes knew that the order of their gods was of recent origin and could not be traced beyond the age of the epics. The time span surmised by Herodotus places the event, at the earliest, in the ninth century B.C. And second, they were convinced that the myth had not grown anonymously over a long period of time, but had been created by definite persons, the poets."[6]

All of this is very important, not only for what it teaches us about Homer and about Greece, but also because this eminent example alerts us to the fact that there is no collective intellectual or spiritual invention, but that it is individual human beings who are the primary cause of human works, even if the record has not left us distinct particulars of dates and places of birth and death, biography, physiognomy, and so on. Let us not be as obtuse as Polyphemus who, when he was asked, "Who is doing that?" answered that it was "Nobody!" That is just what we say when to the question of who fashioned the *Iliad* or Homeric religion, we answer that it was Mycenaean or Pelasgian or Aegean civilization, it was this or that collective name. That Homer and Hesiod elaborated the theology of the Greeks encourages us to dedicate ourselves to our own task, which is to attempt to understand what they did. There is in what they did a meaningful statement that is up to us to receive and to clarify.

This meaningful statement is a certain description of the human world, of the human order (including its disorder). In this order, the gods play a great role; they are the guarantors and in the end they are the authors. The power of Zeus, father of all things, is irresistible. The human order is a subordinate part of the divine order. At the same time, the human world penetrates the divine world, human passions stir the goddesses and gods, which prompts the Socratic demand to correct the "models of theology" and incites us to regard the divine world rather as an extension, an amplification—of course, a poetic one—of the human world. If we speak in very general terms, there is in the Homeric text much material to justify a "religious" reading as well as a "humanist"

reading of the poems that educated Greece. Whether we adopt one reading or the other will not lead us far, or rather on the contrary it will lead
us too far too quickly.

By so mixing humans and gods, by holding on the one hand that humans do nothing important that is not in the end accomplished by the
gods, that their victories are the work of the gods, or on the other hand
that the gods are moved only by human motives, or motives indistinguishable from human ones, Homer means to say something that would
be immediately lost in a religious interpretation as well as in a humanist
interpretation. We can attempt to draw closer to this "something."

To orient themselves in the world before the development of philosophy and the sciences, humans had recourse to a tripartite division that
we can say was universal: animals, humans, gods. This prephilosophical
regime—I am tempted to say this "natural" regime—of the human mind
is characterized by a twofold undertaking that appears to us necessarily
contradictory. On the one hand, one proceeds by disjunctions: what characterizes humans is that they *are not* animals and also that they *are not*
gods; humans are characterized by what they *are not*. On the other hand,
the dynamic law of this tripartite world is the *metamorphosis* of animals, humans, and gods transforming themselves into one another—a
god with the head of a dog, a human with the body of a horse, and so on.
The three great elements of the world exist only in becoming what they
are not, or in joining themselves to what they are not. The philosophical
revolution, under whose mysterious empire we still live, perhaps more
and more, consisted in saying that a thing is what it is, that it exists in
conformity with its definition, or the definition of the class to which it
belongs. The philosophical revolution consisted in saying that a thing—
animal, human, god—is its being, or its essence, or its definition. What
do being, essence, definition mean? We are still seeking, but once the
philosophical proposition has been advanced that each being is what it
is, that each being is its essence, the natural world of disjunctions and
metamorphoses, the natural world of the "mythologies" is condemned
to disappear more or less quickly, but irresistibly.

I have just spoken of the philosophic revolution under whose mysterious empire we still live, perhaps more and more. In what sense do I mean
"more and more"? In the sense that we have a more and more strict, a
more and more rigorous conception of what a thing is, of its essence.

For us, for us "Moderns," not only is a thing what it is, it is *only* what it is. The chief illustration of this movement is to be found in the critique that modern physics addresses to ancient physics, particularly Aristotle's. By its teleology, we think, ancient physics makes every being depend on its end, defines it by its end, that is, by something other than what the being properly and strictly is.

Homeric poetry no doubt belongs to the prephilosophical world, the world of mythologies. Indeed, as we have just seen, Homer, with Hesiod, was in fact the author of Greek mythology. But Homer was an odd mythologist. Here I limit myself to a very simple remark. In the "mythological" tripartition of the human world, Homer did not make room for animals and thus he does not concern himself with metamorphoses.[7] Regarding animals, the *Iliad* knows only the horses of the warriors or the bulls and sheep of the sacrifices, thus animals that are only what they are. Comparisons with animals—with the eagle, the mountain lion—are indispensable to the poem's intent, but in reality the poem knows only humans and gods. One would have to say this is a great simplification in comparison with other mythologies or even non-Homeric Greek mythology.

And since the gods are moved by the same motives as humans, one is tempted to recognize another, and ultimate simplification: there would only be humans. But no. If humans and gods resemble one another to the point of being indistinguishable at times, often by their behavior, there is a difference between them that nothing can attenuate or obliterate, a difference that runs through the poem and gives it its extraordinary tension. This obvious difference is that humans are mortal while the gods are immortal. Homer did not discover that humans are mortal, but the *Iliad* is throughout, so to speak, a confrontation with mortality as there was never before and will hardly be after. The proof is that as "heroic" and "aristocratic" as the world of the *Iliad* is, death, or the threat of death, equalizes all mortals, including the greatest of all, the son of an immortal, Achilles, who confronted the alternative of a long happy life without glory or an early, but glorious, death.

One further remark to echo the "logical" considerations I presented above. Not only are humans mortal (adjective) but they are *the* mortals (substantive). To say *brotos* is at the same time to say "mortal" and "human."[8] Thus, in the mind-set prior to definitions, mortal is the "definition" of the human, or rather the "disjunction" by which the human is designated in contradistinction to the gods. Now, once the system of definition is established, philosophy will not keep the designation "mortal" to capture what is proper to humans. What is proper to humans will be sought in the intellectual faculty, and Aristotle will fix the definition of humans with which, in spite of all the shifts and transformations it has undergone, we still live: the human is a rational animal (which includes political animal). One can see how the philosophical definition refurbishes the Homeric disjunction: the intellectual faculty tends to fill the gap between humans and gods since it naturally looks to what does not change, what is eternal—"natures," "essences," "ideas"—and as such is "divine." Over the ravine or the "dark valley" of death stretches the bridge of the intellectual grasp of the eternal order, the bridge of reason that for philosophy is the only thing that is truly "divine." But if reason is divine, or points toward the divine, what is its starting point, on what does it rest, what pole opposite the divine does it join to the divine? The animal, of course. Philosophy revives this element of the mythological tripartition that Homer had left behind, and it can do so without risk since the definition, particularly the definition according to common genus—animal—and specific difference—rational, political—makes it impossible to restore the circle of metamorphoses.

However summary these remarks may be, they find striking confirmation, it seems to me, in the later development of modern philosophy. The philosophers who place death at the center of their approach to the human phenomenon always end up privileging poetry and metaphors over philosophy and definitions. This can be verified in authors as different as Montaigne and Heidegger. It is, in short, Homer's revenge.

The *Iliad*

If we now consider the *Iliad* as a whole, what shall we say? How shall we define this work from before the age of definitions? Simone Weil's answer is that the *Iliad* is "the poem of force." This can be our starting point.

Simone Weil's text begins as follows: "The true hero, the true subject, the center of the *Iliad* is force. Force employed by man, force that enslaves man, force before which man's flesh shrinks away. In this work, at all times, the human spirit is shown as modified by its relations with force, as swept away, blinded by the force it imagined it could handle, as deformed by the weight of the force it submits to."[9] This is an impressive and exact characterization of the poem. It is also partial, and what follows only deepens this partiality. A few lines later we read: "To define force—it is that x that turns anybody who is subjected to it into a *thing.*" This is no longer altogether exact. And as the text continues, Simone Weil will give us yet again a profound, but partial or unilateral, view of the *Iliad,* where humans are but the victims of force—victims of force because they are blinded by it: "By its very blindness, destiny established a kind of justice. Blind also is she who decrees to warriors punishment in kind. He that takes the sword will perish by the sword. The *Iliad* formulated the principle long before the Gospels did, and in almost the same terms: 'Ares is just, and kills those who kill' " (13). Under the sway of force, a moderate use of force is, so to speak, impossible: "A moderate use of force, which alone would enable man to escape being enmeshed in its machinery, would require superhuman virtue, which is as rare as dignity in weakness" (19). Simone Weil adds lucidly: "Moreover, moderation itself is not without its perils, since prestige from which force derives at least three quarters of its strength, rests principally upon that marvelous indifference that the strong feel toward the weak, an indifference so contagious that it infects the very people who are the objects of it" (19). Whence the sort of theorem with which Simone Weil sums up her thought: "Such is the nature of force. Its power of converting a man into a thing is a double one, and in its application double-edged. To the same degree, though in different fashions, those who use it and those who endure it are turned to stone" (25).

One understands that humans cannot free themselves from such an empire of force, and that they become obstinate and entrenched in the ways of war to the point of exhaustion. This is how Simone Weil explains the duration of the Trojan War: "But actually what is Helen to Ulysses? What indeed is Troy, full of riches that will not compensate him for Ithaca's ruin? For the Greeks, Troy and Helen are in reality mere sources of blood and tears; to master them is to master frightful memories" (23). Explaining the duration of the Trojan War by its very weight is certainly too general; it is in any case obviously colored by the recent experience of the Great War:

Regularly, every morning, the soul castrates itself of aspiration, for thought cannot journey through time without meeting death on the way. Thus war effaces all conceptions of purpose or goal, including even its own "war aims." It effaces the very notion of a war's being brought to an end. To be outside a situation so violent as this is to find it inconceivable; to be inside it is to be unable to conceive its end. Consequently, nobody does anything to bring this end about. In the presence of an armed enemy, what hand can relinquish its weapon? The mind ought to find a way out, but the mind has lost all capacity to so much as look outward. The mind is completely absorbed in doing itself violence. Always in human life whether war or slavery is in question, intolerable sufferings continue, as it were, by the force of their own specific gravity, and so look to the outsider as though they have deprived the sufferer of the resources which ought to serve to extricate him. (22)

We ought to envisage an explanation that is not essentially different but that is more specific. Despite the unilateral character of her thought, Simone Weil grasps certain fundamental aspects of the *Iliad* in a very fitting and striking way:

However, such a heaping-up of violent deeds would have a frigid effect, were it not for the note of incurable bitterness that continually makes itself heard, though often only a single word marks its presence, often a mere stroke of the verse, or a run-on line. It is in this that the *Iliad* is absolutely unique, in this bitterness that proceeds from tenderness and that spreads over the whole human race, impartial as sunlight. Never does the tone lose its coloring of bitterness; yet never does the bitterness drop into lamentation. Justice and love, which have hardly any place in this study of extreme and of unjust acts of violence, nevertheless bathe the work in their light without ever becoming noticeable themselves, except as a kind of accent. Nothing precious is scorned, whether or not death is its destiny; everyone's unhappiness is laid bare without dissimulation or disdain; so man is set above or below the condition common to all men; whatever is destroyed is regretted. Victors and vanquished are brought equally near us; under the same head, both are seen as counterparts of the poet, and the listener as well. If there is any difference, it is that the enemy's misfortunes are possibly more sharply felt. (29–30)

Thus the supreme charm and virtue of the *Iliad* reside in its "extraordinary sense of equity," of which "there may be, unknown to us, other expressions . . . ; certainly it has not been imitated. One is barely aware that the poet is a Greek and not a Trojan" (32).

On this point, one has to agree with Simone Weil but also correct or complete her. There is no doubt that the "humanity" of the Trojans, as we would say today, is recognized by the poet as equal to that of the Achaeans. The image of the Trojans seems even more likeable than that of the Greeks, more completely "human," if only because of the presence of attractive or touching female figures—Helen (Trojan despite herself), Andromache, Hecuba. If readers retain only one scene of the *Iliad,* it is always Hector's farewell to Andromache. And Hector has always been more "popular" than Achilles. Although this is important, nonetheless there is no doubt that the Greeks are presented as superior to the Trojans, something that is yet more important, since it is a window onto the first self-awareness of the Greeks. In what sense are they "superior"? Don't we know that civilizations are equal and beyond comparison, that there is no common measure, no objective criterion that allows civilizations or "cultures" to be compared and classified? Well, even so, Homer does not hesitate to provide us with both the classification and the criterion.

I cannot deal with the matter of animal comparisons—for example, of the Greeks to bees, the Trojans to grasshoppers—that are nonetheless always so interesting in Homer. I will limit myself to a few points that seem to me fundamental.

Perhaps one ought to begin with the fact that the Achaeans, unlike the Trojans, are capable of silence (3.79; 4.105). Not only do they go into combat in silence, but they are able to keep silent to listen to the proposals and arguments of their leaders, when everything should incite them to abandon themselves to noisome agitation, as is emphasized in book 2. This capacity for silence, which is the capacity for listening, allows not only for better military discipline, to be sure, but also more generally for more rational deliberation.

It is worth remarking that although this capacity for silence is the means of maintaining military discipline, it is not its result or effect. The silence of the Achaeans, in military actions as in councils, is not imposed upon them, but is a demeanor that is freely adopted as both the most useful and the most noble. The proof is that furthermore the Greeks express their emotions freely and publicly, while such expressions are severely controlled at Troy. The great Priam does not permit lamenting at funerals (7.494).

Another aspect of the Achaeans' capacity for superior collective action resides in the felicitous relationship between individual interactions and common action. This harmony rests on the role of *aïdôs*, the sentiment of shame or honor before one's companions. There is nothing "holistic" in the Greek expeditionary corps. It has no idea of the fusion of the individual in the group. The common energy is the result of the affects that flow from companion to companion. When at the beginning of book 3 the Achaeans advance in silence against the Trojans, their hearts are on fire to help one another (3.9). And in book 5, the supreme leader, Agamemnon, calls upon the warriors—his *philoï*—to be men— "aneres este"—not by devoting themselves to the whole, the collective corps, but by experiencing shame before one another—"allèlous t'aîdeisthe." This is because when warriors have a sense of shame— "aïdomenôn d'andrôn"—many more among them survive than are killed (5.610–614).

These moral dispositions are particularly salutary when the warriors beat a retreat or are on the defensive, for that is when it is vital for each one to take care of his companions (whereas the instinct for preservation enjoins him to think only of himself). The Achaeans know well how to place themselves in a defensive position by joining their shields and arraying their spears. They often exert every effort to come to each other's aid and even to preserve a companion's corpse from the abuses of the enemy. In book 17, Homer describes at length the admirable efforts of the Greeks (and in particular Menelaus, who is certainly not the most "heroic" among these "heroes") to protect the corpse of Patroclus.

This superiority of the Greeks not only reveals itself in collective action, but shines even more in individual action, when the protagonists are no longer protected by the group. This is seen in a particular way in the wonderful book 10, the Doloneia, that certain commentators inexplicably consider an adventitious episode posterior to the rest of the poem. In the Doloneia Homer sets up a contrast between two symmetrical and simultaneous nocturnal spy operations in which Diomedes and Odysseus on the Greek side and Dolon on the Trojan side engage in reconnaissance missions behind enemy lines. Diomedes, who is probably the purest hero among the Achaeans, volunteers, but suggests that a companion join him, not out of fear but to ensure the success of the mission. As heroic and swept up in emotion as he is, Diomedes is equally prudent, or, as we might say today, professional. This is not the case with poor Dolon, his Trojan counterpart. He is certainly courageous, or at least ardent and desirous of distinguishing himself, and also of winning the reward promised by Hector. But he goes off rashly and alone into the night. Diomedes and Odysseus will easily make short work of him.

It should be noted that Homer takes pains to sketch the portrait of the unfortunate Dolon. He is a rich young man, a swift runner, but uncomely in appearance: "eidos kakos." We would say, in the terms of magazine psychology, that he is the rather conceited young man of means with a need to compensate for his ugliness. But the most important trait perhaps is that he is an only son with five sisters. In other words, he is a boy who is superlatively spoiled by his mother and sisters, spoiled by women.

I believe that Homer here is suggesting something that goes well beyond Dolon himself. His character defects and Hector's almost unbelievable imprudence in placing such a delicate mission in such inexperienced hands are both indications of how weak the Trojans are in relation to the Achaeans. I am tempted to say that the Trojans remain tangled up in the familial and sexual order. In a sort of short circuit, the Doloneia episode meets up with the central theme of the poem, the battle over Helen and for Helen.

There is no question of considering here this theme for its own sake, of inquiring into the "causes of the Trojan War," but simply of showing that at least in some part, but an important and perhaps decisive part, the war stems from the asymmetry of Greek and Trojan civilization, and first of all from the asymmetry regarding familial and sexual order. To put it in the simplest terms, this war is absurd since the Trojans, being decent people, should long ago have returned to Menelaus his rightful queen and his stolen treasures. It is clear as day to all eyes, and first of all to the Trojans, that Paris, in taking Helen and Menelaus's treasures, violated the law of nations, in this case the most sacred laws of hospitality. The Trojans, first among them Paris's own brother Hector, despise and condemn this disastrous playboy. Helen herself, so decent, so modest, so ashamed of the whole story, is not far from thinking the same thing, but she is a slave of the sexual dependence that she hates (3.460–478). I do not believe that book 3 can be interpreted as a celebration of Eros even if Paris asks his brother not to insult Aphrodite (3.77–79), even if the Trojan elders, dumbfounded by the beauty of Helen on the ramparts, *seem* to consent to a war waged for the possession of such a beauty.[10] The Trojans offer us the spectacle of a chain slavery. The noble city of Ilion, Ilion of the broad streets, Ilion beaten by winds, is subject to its royal family, to Priam and his fifty sons. These Trojan rulers are themselves subject, despite themselves, to the least worthy among them, to Paris, the smug youth with the handsome curls. And Paris himself, who is not really a bad person, is despite himself subject, as we have just said, to an irresistible sexual attraction. A chain of weaknesses, running the familial and sexual gamut, links the destiny of Troy to an erotic adventure without illusion and without nobility. One could say that the human chain is here the prisoner of its weakest link. The whole is held captive by its least loyal member, the one that is most indifferent to the fate of the whole. And our sympathy for the "endearing" humanity of the Trojans stems from the weakness we ourselves have for this weakness.

Let us now compare the relation between Paris and Helen, his illegitimate possession, to that between Achilles and Briseis, his legitimate possession. One cannot imagine a more striking contrast. As we have just seen, Paris is incapable of giving up Helen, and Troy neither can nor wants to impose on him this surrender, which nonetheless would save the city and its inhabitants. On the contrary, Achilles, proud Achilles, the son of a goddess who makes himself equal to the gods, the most handsome and the mightiest of the Achaeans, at the command of Agamemnon, hands over to him Briseis, his legitimate captive whom he loves and by whom he is loved in return. To be sure, Agamemnon's demand arouses Achilles's terrible wrath, the immense sulk that with all its consequences is the subject of the *Iliad*. But if Achilles does not accept the injustice done to him and is prepared to ruin his companions to avenge it, he accepts being parted from Briseis because it is the order of his legitimate leader. He accepts this physical separation with a kind of ease (1.390–415), an almost incomprehensible ease if one considers the unquenchable wrath he has begun to experience. In brief, to go right to the conclusion I have tried to suggest, Troy stands for the familial and sexual dependence from which the Achaeans are freed. Troy, with all its endearing humanity, means the slope toward passivity and the power of bodily proximity while the camp of the Achaeans, with all its repugnant brutality, represents the tense movement toward activity and the power of spiritual distance.

I have just spoken of the camp of the Achaeans. It is not a city as such. The only city in the *Iliad* would be the one that gives its name to the poem, Ilion. But it has in it nothing of a city in the classical and political meaning of the term, governed as it is by a king and innumerable princes, his sons. The Achaeans could appear to be but an expeditionary corps. In reality they are more and something other, just as their camp is more and something other than a camp or military base. Homer gives many precise indications of the spatial layout of men, ships, and installations. The Achaeans have even built for themselves a rampart that one crosses through enormous doors. Moreover, they do not seem to have any difficulties with supplies: wine and fat oxen are available in abundance for libations and sacrifices to the gods as well as for the feeding and refreshment of the men. These men who have settled along the coast of the "wine-dark sea" for nine years now seem to have attained self-sufficiency. They are not an army properly speaking, but a complete warrior society, with its political leaders, its "princes," who are equally its military leaders. It has a very marked but also very complex hierarchy about which Homer instructs us as he makes it live before our eyes. This gathering of the flower of the Achaean kingdoms, this extraction of their quintessence, fashioned by circumstances, does not constitute a city as such. But one can recognize in it a heroic or aristocratic republic, this republic of quarrelsome persuasion that is the invention of Greece and whose virtues democracy will spread and develop. In short, the camp of the Achaeans, the city "in speech" whose founder is Homer, was the common mother of the "real" Greek cities.

The Hero, War, and Death

The life of this city is limited to war, and, one can add, to the sort of diplomacy that war implies (truces, embassies, etc.); it is limited to external action. These warriors are away from home and devote themselves exclusively to external action, to an aspect of politics, one is tempted to say, and perhaps not the most interesting aspect. After all, it will be of little interest to the philosophers. Plato and Aristotle have little to say about war and foreign policy; they tend to recommend that the city's external relations be kept to a minimum. But in barbarian times politics and war are one and the same; the progress of civilization is measured by the progress of the arts of peace and the development of internal politics. Even Rousseau, the enemy of modern civilization and promoter of ancient virtue, will praise a Geneva where if citizens are trained for the use of arms it is more for the beauty of the deed than for a real military need, "rather to maintain in them that warlike ardor and that spiritual courage which suit freedom so well and whet the appetite for it, rather than from the necessity to provide for their own defense."[11] External war returns to absorb all the energies only at the decline of civilization, in the case of Greece at the time of the Peloponnesian War of which Thucydides writes. From this perspective, one would say that Homer's poetry describes the city before the city, whereas Thucydides's history describes, if not the city after the city, at least the city on the way to destroying itself.

This civilized and enlightened point of view is in turn partial. It overlooks the meaning and the import of Homeric war. As we have already suggested, war is the condition and the consequence of the self-discovery of "mortals." That is why the *Iliad*, while it speaks of nothing but war, nonetheless says everything about human life, or at least considers it in its entirety. Condition and consequence: this means that war produces the discovery of the self as mortal, which in turn produces war. How can this be? In war, death appears as the greatest possibility of human life since war holds for every man both the greatest possible action—inflicting death on the enemy—and the greatest possible passion—suffering death. And the true life, which is here the noble life, the heroic life, consists in constantly standing on the cutting edge of this twofold possibility.

In Homer there is no embellishment or dulling of death whatsoever. Death is never accompanied nor followed by any consolation, only the poet's recalling the irreparable loss it signifies for everyone. The value of ordinary life, the sweetness of peace, are recognized and stand out as even more attractive and desirable, in contrast with the atrocity of a warrior's rage. Homeric poetry does not present any artificial or complacent heroicizing of human life, but lets each aspect of the human phenomenon have its place, its integrity, and its breadth.

At the end of the poem, Achilles has no living interlocutor. He is no longer concerned with anyone living, but with two corpses, those of Hector and Patroclus, Hector the enemy and Patroclus the friend, the brother, the other self. Hector's corpse represents Achilles's greatest feat—dealing death to the one who is Troy's pillar of strength; Patroclus's corpse represents Achilles's greatest passion—receiving death, Achilles's own since Patroclus is another self, and his death heralds the coming death of Achilles and is already as it were melded together with it. For days on end Achilles deals with Hector's corpse as he dealt with Hector while he was living. He injures him, does violence to him, and insults him until Priam's visit and supplications bring him to accept that Hector's corpse will receive at Troy the rites and honors that Achilles rendered to the corpse of Patroclus in the Greek camp. The death of Patroclus will haunt him painfully until his own death, which, once again, is melded together with it.

The ending of the *Iliad* is extraordinarily powerful emotionally, but it also has a complex and precise design. One must not lose sight of this complexity and precision by giving way to emotion, by giving the last two books, particularly the last, a sentimental interpretation. Priam's visit to Achilles, Achilles's agreeing to let the old king bring Hector's corpse to Troy for burial rites, the corpse that he had abused without end and meant to abandon to the dogs and vultures; these have nothing to do with the hitherto irreconcilable enemies discovering their common humanity in a flow of emotion that envelops the reader or hearer. *Our* emotion is irresistible, and as such it is legitimate, but it is not shared by the two protagonists, who do not forget their enmity for a single moment, even if Achilles—sensitive to the likeness in age and condition between his own father, Peleus, whom he will not see again, and Priam, who dares to come before him—takes the aged Trojan under his protection. In truth, if there is emotion or passion in the soul of Achilles, it is always his wrath toward Hector and the Trojans, which would take little to rekindle at the expense of Priam's life and that will be unleashed anew, we know without any doubt, once Hector's funeral is over. Achilles has changed. Indeed, he is able to keep his wrath at bay and be motivated by something else. By what? Not by compassion or humanity, as we have just said, even if keeping his wrath under control allows for deeds and actions that among us would reveal compassion and humanity. One would have to answer that it is by his reason, by which is meant the more complete awareness he has gained of his mortality, and in general of the fact that men are mortal.

Let us then consider more precisely Achilles's relation to the corpses of Hector and Patroclus. He subjects them to opposite treatments, heaping abuses on the first and honors on the second, or on his ashes. These are opposite treatments, but they are equally monstrous in relentlessness and excess. Every time he thinks of the death of Patroclus, he drags the corpse of Hector behind the chariot to which he has tied it. On his friend's funeral pyre he massacres twelve young Trojans he had taken prisoner for this express purpose. But his monstrous behavior is at the same time "natural." Achilles is merely obstinately extending his hatred and his love, abusing the corpse of Hector and venerating Patroclus's. He multiplies deeds and words over human forms that are now only immobile and silent. This contrast between love and hate contributes powerfully to an impression of monstrosity, but it does not mean that Achilles is a monster, only that he has not grasped that Patroclus and Hector alike are dead.

It is not enough then to be ready to kill and ready to die. That twofold disposition leads simply to Achilles's heroic or monstrous fits of anger if it is not completed by another disposition, one that is difficult to define and that I would approach in the following way. Every human being can kill; he can also expose himself to death, sacrifice himself. These are, one could say, the two supreme human actions. But no human being can bury himself or, once dead, care for himself.[12] The two supreme actions of the warrior, the hero, have a limit. As courageous as he is, something is beyond his grasp. Something remains, the corpse. The self-sufficiency of the hero, the driving force of his pride and the motive of his glory, is incomplete. Something confounds or contradicts his self-sufficiency, and that is the hero's corpse. Nothing less is needed than the corpse of his worst enemy along with that of his closest friend, his brother, and the visit of Priam that in some way gives this twofold death its meaning for the hero par excellence to become aware of this limit, of his limit. It is thus necessary that words and gestures accompany the one who can no longer speak and move himself: burial rites. Achilles of course had surrounded the corpse of Patroclus with many and grandiose rites. But that was an extension of his heroic actions; he was extending himself, extending his being (on the funeral pyre of Patroclus, he was still killing Trojans). He did not want to recognize the death of Patroclus. And, to be sure, he sets himself against the corpse of Hector—he does not stop killing him; he goes on killing him; he refuses to recognize his death. It is only when he is willing to abandon his enemy's corpse that he suspends the movement of his heroic life and recognizes the limits of his force and courage, even of his glory, and thus recognizes death for what it is, that he recognizes that he is mortal. Being fully ready to die (as Achilles is just after he has killed Hector) does not suffice for one to recognize that one is mortal. It is not really different from being ready to kill. One still remains a monstrous hero. It is only when one recognizes that honor is due to all corpses, including those of the enemies, that one is at last a man. Achilles, the son of a goddess and a mortal, was born a hero. He lived as a hero. At the end of the *Iliad,* as his death nears, he has completed his education, his education in humanity. He has become a man; he is at last a mortal.[13]

The Greeks were greatly concerned with the rites meant to honor soldiers fallen in battle, at times to the detriment of military effectiveness, as the aftermath of the Arginusae affair shows. There is a tension between the well-being of the city and the care due to the corpses of the city's defenders. In instructing the citizens on the limits of the city, Homer, the educator of the Greeks, risks putting the city in danger. Enlightened statesmen, concerned with the city's well-being, will make efforts to free it from Homer's authority. Shortly after saying that his city was the school of Greece—"tès Ellados païdeusen"—Pericles, in his funeral oration, declares somewhat brutally, "we do not need the praises of a Homer."[14] Athens had become its own poet, and Pericles's proud speech celebrates this achievement. Leo Strauss remarks that in this speech meant to honor the war dead, Pericles avoids the words "death," "die," or "corpse": "only once does his Pericles speak in the Funeral Speech of death and then only in the expression 'unfelt death,' *'anaïsthètos thanatos.'*"[15]

By his awareness of mortality, by the way he arouses awareness of mortality, Homer differs not only from Pericles but also from Pericles's great critic, Socrates. Socrates himself, in the *Apology,* compares himself to Achilles, to one who thought little of death when it came to doing an honorable deed (28b–d). And in the *Phaedo* the death of Socrates appears as a death without trouble or pain, and that leaves behind no corpse, so to speak. His last words are not about the care due to his remains, but about the cock he owes to Asclepius. The hero of philosophy, the new Achilles, is only a soul that is indifferent to his mortal body, a soul that does not cease to reason and to speak until the moment of death. Then his disciples remember his words and thoughts, repeat them, extend them. The Socratic hero, unlike the Homeric hero, leads a life that, I dare say, leaves behind no remains. His body dissolves in his words.

To be sure, the image of Socrates drinking the hemlock and talking serenely with his distressed disciples is a representation of death that has certainly and profoundly marked the European spirit, more even than the image of Hector dragged by Achilles beneath the walls of Troy. But the representation of death that is the most widespread in the West—let us not say the most influential; we know nothing of that—is not the image of the old philosopher or of the young warrior dying or dead. It is nevertheless the image of a young man dying or dead. It is in no way our subject, but it is impossible here not to point out that, unlike Greek philosophy, the Gospels, like the *Iliad,* culminate in the death of a young man. I will limit myself to just one remark. Jesus is both Patroclus and Hector. More precisely, in the Christian representation, Jesus is for each person what Hector and Patroclus are for Achilles: the enemy he has pierced with blows *and* the friend, the brother, who was pierced with blows for him.[16] This is where I would see the paradoxical proximity between Homer and the Gospels, as much as or more than in the impartial and pure appreciation of human misery where Simone Weil sees it.[17]

Now I would like to take up a more general inquiry concerning war and heroism. Not only the Greek tradition but nearly all human traditions begin with an epic, a heroic poem, peopled with splendid warriors. Why is this? This is a question that is not often raised because we think it need not be raised. We are, on this point as on many others, spontaneously progressive, and thus, since these warrior beginnings have given way to political and moral forms that appear to us more satisfying, more reasonable, more humane, we are hardly motivated to inquire into the human meaning of heroic beginnings. We willingly qualify them as primitive, or even barbaric.[18] The standard and almost universal progressive perspective sees humanity developing along an axis that leads from the age of the warrior to the epoch of commerce. Benjamin Constant expressed this idea in a way that is striking by its synthetic brevity, and also, if I may say so, by its revealing naïveté:

We have finally reached the age of commerce, an age which must necessarily replace that of war, as the age of war was found to precede it. War and
commerce are only different means to achieve the same end of possessing
what is desired. Commerce is simply a tribute paid to the strength of the
possessor by the aspirant to possession. It is an attempt to obtain by mutual agreement what one can no longer hope to obtain through violence. A
man who was always the stronger would never conceive the idea of commerce. It is experience, by proving to him that war, that is, the use of his
strength against the strength of others, is open to a variety of obstacles and
defeats, that leads him to resort to commerce, that is, to a milder and surer
means of getting the interests of others to agree with his own.

   War then comes before commerce. The former is all savage impulse, the
latter civilized calculation.[19]

I have on other occasions analyzed this text that is so revealing of the
self-awareness of the society of commerce that is ours. I will focus here
on just one point. Human things are complex, obscure, and legitimately
give rise to uncertainty and doubt, but if there is one thesis on human
things that has no chance of being true, it is Constant's thesis on war.
Let us admit that there is at bottom no difference between the intent to
seize something by doing violence to its owner and that of obtaining it by
freely given consent, since it is in both cases a matter of possessing what is
desired. But there is no place in Constant's definition for the desire to
prevail over someone considered an enemy, to beat him and rejoice in
the honor or glory of victory. By making war simply a means to possess
what one desires, Constant forgets that war is also desired for its own
sake, that it can itself be the object of desire because it is only in war that
certain human dispositions find their expression and that certain human
experiences can be had.

   War is a form of human conduct that is too common not to have a
specific, proper meaning all its own. If war, with all the frightening woes
that come with it, had no meaning for humans, no desirable, at times
even irresistible, meaning, I dare say very simply that they would not
make war, that they would even be altogether unaware of it. In speaking
of the human meaning of war, I do not have in mind any philosophy of
history, any justification for war that would lead us to conclude that at
the end of the day, all things considered, war is not an evil, that it is even
perhaps a good. The human meaning of war resides very simply in what

takes place in the soul of the one who wages war. What takes place there? Well, in varying degrees and modes, it is what takes place in the soul of Achilles, which Homer has made it possible for us to perceive. Let us return to that briefly.

As I have said, in war death appears as the greatest possibility of human life, since war holds for each man both the greatest possible human action (the "greatest" in the sense of "producing the greatest effects"), inflicting death, and the greatest possible passion, suffering death. The true life then can only be the noble life, the heroic life that consists in constantly standing on the cutting edge of this twofold possibility. This greatest of possibilities cannot but have the greatest power over the soul. If death—death received and given—is the most extreme possibility of life, then true life, the life that is most fully alive, is the life under the spell of death, the life of the warrior, the heroic life.

There is, of course, a difficulty in this that even seems to be a contradiction: heroes die young. The highest possibility in life coincides with the greatest threat to life and finally with the destruction of life, of the liveliest life, of the young life. There is something awry in heroism.

That something is awry in heroism is just what we Moderns think. Indeed, a good definition of modern people might be that they are ones who have seen through the contradiction in heroism and do not let themselves be taken in by heroes. Heroism rests in some way on an erroneous interpretation of the extreme possibility of human life that is death. Death is indeed the extreme possibility of life. On this point the heroes and the poets who sing of them are not mistaken. But death reveals itself to the soul in the experience of fear, of the greatest fear, the fear of violent death at the hands of others, the passion of the soul before which all the other passions and dispositions pale. This is the diagnosis of Hobbes, who also provides the remedy for the sickness of human life. People must organize themselves by recognizing that they fear death and by taking their bearing from this fear. For Hobbes, life, true life, does not consist in confronting death heroically, not even simply with courage. It is on the contrary a flight from death or a race against death, and the good political institution, the good city, is the one that recognizes and preserves this true nature of life, that not only protects life but also the capacity of life to find on its own the best ways to protect itself. It rests on the protector of life, property, and liberty, which is our State.

It should be noted that if Hobbes turns heroism on its head, so to speak, he places himself on the same terrain as heroism. The nub of his argument is not about the protection of life in general, or even the fear of death in general, but about the fear of violent death at the hands of others. He gives a voice of some kind to the victims of Achilles by rebuffing those who fancy themselves as Achilles and whom the Book of Job calls "the children of pride." The Hobbesian State carries out an implacable critique of heroism and heroes. It brings heroes, or those who aspire to be heroes, into line.

The Hobbesian State has prevailed over heroes. The modern State has prevailed over warrior aristocracies in such a complete way that Constant's thesis, at least in its descriptive part, appears to be beyond doubt. It is the case that we have gone from being a military society to a commercial society, from a heroic society to a human society, and that we are satisfied and, so to speak, relieved with the change. At the same time, war and heroes, those "anachronisms" according to Constant, are still with us, not only in the warlike outbreaks that punctuate the history of modern political bodies, but also in the chronic dissatisfaction of democratic societies, in the muted and ongoing revolt against the tedium of bourgeois peace. Were not this dissatisfaction and revolt in part sparked and sustained by images of ancient heroism, by the Greek and Latin authors against whose influence Hobbes so keenly warned us? Contrary to Constant's assertions, the quarrel between heroes and people has not been decisively settled.

The problem could be formulated in the following way. Humanism does not succeed in establishing itself firmly, quietly, and decisively on the human plane as it demands and claims, on the plane that is wholly human and nothing but human, and where heroes would be truly forgotten because they would no longer have any meaning or attraction. In an emblematic way, Montaigne, who is the most consistent humanist because he is the most merciless destroyer of all human attempts to flee oneself by rising above oneself, could not do without Cato, who shows him all that human nature is capable of, to what height it can rise. To grasp his own humanity, Montaigne must elaborate his moderation, or mediocrity, in the light of Cato's excess and excellence. To attain his "nonchalance," he needs to keep his eyes fixed on the tension of Cato, who is "always mounted on his high horse."

The limits of humanism can be seen in social and political life. The quarrel of people and heroes is coextensive with our history, even if they are at times hard to recognize beneath their metamorphoses. Their polarity remains active even in the low tides of history seemingly peopled only with satisfied men.

Let us attempt to illustrate this in concrete historical and political terms. One could say that the matrix or the first form of European life is the "heroic republic" constituted by a small number of "noble" or "good" or "excellent" people, and a great number of "nameless" or "bad" or "good for nothing" people—of a small number of the "more than human" and a great number of the "less than human" or "less than nothing." It is hard to speak here of a city; in Plato's terms, one can say there are here two cities forever at war with one another. At times even, the "few" swear unending hatred for the masses. The heroic republic rests on war of a particular kind. The city of Sparta waged chronic war against subject peoples, Helots or Messenians. Part of the civic education of young Spartans consisted of carrying out punitive expeditions against the poor wretches.

What we call "class struggle" is but the pale remnant of this war, reduced to the rivalry of interests between the rich and the poor. It is a war, or a struggle, that now takes place simply among people. Yet the heroic matrix lies beneath the surface. Marx reactivated it with marvelous ingenuity. He reversed the dialectic of people and heroes. The proletarians who are but people, and moreover people deprived of all the goods that make life human, who are so to speak "deprived of humanity," are for that very reason in a position to recover for themselves and for others the fullness of humanity, a humanity incomparably fuller than what they could until then have experienced. Being less than human, the proletarians for that very reason can become more than human. They are the heroes. Marxism prolonged or revived a heroic horizon that was a great principle of strength and prestige for communism.

Politicization and Pacification

I now return to the original city, the city before the city, or the heroic republic, which I call a "republic" by anticipation, since the group of heroes has no idea of the "public thing." Yet it is from that group that it will be born. Christian Meier reckons that the virtues proper to the Greek city derive from the fact that the city achieved the immediate and direct participation of the many in the aristocratic "values" of the few without the precondition or mediation of the State.[20] Warfare between heroes and people gives way to people's participation in the heroic life, not without conflict, but without any need to have prior recourse to the peacemaking of the State. The Greek city is the result or the process itself of this transformation. This politicization of the original warfare, this participation of the many in the heroic life of the few without the pacifying intervention of the One, is an extraordinary and truly unique phenomenon.[21]

What did this transformation consist of more precisely? How was this war domesticated? Political philosophy, in particular Aristotle's, offers a very convincing interpretation, if not of the process, in any case of its result, which is *political life*. We will soon say more about this interpretation.[22] Let it suffice to say here that Aristotle shows us the transformation of the war between two groups that have *nothing in common* but their mutual hatred into the conflicting confrontation of their respective claims to govern *the* city—the same city that they now share. These claims are of course incompatible and in this sense the condition of war persists, but the parties work to find a method for adjudicating these incompatible claims, for evaluating them according to a common standard, which is precisely that of the *common good*. The process of adjudication and evaluation is what Aristotle calls political justice or "political right."[23] War gives way to political justice, which replaces it very advantageously. But it is important not to forget that justice is something that succeeds war.

We will better understand this transformation by considering the polarity between Sparta and Athens. Each has eminent claims to the glory of being the Greek city par excellence. Sparta was that city to the extent that it was the most typical, the most purely warlike city. It was continuously at war not only externally, against the other Greek cities, but also, as I have mentioned, internally, in the hidden war against subjected but rebellious populations. As the Greek city par excellence, it prevailed over Athens in the Peloponnesian War. As for Athens, it was, of all the Greek cities, the one where internal war was the least bitter—the most visible perhaps, but the least bitter—because it was the one where the people took the greatest part in the life of the city.[24] Its greater internal pacification and democratization gave Athens forces for external expansion that were unknown elsewhere. Democratization and imperial expansion proceeded in Athens from the same movement, with tributes of the conquered cities making it possible to pay poor citizens to engage in their tasks as citizens in political, judicial, or military offices. Athens was the least warlike, in any case the least "military," and nonetheless the most powerful of the Greek cities for the same reason, because it was the most political. It brought the politicization of the polis to its highest degree of actualization.

As we pass from Sparta to Athens, the warrior trait of the few fades. They tend to become "the rich." They even often engage in commercial activity, making Athens in a certain measure as much a commercial as a warrior city, an exception that Montesquieu and Constant are glad to recognize in the opposition they strike between ancient war and modern commerce. But this is a late development, for, to speak in general terms, the rich or the "owners" of heroic times had hardly any commercial holdings. In reality a great part of their wealth bore no resemblance to what we understand by that term. They indeed had lands but their titles consisted of ancestral tombs, of religious shares. The few were mainly proprietors of rites—funeral and marriage rites—while the many had only the nakedness of their animal nature. The many were outside the *genos* or order of "families," as later the foreigner, "strictly speaking," will be a stranger to the city. Their first claims were not, it appears, to goods or powers, but to the right to take part in burial or marriage rites, about which, as we shall see, Vico has much to say.

In heroic times, among the possessions of the few must be counted all those goods that come as spoils of war or plunder. Aristotle, although he is the mildest of the Greek philosophers, still includes the art of war among the natural arts of acquisition.[25] In heroic times, war is general, but that does not mean the "war of all against all" according to Hobbes's characterization of the state of nature. The Hobbesian state of nature is a state of violent nondifferentiation, where everyone threatens everyone, where the weakest can always kill the strongest, and out of which no order can emerge naturally. The only order that can be envisaged is a deliberate, artificial, fabricated order. Taking stock equally and together of their unbearable natural condition, the members of society elaborate the political construct that will heal the evils of the state of nature. The political condition and the natural condition are both conditions of equality. In the one, men are equally threatened; in the other, men—citizens—are equally held to obey the sovereign maker of peace. In heroic times, war does not give way to peace, war does not cease to reign, and inequality also reigns. There is a first circle or active core, the group of warriors, who are, to be sure, at war against the other groups of warriors, but also against their own dependents, against "the people" if you wish—one could not say "their" people, since they perceive the people as their enemy. They are also in latent war against one another within the group, every man always ready to engage in a duel to get blood vengeance for any offense against his honor by one of his companions. These are three kinds of war, but every joint of the heroic order is warlike.

It could be said that our political history consists for the most part of the successive, though imperfect, pacification of the three kinds of war. First, the pacification of the struggles for honor among noble warriors by the leveling sovereign; then the metamorphoses and pacification of class warfare between the few and the many. At the end of this twofold process, the democratic nation-states are essentially pacified from within, and war—more and more rare but more and more violent—is relegated to the border that separates each nation from foreign ones. The phenomenon of the border becomes more and more significant; border separation becomes more and more marked at the same time as the distinction between war and peace becomes more clear-cut, with peace being ever more mild and war ever more violent. The progress and deepening of peace and the aggravation or exacerbation of war paradoxically go hand in hand. The more peace is the natural condition of the members of society, the more war, when it breaks out, is violent, unlimited, unnatural. Men are thrown without rules or direction into an element that has become altogether foreign to them, and they are then liable to adopt ways or fall into behaviors that would have seemed absurd or monstrous to their ancestors of the warrior generations. It suffices to think of the trenches of 1914, and of the type of war of which they were the setting and expression. From the heroic to the bourgeois or democratic age, the political process has made us leave behind a situation where war, with its internal differences and under its three forms, was the natural way of life for men, and thus entailed in general the rules and limits that go with this condition—of course, since war necessarily entails the exaltation of some parts of the soul that are difficult to master once they are aroused, it necessarily implies getting carried away, excess, gratuitous violence, cruelty—Achilles. It has brought us to a situation where war has become completely foreign to normal life and is thus prone to becoming unlimited, for which the First World War set the example.

With the "hyperbolic wars" of the twentieth century, to use Raymond Aron's expression, an extreme point was arrived at. It was impossible to return to a "normal situation," to war "as usual." In Europe, the situation tipped toward what one is irresistibly tempted to call a hyperbolic peace. There was no longer any enemy; borders were erased; and war became "unthinkable." It is of course an open question whether this hyperbolic peace will last.

Recent events in any case prove that war is still susceptible to taking unprecedented forms. As it happens, they take us back to very ancient forms of warfare, to private war—*feud, Fehde*—or to a mixture of private and state war without precedent, the Afghan state, for example, being seized by the Taliban, who in their turn were bribed or co-opted by bin Laden and Al-Qaeda.

Let us return to the border between internal and external that is also the separation between war and peace. It will help to draw the form and, so to speak, to find the rhythm of one of the principal articulations, perhaps the principal one, of the human world. I will represent it by the following two parallel series:

war	external	unknown	nature	world
peace	internal	known	law	city

It is not possible for me to comment on each polarity and so to fully justify the parallelism. I count on the presentation's power of suggestion. A mental experience might provide, if not the proof, at least an argument in favor of the solidarity or mutual dependence of the polarities. Let us imagine that the movement toward pacification was to spread from Europe to the rest of the world and only peace without war would remain. Then the external and the unknown, which would no longer pose a threat, would join with the internal and the known. All people are *tourists* for one another. To regulate their lives, they have only to take into account the law, the internal law. No signal—no call or threat—comes to them from the outside since there is no longer, properly speaking, an outside. We could say in other words that the city would merge with the world. This very brief evocation of what a "world State" would entail shows how several fundamental articulations of the human world are intrinsically linked to the war-peace polarity, which in one sense combines with the external-internal polarity and brings out by contrast the "phenomenological" or "anthropological" coherence of the original or heroic stage. While there would be only peace and the interior sense of self in the world state, in the heroic age there tended to be only war and external affects, especially the "glory" attached to "victory."

One last but very important remark is in order. It can be seen that philosophy, in revealing the distance between law and nature, the city and the world, preserves or restores in the element of peace what war brought to light but without understanding it.

The Greek Camp

I would like to conclude this lengthy Homeric journey by going back to the beginning of the *Iliad* and briefly describing the sort of city that the Greek camp constitutes. We shall see living outside the walls, in conditions of external war, the same elements, or at least some of them, that will animate the city within its walls, and this will help us to discern what the Greek camp lacks to be truly a city.

Here is how the *Iliad* begins. Agamemnon has offended Chryses, the priest of Apollo, by refusing to hand over the priest's daughter, Chryseis, although Chryses had come bearing an immense ransom and with the god's insignia in his hand. Apollo then sends plague to the camp of the Achaeans. For nine days the epidemic rages. On the tenth day Achilles calls the men to assemble. Calchas, the best of the diviners, after receiving from Achilles assurance of the safety of his life, explains to the assembled Achaeans what the readers and hearers already know, that the cause of the catastrophe resides in Agamemnon's behavior.

Such is the starting point. The debate bears on the share that belongs to each man, to which each man has a right, and here especially on Agamemnon's share. Chryseis was his portion of the plunder, and therefore, according to the mores and measures of the time, his legitimate portion.

It is not clear that justice required Agamemnon to hand her over to her father when he came to claim her by bringing an enormous ransom, even if the crowd of Achaeans was in favor of the transaction, moved as it was by respect for the priest and greedy amazement at the size of the ransom. The demand for justice may be imperious, but the law here is vague. What can probably be said is that, even if Chryseis legitimately belongs to Agamemnon, he lacked respect for Apollo in refusing to hand her over in exchange for ransom to her father, the priest of Apollo. Thus what characterizes Agamemnon's behavior here, like that of every human being, is an extreme and excessive attachment to what is his. (Of course, the young captive, as a sign of glory, a portion of the plunder, and an object of sexual possession, combines in her person the strongest human attachments.) If Agamemnon has committed an injustice, it is with regard to the gods. But what is the portion of the gods, their legitimate portion? At the beginning of this whole immense affair there is uncertainty regarding what to apportion to humans and what to gods.

Let us come back to the assembly. By identifying the causes of the evil, Calchas has also pointed to the remedy, the only remedy. The girl must be handed over to her father, without ransom and with a magnificent sacrifice to Apollo. Upon hearing this, Agamemnon is furious, but he immediately sees that he has no choice. At the same time that he emphasizes how strongly attached he is to Chryseis, he says he is ready to hand her over for the people's well-being. He thus makes known how willing he is to sacrifice himself. But this sacrifice lasts only a very short time. At the same time he hands over Chryseis to her father, as he lets her go with one hand, with the other hand he takes another captive—at least he asks for and demands her. He has a solid argument: he cannot be alone among the Achaeans without his share of honor and plunder, a share to which he has a right (the repetition of the word *geras* punctuates Agamemnon's speech). To repair a lack of respect toward Apollo, a blatant injustice toward the chief of the Achaeans would be committed.

The assembly clearly finds itself confronted with a very delicate problem of justice. Achilles, whose hostility and jealousy toward Agamemnon have been palpable from the beginning, formulates the difficulty very well. The matter is simply impossible. Where is the compensation that Agamemnon requests, the equivalent share that he demands, to be found? It simply does not exist, since the distribution has already been made. In making his request, Agamemnon is in effect asking to return to the time when the distribution had not yet been made, which is obviously impossible. Achilles's argument of course assumes that all the plunder has been distributed and that nothing remains. That is in fact what he states explicitly with rigorous reasoning one would not expect from this passionate warrior: "I know of no troves of treasure, piled, lying idle anywhere [kunèïa keimena polla]" (1.145). These words reveal what the Greek camp lacks that a city would have: there is nothing held in common, as line 145 could be rendered. All the plunder the Achaean army took has been portioned out and taken possession of. This is how we measure the exploit the city accomplishes every day without our noticing it, which is to ensure a continuous distribution, an unending flow of goods. We become aware that the flow of private goods requires in one way or another the presence and the resources of a common good. In the circumstances of the Achaean camp, the only thing that can be done, as Achilles emphasizes, is to wait for the next distribution, that is, for the next pillage. Achilles concludes his legal consultation by inviting Agamemnon to be patient.

Agamemnon will not hear of it. Achilles's argument is compelling, but Agamemnon, urged on by the furious desire to keep his portion, or to regain an equal share, quickly fires back that Achilles's argument implies that, while he would keep his portion, Agamemnon would surrender his. Nothing justifies such an unequal treatment He then grows more threatening and claims a portion of equivalent value—"geras . . . antaxion (1.159–160). Achilles, now threatened with losing his portion, replies by widening the terms of the debate. Leaving aside the particular question under consideration until now—*this* portion of the plunder and its prospective equivalent—he puts Agamemnon on trial. It was for Agamemnon and his brother Menelaus, and only for them, that Achilles came to fight the Trojans, who had done him no harm. For the first time and not the last, Achilles declares he has nothing to do with this war and announces he will go home. And though the Achaeans are fighting for him, Agamemnon always takes the greatest share of the plunder. For the question raised by *this* particular division (Chryseis), Achilles substitutes the question of the division of the plunder in general, in short the question of the regime in the camp of the Achaeans: "when it comes to dividing up the plunder the lion's share is yours and back I go to my ships, clutching some scrap, some pittance that I love [soï to geras polu meizon, ego d'oligon te philon]" (1.195–197).

Now that Achilles has widened the field of debate and raised the question of the regime, Agamemnon replies in kind: he will take Briseis in order to punish Achilles's insolence, and let him who has ears hear. Thus the discussion has gone from the particular question of this share to the general question of the plunder, then from the general question of the plunder to the question of the prerogatives of command, the political prerogatives.

And so Agamemnon returns Chryseis and has Briseis seized in exchange. Achilles weeps to his mother, the goddess Thetis. She goes to supplicate Zeus to avenge her son by granting the Trojans victory until the Achaeans and Agamemnon recognize their error and restore the honor of Achilles. Zeus consents to her plea. To achieve this result, Zeus sends Agamemnon a deceptive dream. The dream enjoins him, in the name of Zeus, to call all the Achaeans to arms, for the hour has come for him at last to capture Troy.

Agamemnon then orders the heralds to convoke the assembly of the Achaeans, agorèn (2.60). But first he convenes the council, the boulè: "he called his ranking chiefs to council" (2.62). We have before us the articulation between the many and the few, the agora and the boulè, that will form the dialectic of the city.

Before the council, Agamemnon explains how he intends to proceed. He will practice on the assembly a sort of well-meaning lie; more precisely, he will tempt or test the Achaeans by inviting them to flee, to board their ships and make for home. He expects the members of the council to play their role as leaders and hold them back with their words. This procedure, which cannot fail to appear curious, even bizarre, to us, was, it seems, common, since after announcing that he was going to tempt or test the Achaeans, Agamemnon adds, "according to time-honored custom [è themis estin]" (2.86). However legitimate and recognized his power is, however grandiose the epithets that qualify him, Agamemnon does not think it is enough to issue his orders to be sure that he will be obeyed. He is so far from thinking so that he expects, on the contrary, to be met at least with opposition, if not with disobedience. Thus, by advocating black, he will make them crave white. This is not our idea of an absolute ruler. The Achaeans need to be persuaded.

Leaning on the scepter Hephaestus fashioned long ago, Agamemnon then addresses the army, the crowd that did not attend the council (2.129ff.). Hearing their leader despair of ever capturing Troy and invite them to flee toward their home shores, the distressed Achaeans run to the ships shouting their desire to go home. Agamemnon's clever trick has succeeded only too well. Taking stock of the impending disaster, Hera urges Athena to intervene. From the heights of Olympus, Athena leaps down to the Achaeans' vessels. There she finds Odysseus, "a mastermind like Zeus [Dii mètin atalanton]" (2.197).

Among the heroes of the *Iliad,* only Odysseus receives this qualifier that distinguishes him from all the others, Achaeans as well as Trojans. There is no Odysseus among the Trojans, a point that is of course decisive for confirming the superiority of the civilization of the Greeks. Odysseus represents a human possibility that until then has emerged only among the Greeks. Agamemnon exercised his legitimate power in accord with custom. His typical trick has failed lamentably. He is at the end of his power. The only recourse resides in the prudence, or wisdom, of Odysseus. Only the wisdom of Odysseus is capable of confronting the exceptional situation, or the state of emergency. In this sense Odysseus, and not Agamemnon, is the true sovereign.[26]

This does not mean that Agamemnon really relinquishes his sovereignty in favor of Odysseus. But in the circumstances and for the occasion, in order to deal with the exceptional situation, he passes his scepter to him, the hereditary and indestructible scepter.[27]

Thus equipped with the scepter, Odysseus briskly goes into action. Homer insists how Odysseus treats the few (2.218ff.) and the many (2.229ff.) very differently. He deals with the few with gentleness and by persuasive means; and with the many with brutality and by forceful means. He rebuffs them and even strikes them with the scepter. He apparently appeals to the intelligence and pride of the few and to the habit of obedience and feeling of inferiority of the many. In this sense Odysseus's speech is grounded in social difference, which he confirms and reinforces.

But there is another aspect, more difficult to grasp. In addressing the few, Odysseus invokes Zeus three times (2.226–229); in addressing the many he mentions him only once without naming him, calling him "the son of crooked-minded Cronus." To the few he makes a theological or theologico-political speech; to the many, the *laos,* he makes a secular speech.[28] He speaks to the fear and wants to awaken the humility of the few by combining Agamemnon and Zeus in one and same threat; and he speaks to the reason of the many to make them consent to an argument of political prudence, or wisdom. One could call this wisdom Hobbesian. Lines 235–236—"Too many kings can ruin an army—mob rule! Let there be one commander, one master only"—will be one of the great authorities in the European monarchical tradition. Odysseus endeavors to frighten those he has called courageous by bringing to bear a sublime, even divine, conception of monarchical power; he appeals directly to the reason of those he has dealt with as cowards. Thus he takes into account that in some circumstances at least, the many are "more reasonable" than the few.

There is no use in pushing our point any further. We see how this scene in the camp of the Greeks contains, so to speak, the seed of all later developments. More precisely, it puts in place all the elements that the Greek city and Greek political philosophy will ceaselessly work on and combine. Which elements are these?

First, of course, there is the tripartition according to number: the many (democracy), the few (oligarchy), and the one (monarchy). But also there is the hard to define but fundamental element that Odysseus stands for—the political wisdom or prudence that has no established place in the human association, that as such does not belong to the one, the few, or the many. It is given by nature, but in a haphazard way, so that the wise man really has no name and thus it is not a coincidence that Odysseus's other name is *Nobody*. Odysseus, so to speak, has no patronymic (in the *Iliad* Homer calls him only Odysseus, even though the other characters call him "son of Laertes").[29]

Homer's text offers us yet another element. Odysseus succeeds in restoring calm, and the warriors return to the assembly from the ships and shelters, and agree to take their seats again. Only Thersites continues to hold forth and mock. He violently lays into Agamemnon, giving voice in some fashion to the resentment against the prince, the man in power, that the other warriors repress in the depths of their hearts. And so Odysseus rebukes him very harshly and cruelly strikes him with the scepter. The Achaeans are pleased to see the mocker chastised. He gave voice to their resentment but his chastisement satisfies their respect for authority and wipes away their unhappiness over this apparently unlimited disrespect.

Who is Thersites? He is, as I have just indicated, the disrespectful person, the critic of power who surrenders wholly to the movement of criticism and speaks truths that are better left unspoken. But this means that he sees them. He thus has some important things in common with Odysseus, first of all a freedom of outlook that stems from independence of mind with respect to social ties. Seth Benardete remarks that Thersites is even more anonymous than Odysseus, "his closest rival in anonymity,"[30] since his father and his homeland are not named. One could say that Thersites is the spirit of comedy, or at least the base part of this spirit, which is no less precious for that. (Is not comedy the "low genre"?)

Thus, as we see, the *Iliad*, that with Achilles and Agamemnon contains the source and the model of all later tragedy, and with Odysseus the prototype of the wise man and we might say the first version of Socrates, with Thersites also contains the living seeds of comedy. Homer was indeed in every sense the educator of Greece.

3

THE CIVIC OPERATION

The first part of our inquiry was devoted chiefly to war, more precisely to the warlike condition that precedes and prepares the civic condition, the life of the city. With the help of Homer we have studied the range of phenomena that modern political philosophy sums up by simplifying them under the rubric of the state of nature, or the state of war. It is now time to examine what the same modern political philosophy calls the civil state, which succeeds the state of nature as peace follows war. But the peace that the ancient city offered was a less complete or less univocal phenomenon than the peace expected by modern political philosophy and largely achieved by the modern State. It has been said that the modern State, with its monopoly on legitimate violence, overcame the natural state of war thanks to a "homeopathic" use of violence. But the ancient city did not deal so directly with the condition of war that preceded it. It largely overcame it, it is true—otherwise there would be no city— but by transforming it in a way that was both more subtle or profound and less complete. Our view of these things is necessarily conditioned both by the univocal character of modern political philosophy that makes us pass from a state *defined* by war to a state *defined* by peace, and by the corresponding effectiveness—that corresponds to this univocal character—of the modern State that in effect brings an unprecedented peace. We are speaking of a complete transformation here, since it makes us pass from one pole to another or from one opposite to another. At the same time, this complete transformation of the state of humans does not constitute, or does not imply, a profound transformation of their nature since it is essentially the same human being who lives in the two states, namely the individual who craves security: if we were not dealing with *the same human being,* the state of nature would not bring to light those human rights that the civil state must thereafter guarantee. Unlike the modern State, the ancient city presupposes and produces, as I have said, a transformation of human nature that is both more profound and less complete: less complete, for war persists or is felt more in the ancient city than in the modern State; more profound, for the transformation is not accomplished by a State that remains in some way outside individuals, but directly concerns the individuals themselves whose nature is transformed since they become participants in a *common thing.* The modern political condition is oriented by the question of the means of achieving civil peace, or, more broadly, the means to guarantee human rights. The ancient political condition is oriented by the question of who participates in the common thing, which is inseparable from the more radical question: what is the common thing?

These two types of questions surely are not mutually exclusive. Ancient politics was not unaware that the city guaranteed rights; modern politics is not unaware of the problems raised by participation in the common thing. Yet they orient two very different orderings of common life, one by the construction of more and more serviceable external instruments, the other by the elaboration of a more and more refined internal tension.[1] The modern politician is an expert in constitutional law, concerned with improving the mechanisms of representative government; the ancient politician was an inseparably political and moral educator who strove to arouse in the soul of the citizens "the most noble and most just" moral dispositions. We need to speak a little more about the difference between ancient and modern political science.

Politics and the Question of Number

The heart or soul of ancient political philosophy resides in the analysis and classification of political regimes. These regimes are particularly delineated in Plato and Aristotle, but we have already met with some elements of analysis in Homer. In this classification, number plays a decisive role: according to whether one or a few or the many govern, the regime of the polis, that is, the form of common life, essentially changes. Human life changes profoundly depending on whether one lives in a monarchy, an oligarchy, or a democracy. This threefold division finds numerous refinements in Aristotle as in Plato, but they do not affect the central character of the question of number for Greek political philosophy. By contrast, modern political philosophy is not very interested in the question of the political regime because in its view the number of the rulers does not seem to be a decisive or even a particularly interesting factor. It replaces debate about the respective merits of the one, the few, and the many with the affirmation of the exclusive legitimacy of "all." It tends to reduce the classification of regimes to the polarity between representative and nonrepresentative regimes, or between democratic and nondemocratic regimes—dictatorship, authoritarian, or totalitarian regime, according to times and circumstances. It is true that Montesquieu elaborated a famous and more refined political classification, but, as we have seen, it is not properly speaking a classification of political regimes, but of political and historical forms: "despotism" is essentially the Oriental type of empire; "republic" is essentially the ancient city; "monarchy" is essentially the modern nation. In this classification, number does not play a decisive role since the republic can be aristocratic or democratic, and monarchy and despotism are equally the government of one alone.

If modern political science has so little interest in the classification of regimes, it is surely because for it there is only one legitimate regime, the democratic regime, which is founded on the participation of "all" to the extent that no one, barring legal sanction, is deprived of civil rights. In practice, the majority governs, or decides who will govern. The substitution of the majority for the whole or for unanimity is a delicate passage for democratic theory. If legitimacy resides in "all," in unanimity, and if the latter is lacking, one does not see why the legitimacy that no longer exists could be found in one group, the majority, rather than in another, the minority. But that the majority is closer to unanimity than the minority and is thus the depository of democratic legitimacy is an irresistibly plausible argument, yet one that is valid only in a very narrow arithmetical sense.

No one will deny the prodigious practical fruitfulness of the majority principle. All the good things that we owe to modern democracy we owe in the end to the resolute and methodical implementation of this principle; we owe them in the final analysis to the procedure of election by majority. There is good reason to admire the immense effects of such a small cause. But the overwhelming victory of the democratic reality must not deter us from examining the theoretical problems inherent in the democratic principle. As Aristotle says in a related context, there is difficulty here and matter for political philosophy.[2]

The modern democratic arrangement contains three moments or aspects that one is tempted to say are numerical: unanimity, majority, minority. However, unanimity is not a real, effective number: unanimity is never active as such. The active number is the majority. But here again one must beware. The majority as number or the number of the majority does not exist as such. What makes the majority is its positive difference with the minority. The only real, effective, active number here is the difference between the majority and the minority, a difference that keeps its full validity even when it is reduced to one: the one who is elected is the one who has *at least one* vote more than his opponent. The only real, effective, active number is in the end the unit of counting, the unit that is used to count, which is not properly speaking a number even if it is the constitutive element of all the numbers. Modern democratic politics is founded not on number, as is often said, but on counting. It is a matter of counting to the end, of going to the end of the count, since the outcome is liable to result from the last vote counted, from the last and smallest difference. Neither the majority nor the minority exist as real, effective, active numbers as long as they are not in effect counted, and then what effectively exists is their difference, which can be reduced to one unit of counting.

These apparently abstract considerations help us by contrast to gauge the role of number in the ancient civic ordering. This ordering appears then as an articulation of one, of several (a small number) and of many (a great number). We are dealing with three real numbers here. The "monarchic" *one* is not a unit of counting, since nothing can be added to it without destroying it; it is a unit that exists solely as a unit. *Several* and *many* also exist in reality; they are also real numbers. Unlike the majority and minority, they do not exist according to their numerical difference, even if of course there is a numerical difference between them. The paradoxical proof that they are real, effective, active numbers is that there is no need to count them. How many are *several?* One does not know exactly; one does not need to know: the few are the few, and that is in fact a qualitative determination. How many are *many?* One knows with even less exactness, and one needs even less to know.

In the classical tripartite division, there are three real, qualitative numbers that do not need to be counted in order to be defined in themselves and in relation to one another. In this sense it is a natural tripartition that belongs necessarily to human things. But if this is the case, it ought to be present and active among us, as in ancient politics. But we have seen that the modern democratic arrangement is altogether different, founded on counting the majority, that is, the difference between the majority and the minority. Must we think that the modern arrangement has simply succeeded or replaced the ancient? If that were the case, the classical ordering would have no right to the qualifiers "natural" and "necessary" that I have used; it would be simply a historically determined ordering that today has been replaced. However, it takes very little attention to acknowledge that the ancient arrangement is still present, effective, and active beneath the modern. After all, the few and the many, although they have no place in the constitutional mechanism, play a considerable part in the social and political life of modern peoples. When not so long ago in France there were denunciations of the power of the "two hundred families," that number did not result from a count; it was not subject to a statistical refinement concluding that the exact number was rather 192 or 207. This number, which had only a qualitative meaning, designated the "few," whose real political influence was judged largely independent of the electoral play between majority and minority and of constitutional mechanisms. Likewise, when one spoke of the "workers" or the "masses," one did not mean either a majority exactly determined as the outcome of a count as in the case of an electoral majority, or the unanimity of citizens since on the contrary the "workers" or "masses" excluded the "exploiters" and thus the "two hundred families." One meant, and everyone understood, "the many" as opposed to "the few."

One could of course say that these themes and terms were "partisan," that they did not give an account of objective reality or that they gave excessive place to provisional phenomena that may not have disappeared but are at least much less salient today. However that may be—and we could discuss this at length—one must also observe that the modern arrangement as such, in its explicit structure if I may say, reveals the classical threefold partition or offers a mode of that partition. Does not the "one" reappear in the executive power, the decisive invention of modern politics? Do not the "few" appear anew in the "educated," the "productive," or the other "deserving" members of the modern "meritocracy"? As for the "many," do they not reappear in the "broader public," which cannot be counted precisely but by its "opinion" exercises so much influence on the character of contemporary life? One could suggest still other modern embodiments of the three "numbers."

As one can see, modern democracy juxtaposes, superimposes, and mixes the modern bipartition and the classical tripartite division, the precise numbers one can count to the last unit, and the qualitative numbers that are not calculated or not counted. In this way the transhistorical validity and the necessary and natural characters of the classical tripartite division are confirmed. This is a powerful reason for us to consider it with renewed attention.

As I have said, the one, the few, and the many that constitute the classical and natural tripartition of political life each represent a qualitative number that is real, effective, and active. If this is so, and although to be sure they exist naturally one with the other and one in rapport with the other, they are susceptible of existing by themselves or separately, independently of one another. The close examination of ancient life seems to confirm this fact.

Becoming Human, Becoming Citizen

It is natural to begin with the *one*. It seems necessary that properly human life began with the *one*. The human world has to appear with the unity that makes it precisely "a world." This *one* in any case is to be found in the beginning, with the first fathers of families that Homer and following him Plato and Aristotle describe under the figure of the Cyclopes.[3] Vico, who along with Rousseau was the political philosopher who scrutinized with the greatest attention the transition to humanity, the coming-to-be-human of the first "men," often returns to these Cyclopes—*polifemi*—"who lived separately and alone in their caves with their wives and children, never concerning themselves with one another's affairs, as Polyphemus tells Ulysses in Homer."[4] In the life of the Cyclopes, one, the father, encompasses and determines every plurality: since no one concerns himself with another's affairs, each cave constitutes, so to speak, a unit of justice.[5] In other words, this savage independence can be interpreted as a "primary justice," a justice "toward Jove."[6] The Cyclopes' caves, Vico goes on to say, protected the modesty of the first properly human couplings.[7] One is not required to follow Vico in all his conjectures, nor Homer or Plato for that matter. What is not conjectural but confirmed in all sorts of ways in the whole breadth of the historical field is the pervasiveness of this type of human association, dedicated to intense unity, if I may say so, under the pressure and attraction of paternal power. I have not said enough for our purpose about the original mode of the independent or separated and substantial *one*.

It seems more difficult to ascertain the separate existence of the many, the effective and active great number in its substantial indetermination, so to speak. Here too Vico offers some very suggestive conjectures concerning those he calls the *famoli*. Did not the fugitives, the bandits, the wanderers, all those beings with no faith or law, with no hearth or home, without marriage or burial rites, who found asylum in the cities constitute a very important element of the prepolitical condition of humans? Even more, is not the definition of the first cities, or at least of some of them and especially the most famous among them, that they were the "first asylums"?[8] The phenomenon of refugees or wanderers is not limited, of course, to the most primitive epochs. It is as it were coeval with human history. It does not necessarily concern "large numbers" in the quantitative sense, but it possesses the qualitative characters of indetermination—how many are they?—of opaqueness, alienness, recalcitrance, and threat of the "large number."

Thus the separated *one* along with the separated *many* are registered, constitutive phenomena of prepolitical human experience. But they count for little by comparison with the phenomenon of the separated *few*, the separated *several*, that, because it engenders politics as such, also engenders the phenomena of the political one and the political many or joins them to itself, thereby instituting the city that is articulated according to the threefold division of the one, the few, and the many. We have already said much about the phenomenon of the separated few, the group of warriors, heroes, whose depiction by Homer was the education of Greece. The paradox of the heroic group is that something like the common good arises from psychic or moral dispositions that seem to exclude any notion of a common good. How is that? How could the likes of Achilles recognize, or elaborate, something resembling a public thing? Vico helps us to discern the paradoxical political fruitfulness of the heroes' unlimited egoism, as it were.

First of all, this egoism extends the savage independence of the Cyclopes that, as we have pointed out, made a decisive contribution to the moral education of humanity—or rather to the coming-to-be-human of the bestial being that preceded him—by ensuring the "guarding of the confines." The "infamous promiscuity of things in the bestial state" had nothing of a republic, nothing of a common thing.[9] When everything was common, nothing was common. In this way Vico suggests that the common is not simply the absence of the proper or particular; in order to come into being, it needs the prior activation of the proper or particular. Only one who has first thought of the proper or in whom the thought of the proper is active can think of the common. How could this come about in reality? Let us read the end of paragraph 629:

> And at their very birth providence causes the commonwealths to spring forth aristocratic in form, in conformity with the savage and solitary nature of the first men. This form consists entirely, as writers on political theory point out, in guarding the confines and the institutions, so that peoples newly come to humanity might, by the very form of their governments, continue for a long time to remain enclosed within these confines and institutions, and so forget the infamous and nefarious promiscuity of the bestial and feral state. But the minds of men were preoccupied with particulars and incapable of understanding a common good; they were accustomed never to concern themselves even with the particular affairs of others, as Homer makes his Polyphemus tell Ulysses (and in this giant Plato recognizes the family fathers in the so-called state of nature preceding the civil state). Providence, therefore, by the aforesaid aristocratic form of their governments, led them to unite themselves to their fatherlands in order to preserve such great private interests as their family monarchies were (for this was what they were entirely bent upon), and thus, beyond any design of theirs, they were brought together in a universal civil good called commonwealth.[10]

The "providential," in fact intensely natural mechanism that Vico describes here makes us think of course of the mechanism invoked by the theoreticians of the social contract: the political institution is rooted in the private desire or need for self-conservation. The important point, however, resides in what differentiates Vico from these theoreticians. The decisive point here is that this is a matter of "great" private interests, so great that they are called "monarchies." These interests do not belong to a republic since there is nothing common yet, but they are already political by their scale or amplitude. It is not in vain that the imagination represents these exemplars of the political *one*, of which I was just speaking, as giants. In their caves under the sky, with their flocks, their wives, and their children, they deepened and extended the sphere of the proper to the point where, paradoxically, it became big enough to enter, as it were, a "republican" edifice. The paradox is that what maximizes the proper is also what prepares or makes possible its overcoming.

It remains that we still do not see well what circumstances could in effect lead the Cyclopes, or the heroes, to surrender even in part their enormous self-sufficiency, their "familial monarchy." In an earlier paragraph Vico proposes an explanation that makes us witness in some way the birth of the city, that is, the joining of the one, the few, and the many in the crystallization of the tripartition that is constitutive of politics. The role of catalyst is played by the many, in Vico's language the *famoli,* the faithless, lawless wanderers who took refuge under the protection of the heroes, the monarchic heads of families, a protection that in reality merged with harshest servitude. Now, in the terms of Vico's perhaps borrowed formulation, "subject man naturally aspires to free himself from servitude."[11] Thus the *famoli* mutinied against the heroes. Therein lies the catalyst of political crystallization, into a city of the one, the few, and the many:

> For at this point, under pressure of the emergency, the heroes must by nature have been moved to unite themselves in orders so as to resist the multitudes of rebellious *famoli.* And they must have chosen as their head a father fiercer than the rest and with greater presence of spirit. Such men were called *reges,* kings, from *regere,* which properly means to sustain or direct. . . . Such was the generation of the heroic kingdoms. And since the fathers were sovereign kings of their families, the equality of their state and the fierce nature of the cyclopes being such that no one of them naturally would yield to another, there sprang up of themselves the reigning senates, made up of so many family kings. They found that, without human discernment or counsel, they had united their private interests in a common interest called *patria,* which, the word *res* being understood,

means "the interest of the fathers." The nobles were accordingly called patricians, and the nobles must have been the only citizens of the first *patriae,* or "fatherlands."[12]

Thus it can be seen that the first political monarchy was but the instrument and so to speak the annex of familial monarchy. It does not alter the essentially aristocratic character of the first "public thing." Its most substantial legacy resides probably in the name of *king.* The family monarchies unite, without profoundly transforming themselves, in this first republic, which is in effect a patriciate, a senate of fathers.

There now is indeed a fatherland, but does this fatherland entail or imply a truly common good? Vico chose his words with great care, but he does not end our perplexity: "They found that, without human discernment or counsel, they had united their private interests in a common interest called *patria.*" It is certain that the fathers at the beginning think only of their private interest. It is no less certain that henceforth they have a common interest. But what is the relation between the subjective dispositions of the fathers and the objective reality of their common interest? Does the latter transform the former? Does the family king, the selfish and proud father, now become concerned with the common interest as such, as common? In short, does the family king become a citizen, and to what extent?

Perhaps the very terms of our question render a serious answer impossible, by setting before us the following alternative: either the patrician remains a selfish and self-interested family king, or he becomes a disinterested citizen, that is, interested exclusively or principally in the common good. This alternative, which has been so familiar ever since we assimilated morality to selflessness, hardly helps us to conceive the transformation of soul by which the father becomes citizen. Vico has some suggestions that lead us to abandon this alternative. Speaking of family kings, he says:

> They were led to observe their laws by a sovereign private interest, which the heroes identified with that of their fatherlands, of which they were the only citizens. Hence they did not hesitate, for the safety of their various fatherlands, to consecrate themselves and their families to the will of the laws, which by maintaining the common security of the fatherland kept secure for each of them a certain private monarchical reign over his family.

Moreover, it was this great private interest, in conjunction with the supreme arrogance characteristic of barbarous times, which formed their heroic nature, whence came so many heroic actions in defense of their fatherlands. To these heroic deeds we must add the intolerable pride, profound avarice and pitiless cruelty with which the ancient Roman patricians treated the unhappy plebeians, as is clearly seen in Roman history precisely during that period which Livy himself describes as having been the age of Roman virtue and of the most flourishing popular liberty yet dreamed of in Rome. It will then be evident that this public virtue was nothing but a good use which providence made of such grievous, ugly and cruel private vices, in order that the cities might be preserved during a period when the minds of men, intent on particulars, could not naturally understand a common good.[13]

This is a remarkably interesting and deeply troubling text. The last lines give a particularly vigorous and almost violent expression to an idea that recurs often in Vico and that we have already encountered several times, the idea, we could say, employing the phrase Adam Smith would later make famous, of an "invisible hand" that guides men to produce public benefits by following their private vices—now citing Mandeville's terms. This type of thinking became current with the emergence of the commercial society, to whose simple and powerful wellspring one thus purports to point. But Vico's thesis here concerns the other extremity of political development, its beginnings, far removed from the society of commerce that presupposes equality and knows of sympathy. When Mandeville spoke of "private vices," he had in mind only the taste for comfort and luxury, ostentatious vanity, the desire to please and to entice—in short all the passions that by inducing spending feed the economic system and maintain the social engine. Vico here speaks of "intolerable pride," "profound avarice," "pitiless cruelty," of "such grievous, ugly, and cruel private vices." There is no doubting we are far from any disinterestedness and from all civic virtue. At the same time, we are told of "so many heroic actions in defense of their fatherlands." Vico suggests, it seems, an *identification* between the patricians' private interest and public interest, with the dedication to what is common that the latter implies, an identification that is made possible by the fact that the patricians were at that time still the only citizens. The key to the enigma resides perhaps in the "supreme arrogance" that Vico says is "characteristic of barbarous times." Could one not suggest that the supreme arrogance that is inseparable from this "private monarchical reign over [the] family" finds a kind of extension, a supplement, and also, in a sense that is in no way "moral," a sort of corrective in this undoubtedly exhilarating discovery of the fatherland, however limited it still is? The common thing that begins to appear, however narrow it is—but this narrowness is the condition of its birth—in some way stimulates selfish pride just as bellows make a fire burn more fiercely.

Such is the explanation that I would propose of this fascinating passage of Vico, which is a contribution of the first order to a question that has not ceased to occupy modern political philosophers and that became an obsession in the eighteenth century: how does one explain the extraordinary civic dedication—or what appears to be such—of the Greeks of the cities and the Romans of the republic?

Here it would be worth comparing Vico's suggestions with the views of Montesquieu and Rousseau, who set, so to speak, the two poles between which the modern interpretation of ancient city life will oscillate.

Civic Virtue according to Montesquieu

Let us begin with this text of Montesquieu that I have previously discussed elsewhere:[14] "Love of the homeland leads to goodness in mores, and goodness in mores leads to love of the homeland. The less we can satisfy our particular passions, the more we give ourselves up to passions for the general order. Why do monks so love their order? Their love comes from the same thing that makes their order intolerable to them. Their rule deprives them of everything upon which ordinary passions rest; what remains, therefore, is the passion for the very rule that afflicts them. The more austere it is, the more it curtails their inclinations, the more force it gives to those that remain."[15]

This astonishing text, which includes a psychological interpretation not only of the ancient city but also of the Christian Church and perhaps even of morality as such, rests entirely on the polarity between particular and general passions, that is, between the particular and the general, since the passions are here the "common factor." There is in the human soul as it were a "fixed quantity" of passions that can moreover take on qualities or take directions that are different and even opposed. These qualities or directions do not have the same standing. Montesquieu's analysis presupposes that the primitive or "ordinary" passions, which one perhaps could rightly call "natural," are "our particular passions." The general passions are, so to speak, an "extraordinary" modification of the particular or "ordinary" passions. Now, the boldness and even the insolence of Montesquieu's thought lies more precisely in the fact that this modification, which seems essential, radical, qualitative, since it makes us pass from the particular to the general, from what is selfish, self-interested, and often culpable to what is in principle moral, results from a mere displacement of the energy of the passions: the more one subtracts from the particular passions, the more one adds to the general passions. In reality, it is by subtracting from the sum of the particular passions that the general passions are produced, which those who "in all countries of the world love morality" call by the name of "virtue."

The analogy Montesquieu makes between civic virtue and monastic rule is certainly striking. Let us for the moment set aside the brilliant antireligious epigram contained in these lines. The analogy implies that the intention, the aim of those who practice religious or civic virtue does not in any way determine the actual dispositions of their soul: whether they aim at God, the divine law, or the city, the public thing, does not really matter, since in both cases the same mechanism or system of the passions is at work. If what the soul consciously aims at, what it is "open" to, has no effect on its actual life, but if on the contrary what it aims at, or believes it aims at, is the effect of its internal mechanism or system, then this soul is a closed soul; it functions, so to speak, only internally.

The monastic analogy then has the value of a mathematical maximum: if obedience to the law of God, the "greatest" Being, is the effect of the internal mechanism of the soul's passions, it becomes very plausible to also consider obedience to the law of the city as an effect of this sort.

I characterized these lines of Montesquieu as an antireligious epigram. Indeed, the loving obedience to the divine law that defines monastic life is here reduced to an internal mechanism of the soul, in the development of which the soul has no other object than itself—the soul is without object. At the same time these lines can be read as an antireligious version of

Augustinian psychology. For Augustine, the fundamental disposition of the soul, its movement, gravitation, and weight, is love—a capacity that is also a will to love. "Amor meus pondus meum."[16] Montesquieu here explains to us that when we cannot love what gives us pleasure—when we cannot satisfy our particular passions—we love what makes us suffer; for example, the law that deprives us of what gives us pleasure. The implied major premise of the syllogism would be that we cannot stop ourselves from loving, that we prefer to love what gives us pain than not to love at all.

One could add that the antireligious epigram contains a further irony. For Machiavelli, the first modern political thinker, the manly virtues of the ancient city were advantageously opposed to the "effeminate" virtues of the Christian Church. Now Montesquieu, who on many scores stands in the Machiavellian tradition, here assimilates the civic virtues to the monastic virtues, ancient civic life to monastic life, that aspect of the Christian world toward which Machiavellian politics felt the keenest antipathy. One can wonder to what extent Montesquieu himself perceived the irony in this: that the life that once was assumed to be the most manly was now confused with the life that was always taken to be the most effeminate. The political and moral opposition between the ancient world and the Christian world necessarily fades while the redefinition of the soul as something closed and obedient to itself takes shape and gathers strength.

I have not raised the question of the validity of Montesquieu's analysis. It is certainly plausible for us today, who are so familiar with the psychology of frustration and sublimation. But if it seems plausible once the city, or the Church, has been instituted, that is, once the general law has been defined and promulgated, it is much less so if one looks at it in the situation Vico considered, that is, before the institution of the common or the general, when there was only what is proper or particular. How could the general be born where there is only the particular?

Politically, Montesquieu's purpose was to make the ancient city distant and foreign to us, to render it repulsive just as monastic life was repulsive in the eyes of his contemporaries of the Enlightenment age, in order to open up the way for modern liberty. Rousseau's intention seems to be rigorously opposite, since he contrasts ancient virtue—still admirable—with modern corruption.

Civic Virtue according to Rousseau

How does Rousseau define the civic virtue he readily calls "patriotism" or "love of country"? Let us consider a text that receives less attention than others but that contains the most direct and most complete analysis of the love of country, the *Discourse on Political Economy*.

The conception of civic virtue proposed by Rousseau seems very close to the one Montesquieu extracted from his analysis of the ancient city. I cite Rousseau: "Do you want the general will to be accomplished? Make all private wills be in conformity with it. And since virtue is merely this conformity of the private to the general will, in a word, make virtue reign."[17]

The only important difference seems to be that where Montesquieu spoke of "passion," Rousseau speaks of "will." A few lines later, we see this difference fade and disappear: "It is certain that the greatest miracles of virtue have been produced by the love of country. In joining together the force of self-love and all the beauty of virtue, this sweet and lively sentiment takes on an energy that, without disfiguring it, makes it the most heroic of all the passions."[18]

We remark in passing that for Rousseau, as for Vico, civic life is not intelligible outside a certain "heroic" perspective. Now, how does Rousseau analyze the functioning of "the most heroic of all the passions"? A few pages later he explains what must be done to arouse this passion in the hearts of citizens:

> A man who had no passion would certainly be a very bad citizen. But one must agree that even though men cannot be taught to love nothing, it is not impossible for them to learn to love one object more than another and what is truly beautiful more than what is deformed. If, for example, they are trained early enough never to consider their own persons except in terms of being related to the body of the state, and not to perceive their own existence except as part of the state's existence, they will eventually come to identify themselves in some way with this larger whole, to feel themselves to be members of the country, to love it with that exquisite sentiment that every isolated man feels only for himself, to elevate their soul perpetually toward this great object, and thus to transform into a sublime virtue this dangerous disposition from which arises all our vices.[19]

This passage is just as fascinating as Montesquieu's that we read a moment ago. It deals with the same object in the same radical way: how the human passions become civic virtue. It is true that Rousseau introduces an element Montesquieu did not mention: "what is truly beautiful."

Comparing these two texts leaves us perplexed. It seems that Rousseau says the same thing as Montesquieu, and also the exact opposite. The same thing: civic virtue results from a modification of the ordinary economy of the passions. The opposite: whereas Montesquieu had civic virtue born of the frustration, repression, or negation of the particular passions, the virtue Rousseau sketches seems to be a culmination of the particular passions since it consists in the identification of the particular with the general or the individual with the whole. Where Montesquieu defined love of country as "this passion for the very rule that afflicts" citizens, Rousseau compares it to "that exquisite sentiment that every isolated man feels only for himself." For Montesquieu love of country resides in the negation, not without a certain bitter pleasure, of one's own individuality, whereas for Rousseau it constitutes the delicious fulfillment of the sentiment of one's own individuality. Nevertheless, this opposition is more apparent than essential. It is more a difference in accent, depending on whether the sentiment of the self, the sentiment of one's own, appears to be exalted by the repression of the particular passions, or rather by the identification with this greater individual that is the city. Indeed, does not the education in identification Rousseau speaks of here presuppose the repression of the proper that Montesquieu spoke of and that Rousseau himself evokes elsewhere rather fiercely?

Montesquieu and Rousseau share essentially the same psychology, a mechanistic psychology of the homogeneous soul, the soul defined exclusively by love of the proper and in which the common, or rather the general, can only arise as a modification of the proper or particular, which alone is natural. I mentioned briefly an element present in Rousseau, even emphasized by him, and which is not found in Montesquieu: the aim of legislation is to teach people to love "what is truly beautiful more than what is deformed." The "beautiful" here is not a matter of what we call aesthetics. Rousseau characterizes it not much later when he speaks of "this larger whole," "this great object," the love of which defines the "sublime virtue." The "beautiful" then is this "great object"— the city, of course—the love of which enlarges and elevates the soul. The nature of the soul does not change; it is always self-interested love; but what changes is its quantity, its extension, and what Rousseau immediately after calls its "direction." Thus "this dangerous disposition from which all our vices arise" is "transformed into a sublime virtue."

Rousseau here keeps very explicitly to the terms of the mechanistic psychology of the homogeneous soul of which we were speaking. At the same time, the mechanistic transformations that he describes—extension, direction—induce a transformation whose qualitative character he emphasizes and celebrates. It is not that vice is transformed into virtue; what is so transformed is a "disposition" that is itself neutral but "dangerous," for "all our vices arise" from it. The soul is always self-interested, but its objects are more or less interesting. Reduced to itself, to its private interests, it becomes irresistibly vicious. Interested in something greater than itself, it becomes as it were greater than itself and capable of "sublime virtue." It would overcome its self-interested nature if that were possible.

In this way Rousseau rediscovers some possibilities of the soul that the moderns had decried and repressed, organizing themselves in such a way that these possibilities could not be deployed. Modern society and "English psychology" belong to one another: the society of commerce and equality and the psychology of self-interest and vanity belong to one another. Together they produce and formulate a prejudice that, according to Rousseau, is fatal to both the happiness and the virtue of men. What is that prejudice? The prejudice according to which to live is for each man to compare himself, the prejudice of the man Rousseau calls the "bourgeois" and that Allan Bloom characterizes as the man who, in his relations with others, thinks only of himself and, in his relations with himself, thinks only of others. The bourgeois lives torn between himself and others. Rousseau maintains that one can escape this in-between; one can live in oneself without thinking of others; one can live with others in the city without thinking of oneself. He rediscovers the full extent of the soul's possibilities, and consequently the full extent of the transformation the soul can undergo. He asks anew the question of the form and dimensions—extension, height, or grandeur—of the soul.

Rousseau thus defines the nature and breadth of our soul by the following twofold possible identification: identification with the self and identification with the Whole. We understand that this twofold identification is made possible by the soul's plasticity, by the capacity that is proper to it to circumscribe itself on the one hand and to enlarge itself on the other. But how can one prevent these two identifications from becoming contradictory or from impeding one another, and so making us fall again into the in-between of bourgeois life? How can one live in the self all the while living in the Whole?

The law is what accomplishes this miracle, but law understood in a novel way. It has always been a principal part of the role and function of the law to hold together the citizens in the city, the individuals in the Whole. It was assumed that they were all they should be once they obeyed the law. Rousseau was brought to ask something more of the law: it must hold together and even join the two extremities of the soul, the two extreme possibilities of identification with the self and identification with the Whole. He was thus brought to change, and to change radically, the meaning and definition of law. In order that living in oneself be the same thing as living in the Whole, it is necessary and sufficient that the law of the Whole coincide with the law of the self, that in obeying the law of the Whole I obey myself at the same time; I obey the law I give myself, an obedience to oneself that Rousseau identifies with freedom. To resolve the unprecedented problem posed by the extension of the soul's capacities that he discovers or proposes, Rousseau proceeds to redefine the law, which becomes a law one gives oneself, a command by the self to the self. Thus Rousseau encloses the essentially open soul which he had, so to speak, taken back from English psychology between command by oneself and obedience to oneself. He thus substitutes an entirely determined, as it were calculable relation of self to self for the twofold relation—to the self and to the Whole—of the extended soul, for the incalculable angle of the open soul. It seems then that all the benefit of Rousseau's rediscovery of the "heroic" dimensions of the soul is lost.

At the same time it appears that in practice the law is the work not of each person, not of all people, nor of the Whole, but of the "legislator" who is outside the city and who obeys only his "great soul"—the "great soul," one might think, that gives the legislator the desire and the capacity to teach the people he forms for civic life to "love one object more than another and what is truly beautiful more than what is deformed" and so "to identify themselves in some way with this larger Whole" that is the country. In this way obedience to oneself hangs on obedience of the Whole to the external legislator; the most internal rapport derives from the most external dependence. What is going on here? Why does Rousseau, after rediscovering the soul's extension, not only reduce it to the obedience to oneself that is freedom, but also reduce this freedom to superstitious obedience to the legislator? All these maneuvers—which are otherwise so brilliant that their analysis has spawned innumerable commentaries—have as their goal to cast a veil over and to prohibit the only approach that would allow Rousseau to explain in a coherent way his rediscovery of the soul's extension, which was to take account of the "few" between each and all, or the Whole. One could say that all the difficulties of *The Social Contract* derive from the deliberate and fundamental exclusion of the "few" that Rousseau effected in that work.

Rousseau knew what he was doing. By the genre to which it belongs, *The Social Contract* is more the work of a jurisconsult or a theoretician of public law than of a political philosopher. As a theoretician of public rights, Rousseau had good reasons to exclude the few from his consideration: the political law he wished to promote is an equal law.[20] On the other hand, when he is a political philosopher, in particular in his work that he himself calls "the most philosophical," *The Second Discourse,* he gives a decisive and central role to the "few" not only in the formation of the body politic but in its definition. How does he manage to conceal or to mask the contradiction between the two approaches? By shouting very loudly. By railing against those he calls "the rich," he glosses over the troubling fact that he gives them the decisive and central role I have just spoken of.

Let us quickly proceed with the help of some citations. First, the strident condemnation of the rich: "The rich, for their part, had scarcely known the pleasure of domination when they soon disdained all others, and using their old slaves to subdue new ones, they thought only of subjugating and enslaving their neighbors: like those famished wolves which, having once tasted human flesh, refuse all other food and thenceforth want only to devour men."[21]

In reality, however, Rousseau's description of the prepolitical stage is much more impartial than these words would suggest. Let us read what follows immediately after: "Thus, as the most powerful or most miserable made of their force or their needs a sort of right to the goods of others, equivalent according to them to the right of property, the destruction of

equality was followed by the most frightful disorder; thus the usurpations of the rich, the brigandage of the poor, the unbridled passions of
all, stifling natural pity and the as yet weak voice of justice, made men
avaricious, ambitious, and evil. Between the right of the stronger and the
right of the first occupant there arose a perpetual conflict which ended
only in fights and murders. Nascent society gave way to the most horrible state of war."[22]

In the period of people coming together that precedes and conditions
the appearance of political life, the order, which is rather a disorder, but
which is nevertheless an order since it will provide the nucleus of political order, forms itself around the hinge of domination—servitude. Rousseau's rhetoric, like our finer feelings, must not blind us to the fact that
the two opposing groups in this articulation are equally deprived of legitimacy, or legality, or moral justification, as one would say, in the eyes
of Rousseau the political philosopher. To the "usurpations" of the rich
corresponds the "brigandage" of the poor. To the "right of the stronger"
of the first, which is not a right, there corresponds the "right of the first
occupant" of the second, which in short is but an attenuated version of
the right of the stronger. Rousseau leaves us without any doubt: in a state
of war where "all" are prey to "unbridled passions," no one, rich or
poor, is within his rights; justice is on neither side.

It would seem that this "horrible state of war" Rousseau speaks of ought
to have broken down these beginnings of coming together, definitively forbidding people to have access to social life, to form themselves into political bodies. The opposite happened. The very gravity of the evil, the urgency
of the situation, led them "at last" to find the remedy, in any case a remedy.[23] No, the term "remedy" decidedly does not fit, since the root of evil
will not be removed, but on the contrary, so to speak, conserved. Only the
symptoms will be attenuated, at the same time masked and stabilized. The
patient will be kept alive, without seriously treating his illness but on the
contrary consolidating it, by consecrating it, that is, by institutionalizing it
as political justice or law. How can this be? How is one to conceive of this
process that is nothing less than the birth of political life?

Reason plays a decisive role in this process, reason conceived as "reflection" on the "situation" in which people found themselves. Here,
Rousseau is not content to say, as Aristotle had said, that the human is a
"rational animal" who is thus able "to reveal the advantageous and the

harmful and hence also the just and the unjust."[24] (On this point, Hobbes himself, as critical of Aristotle as he otherwise is, shares his perspective: civic life flows from the action of the rational faculty of humans, a faculty that by Hobbes as well as Aristotle is attributed to humans in general, or to humans as a species.)[25] Reason may well be a general human faculty; its actualization, its actual implementation, is first of all the act of a particular group, which is the "few," or, in the language of Rousseau, the "rich."

Before attempting to see more precisely what Rousseau has in mind and in order to help us overcome or master our nascent indignation at the suggestion, in truth the affirmation that civic reason is in short the invention of the rich, we need to measure the difficulty that Hobbes for example had left us to face. Contrary to the impression that Hobbes's description of the state of nature wishes to produce, the fact that all humans share the same condition and find themselves in the state of war makes it more difficult and not more easy to leave this state. To be sure, everyone and all humans would equally have an interest in leaving it; but everyone and all humans find themselves equally in a situation that necessarily produces in them actions that extend and aggravate the state of war. Who will have the intelligence or the boldness to raise themselves *above* their situation to conceive and propose to their companions in misfortune, that is, to their enemies, what Hobbes calls "convenient articles of peace"?

Thus Rousseau does not make political reason, justice, or law derive from a general reflection on a general situation, from a gradually expanding awareness of a situation that is disastrous for all. He makes it emerge from a particular reflection on a particular situation within the general calamitous situation. There is paradoxically an original bond between reason and a certain particularity or partiality because reason is reflection, that is, always in some fashion a return toward the self. Such a return presupposes, then consolidates and consecrates, the existence of such a self. Thus public reason for its birth presupposes a particular group existing beforehand, a group whose particular situation distinguishes and separates it from all others, a group whose situation is particularly problematic. That group is the rich.

What is proper to the rich? Of course, it is the fact that they are rich. Now that means that they are paradoxically more vulnerable than the others. They are more exposed than the others in a situation where "the risk of life was common to all while the risk of goods was theirs alone."[26] A few pages later, Rousseau makes us aware of the particular sensibility of the rich as it derives from their specific vulnerability: "The rich being so to speak vulnerable in every part of their goods, it was much easier to harm them."[27] In short it is a question of surface. Like a larger boat with a larger sail, don't the rich expose a larger surface to the winds and blasts of fortune? They are more exposed because they are more extended.

The more extended being of the rich is thus decisive for the birth of political reason. Such is the mystery of the city in full light: those who are manifestly the strongest are at the same time and for that very reason—it is the reverse side of their strength—the weakest. They have an urgent need to utilize the strength of the others, to turn it to their advantage. We now understand why, in the second prologue to the *Discourse*, Rousseau could present the purpose of this work in the following terms: "Precisely what, then, is at issue in this Discourse? To indicate in the progress of things the moment when, right taking the place of violence, nature was subjected to law; to explain by what sequence of marvels the strong could resolve to serve the weak."[28] The poor of course are not strong only because, deprived of goods, they carry their whole being with them, unlike the rich whose goods give them so to speak a second body, more extended than the first, and thus more vulnerable. But how did the rich go about turning the strength of the poor to their advantage?

On first impression it appears indeed the result of a "marvel." Since the natural inclination of the poor is to pillage the rich, how could the poor be brought to be the defenders of the rich? By persuasion? But how could the rich persuade the poor, or even get them to listen? Indeed Rousseau insists on this point: in no way can the rich justify their particular situation, their particular advantages. All the reasons they could advance would in the end come down to their being the stronger. Yet they are not the stronger since they are asking for help. And anyway, might does not make right.

Rousseau shows how radical he is by reducing all the reasons advanced to justify the particular advantages to one version or another of the right of the stronger. Even "labor," which a few pages earlier was said to be at the origin of the idea of property, is now dismissed in these terms: "by virtue of what do you presume to be paid at our expense for work we did not impose on you?"[29] As one can see, Rousseau here turns on its head the argument Locke put forth in favor of the rights of the "industrious and rational" and against the "quarrelsome and contentious." In sum, he takes the side of the latter because in his eyes no right can rest exclusively on what the beneficiary of that right is, or does. As he is in the habit of doing, Rousseau gives his idea an extreme expression: "Do you not know . . . that you needed express and unanimous consent of the human race to appropriate for yourself anything from common subsistence that exceeded your own?"[30] One could state this more calmly by saying that no particular reason can be truly valid unless it is sustained and enveloped by the general or public reason. In this sense, and in an unexpected way, while categorically affirming the original dispersion of men and the artificial character of human reason, Rousseau rediscovers the necessity and eminent dignity of common reason. Each one of us lacks strength as well as reason. Each needs to be strengthened and justified by public force and common reason.

The rich then, carried away by the "pleasure of domination," ceaselessly increase their goods, the "surface" of their domination and of their weakness in the same proportion. I am mistaken in saying "the rich" in the plural. They do not form a united group of equals susceptible of joining their forces against the "brigandage of the poor." Their "mutual jealousies" prevent them from doing so. It is the rich person, the individual subject, and not the rich as a group that is the author of these "decisive" reflections on the "situation." How could it be otherwise in this period of "nascent society" that tends irresistibly toward the "state of war," where each is pressed to first think of himself, where social groups do not yet exist since society does not yet exist? How could parties exist when the whole does not exist? The decisive reflection finally comes into the mind of the rich man when he sees himself "alone against everybody": "the rich, pressed by necessity, finally conceived the most deliberate project that ever entered the human mind. It was to use in his favor the very forces of those who attacked him, to make his defenders out of his adversaries, inspire them with other maxims, and give them other institutions which were as favorable to him as natural right was adverse."[31] Never has a friend of the rich given him such striking and penetrating praise as Rousseau has here.

Nevertheless, as we read on, we soon ask ourselves if this move by the rich was truly the exploit Rousseau has led us to conceive it to be. In fact, after sketching, in a direct speech, what might have been the rich man's wondrously persuasive speech, Rousseau adds:

> Far less than the equivalent of this discourse was necessary to win over crude, easily seduced men, who in addition had too many disputes to straighten out among themselves to be able to do without arbiters, and too much avarice and ambition to be able to do without masters for long. All ran to meet their chains thinking they secured their freedom, for although they had enough reason to feel the advantages of a political establishment, they did not have enough experience to foresee its dangers. Those most capable of anticipating the abuses were precisely those who counted on profiting from them; and even the wise saw the necessity of resolving to sacrifice one part of their freedom for the preservation of the other, just as a wounded man has his arm cut off to save the rest of his body.[32]

Thus, what at first appeared as the brilliant initiative of the rich acting individually in achieving this masterwork of persuasion now shows itself as a sort of unanimous chorus, with the poor being so easy to persuade that they run to their chains. The two aspects, in appearance contradictory, must be kept in mind together. The kind of irresistible pull of half-socialized people, or, more precisely, of people bound in the knot of domination and servitude is clarified and resolved in the great act of reflection that Rousseau depicts in such solemn terms. Reflexive reason emerges at the same time that nascent society takes shape by closing on itself and becoming a properly political association. For Rousseau too, people become rational at the same time that they become political. This twofold and unique transformation takes place once people who are still rude yet already dependent turn toward and bring their forces to those few who, as a consequence of the extension of their being, are led to imagine a still greater extension, one that envelops not only themselves and their goods but also themselves and others, the rich and the poor, the few and the many, in short an extension that for the first time envelops and defines a whole, that is, a city. In Rousseau's eyes, the city will never fully escape the partiality of its genesis. It results from a social domination that it covers over and from which it does not cease to live.

How could the common ever completely escape the partiality of the self, of which it is but an extension produced by reflection?

Political Institution and Social Domination

The genesis of the city proposed by Rousseau is at the same time very close to and very far from the one proposed by Vico. It is very close because, for both authors, the city is born of the few to whom the many are joined. It is very different, notably because Vico gives a decisive role to the "monarchic" unity represented by the "father" or the patrician who is fiercer and more determined than the others and so capable of leading his peers in confronting the *famoli*. Why does Rousseau not have any place for this "monarchic" figure? As we have seen, he evokes the "mutual jealousies" that prevent the rich from uniting by deferring to the authority of one among them. Surely there is in this a phenomenon abundantly documented in political and social history and that is not Rousseau's invention. But if Rousseau does not envisage this "monarchic" possibility, it is more generally because the "political numbers"— not only the one, but also the few and many—lack substance of their own and thus do not play a decisive causal role in his political analysis. The rich themselves, who, as we have just seen, are at the origin of political society, act only as rich individuals, and not as a group or class. The decisive reflection that they inaugurate is that of the individual, whose goods produce an extension of his own body along with the increased vulnerability that this brings. "The most deliberate project that ever entered the human mind" arose out of the condition and the reflection of the rich *individual*.

It can seem artificial to make the city emerge out of individual domination. But, Rousseau could reply, one cannot say that the rich share a like social or political position when there is as yet no society. They will hold the same position, they will have something in common, after the city has been formed to protect the individual domination of the rich, transforming it into social domination. Rousseau's thinking on this is subtler than Marx's. The latter made political authority the expression or instrument of social domination. For Rousseau this is only half of the truth, for the reverse is equally true, that social domination is the result and the effect of the political institution as much as or more than its cause.

However, even if it is a cause as much as or more than an effect, and the political institution is essentially linked to social domination, it could not really detach itself from it.[33] The beginning of the city thus contains its entire history, including its end. Since the point of the city is to crystallize domination, its history is the history of ever-worse domination. The rich have the passions and thus the thoughts of the rich. The poor have the passions and thus the thoughts of the poor. These dispositions of both groups have no other future than to grow stronger, get worse, and become embittered until "the last degree of inequality" is attained.[34] Finally, the city described by Rousseau has no properly political history. We need to pause on this point.

Let us consider anew the city's point of origin, the overextended and thus especially vulnerable rich. In order to erect the body politic that can protect his own dangerously exposed body, the rich man turns to the poor. Rousseau makes us listen to the rich man's speech, the speech by which he, so to speak, encompasses and turns the poor toward himself and thereby regains possession of his own being. The rich man's speech protects his extended and vulnerable being. But what is this speech?

As we have seen, Rousseau presents it successively and indifferently as supremely persuasive and as having no need at all to persuade, as doing everything and as having so to speak nothing to do. Therein lies the visible fault line of his supremely competent, suggestive, persuasive description. Is this speech, which he says is decisive, truly a speech? A speech that aims to persuade *advances* arguments and reasons. Before considering the nouns, I emphasize the verb. Unlike the inarticulate cry that is simply expressive, and so is not really separate from the one who emits it, articulated language, speech, detaches itself from the one who emits it. Even when he seeks to express his most personal thought, even the most self-interested if one likes, the speaker delivers to his audience something that escapes him and over which they immediately have power. Speech exposes in more than one sense. This is why it is so difficult to speak in public. Everyone is "timid" in public, because everyone is naturally afraid to put himself in view. Arguments open a space over which the one making them has no mastery. Speaking draws one out of oneself, and when one is outside oneself, one is exposed and threatened.

These very elementary remarks suffice in any case to establish that the speech of the rich, from the start exclusively meant to protect him, exposes him in another way even if at first it achieves its intended result. He has entered the domain of argumentation over which he has no mastery. He is, as I have said, outside himself. He is decentered. This profoundly modifies the human geometry that Rousseau has presented us with. By the imagination that identifies him with his property, which is more extended than his own body, the rich man remains at the center of the sensible surface of his being. He only lacks the forces to defend it, the forces he persuades the poor to bring to him. But Rousseau neglects the fact that, once he has begun to speak, the rich man necessarily transforms this situation. Hence his speech, starting admittedly from the center of his sensible being, aims at and defines another center, which is the point where the poor, moved by its persuasive power, congregate. These two centers come together, it will be said, since it is toward himself and for himself that the rich man unites the forces of the poor. Yes, but as the hypothetical speech elaborated by Rousseau himself indicates, the rich man directs the gaze of the poor toward this "supreme power" whose function is certainly to protect him,[35] but that conjures the image of a common point that is distinct from each individual and the guarantor of general concord. However favorable it may be to the interest of the rich man, the city has a center of its own that is distinct from the center of identification to which the rich man seeks to relate everything. The speech that is meant to close the circle of domination is constantly reopening it. At least it necessarily always holds this possibility.

The objection I am raising to Rousseau could be summarized in the following way. Let us allow that the rich person, who is the owner, becomes a citizen *in order to* be assured of his ownership. But once he is a citizen he is no longer simply an owner. Citizenship cannot be only a means; it is a new determination of being. Let us also allow that once he is a citizen, the rich man still thinks only of himself, of his property, his goods, but he must nevertheless take into account this new extension of his being that civic life implies. Perhaps against his inclination his soul is open to a possibility that it cannot again close at will.

Precisely because he is so convincing, or so persuasive, in his description of the soul as capable of extension, or expansion, Rousseau makes us sense all the more the limits of a thesis that would make the more extended soul—the soul of the citizen—the instrument of the less extended soul, the soul of the owner. In other words, he makes us sense the limits of a thesis—his own—that would imply that the political arguments—the arguments of political justice—are simply or ultimately what today we call rationalizations. Assuming that the activity of reason *begins* as rationalization, its development necessarily emancipates it from this beginning. As we have seen, public speech draws the speaker out of himself. Each speaks to defend his interest, to justify himself, to account for his position, of course; but how each one, persuaded of the rightness of his view, is unpersuasive. The argument that seemed to him irrefutable is thrown back at him as confused, or contradictory, or immoral. He lives mainly with those who share his condition and his opinions; he strives to avoid encountering others and their inadmissible opinions, but neither side can change the fact that they share the same city. Both want only to win but willy-nilly there emerges a dialogue among them, though often superficial and brutal, about political justice. They largely use the same terms and notions even if at first not with the same meaning or the same intentions: merit, equal, unequal, just, unjust, and so on. Their partisan notions communicate enough to constitute a public layout that is somewhat intelligible to each, and in the end more acceptable, more "reasonable," than the partisan admits to himself.

Are we capable of perfectly selfless thinking in the city? I do not know. We can even grant to Rousseau that a negative answer is very plausible, that the rich, as I have said, have the passions, and therefore the thoughts, of the rich; the poor the passions, and therefore the thoughts, of the poor. But both are constrained, and thus able, to live together, in some way to share the same city. How? Why? Because reason, however partisan its ordinary arguments may be, is more extended than the most extended imagination of the richest proprietor. The most extended imagination has its center in the body itself, in the sentiment of self, the sentiment of the existence of the human individual, whereas the least active reason, the one most constrained by the needs, the passions, the sentiment of the self, involves a decentering movement toward a point that exists only through it, the point of justice or the common good. Becoming a citizen and becoming a rational agent in this sense go together. Reason is not reducible to the activity of rationalization for the same cause that citizenship is not reducible to property or the protection of property.

These considerations incite us to invert Rousseau's approach. Rousseau reduced the civic debate to the prepolitical confrontation, devoid of any justice, between the rights of the stronger and the rights of the first occupant. Let us try to reestablish its political meaning. It is always a matter of having or not having, of belonging to the "haves" or the "have nots." But the deployment of these two possibilities in the framework of the city modifies their nature and meaning. The rich are not content to enjoy their property that is now solidly theirs, to taste the pleasure of declaring themselves the legitimate possessors of their considerable goods; they argue from their property to claim exclusive government of the city. The poor, on their side, are not content to remind the rich that they are there and have the right to be there; they explain that being there—being citizens—is the necessary but sufficient condition to having a share in the government of the city. The elements are the same as in the situation described by Rousseau, but everything has changed because the whole has changed, or rather because there now is a whole: the city. One can well say that social domination remains the fundamental fact, but the meaning of this fact has changed. Whereas in the prepolitical state the "social" situation was the principle and the goal of all human movements, in the civic state of the city, it is also the starting point of a vast and very complex, an unprecedented category of human movements, those that are proper to the citizen. And the city, or the public thing or the common good, is the object and the goal of these movements.

Once again, Rousseau overlooks, so to speak, this second movement. Very attentive and even prodigiously sensitive to social domination, he overlooks the class struggle and its political dynamism. For him social domination is present at the beginning and at the end without any development other than its aggravation. He does not cease to emphasize the reality of the rich and the poor, but he does not show us the two groups engaged in and mobilized by the movement of the question of who governs and by what authority or what right. Yet this is the question that frees men from the repetition of domination and makes them enter political history, an open history. Even if at first it is for themselves, for their own interests, that the rich and the poor want to govern, engagement in the debate over the question of who governs draws both groups out of their social nature to engage them in the properly political adventure. Why is Rousseau so little open to this perspective, or even why does he so carefully exclude it? Let us read what he has to tell us on this score in the framework of the very city of which he proudly proclaims himself a citizen.

As is well known, the *Second Discourse* opens with a very lengthy dedication "To the Republic of Geneva" and its magistrates. This text is among other things a careful description of contemporary Geneva as a perfect or nearly perfect city or republic. Not long before, the city of his birth experienced lively and even violent dissensions between the few and the many, disorders about which Rousseau was surely perfectly well informed. This evocation of Geneva is thus the expression of a wish more than the description of a reality. In a manner that is flattering to the Genevans, Rousseau strives to reconcile the democratic and the aristocratic parties by sketching the great traits of a republic where the legitimate demands of both would be satisfied. This dedication is in sum the "elegy" of the one who would be the Solon of Geneva. Thus Rousseau's entire political philosophy as a practical science is sketched in these few pages that give us a clear enough idea of what he understood as a "wisely tempered democratic government." Such a regime binds tightly together the strictest equality between the few and the many with the fullest deference of the many toward the few who are the legitimate magistrates, a deference to which the magistrates answer in turn with "a kind of gratitude." This extraordinarily tight knot of social affects is perfectly described in the following sentence: "It does not behoove me and, thank heaven, it is not necessary to speak to you of the consideration which can be expected from you by men of that stamp: your equals by education as well as by the rights of nature and of birth; your inferiors by their will and by the preference they owe your merit, which they have accorded it, and for which you owe them in turn a kind of gratitude."[36]

This republic of Geneva bears little resemblance to the nascent city of the *Second Discourse*. The two communities however share a very striking trait: they have no class struggle. In the virtuous city as in the one born of corruption, there is full consent to inequality—a consent resulting from the deception of the rich and the vices of the poor in the first case, from the merit of the rich and the virtue of justice of the poor in the second, but a full consent in both cases. Once again, Rousseau detests, one is tempted to say he censures, class struggle even as he places class domination at the center of his perspective, even as this "democrat" proclaims an iron law of the oligarchy. Admittedly, when the people rise up, they have the right to do so, but then they become a seditious populace; they give free rein to their cupidity, their injustice, their self-esteem; they start to resemble the rich. One could say it is by their deference for the rich, when these merit it ever so little, that the poor rise above their condition, and in truth above even that of the rich.

To summarize this point: although Rousseau is so to speak obsessed by the problem of inequality, he does not consider class struggle for itself. He sees in it only a mode, which is particularly antipathetic to him, of the corruption induced by inequality. The phenomenon of inequality that interests him, the one he studies in the *Second Discourse,* is the one that runs though an otherwise homogeneous society and involves the mediation of individual psychology, not of class psychology: "If this were the place to go into details, I would easily explain how, even without the involvement of government, inequality of credit and authority becomes inevitable between individuals as soon as, united in the same society, they are forced to make comparisons between themselves and to take into account differences they find in the continual use they have to make of one another."[37]

The phenomenon that Rousseau does not consider or that he wishes to prevent is the movement by which each class separates itself, affirms itself, becomes aware of itself, and claims for itself all or part of the political power. This movement, to be sure, is the effect and the cause of all sorts of passions that Rousseau has good grounds for wanting to prevent. But these movements of the soul are also motivated, amplified, and finally corrected by the rational arguments that the different classes advance in support of their political claims.

In the Geneva that Rousseau limns, the knot that binds the classes is so tightly tied that each is held in a happy immobility where it can enjoy itself. The envy of the poor is precluded by their deference to the rich; the disdain of the rich is precluded by their gratitude to the poor: the alienating passions thus deprived of nurture, each person can be what he is and give himself over to the sentiment of existence without any trouble. But this is not how things happen, including at Geneva, as Rousseau knew very well. The rational animal does not let himself be immobilized in this way.

The Two Democracies

The members of the nascent city are thus distributed and divided into two great categories: the rich, whose imagination extends widely beyond their own body and who experience a prideful satisfaction from this extension of their being; and the poor, whose imagination is constricted within the limits of their own body, a body whose integrity is at times wounded by heavy work and privations, and its appearance by shabby and worn clothing, and who from this constriction of their being experience a variable mixture of humiliation, resentment, and anger. As they become aware of their citizenship, the rich see themselves as and want to be members of a city of the rich—only the rich, of course, are truly citizens; the poor see themselves and want to be members of a city of the poor—only the poor, of course, are truly citizens since the rich can purchase their stay in any city whatever. But however selfish and partial the members of both groups may be, however their passions and undertakings may be rooted in the identifying imagination—we alone are the city!—there necessarily emerges between them a debate on the definition of the city. Perhaps in spite of themselves they are more than what they are.

The rich person wants more than to guard or increase his property. The poor person wants more than to seize the property of the rich or have it distributed. The rich wants to set the tone for the city, to be recognized as one of its *first* citizens. The poor wants to have a share in the city, to participate in it, to give his opinion with as much right as the rich, in short to be recognized in his *dignity* as a citizen. The movement of politicization, by which the one and the other become citizens, transforms the nearly animal confrontation between those who have and those who have not—it is "animal" because the sentiment of the body plays such a large role in it—into a contest over "honors" or "dignity." The city engenders itself in this movement where cupidity develops into pride. The city takes its form from the development of the human form. In the city, one constitutes oneself by deploying and moving through one's being from the body to the soul.

Let us take a closer look at the process by which the city extricates itself from the social domination in which it is rooted. What makes one worthy of governing is, to begin with, in the eyes of society's members who are necessarily partisan, a social quality, a "prepolitical" quality, which is chiefly wealth or free birth. Then as the city emerges, as the polis becomes, if I dare say, more political, what makes one worthy of governing is more and more a properly political quality that Aristotle calls precisely *political virtue*.[38] This movement from partisan claim to political virtue is described in the most sober and at the same time subtlest manner in book 3 of the *Politics*. Let us briefly consider the heart of the argument in chapters 9 to 13.

Aristotle, as we shall see, is not the enemy of democracy, but he is very different from the modern democrats, or republicans, who are terribly concerned with our morality, hound our egoism or our individualism, and summon us in a pressing way to all kinds of sacrifices. Aristotle is more preoccupied with the limits of our intellect than with the weaknesses or vices of our will. (This is why reading him is so calming and so enlightening.) The problem with us, he says, is that, rich or poor, we judge ill of our own affairs and that both parties "by speaking to a point of a kind of justice in a sense, consider themselves to be speaking about justice simply."[39] Each partisan thesis on justice has its own limits, which Aristotle discloses without any polemical bitterness. What interests us here is the limit that they share, so to speak, the defect that is common to both. They are arrows shot with vigor (the vigor of the conviction that one is right), but they do not hit the target; they fall short of it, for the archers aim too close. The theses that are directed to the city do not reach the city. Aristotle's critique is very simple and very effective. The word "critique" is almost too aggressive. Aristotle does not oppose an impartial ideal to these diverse partisan claims. He limits himself to showing how these claims outline cities that do not resemble the city—not the ideal city but those same cities we have under our eyes. It is the city itself, the very phenomenon of the city, what "we see every day," as Montesquieu would have said, that constitutes the critique of these partisan theses on the city.

More precisely, these partisan theses imply and outline associations where the holding of things in common, the degree of *commonality*, if I may say, is visibly inferior to that of the city. The city of the oligarchs, for example, resembles a joint-stock company: to each according to his capital. It is not truly a city. As for the city of the democrats, it resembles more "an alliance to prevent their suffering injustice from anyone."[40]

One could also call a "city" a zone of commercial exchange or a forum of intermarriages. In all these cases, the life of the "city" has nothing properly civic. Yet the city, since it exists, must have a life of its own. "Political life"—the life of the polis—must have a content of its own. What is this content? We know Aristotle's answers: sharing in happiness ("to metechein eudaïmonias"), life according to deliberate choice ("to zèn kata proaïresin"), or life for the sake of noble actions ("tôn kalôn praxeôn charin").[41]

These affirmations of Aristotle are justified, in any case clarified, elsewhere in his political writings, especially in *Nicomachean Ethics*. At the same time we cannot help thinking that Aristotle makes a leap here. We are convinced that the city has a life of its own, but we are perplexed when it comes to the definition of this life: are there not as many different political lives as there are cities, at least types of cities? The more competent one is, it seems, the more one is able to distinguish the types of cities, as does Montesquieu:

> Although all states have the same purpose in general, which is to maintain themselves, yet each state has a purpose that is peculiar to it. Expansion was the purpose of Rome; war, that of Lacedaemonia; religion, that of the Jewish laws; commerce, that of Marseilles; public tranquility, that of the laws of China; navigation, that of the laws of the Rhodians; natural liberty was the purpose of the police of the savages; in general, the delights of the prince are the purpose of the despotic states; his glory and that of his state, that of monarchies; the independence of each individual is the purpose of the laws of Poland, and what results from this is the oppression of all.
>
> There is also one nation in the world whose constitution has political liberty for its direct purpose.[42]

Moreover, Aristotle suggests as much, when, after recalling that a city is "the partnership of families and villages in a complete and self-sufficient life," he adds immediately, "this, we assert, is living happily and nobly."[43] "We assert" can refer to the particular doctrine of Aristotle and his school but also to the current usage of the Greek language at the time, in which case *eudaimonïa* and *kalon* become for us words that strictly speaking cannot be translated, words that have their full meaning only in a Greek mouth and for Greek ears. It would then be incompetent to want to generalize or universalize Aristotle's theses. However, these reservations and questions, which need to be kept in mind, must not prevent us from considering more precisely the elements of Aristotle's answer—namely, "deliberate choice," "happiness," and "noble actions"—and to attempt, not to generalize them, but at least to appropriate them to ourselves.

With "deliberate choice" we have no difficulty in principle, even if we do not necessarily understand it as Aristotle did. We are in an element familiar to us, we who aspire to a rational society and who strive to understand individual and collective life on the model of the rational agent. The rational agent, the rationally organized society, presupposes of course self-government and civic life. On all these points, we are squarely with Aristotle. However, one must not overlook an important difference. For Aristotle, deliberate choice finds its most proper framework in political life. Now, in what way is political life more "proairetic" than, for example, economic life? We would rather think the contrary, we who often demand that the country be governed, no, "managed like a business," which suggests that business leaders act rationally while politicians are moved by passions, by ideologies, or simply a too-pressing desire to be reelected. However, even without going further into the subject, it is not difficult to discern at least some of the reasons why Aristotle saw in political life the framework par excellence of *proaïresis*. In a word, the stakes here are vaster than in any other domain, since they concern the whole, the life and death of the whole. There is a qualitative difference between the failure of a business and the disappearance or destruction of a State. Hence it is in political life that the latitude for action is the greatest and "deliberate choice" encounters the most anguishing uncertainties. The latitude for action is so great and the "deliberate choice" so uncertain that citizens never stop splitting into opposing, even enemy parties. Perhaps, when we call for the country to be governed "like a business," we are in truth backing off before the breadth of political possibilities that *proaïresis* strives to master.

The other element belonging to political life according to Aristotle is "happiness" and "noble actions." On this point, we are squarely skeptical, or worse. We willingly say, like Benjamin Constant, "Leave justice to the government, we will take charge of our happiness." Or if the government is to concern itself with our happiness, let it be to guarantee our "inalienable rights"—according to the Declaration of Independence of the United States—"to the *pursuit* of happiness." As for nobility,[44] what is more relative, more subjective in our eyes? Do we imagine an election platform that would promise us "noble, beautiful actions"? At the same time, it is not impossible for us to give a political meaning and significance to this notion. After all, the noble, or the beautiful, is what many people admire; likewise, what many do together rarely lacks a certain nobility, or beauty. In this sense, what is more noble than a common action or an action for the common? What is more noble, or beautiful, than the city? And the beauties of art will be found eminently in the faithful imitation of great common things or things made for the common, particularly great actions. Whereas the Greeks situated beauty in things themselves, we situate it more in the eye of the beholder or the artist, and thus beauty for us is divorced from any explicit idea of greatness: since beauty is in our eyes, the smallest things—for example, three plums in a fruit bowl—can be the most beautiful. But if we detach ourselves even a little from the complacency or laziness of the spectator, from the desire that everything be smaller than our view, we will find meaning in the series of notions that are joined in Aristotle's definition: self-sufficiency, perfection, happiness, and beauty. Herein human life gathers itself, and the notions just enumerated are so many aspects of this gathering. Those who make the greatest contribution to this gathering contribute most to the city, and for that they are said to have more "political virtue."[45]

Of course this gathering is not a given. It must be instituted. The different modes of this institution are the different regimes. We are back to the few and the many. I will not repeat how the city is rooted in the social division and strives to overcome it, although always imperfectly. But it remains for me to underline a capital aspect of the process. The true city comes into being, or rather strives to exist, through the effort of the many to have a share in the city of the few. In this sense politicization is identical with democratization, the city with democracy, more exactly with the movement toward the democratic regime. But pay attention. It is not just any "many" that is capable of having a share in the true city, the city that also has room for the few who are rich and the fewer yet who are "excellent" or "virtuous." This is the circle of the city and the democracy that Aristotle explores with incomparable tact in these developments of book 3: the city in which the people do not participate is not a true city, but in order for the people to participate in the city without destroying it, it must be rendered capable of having such a part. The good city educates the people who are capable of sharing in the life of the city.

The modern political cycle took up, broadened, and profoundly transformed the Greek political cycle. In both cases, to be sure, the vector of political history is a vector of democratization. But in the modern European nations, unlike what took place in the Greek cities, the confrontation between the many and the few was decisively mediated by the one, that is, by the State, which was at first royal and later republican, but always "monarchical." This active interposition of the State has very deep consequences that are not yet exhausted. The people ceased to be the many to become simply *all*. In the eyes of the One, all became the people, all were equal. The modern State signifies, by imposing it, this *plane of equality* on which we have been living for two or three centuries—the plane of equal human rights, the plane of the equal or similar human condition. Henceforth, the few as few no longer have any admissible claim. Any political or moral argument, any human argument, is acceptable only if it can be generalized or universalized. Henceforth democracy is the only legitimate political regime.

Must we then lament the fate of the few? Not exactly. Unlike what took place in the Greek city, the poor no longer massacre the rich, with rare exceptions (in nineteenth-century France it was even rather the reverse), and above all the rich can at last become as rich as they desire. No more sumptuary laws. How did this come about? Social and political life, that until then was intent on distinguishing and affirming one or another version of the "noble life," turned to the "relief of man's estate," the "bettering of human condition," through the work of all. But if everyone's task becomes the improvement of everyone's condition, or of the general human condition, then the differences of condition among men lose their organizing power. It now is a matter of accumulating goods and services in order—in Hobbes's striking expression—"to assure for ever the way of [our] future desire." Now, it was the chance of the rich, or, if one wishes, the few, that such an accumulation has no more effective instrument than the capitalist system embodied in the joint-stock company. You will recall that this is what for Aristotle defines the oligarchic idea—partial and partisan, but only up to a certain point—of the city. This oligarchic city triumphs usefully, under the form of capitalism, in the midst of democracy. This industrial oligarchy is not as such linked to a particular political framework: its natural domain of action is the world, the world market. Of course, as a consequence of its inclusion in a democracy, this oligarchy ignores the privilege of birth. Its members include anyone who exercises the skills that the market needs.

Thus, in the contemporary system democracy has overflowed the limits of the city—I mean the nation. Equality triumphs in this unlimited democracy where everyone is like everyone else. But oligarchy too has overflowed the limits of the city, or the nation, and inequality triumphs in this competition where there is no limit to the price we are prepared to pay for the people that we prize. In brief, all are equal and everyone has his price.

The problem then is not precisely that society is too equal, to the point where there are no more differences—even if this critique of "the Right" is not without reasons—nor that it is too unequal—even if this critique of "the Left" is also not without reasons. It is rather that this equality and this inequality are deployed in two parallel affirmations that envelop the whole human world but that never meet, so to speak, or do so less and less since they more and more overflow the framework of any possible meaningful dialogue—the properly political framework. I would like to conclude on this point.

All of us today live under a twofold and contradictory challenge to be as equal as possible, ever more equal, ever more alike; and to be as unequal as possible, ever achieving more, ever more "valuable." Now these two modes of humanity—it is not without reason that I employ Spinoza's language—no longer have a political structure—a form and a regime—capable of combining them in good proportion. They mix only in the individual subject who, as I have just said, is constantly challenged to show signs of equality as well as inequality. The hero of our time is both compassionate and competitive. To be compassionate but competitive, to be competitive but compassionate: such is the twofold imperative under which we strive to advance.

Now, does the pressure of this imperative form a truly complete or at least a sufficiently defined human type to give a form or a physiognomy to contemporary democratic humanity? Most of the earlier human types rested on the social division they transfigured. Their moral disposition was both a refinement and a correction of a social position. The master, educated to greatness, corrected by justice or humanity, became the patrician worthy and capable of governing, or could even become simply the magnanimous person. The servant, educated to obedience, straightened up by pride, became the citizen worthy and capable of sharing in government, or could even become simply the just person, or the moral person. These notations are excessively summary. What I mean to say is that equality as well as inequality entered into the composition of our moral being only by explicitly taking one another into account and in two ways: by defining one against the other, and by allowing one to be corrected by the other. Henceforth, equality and inequality are detached from this reciprocal conditioning, and thus are affirmed unconditionally: they claim the whole human being, one as the principle of identification, and the other as the principle of differentiation. The individual is indeed freed from the necessity of being master or servant, from the trying confrontation of the few and the many, but is rent by the agonizing contrast between a boundless equality and an unlimited inequality.

II

THE ENIGMA OF ROME

4

ROME AND THE GREEKS

Our inquiry is propelled and oriented by the question of political forms. The two great political forms, the two mother forms of the ancient world, are the city and the empire. They are the mother forms, but they are also the polar forms: the city is the narrow framework of a restless life in liberty; the empire is the immense domain of a peaceful life under a master. It is fairly obvious that it is impossible to pass directly from one form to another. In the Greek world, if the empire of Alexander "succeeded" the city, it did not come out of one or the other of the two dominant cities, Athens and Sparta, or Thebes, but it came out of the "tribal monarchy" of Macedonia. It is moreover a sort of general rule, a law of the physics of political forms, that they do not directly transform themselves one into the other. We have the example close to us of Europe itself: the modern nations were born not of the medieval cities but of those strange political bodies that were the national monarchies, produced by a political operator proper to Europe, the "Christian monarch." The Greek historical experience, like the European experience, establishes that the political forms are truly forms; that is, if they each indeed have their genesis, they are not moments or aspects of a process; they exist by themselves and from one to the other there is not continuity but rupture. Now, there is one exception to this rule or law, a unique example of a political form transforming itself directly into another political form, of a city transforming itself directly into an empire. At Rome, or starting from Rome and under the name of Rome, a properly unique political phenomenon developed, a phenomenon contrary to the ontology itself of politics—I dare say—namely, the effective and direct continuity and communication between the two mother and opposed forms, the city and the empire.

Why was the development of Rome, which also began as a city, so different from that of Athens? This is a question that historians necessarily encounter but that is rarely treated as a theme by political science, although it touches on a fundamental question of political order. Wherein resides the difference between the dynamics of Athens and those of Rome? This is the question we need to raise.

Athens and Rome

For this "comparative political physics" inquiry, we can start from a very revealing phenomenon of opinion: in spite of the terrible calamities attached to its history, Rome enjoyed an immense prestige across the centuries, whereas in spite of the glory of its philosophers and artists, Athens was never considered as a political object worthy of imitation or even, before the nineteenth century, of admiration. We find a particularly eloquent expression of this unequal treatment in the document that lays out and justifies the first republican foundation of modern times, *The Federalist Papers*.[1]

Let us take *Federalist* number 9, written by Hamilton, and read the first paragraph:

> A firm union will be of the utmost moment to the peace and liberty of the States as a barrier against domestic faction and insurrection. It is impossible to read the history of the petty republics of Greece and Italy without feeling sensations of horror and disgust at the distractions with which they were continually agitated, and at the rapid succession of revolutions by which they were kept in a state of perpetual vibration between the extremes of tyranny and anarchy. If they exhibit occasional calms, these only serve as short-lived contrasts to the furious storms that are to succeed. If now and then intervals of felicity open themselves to view, we behold them with a mixture of regret, arising from the reflection that the pleasing scenes before us are soon to be overwhelmed by the tempestuous waves of sedition and party rage. If momentary rays of glory break forth from the gloom, while they dazzle us with a transient and fleeting brilliancy, they at the same time admonish us to lament that the vices of government should pervert the direction and tarnish the luster of those bright talents and ex-

alted endowments for which the favored soils that produced them have been so justly celebrated.[2]

The political judgment is unequivocal: "perpetual vibration between the extremes of tyranny and anarchy."

I next cite number 10 of *The Federalist Papers,* written by Madison: "From this view of the subject it may be concluded that a pure democracy, by which I mean a society consisting of a small number of citizens, who assemble and administer the government in person, can admit of no cure for the mischief of faction."[3]

No cure! A little later, Madison explains that, thanks to political representation, we are in a position to remedy the otherwise incurable malady of democracy: "A republic, by which I mean a government in which the scheme of representation takes place, opens a different prospect and promises the cure for which we are seeking." And he explains how a republic differs from a pure democracy—what we would call, rather, direct democracy: "The two great points of difference between a democracy and a republic are: first, the delegation of the government, in the latter, to a small number of citizens elected by the rest; secondly, the greater number of citizens and greater sphere of country over which the latter may be extended."[4]

We cannot here dwell on the very interesting question of representative government, *the* great modern political invention. Let us stay with the comparison between Athens and Rome. We have seen that Hamilton did not include Rome in the "petty republics of Greece and Italy." It is not that he necessarily had much sympathy for Rome, which, in *Federalist* number 6, he said, "was never sated of carnage and conquest."[5] But Rome no doubt constituted a different case since, in *Federalist* number 34, after analyzing an apparently damning flaw of Roman political institutions—the fact that legislative authority resided in two independent legislatures representing opposing interests, the Comitia Centuriata and the Comitia Tributa—Hamilton concludes: "And yet these two legislatures coexisted for ages, and the Roman republic attained to the pinnacle of human greatness." Whatever its faults or vices, Rome was not petty.

If we wanted to give a somewhat more complete idea of the Founding Fathers' appreciation of Rome, we would need to cite *Federalist* number

63, probably by Madison, one of the papers devoted to proving the usefulness of a senate.

Our point here is not so much to recapitulate the opinion of Rome held by the wisest republicans of modern times, but to gauge the disdain they had for Athens as a political body. We cannot of course be content with this opinion, however authoritative it may be. We cannot be content to say that a city like Athens was prey to factions and perpetually oscillating between tyranny and anarchy, which besides is not accurate, as the indications I gave in part I suffice to suggest. We need to form a somewhat more precise idea of what Athens was politically. Without in the least entering into a historical account, we must attempt to recover the dynamic scheme of Athenian history. We will in that way have a term of comparison that will then permit us to better grasp what the Roman political development had that was its own and unique.

Athens and Rome had many traits in common, both being independent cities and free republics. What did they have most in common—what trait, what characteristic? As Plato noted, "each [city] is very many cities, but not a city.... There are two, in any case, warring with each other, one of the poor, the other of the rich."[6] In modern terms, we would say that the principle of movement, in both Athens and Rome, was class struggle, or class warfare. But this warfare took very different forms in the two cases. Let us first consider the history of Athens in this perspective.

The most suggestive summary of the political history of Athens, and the most enlightening for our purpose, is to be found in Aristotle's *Constitution of Athens*. In the text that we have (the beginning of the treatise is lost), Aristotle's exposition begins with Solon. Solon, he tells us, "was the first to become a leader of the people [tou dèmou prostatès]."[7] Before the reforms he introduced, there were dissensions between the nobility and the people. The regime—*è politeïa*—was in effect oligarchic: the poor, with their wives and children, were slaves, or serfs—*edouleuon*—of the rich. In Aristotle's striking terms, "they had, so to speak, no share in anything [oudenos ... metechontes]."[8] It comes as no surprise that the people should revolt against the nobles, and that dissensions became violent. Finally, the two parties, by common agreement, chose Solon as mediator and archon, and entrusted the State—*tèn politeïan*—to him. This happened just when he had composed a poem—an "elegy"—on the situation of his country, in which, Aristotle says, "he fights for both parties against both parties."[9]

There would be no profit for our purpose in discussing Aristotle's exposition in detail. I would like only to bring out a few points. Aristotle notes that Solon "in general attaches the blame for the conflict [stasis] to the rich."[10] A little further, commenting on a charge against Solon—in brief he was accused of "insider trading"—Aristotle says that "the version of the friends of the people appears much more trustworthy."[11] And he makes a list of the democratic measures Solon promulgated for the people's relief. The most famous is certainly the cancellation of debts (seisachtheïa). In emphasizing the most democratic traits of Solon's constitution, Aristotle accords a particular place to the right of appeal to a jury court, for, he says, when the people are master of the vote in the courts, they become the masters of the State—"kurios tès politeïas."[12] Solon's most proper trait is the fact that he was at once the leader of the people and the impartial arbiter or mediator between the people and the rich or nobles. As such he provides the key—the tonic key—of all the subsequent political history of Athens. From that time onward, Athens moves in the direction of democracy, that is, a democracy that is ever more democratic, with its best citizens seeking just arbitration between the pretentions of the few and those of the many. Rome will organize the same elements—the rich, the poor, and their dissensions—in a different way and above all will propel them with an altogether different movement.

The leitmotif of the account of Athens's development after Solon's reforms is indicated by the adjectives and verbs deriving from the noun dèmos—for example, the verb dèmagôgein—the most revealing morphology being the comparative or superlative of the adjective dèmotikos—"popular." The winner is always the one who is the more dèmotikos. Aristotle then carefully describes—this is the second knot of the account—how Pisistratus introduced tyranny in Athens. The question of the tyrant and tyranny in Greek political experience and reflection is obviously very complex, with extremely diverse political phenomena falling under these terms. As is well known, the psychology of the tyrant and the tyrannical man was of great interest to the Greek philosophers, in particular Plato.[13] It also greatly interested the tragic poets whom Plato otherwise blames because "they [made] hymns to tyranny."[14] It is not necessary here to enter into the quarrel between philosophy and poetry that was so important for the Greek philosophers. We can, I believe, without being rash, summarize the "Greek perspective" on tyranny in the following verse of Sophocles: "Pride breeds the tyrant [hubris phuteueï turannon]."[15] Now, precisely, it seems that Pisistratus was not by nature very "hubristic." He employed the techniques of tyranny, and he contributed in some way to make them "classical," without himself being a truly tyrannical man. In any case Aristotle emphasizes that Pisistratus's government of Athens "was moderate . . . and more like a constitutional government than like a tyranny." He was even "benevolent [philanthrôpos] and kind and readily forgave those who had committed an offense,"[16] to such a point that it became a current expression to say that the tyranny of Pisistratus had been the Golden Age,[17] for, when his sons succeeded him, tyranny became much more harsh.

The point for us to note here is that although Pisistratus at the start of his career aroused the hostility of Solon, who alerted the Athenians to his tyrannical aims, all in all he practiced the policy that the legislator had formulated and undertaken, that is, a moderate policy aimed at a certain impartiality—"the majority both of the nobles and of the common people were in his favor"[18]—and for that very reason including a democratic tone. To grasp the political meaning of Greek tyranny, we can compare it with the modern State. Between the two there is at least a functional analogy. In both cases it is a matter of introducing a mediation between the many and the few and thus of opening the possibility of a properly political or public action by putting an end to the paralysis induced by class conflict. For example, Pisistratus initiated various "public works." Of course, in both cases the mediation was accompanied by extreme ambivalence. The ancient tyrant, like the modern State, can go from the greatest good to the greatest evil, can be an almost divine benefactor—*l'État providence* as the French call the welfare state—or on the contrary a destructive monster (Nietzsche famously characterized the modern State as "the coldest of all cold monsters"). Tyranny was the instrument or the means by which the Greek city was democratized, as the modern State was the instrument of the equalization of conditions in Europe. With this equalization or democratization there comes in both cases a certain depoliticization: the State as well as the tyrant tends to monopolize public action, sending the citizen back to private affairs. Aristotle explains that Pisistratus loaned money to the poor so that they could earn their living by working on their farms: thus, they would not spend their time in the city but would on the contrary live dispersed over the whole territory; and, being moderately at ease and preoccupied by their own affairs, they would have neither a strong desire nor the leisure to concern themselves with common affairs.[19]

Aristotle later describes how, after the reforms of Cleisthenes, the Athenian regime became "much more democratic" than it had been in the time of Solon; how, after Marathon, the people, who now were confident in their powers, for the first time made use of the law concerning ostracism; how, after the wars with the Medes, the city made great progress, becoming stronger and stronger with the advance of democracy; how—and Aristotle emphasizes once again the growing self-confidence or even the boldness of the city—Aristides counseled the Athenians to seize "[maritime] leadership" and abandon the fields to come live in the city—they would in this way earn their living, "some by participating in military expeditions, some by doing garrison service and still others by participating in public affairs; and in this way they would keep hold of the hegemony."[20] Once they followed this counsel and seized the empire, they began to treat their allies as *despotikôterôs*—as though they were their masters.

We thus see emerge the arc or circle of Athenian political development. After Solon gave the tonic note I mentioned, after the tyrant Pisistratus began to undertake public action that favored the people, the people became stronger and bolder. At the same time that the people grew stronger internally, the entire city grew stronger externally to the point of becoming a "despot" over other cities. The people that Pisistratus sought to keep busy far from the city were in the end invited by Aristides to come settle in the city in order to occupy the political and military offices of empire or, rather, of "hegemony."

One final remark on Aristotle's account. He notes that after the death of Pericles, the situation degenerated considerably because the people for the first time chose a leader who did not have a good reputation among the upper classes who was not respected by them.[21] He means of course to speak of Cleon, whose very bad manners he describes a little further. And he rapidly reviews the leaders worthy of esteem who successively guided the Athenian people: "The first leader of the people, in the very beginning, was Solon, the second one was Pisistratus, both of whom belonged to the aristocracy of birth. After the overthrow of the tyranny, it was Cleisthenes from the noble family of the Alcmeonidae. . . . After this Xanthippus was the leader of the people, and Miltiades the leader of the aristocracy. Then Aristides and Themistocles [were the leaders of the people]. After these, Ephialtes. . . . Then Pericles was the leader of the common people."[22] Aristotle here gives us what I am tempted to call the "axis of good" in the history of Athens that runs from Solon to Pericles. This axis was formed by the almost uninterrupted succession of the leaders of the people. What gives the Athenian political development its specificity, its direction, and its wellspring is that it consisted in the growing power of the people thanks to a succession of eminent men who sided with them in order to guide them.

If we now turn to the history of Rome, we are obliged to observe that it has nothing of the sort. The *elements* of its history greatly resemble, as I have said, those of Athens. In both cases one finds the many and the few, their dissensions, and those eminent men of whom some are leaders of the party of the people, others of the party of the nobles. One can in addition say that at Rome also, the claims of the people, of the plebeians, provided the energy of the collective movement. But one could not describe the axis of Roman history as formed by a succession of patrician leaders of the plebeians.[23] Leaving aside Marius, whose political talents were mediocre and who moreover did not belong to the nobility, one could almost say that Caesar was the first and the last among them, while the Roman republic was in agony. Class warfare developed very differently in Athens and in Rome. If one tries to condense the difference to a few words, one could say that whereas in Athens the growing power of the people was *guided* by a brilliant succession of leaders of the people of generally aristocratic origin, in Rome, it was *controlled*—that is, at once used and checked—by an aristocratic body that resembled nothing in Athens, namely the senate.

After the golden chain was broken by the death of Pericles and Sparta emerged victorious in the Peloponnesian War, democratic Athens was set on a course of decline that would be definitive in spite of more or less energetic and enduring efforts to recover its influence and its strength. But if it had to suffer the domination of the Macedonian monarchy that superimposed on the Greek cities a sort of "federal state," in the phrase of Pierre Lévêque, it never changed form. It remained a city. Rome's destiny was altogether different. The republic, though bruised within by the bloodiest strife, instead of foundering over itself engaged in a new career, or rather pursued its expansion, but under an altogether new form, the imperial form.

In spite of its tormented history, in spite of the great transformations produced by regime changes, by the modification of domestic and foreign circumstances, Athens, as a living entity and as a lasting "whole" that keeps the name of Athens, never ceased being a city. Moreover, if Athens "invented politics," it gave this strange activity the name of the political form it exemplified—the polis—because this activity appeared as essentially linked to this form. Even at the height of its power, while it exercised a very rigorous domination over a good part of the Aegean Sea, a domination that thus extended far beyond the limits of its territory, Athens remained a city. At the head of a maritime empire, the city of Athens did not transform itself into an Athenian empire. Its action was imperial, or imperialist, but its form remained "civic" or "political."

Aristotle's very complete and very subtle analysis of political life is concerned exclusively with the city. It takes place wholly within the limits of the city. As I remarked at the very beginning of this book when I introduced the notion of political form, Aristotle does not ignore the existence of other forms of human association.[24] He does not ignore the fact that the Persians live in very different conditions. Yet one would hesitate to say that for him the Persians lived in another political form since, under the great king, political life could not properly develop. My usage of the expression "political form" would not meet with his approval. It is very significant that in his exhaustive treatment of political things, at no point, however briefly, does Aristotle consider the new political form that was being deployed under the quite visible direction of Alexander. Aristotle, who knew everything and whom nothing escaped, does not seem to have remarked that an enormous Greek empire was developing right under his eyes. I have already pointed out that Aristotle's silence on this point is very puzzling. What we can say is that this silence suggests at least a certain perplexity on his part, perhaps a decided hostility, regarding a political form that extended the territory of the body politic indefinitely and that also multiplied indefinitely the number of citizens, although the term is not appropriate since they must henceforth follow a combination of Greek and barbarian customs under the power of a ty-rannical king.[25]

Understanding Caesar

Rome's uniqueness resides not only in the fact that under the same name it prospered, first as a warrior republic and then as an immense empire, but also that the latter came out of the former. The self-destruction of the republican city was in a certain sense the cause of the empire coming into existence. In the case of Rome extreme corruption did not signify death or the end, but the introduction to an unprecedented metamor-phosis. Whereas Athens had consumed itself, so to speak, Rome re-newed itself entirely. The fact that only in Rome was extreme corruption not fatal means that Rome is a phenomenon that contradicts not only the ontology of politics, as I have already said, but even ontology *tout court*. In Rome death was not deadly.

If the transformation or metamorphosis of city into empire is at the cen-ter of the "Roman question," then that question comes together or is summed up in the figure of Julius Caesar—who became more, and some-thing other, than a Roman citizen, as eminent and glorious as one imagines him, yet without however seizing the royal crown that was offered him and that he apparently coveted so much. In "missing" the royal crown, he founded a new kind of monarchy, not only because he was the true founder of the Roman Empire, but also because he gave his name to an unprecedented phenomenon, "Caesarism." What is Caesarism? It is a mon-archy that follows a republic no longer able to govern itself. "Follows" is the important word here. "Normally," in the usual order of things, the re-public succeeds monarchy: that was the case in Greece and Rome; it was also the case in most countries of Europe, beginning with France. Caesa-rism, in France as in Rome—though unknown in Greece—is the monarchy that *follows* a republic that had *followed* kingship. A new historical se-quence is added, one that was absent from the Greek experience.

If then one considers the "Roman" phenomena of empire and Caesa-rism or the empire introduced by Caesarism, but also the European monarchy in which the ruler is "emperor in the realm," one will say that "Rome" gave rise to these monarchical experiences or made them pos-sible, experiences of the government of one alone that, good or bad, had remained foreign to the Greek city and even to the Greek world in spite of the empire of Alexander. One could say that *the* limit of the Greek city is the limited character of its experience of monarchy.

Are the limits of the Greek political experience also the limits of Greek political science? At the very beginning of our inquiry, I pointed out that this question would not cease to be with us. If experience provides the matter and so to speak the motive of science, science ultimately seeks to give an account of every possible experience and thus to emancipate itself from the original experience. Otherwise the very notion of science would lose its meaning. One can then maintain that on the admittedly limited basis of the experience of the city, Greek political science elaborated an explanation of the political phenomenon that is so complete that it could be said to be exhaustive. Besides, one could dispute that the experience of the city might be said to be "limited," if it is in the framework of the city that the political phenomenon concretizes and deploys itself according to the diversity of the regimes of which one can make an exhaustive classification. If the city is the original form of politics, it contains in some way the whole of politics. The apparently new phenomena, which are in fact new, such as Caesarism, or more generally all those that can be gathered under the rubric of "Rome," would however still be accounted for by Greek political science, which, if it did not take them into account explicitly because it did not encounter them in such characteristic form as they took later, provides all the elements to give an account of them in a satisfactory way. If that is the case, our inquiry is in vain since "Rome" would not designate any radically new political phenomenon that was not already identified and illuminated by Greek political science. Now, at this point of our inquiry, our hypothesis is indeed that "Rome" designates unprecedented political phenomena. It is in order to make this unprecedented character appear that we have set the stage with the Greek civic experience as Aristotle elucidates it, a complete experience or a complete cycle of experiences, where the political phenomenon—"politicization" and "democratization"—is deployed in a manner that, I dare say, leaves nothing to be desired. This is then our perplexity: if "Rome" seems to offer us the example of a very unique development, we do not know if a deeper examination will confirm this impression. This uncertainty is the condition of the freedom of our inquiry and of the validity of its results.

To get right to the subject, the best way is to let speak an author who experiences none of the uncertainties I have just acknowledged, but who categorically affirms that Greek political science is indeed exhaustive and that, therefore, "Rome" does not designate any radically new political phenomenon. I am speaking of Leo Strauss.

Nowhere does Leo Strauss deal with the question of "Rome" in general, or according to the range of the political phenomena the word covers. But he deals with it very directly and very clearly with regard to a particular political phenomenon that it would be hard not to call "Roman" since it precisely concerns "Caesarism." He does this in the context of a reply to Eric Voegelin, who, in a review of Strauss's work on *Hiero,* Xenophon's dialogue on tyranny, had maintained that the classical concept of tyranny is too narrow because it does not cover the phenomenon known by the name of Caesarism.[26] I have already sketched Voegelin's argument, although he himself does not use the term Caesarism, when I underlined the importance of chronology. Strauss summarizes it as follows: when we say of a certain regime that it is tyrannical, we imply that a "constitutional" government would be a viable solution in place of this tyranny; or Caesarism appears only "after the final breakdown of the republican constitutional order"; consequently, Caesarism, or "postconstitutional" government, cannot be understood as a subdivision of tyranny in the classical sense of the term. Having summarized Voegelin's argument in this way, Strauss adds this that formulates the terms of the problem perfectly: "There is no reason to quarrel with the view that genuine Caesarism is not tyranny, but this does not justify the conclusion that Caesarism is incomprehensible on the basis of classical political philosophy: Caesarism is still a subdivision of absolute monarchy as the classics understood it."[27]

The reason why genuine Caesarism is not tyranny is clear enough: "If in a given situation 'the republican constitutional order' has completely broken down, and there is not reasonable prospect of its restoration within all the foreseeable future, the establishment of permanent absolute rule cannot, as such, be justly blamed; therefore it is fundamentally different from the establishment of tyranny."[28] Whenever Caesarism is the least bad practical solution, it is for that very reason the best solution. By this same measure, it is "good," which is something one would never say of tyranny.

This absolute government, which is in its principle good in light of circumstances, can be exercised in a good way, by a good ruler, in which case we would be dealing with a "royal" Caesar; or in a bad way, by a bad ruler, and we would be dealing with a properly tyrannical Caesar. With regard to the first to bear the name of Caesar, Julius Caesar, Strauss mentions the defense of Caesar by Coluccio Salutati against the accusation that he was a tyrant.[29] What interests Strauss here is not the case of Caesar as such but Salutati's line of argument, which, he says, "in all essential points is conceived in the spirit of the classics."[30] If it can be established that Caesar was not a tyrant by appealing to the principles of classical political philosophy, what better proof is there that "contrary to Voegelin's thesis, "the distinction between Caesarism and tyranny fits perfectly into the classical framework"?[31]

Now, that one can elaborate the distinction between Caesarism and tyranny on the basis of classical principles does not suffice to prove that this elaboration, or this interpretation, is valid or that it is the best. All that Strauss has proven up to this point is that there is or there can easily be conceived a classical interpretation of the distinction that is plausible or defensible. But is it better, that is, is it more true than the modern conception as put forth by Voegelin here? As Strauss himself says very well, "The question thus arises whether the current concept or the classical concept is more nearly adequate."[32]

Strauss identifies two elements of the current conception, which is also Voegelin's, that he says have their origin in nineteenth-century historicism. In the first place, Voegelin appears to believe that "the difference between 'the constitutional situation' and 'the post-constitutional situation' is more fundamental than the difference between the good king or good Caesar on the one hand, the bad king or bad Caesar on the other. But is not the difference between good and bad the most fundamental of all practical or political distinctions?"[33] In the second place, Voegelin seems to believe that "'post-constitutional' rule is not per se inferior to 'constitutional' rule. But is not 'post-constitutional' rule justified by necessity or, as Voegelin says, by 'historical necessity'? And is not the necessary essentially inferior to the noble or to what is choice-worthy for its own sake? Necessity excuses: what is justified by necessity is in need of excuse."[34] Strauss then ties Caesarism to the corruption of the people: "It presupposes the decline, if not the extinction, of civic virtue or of public spirit, and it necessarily perpetuates that condition. Caesarism belongs to a degraded society, and it thrives on its degradation. Caesarism is just, whereas tyranny is unjust. But Caesarism is just in the way in which deserved punishment is just. It is as little choice-worthy for its own sake as is deserved punishment. . . . It is much more important to realize the low level of Caesarism, (for, to repeat, Caesarism cannot be divorced from the society which deserves Caesarism) than to realize that under certain conditions Caesarism is necessary hence legitimate."[35]

Strauss's argument is very impressive. It forces us to rigorously distinguish two points of view that we Moderns are particularly prone to confuse: the point of view of the good (the noble, the just) and the point of view of the necessary. For reasons difficult to untangle and which it is not useful to enter into now, we have persuaded ourselves that human history obeys a law in which novelty and necessity are inseparable. What comes after—for example, empire after republic—is both new and necessary, and good inasmuch as it has this twofold character. We are thus prone to side with Caesar against Cato, about whom Strauss has this to say in the passage I have omitted: "Cato refused to see what his time demanded because he saw too clearly the degraded and degrading character of what his time demanded."[36] Whatever Caesar's merits may be, there is something corrupt and corrupting in our preference.

The point of view of classical science according to Strauss is not however identical with the point of view of Cato. It does not simply defend the noble. It knows how to make room for necessity by recognizing it for what it is, a sad necessity. Why then, as Strauss himself recognizes, were the classics almost completely silent on "postconstitutional" government? Why did they not explain clearly what Strauss here explains very clearly? Here is Strauss's answer: "To stress the fact that it is just to replace constitutional rule by absolute rule, if the common good requires the change, means to cast a doubt on the absolute sanctity of the established constitutional order. It means encouraging dangerous men to confuse the issue by bringing about a state of affairs in which the common good requires the establishment of their absolute rule. The true doctrine of the legitimacy of Caesarism is a dangerous doctrine. The true distinction between Caesarism and tyranny is too subtle for ordinary political use. It is better for the people to remain ignorant of that distinction and to regard the potential Caesar as a potential tyrant."[37]

Thus Strauss concludes his explanation why the classics declined to formulate the true notion of Caesarism, whose principles they firmly possessed. "The classics could easily have elaborated a doctrine of Caesarism or of late kingship if they had wanted, but they did not want to do it."[38]

However impressive, as I said, this line of argument is, questions remain. One can understand very well that reasons of high political prudence would have incited the classics to maintain an almost complete silence on the phenomenon of Caesarism. Strauss shows in a convincing way that the Greeks were equipped to grasp and formulate the *distinction* or *difference* between Caesarism and tyranny. But one can see very well the difference between Caesarism and tyranny—it is the practical difference between necessary evil, which as such is relative good, and deliberate evil—without seeing clearly, or in any case completely, what Caesarism is as a political phenomenon. I have already cited the political definition of Caesarism that Strauss gives at the beginning of his discussion of Voegelin: "Caesarism is still a subdivision of absolute monarchy as the classics understood it." This definition is altogether plausible but it remains on a very high plane of generality or abstraction. Who would disagree that Caesarism is a certain species of the genus of monarchy? The complication is obviously that, among the great notions of Greek political science, monarchy covers the greatest breadth and the most abrupt shifts in meaning. In a word, monarchy can designate just as well the worst and best of regimes. Thus, in order to grasp what is proper to Rome, we are brought again to consider Greece, more precisely to examine the classical concept of monarchy. After consulting him regarding the history of Athenian democracy, we need to briefly consult Aristotle on his evaluation of the place of monarchy in Greek political experience.

Monarchy in Greece

In his classification of political regimes, Aristotle opposes to the three good regimes—kingship, aristocracy, polity—their three "deviations" that are the three bad regimes: tyranny, oligarchy, democracy.[39] In practice, as Aristotle goes on to explain, most contemporary cities are mixtures or composites of oligarchy and democracy, since, as we are well aware, the city is set in motion by the opposing claims of the few and the many. Without wise arbitration, warfare between the few and the many begets tyranny. Thus the most usual and most useful notions for under-standing political life are those of democracy, oligarchy, and tyranny.

What does Aristotle have to say about kingship? It can seem to oc-cupy a large place in the landscape he describes in that he distinguishes no less than five forms of kingship:[40]

1. Laconian kingship, which is a perpetual generalship ascribed to a lineage.
2. The kingships of certain barbarian peoples, which are in fact tradi-tional tyrannies, one could say. Aristotle explains that "because barbarians are more slavish in their characters than Greeks (those in Asia being more so than those in Europe) so they put up with a master's rule without making any difficulties."[41] It is a hereditary tyranny that is not experienced as such on account of the character of the populations involved.
3. The kingship of those who were called *aisymnetès:* these were desig-nated by enemy parties to put an end to civil disorders. They received absolute powers and answered to no one. Aristotle characterizes this kingship as an elective tyranny.[42]
4. The kingship of "heroic times," which was at once over willing sub-jects, hereditary, and in accordance with law.[43]
5. The kingship in which a single individual is ruler of all things—*pantôn kurios*—as each people and each city are rulers of their common affairs.[44] The king is in the kingdom like the father or the master in the household.

This classification is a bit misleading, to the extent that two of the "king-ships" are in reality rather tyrannies of a particular species. In fact, Aris-totle immediately adds, "there are, then, fundamentally two kinds of kingship which must be investigated . . . for most of the others are be-tween these." What are these two extreme kingships between which is stretched the arc of royal regimes? They are Laconian kingship on the one hand, and absolute kingship on the other.

The first is not properly speaking a kingship, because it is not prop-erly speaking a regime, but rather simply a legislative provision: the of-fice of *stratègos* can exist in all regimes. Accordingly, Aristotle says, it can be set aside.[45]

The other species—the opposite species—of kingship is on the contrary a true regime. It is *discussed* at length by Aristotle, whose account is markedly aporetic. It weaves together two particularly embarrassing and thorny questions.

There is the question of knowing what the city does with the individual whose virtue surpasses everyone else's;[46] and there is the question of knowing whether the rule of the best law is more choice-worthy than that of the best person.[47]

As for the first question, Aristotle's reply seems unequivocal: absolute power should be given to such a superior person—or lineage.[48] This argument of Aristotle, which directly ties the political order to a natural order and the political hierarchy ("who governs?") to a natural hierarchy, and which gives absolute sovereignty an ontological foundation, will be very influential; it will be orchestrated in a thousand ways in later European "monarchic" history. Since it seems to be detached from any political context and so to hold in any context, the argument will more easily be taken seriously in a political and theological context extremely removed from the Greek context. But is it appropriate to take this argument so seriously? The reference to Zeus already suggests the rhetorical character of the argument.[49]

To state the terms of the debate more precisely, let us consider the second question, whether the rule of the best law is preferable to that of the best man. The very fact that he raises the question shows, let us note at once, that Aristotle is not satisfied with the reply he gave to the first question. How then does he answer the second?

The argument against the government of laws—and, by the same token, for the government of humans, a fortiori of the best among them, the king—is that laws can only enunciate general rules and are unable to prescribe anything concerning particular situations.[50] That is true, but on the other hand, those who govern must have at their disposal this universal rule.[51] One cannot then do without laws. The virtue of the law is that it is devoid of all passion, while every human soul necessarily contains passions. Thus, the superiority of the government of humans is that it can take into account particular situations; that of the government of law is that it is exempt from passion.[52] One would then have to mix or join together the government of people—or of the best person—and the government of the laws.

All of this remains very general. Let us look at things more closely. The law is incapable indeed of entering into the details of particular circumstances. But is a person more capable of doing that? Certainly not.[53] What is to be done then? Well, the law gives the magistrates a special education in this matter, and trains them to judge and administer the matters it leaves undecided "by the most just opinion."[54] In this way the law, by means of humans—of well-educated rulers—corrects the defect of the law.

Thus, in practice, "they [all] come together to adjudicate and deliberate and judge, and the judgments themselves all concern particulars."[55] Taking into consideration this effective solution permits us to examine more freely the case presented by "the best person," for, although any member of the assembly is individually, by comparison, probably of lesser merit than the best one, the city is composed of many of these people, and as a banquet where the guests bring their share is better than a simple meal offered by one person, a numerous mass judges many things better than one person, whoever that may be.[56] Here appears a type of argument that occurs in several places in the *Politics*, a surprising argument for us, for not only does it have a marked democratic character, but this character seems so extreme that a modern democrat would hesitate to support the argument or would even reject it.[57] The nature and significance of this "democratic argument" needs to be defined. It is not a dogmatic argument that posits, for example, that the politically just is determined by the will of the majority. It is an essentially or intrinsically political argument, by which I mean that it is not only an argument whose object is the political thing, but one whose tenor and so to speak whose life imitates our political condition. It reveals the power of number, more precisely the almost irresistible effects of the human plurality that are characteristic of our political condition. However excellent an individual may be—unlike many modern democrats, Aristotle considers that there are enormous natural differences among human beings—his superiority deploys itself in a dense element, formed by the "crowd" of those who, without being particularly eminent, are not without qualities or talents, and who, together constituting the city, add up in some way those talents and qualities to the point of judging better than the excellent person. As one can see, Aristotle's democratic argument has nothing to do with Rousseau's egalitarian moral argument according to which the conscience of the person with no particular quality is the best or even the infallible judge of good and evil. It rather finds an illustration or an expression of this in the proverb that holds that "Monsieur Everybody has more wit than Monsieur Voltaire."

There is no point in pursuing all the ramifications of the argument. Let us note one, however, that is particularly pertinent for our concern. The very same people who in principle govern alone are not immune to the law of number, or the power of the plurality: "For as it is, monarchs create many eyes for themselves, and ears, feet, and hands as well; for those who are friendly to their rule and themselves, they make corulers. If they are not friends, they will not behave in accordance with the monarch's intention, but if they are friends to him and his rule, the friend is someone similar and equal so if he supposes these should rule, he [necessarily] supposes that those who are similar and equal should rule similarly."[58]

If, earlier, the logic of number was "democratizing," here it is "aristocratizing." Whatever abstract validity there is to the royal argument, the argument of the One, the power of the One, the royal power is subjected to the political condition of plurality under its two determinations, that of the many who, in adding up their virtues, in some way prevail over the virtue of the best person, and that of the few, among whom the friendship of the king diffracts itself and who tend to become so many equals of the king. Thus, it appears that absolute kingship, which was the only royal regime that the Aristotelian classification effectively left to subsist, has in the end no substance of its own in the Greek political experience explored by Aristotle. The notion of absolute kingship is necessary to provide a peak to the pyramid of numbers—the one, the few, and the many—that organizes our political condition and allows us to understand it. Unlike democracy, oligarchy, and tyranny, even aristocracy and polity, it does not designate a political regime that is susceptible of becoming real.

But then, you will say, did Greece, in Aristotle's eyes, completely ignore kingship? In that case, where did its very name come from, and what did it designate? No, Greece did not completely ignore the kingly regime. If we go back to the classification with which we started, we see that Aristotle mentions a kind of kingship about which we have not yet said anything, the fourth kind, the kingship of "heroic times," which was at once over willing subjects, hereditary, and in accordance with law. It was the only effective kingship in the Greek world. Let us consider it a bit more precisely, even though Aristotle deals with it very quickly.

This kingship belongs to the beginning of the life of cities. It rests to be sure on superiority in virtue, but a very modest superiority since it stems from the paucity of excellent persons in these small associations. It is tempting to say that, in these primitive stages of human development, the least physical or moral quality—a noble physiognomy, long hair, courage in war, generosity in peacetime—was enough to make one worthy of kingship. Aristotle suggests that a sort of election, in any case a sort of "aristocratic" process of choosing the best person, underpinned this primitive kingship: the king was a benefactor, and whoever was most capable of doing good, or rendering services, was designated the king.[59]

This modest kingship thus rested on a puny human association, poor in "human resources." But when there appeared many people alike in virtue, "they no longer tolerated [kingship] but sought something common and established a polity."[60] It can be seen that this kingship of heroic times has no consistency of its own: as soon as the able members of society become more numerous—and that is the most natural movement there is—they discard this "king" whose ascendancy stemmed from the mediocre circumstances of the city.

Then, in a few very brief sentences, Aristotle recapitulates the constitutional history—the history of regimes—of cities. The progress of the love of gain led to oligarchies. Then the oligarchies transformed themselves into tyrannies. Finally, the tyrannies gave way to democracy. How did this last change come about? Aristotle suggests that because of its sordid love of gain, the ruling group shrank and so made the masses stronger. With the latter revolting, democracies arose.[61] This extraordinarily concentrated account reveals in all its force and simplicity the principle of political change, the change of the regime of the city. This principle is the play of plurality, the play between the few and the many, the few tending naturally to become fewer, the many to become more. In this presentation, the One, far from constituting one of the three principles of the political and human order, is but the limit of the few. In properly political terms, kingship and tyranny are but two modes—the one, ancient or heroic; the other, coming later and decadent—of oligarchy. Thus, in the Aristotelian analysis of the city, *there is no* regime of the One.

In any case, "now that it has happened that cities have become even larger, it is perhaps no longer easy for any regime to arise other than a democracy."[62] What is the significance of this last remark, which seems to considerably restrict the gamut of our political choices? Would Aristotle here yield to the prestige of necessity as the moderns are quick to do? We remember the assertions of Leo Strauss: the difference between a good and a bad regime is the most fundamental of all practical or political distinctions, more fundamental, then, contrary to what Voegelin seems to think, than the distinction between constitutional and postconstitutional regimes. The consideration of what is necessary must never close our eyes to the consideration of what is good, which must always be first for us. Does not Aristotle here precisely give the advantage to the consideration of what is necessary to the detriment of the good? Does he not explain to us that democracy—which is, according to his classification, a bad regime—is in sum the only regime available to the Greek cities of his time? This would suggest, let it be said in passing, that, contrary to Strauss's thesis, classical political science is not so reticent about evoking the necessary character of a regime that, if it is not simply bad, is in any case less good than the completely good regimes.[63] It seems to me in any case that Aristotle's remark, without implying the least disdain for the difference between good and evil, entails an understanding of necessity that is not the same as the one Strauss suggests—"necessity as just punishment." However summarily, Aristotle sketches a natural history of the city: the development of the city as a political form—its growth in numbers and talents, a growth that is natural—leads so to speak necessarily to a state where a democratic regime is the only possible regime. This regime can be more or less good according to the quality of the people, but it will necessarily be a regime of the many. If the people are very corrupt, it will be a very bad democracy. Nowhere does Aristotle suggest that the latter could lead—even less, that it would necessarily lead—to a "Caesarian" regime, even if he points out that in place of this bad democracy, a tyranny can arise.[64] All his indications go in the same direction: democracy—wholesome or corrupt—is the final regime of the city, the end of its "natural history," or the natural end of its history. This is eloquent: democracies today have taken the generic name of "regime"— what was previously called *dèmokratia* is today called *politeïa*.[65] With this final regime, the city has become all that it can be. All of its possibilities are fulfilled. A "Caesarian" future is not envisaged, because no real inno-vation—no future in the strong sense of the term—is envisaged. Such an innovation would presuppose a transformation of the political form it-self and we know that Aristotle, far from exploring the possibility, multi-plies the arguments to render it properly "unthinkable."

Thus, Strauss's thesis on the practical primacy of the good, while per-fectly acceptable in itself, is by him closely joined to a theoretical propo-sition or perspective on politics that holds that understanding politics comes down to understanding the political regime, and to answering the question of which regime. Now this thesis or proposition is insufficient, for these regimes that can indeed be good or bad do not all exist, I dare say, in the same way. If they are equally subject to circumstances in gen-eral, they depend unequally on a circumstance that is more than a cir-cumstance since it largely determines the number and the nature of pos-sible regimes, namely, the political form. As we have just seen, kingship does not have its place in the city form, except in the beginnings of the city's existence, from which come the "kingly" terms. Thus, it is not only a matter of placing a regime on the scale of the good, but of grasping its articulation with the political form. However desirous one may be to not reduce or subject the political science of Aristotle to the limits of the Greek experience, one would be, I believe, unfaithful to his approach if one detached a few very abstract propositions on the kingly regime in order to extract a science of kingship independent of the political form in which kingship has, or, as it happens, does not have its place.

Montesquieu's Critique of Aristotle

As I stated in chapter 1 of this inquiry, the sense that Greek political sci-ence found its limits in the limits of the Greek experience, more precisely in the Greek ignorance of monarchy properly speaking, played a large role in the development of a modern political science, that is, which understood itself to be modern by opposition to ancient political science, chiefly Aris-totle's. Montesquieu is the most complete master of this modern political science, since he both presents the liberal doctrine in the broadest and sharpest manner and gives the example and provides the tools of what will much later be called the social sciences, which make of politics one param-eter among other parameters, such as climate or religion. Now, Montesquieu discredits ancient political science by enclosing it within the limits of the city. This he does in two senses, by describing it as a simple reflection of the conditions of life in the city,[66] and by emphasizing that it is incapable of grasping the political phenomenon proper to modern Europe, namely monarchy. The Greek experience of monarchy was too meager for the Greeks to have an adequate idea of that government. I would like now to develop the summary indications given in chapter 1.

Montesquieu devotes no fewer than four chapters to the question of monarchy in Greece and in Greek thought, four chapters situated in a strategic place since they come immediately after the account of the English constitution.[67] The first of these four chapters is titled, "Why the ancients had no clear idea of monarchy" (11.8). The following chapter is titled, "Aristotle's manner of thinking." This title seems very innocuous, but it is the only one in the entire work that contains the name of a philosopher. The chapter begins as follows: "An awkwardness is clearly seen in Aristotle's treatment of monarchy." Then he comments on the passages in the *Politics* that we have read. After a short chapter titled, "The manner of thinking of other political men," which is, one would say, separated from the preceding one only to isolate Aristotle and to highlight the critique Montesquieu makes of him, the last in the series of four chapters is titled, "On the kings of heroic times among the Greeks." Montesquieu takes up the elements provided by Aristotle: "This is one of the five kinds of monarchy of which Aristotle speaks, and this is the only one that might arouse the idea of the monarchical constitution. But the plan of this constitution is the opposite of that of our monarchies today." The decisive point is that "in the government of the kings of heroic times, the three powers were badly distributed,"[68] the people having the legislative power, and the king the executive power along with the judicial power. Montesquieu explains:

Among a free people who have legislative power, among a people enclosed within a town, where everything odious becomes even more odious, the masterwork of legislation is to know where properly to place the power of judging. But it could not be placed worse than in the hands of the one who already had executive power. The monarch became terrible immediately. But at the same time, since he did not legislate, he could not defend himself against legislation; he had too much power and he did not have enough.

It had not yet been discovered that the prince's true function was to establish judges and not to judge himself. The opposite policy rendered unbearable the government of one alone. All these kings were driven out.

Setting aside the considerations on the distribution of the three powers, as decisive as they are for Montesquieu, I will dwell on just one nota-
tion: "among a people enclosed within a town, where everything odious
becomes even more odious." The question of political physics is perhaps
just as important as the constitutional question. The city's size is such
that a king will necessarily be odious, and thus ruling power necessarily
fragile. Monarchy as a political regime can only be deployed in a political body of a certain size, and so in a more extended political form than
a city. Aristotle lets us neither know nor even guess anything about this
political form that is more extended than the city. One can think that in
certain circumstances unknown to Greece, the monarchical regime, in
developing itself, in wanting as it were to attain its complete development, produced in some way the political form capable of sheltering it,
namely the nation.

A final word. Following the four chapters about Greece that I have
just commented on, Montesquieu devotes the rest of book 11 to the political history of Rome. I will read only the beginning of chapter 12, the
first of the series devoted to Rome and titled, "On the government of the
Roman kings and how the three powers were distributed in it": "The
government of the Roman kings was somewhat related to that of the
kings of heroic times among the Greeks. Like them it fell, from its general vice, although in itself and in its particular nature it was very good."
One sees how Rome's beginnings resemble those of the Greek cities. Its
kings were not at the head of a monarchy as we understand the notion,
but they participated in an oligarchic regime in which their crown was
subject to election. They belong then by right to the political science of
Aristotle. I have already underlined and it must not be forgotten that
Rome began as did Greece and the moving principle of class struggle,
the interplay between the few and the many, was the same in both cases.
How then was it possible in a popular republic, whose natural tendency
was all in all to become ever more popular, for the power of one only to
finally arise within it, the power of monarchy, which it had never known,
so to speak, and whose principle was in spite of that the object of invet-

erate and implacable hatred? How did such a gap widen between a citizen—Caesar—and his equals, when, as we have seen, the very principle of the movement of the city is the rejection of every superiority considered as "odious"?

The Friendship of Caesar

It will be recalled that Aristotle explains that the city develops starting from the primitive or "heroic" kingship, because the citizens who increase at the same time in number and in skills can "no longer tolerate" a king, and so they seek "something common" and establish a republic, a "polity." Thus there is an intrinsic link among number, equality, and the existence of a common good. Here, however, one needs to pay attention: the "number" that cannot put up with the power of the king is of course the "small number." The king's superiority is odious to the pride of the few. They will thus agree—conspire—to drive him out.

Now soon, or sometime later, the "many," as they increase in number and in skills, will deal with the "few" as the latter dealt with the king. For in their turn they find the superiority of the few "odious." Perhaps they will not drive out the few, but they will at least reduce their power and abase their pride. Such are the efforts of the republic to achieve civic friendship. Accordingly, Aristotle says in the *Nicomachean Ethics* that "friendships and justice" play a much larger role in democracies than in tyrannies, for there are many common things wherever citizens are equal.[69]

The plural here is noteworthy: friendships. Even if democracy is the regime that opens the widest field to civic friendship, that friendship cannot normally cross the "class barrier." Normally the poor and the rich are not friends. The most one could hope for in this regard is a friendship founded on utility.[70] Thus, while a democratic republic calls for civic friendship among all citizens, in practice this friendship is composed of two distinct friendships that do not befriend one another. This situation opens the possibility for a member of one or the other class to break with it in order to make friends with the enemy class and in this way acquire a decisive superiority over his rivals in his class of origin. For obvious enough reasons, this possibility is in effect open only to a member of the "few," who thereby becomes a demagogue.[71] Thus, perhaps the most important parameter in a city living under a republican regime with a democratic tendency is the "state of friendship" among the few. There is an abiding temptation for an oligarch with a modicum of character and ambition to pave his way by seeking support among the people, where his peers disdain to look for it. What such an oligarch will be able to accomplish depends of course on chance, on his talents, and also on a factor that is very difficult to weigh and that I would describe with the following question: what degree of superiority are his equals who are his friends likely to grant him, or is he able to wrest from them? It becomes a question of what degree of inequality is friendship among equals able to accept. One of the most humanly interesting aspects of the "Caesar question" is the question of the rapport between friendship, that of the friendship of unequals, or the inequality of friends.

Let us then rapidly consider the mechanism or structure of friendship. Aristotle remarks that equality is more fundamental in friendship than in justice. In fact, once a considerable disparity arises between friends, whether on account of virtue, vice, wealth, or something else, they cease to be friends and do not even aspire to be friends.[72] Aristotle is not very sentimental about all this. If your best friend from childhood or high school or the army becomes much richer or much poorer than you, or becomes much more learned, and so on, you can bid your fine friendship farewell and you will not even wish that it could be maintained. Even if this statement hurts our finer feelings, we understand it perfectly. We are thus surprised at the statement Aristotle adds immediately, that this is most evident with the gods since they hold the greatest superiority in every kind of goods.[73]

What does that mean? Why mention the gods here? Does Aristotle mean to say that we cannot be friends with the gods because they are so far above us? That statement seems reasonable. Besides, its validity is not limited to the gods of the pagan philosophers, who, happy in their intermundane space, were indifferent to human beings. The God of the Bible is surely very different from the pagan gods by reason of his "philanthropy," and friendship is possible between him and his rational creatures. But that does not go against what Aristotle says here. For Judaism as for Christianity, human beings cannot become friends of God by their own power. God must take the initiative and "condescend" to this friendship. In the language of Christianity, only the grace of God can bridge the infinite distance between human nature and the "nature"—the "supernature"—of God.

However that may be, Aristotle's statement here does not seem to have much to do with theology. He says a little further: "From this an impasse is raised, that perhaps friends do not wish for the greatest goods for their friends, such as that they be gods; for then they would no longer have friends, and so there would be good things they did not have, since friends are good things. So if it was beautifully said that a friend wishes for good things for a friend for that friend's own sake, that friend would need to remain whatever he was."[74] Isn't Aristotle being too subtle here? Or is he not taking a very indirect route to come to a quite obvious conclusion? If we wish all kinds of good things for our friend *for his sake*—which is the definition of friendship—we obviously assume he will remain the kind of being he is; otherwise the idea of *his* good would have no defined or stable point of reference. How could we wish our friend to have no more need of friends? Accordingly, the aporia Aristotle speaks of seems to be resolved by saying that the good that we wish for our friend must be in keeping with his nature and the circumstances of his life.

On the other hand, the desire that our friend become a god is not simply absurd. If it seems contradictory indeed to wish that our friend might become a god and have no more need of friends—for a god is self-sufficient—it is not absurd to make this wish in thinking of oneself. If my friend becomes a god or approaches the divine condition, that is excellent for me, for then he will be so much more able to be helpful to me—provided, of course, he is a "philanthropic" god. Moreover, it is not necessary to suppose that, in my enthusiasm for my friend, I am clearly or deliberately thinking of my own advantage. I love him, and in brief I wish that he might become more and more lovable.

But who has ever seriously wished his friend to become god, or a god? To that one must reply: probably never in our private life, or as a private person, but what about as a citizen, in public life? There is in any case one political episode of immense consequence in which not only did the citizens wish that one of them, the one they loved the most, become a god, but that beloved citizen did in fact become a god. This is not a way of speaking: this citizen did in fact become immortal—immortality belongs to the gods—since he governed the world after his death.[75] Aristotle could not know anything of this extraordinary episode that would take place three centuries later and that seems to contradict his very convincing analysis of friendship. Or more precisely, the extreme and "aporetic" case Aristotle envisaged by reducing in a way the question to the absurd, came to be a reality. I am speaking of course of the death and deification of Caesar as the founding cause of the Roman Empire.

Cicero's Perplexity

This extraordinary elevation of a citizen above those who were his equals presupposes a considerable modification of the form of the city. For such an elevation to be possible, its base—which is the city itself—must first have been considerably extended to be able to sustain this elevation.[76] The surface area of the base, dare I say, must be proportional to the height of the new prince. The narrow city, "where all that is odious becomes even more odious," had to undergo such an extension and deformation, such a distension, that the laws of hate and love, the chemistry of the passions, were profoundly modified.

The consequences of this distension of the city can best be seen in the period immediately preceding the institutionalization of empire, in the "Caesarian" period. The political and moral order becomes blurred or, better, indeterminate. One can sense this blurring or indetermination in a major work of Latin philosophy, in truth one of the most influential works in the moral history of Europe, a work that endeavors precisely to order the moral and political landscape at the time of all the disorders. I am alluding to the *De officiis* of Cicero.

It is a work whose context is both dramatic and touching. Hounded by the hatred of Antony who will soon catch up to him, Cicero lived the last months of his life fleeing from one house to another. For his son Marcus, who was studying philosophy in Athens, he composed this long exposition of his moral philosophy. He presents himself as someone who follows chiefly the Stoics, but not in a servile way. In fact, he frequently corrects Panaetius, who is his principal reference. This very long "letter of a father to his son" is of course also addressed to the Romans in general. At the beginning of book 2, Cicero directly ties the composition of the work to the political situation:

Now, as long as the state was administered by the men to whose care she had voluntarily entrusted herself, I devoted all my effort and thought to her. But when everything passed under the absolute control of a despot, and there was no longer any room for statesmanship or authority of mine; and finally when I had lost the friends who had been associated with me in the task of serving the interests of the state, and who were men of the highest standing, I did not resign myself to grief. . . . And since my mind could not be wholly idle, I thought, as I had been well-read along these lines of thought from my early youth, that the most honourable way for me to forget my sorrows would be by turning to philosophy. . . . Therefore, amid all the present most awful calamities I yet flatter myself that I have won this good out of evil—that I may commit to written form matters not at all familiar to our countrymen but still very much worth their knowing.[77]

It is not my intent here to study the content of Cicero's moral teaching, nor the manner in which he combines the threads of diverse traditions that are all in some way tied to the Socratic source. What concerns us is the relationship between moral philosophy and the political framework. As I have just said, with the distension of the city the order of political and moral things became blurred or indeterminate. How does this appear in *De officiis*?

It appears first of all in the rather vague way Cicero describes the relations between the different *gradus societatis hominum* in 1.17. What the "degrees of human fellowship" are—one could say, the degrees of social intimacy—is not what is uncertain. Cicero enumerates them from humanity as a whole down to the close family circle, passing through the nation, the city, friendship, and so on. The question at hand bears on the manner of classifying these different degrees, of situating them on the ladder of our esteem. Aristotle's reply left no doubt. For him, it was the city that aimed at the highest good and accordingly encompassed the other communities that were clearly subordinated to it.[78] But matters are markedly less clear in Cicero's exposé. To be sure, he concludes, "there is no social relation among them all more weighty, none more dear than that which links each one of us with our *respublica*."[79] But why is this so? Nowhere is a clear justification given, or it comes down to this: "our native land embraces all our loves."[80] Certain expressions suggest that blood ties are closer than civic ties—"artior vero colligatio est societatis propinquorum"—moreover, the "household" *(domus)* is "the foundation of civil government, the nursery, as it were, of the *respublica* [principium urbis et quasi seminarium rei publicae]."[81] It is not lacking respect for Cicero to remark that these vague formulas do not bear comparison with Aristotle's neat analysis of the relation between household and city in the beginning of the *Politics*. Cicero indeed celebrates the merits of friendship between virtuous people as he should,[82] but he says nothing about the complex relation that obtains between friendship and the diversity of political regimes.

Thus, the differences and articulations among the diverse human associations that were brought out so clearly in Aristotle's description dim, weaken, or fade in Cicero's exposition. The landscape becomes flat and at the same time confused. What comes to the forefront is an encompassing notion in which differences tend to be absorbed and lost. This notion of "the fellowship of the whole human race [universi generis humani societas]" is a notion unknown to classical Greek philosophy. In seeking the natural principles of human community and society, Cicero sees the first principle in "the fellowship of the whole human race."[83] The bond—*vinculum*—of this society is "reason and speech, which by the processes of teaching and learning, of communicating, discussing, and reasoning associate men together, and unite them in a kind of natural society [naturali quadam societate]."[84] Later, toward the end of book 1, concluding an enumeration of rules of good conduct, Cicero writes: "In a word, not to go into details, it is our duty to respect, defend, and maintain the common bonds of union and fellowship subsisting between all the members of the human race."[85] These expressions please us as admirable anticipations of our own convictions—of the modern concept of human unity. This sentiment is very understandable, but more important for our inquiry than the anticipation of the modern concept is the rupture with the classical Greek concept that these expressions imply.[86] Let us pause here for a moment.

The phrase "human unity" that I have employed is altogether equivocal. As I have often emphasized, classical Greek philosophy very clearly affirmed the unity of the human species—the more clearly, moreover, in that it invented the very notion of species, that of species in general and of the human species in particular. The human being is a rational animal—an animal possessing *logos*. The Romans received and confirmed this definition, translating, as Cicero does here, *logos* as *ratio et oratio*. The difference between Romans and Greeks resides in the framework in which this specific difference is inscribed and first of all that produces it. Aristotle in some way equates rational animal and political animal, an animal living in a polis, that is, in a determined political form. Of course, those human beings who do not live in cities properly speaking but in tribes or empires also belong to the species, although they are without doubt less accomplished since the framework for the deployment of their *logos* is less favorable. But, in all cases, speech and reason develop in a community that is real, and thus distinct, that can be seen, named, and, so to speak, touched. With Cicero an uncertainty sets in that foreshadows our own uncertainties: do *ratio et oratio* develop in a framework constituted by humanity itself as the universal society of the human race or can they develop by themselves, independent of any determined political framework, in which case the human being could be a rational animal without being a political animal? This is an interesting question from a so-called ontological point of view, but politically it is an idle question. It is impossible to consider humanity as such as a political form. In both cases, human action as *ratio et oratio* tends to detach itself from any political form as well as any political regime. It is no longer located in a concretely determined *political* order but in an order that will later be called *civilization* or what Cicero himself begins then to call the "universal society of the human race." *Ratio et oratio* are independent of any concrete political operation; they are at the service of a general morality, detached from political forms and regimes and thus applicable in all political regimes and forms, in all political conditions, for the citizen of the smallest city as well as the emperor of Rome.

Cicero is not the author of this morality that in *De officiis* he articulates in a way that will be most influential thereafter. As I have already noted, it belongs to "Stoicism," a diverse and complex doctrinal array that, while encompassing highly technical philosophical elements, is characterized by a vagueness or metamorphic indetermination that very often makes it difficult to judge with assurance if a certain point of doctrine, a certain nuance, or a certain statement is or is not of Stoic inspiration. This plasticity of Stoic doctrine corresponds, dare I say, to the plasticity of Hellenistic civilization detached from cities and to the plasticity of the city of Rome that was capable of an expansion whose secret still evades us. Thus, after inspiring or escorting the best of the Roman Republic when Panaetius joined the "circle of the Scipios" in the middle of the second century B.C.E., Stoicism ascended the imperial throne in the second century C.E. with Marcus Aurelius.[87]

In a world where the difference between cities pales, where their self-sufficiency and impenetrability pales, *jus gentium*—the expression itself comes from Cicero—increases in importance and credence. What is the "law of nations"? It carries almost infinite meanings.[88] *Jus gentium* does not refer simply or even principally to international law—the law between nations—but more generally to the array of principles and maxims shared by all civilized peoples (for example, *pacta sunt servanda*).[89] These diverse meanings have in common that *jus gentium* is the law that ignores the distinction between the interior and the exterior of political bodies,[90] or that envelops one and the other.

What Is Proper to Rome

I do not want to suggest that Rome did not know the notion of limit. It suffices to mention the *pomoerium* and the *limes*.[91] But their experience soon made the limit of the *civitas* vague. Rome expands by transforming the conquered into allies and then into citizens, in such a way that with territorial expansion comes a diversity and gradation of the status of persons. On the eve of empire the Romans still speak of their *civitas,* a *civitas* that is enormously, almost monstrously, extended and distended. This flexibility, this plasticity, this malleability of the Roman substance forms a vivid contrast with the firmness and compactness of the Greek civic substance, especially the Athenian. The idea Athens has of itself is condensed in a very expressive manner in the notion of autochthony.[92] On the contrary, Rome comes from elsewhere: Aeneas came from Troy to found Lavinium; his son Ascanius founded Alba, from which came Rome; and at the same time Rome comes from nowhere, for Romulus and Remus wanted to leave Alba:

> They resolved to live by themselves, and build a city in the same place where they were in their infancy brought up. This seems the most honourable reason for their departure; though perhaps it was necessary, having such a body of slaves and of fugitives collected about them, either to come to nothing by dispersing them, or if not so, then to live with them elsewhere. For that the inhabitants of Alba did not think fugitives worthy of

being received and incorporated as citizens among them plainly appears from the matter of the women, an attempt made not wantonly but of necessity, because they could not get wives by good-will. For they certainly paid unusual respect and honour to those whom they thus forcibly seized.

Not long after the first foundation of the city, they opened a sanctuary of refuge for all fugitives, which they called the temple of the god Asylaeus, where they received and protected all, delivering none back, neither the servant to his master, the debtor to his creditor, nor the murderer into the hands of the magistrate.[93]

Whereas the idea of Athens as autochthonous implies that the city of Athens was, so to speak, always already there, the accounts, legendary or historical, of the origins of Rome emphasize that it was born from nothing: those who will make up Rome are nobodies; they are, we would say, outcasts. This city was founded by the cityless. Livy emphasizes that to its still-empty premises "fled for refuge all the rag-tag-and-bobtail from the neighboring peoples; some free, some slaves, and all of them wanting nothing but a fresh start."[94] This mixed crowd in search of something new *(avida novarum rerum)* was the kernel of an expansion and a future without limits.

When Rome became fully aware of itself, that is, when it was capable of comparing its experience to the Greek experience, it understood itself as a process of human gathering, a process of association or consociation whose starting point as well as its development could be known rationally, for they belonged to enlightened times.[95] The fact that it came later and is "secondary" compared to Greece turns to Rome's advantage.[96] In addition to this, so to speak, gnoseological superiority, Rome has a political superiority: "Our commonwealth, in contrast, was not shaped by one man's talent but by that of many; and not in one person's lifetime, but over many generations."[97] We now understand better why Cicero seems to put up with a good deal of vagueness concerning both relations among the different *gradus societatis hominum* as well as the most determining framework of human *ratio et oratio*. Rome is not so much a city to be compared to Athens or Sparta as the dynamic process of human consociation, a process that unceasingly pushes and in the end abolishes the limits of the city form.

This abolition of limits obviously has considerable consequences for the content and for the very definition of political life. When the form of the community becomes blurred, the form of the common good disappears. When what the citizen has a share in becomes indeterminate, citizenship is weakened to the point of changing meaning. Indeed the figure of the citizen is practically absent in *De officiis*. This is not only because all things have come under the domination of one only. It is also because, in his sketch of the desirable political order, Cicero substitutes for the citizen who is both one and double—sometimes commanding, sometimes commanded—the duality of the magistrate and the private person. The magistrate is elevated at the same time the private individual is abased, or, more precisely, the citizen is reduced to the condition of a private individual. As for the first, "it is, then, peculiarly the place of a magistrate to bear in mind that he represents the state [se gerere personam civitatis] and that it is his duty to uphold its honour and its dignity, to enforce the law, to dispense to all their constitutional rights, and to remember that all this has been committed to him as a sacred trust."[98] The role, or in any event the dignity, of the magistrate increases in proportion to the decrease of the concrete presence of the city that, no longer assembled and visible as a whole, no longer present, must be *represented* by the magistrate. Whereas in the limited city the magistrate is simply the governing part of the city, in the extended or distended city the part and the whole have lost their mutual actuality and need the mediation of a third term. This third term, unknown to Athens and to early Rome, is the *persona civitatis*. The city has become, we would say, a "moral person." This transformation allows for the city to be placed on the shoulders of the magistrate who henceforth carries it.

The abstraction of the *persona civitatis* means a loss of substance for the civic body. The good citizen *(bonus civis)* is defined first of all as *privatus,* the "simple citizen" who is expected to live in equality ("aequo et pari jure") with the fellow citizens. As for rapport with the public thing, the citizen is expected to be committed to peace and decency ("ea velle, quae tranquilla et honesta sint"). These are vague terms, to say the least. In any case, they do not suggest an active concept of citizenship.

It seems to me, then, that everything in Cicero's language indicates a displacement of the center of political gravity toward the magistrate, who as the bearer of the "person" of the city is the object of the citizens' trust *(fides)*. For what do they trust him? They trust him to defend the dignity of the republic and uphold the laws, but also to *jura discribere*—to dispense to each his rights. Cicero here proposes a new understanding of republican government that, as the object of the citizens' trust, carefully guarantees their rights. Is this not a sketch of the modern State that, elevated above society and separated from it, returns to it to assign to each member of society his or her rights?

This rapprochement is the more justified in that Cicero, like the Moderns, closely ties the end or goal of the political institution to the protection of property. After severely condemning Philippus who, in his capacity as tribune of the *plebs,* had proposed an agrarian law aimed at equalizing properties, he writes: "The chief purpose in the establishment of *respublicae* and *civitates* was that individual property rights might be secured. For, although it was by Nature's guidance that men were drawn together into communities, it was in the hope of safeguarding their possessions [spe custodiae rerum suarum] that they sought the protection of cities."[99] This sentence does not of course contain Cicero's whole political philosophy, but one cannot fail to see that it leaves little place for a true common good. Nature's causality, its socializing or aggregative thrust, works through the activation of the sentiment of what is one's own.

The insistence on what is one's own, on the particular, was already to be found in Cicero's taking up a thesis of Panaetius. He writes, "We must realize also that we are invested by Nature with two characters [duae personae], as it were: one of these is universal, arising from the fact of our being all alike endowed with reason and with that superiority which lifts us above the brute. . . . The other character is the one that is assigned to individuals in particular."[100] Nature thus has endowed us with two kinds of persona: a *persona communis* that is our rational nature common to all human beings; and a *persona singulis tributa,* a particular or singular persona that is our individual nature, our individual character. What is striking here is how much Cicero insists on this second persona. Unlike Aristotle, who offered us incomparably subtle tools to analyze and bring out the character of every human being in the full range of virtues and vices but showed no visible interest in particularity as such, Cicero makes particularity his theme. Whereas Aristotle studied human beings whose virtues and vices made them indeed very different from one another but which virtues and vices were so many expressions—dispositions—of this common nature, Cicero considers this diversity for its own sake; he detaches individual particularity from common nature, as the distinction between two personas shows. Where there was nature and its virtuous or vicious "dispositions," now there are two "persons."

Cicero first of all mentions the great differences one encounters *in corporibus,* but he quickly adds, "diversities of character are greater still."[101] He gives us a quick tour of a portrait gallery of famous men—Romans and Greeks—with a few words, sometimes only one, to characterize Laelius, Scipio, Socrates, Pericles, Themistocles, Solon, and so on. What interests Cicero in this are not the particular characters in their particularity but, dare I say, the phenomenon of particularity in general. Individual nature, as nature's other face but nature nonetheless, brings about another kind of rule for us. If assuredly we must not do anything against our common or universal nature ("contra universam naturam") but on the contrary preserve it, we must on the other hand follow our own proper nature ("propriam nostram sequamur").[102] Proper nature provides a no less legitimate rule, one that is no less authoritative than the rule included in common or universal nature. Cicero even suggests that the authority of the first trumps that of the second. Even if other *studia* were *graviora atque meliora,* he says, we ought nonetheless to measure or evaluate our activities according to the rule or criterion of our proper nature ("nostrae naturae regula").[103] To be sure, the explanations that Cicero immediately adds tend to turn these theses into statements of good sense: it does no good to aim at the impossible or, more subtly, one cannot attain propriety in one's action, decorum, if one acts in a manner that is contrary or repugnant to one's individual nature ("nihil decet invita Minerva"). But these explanations cannot conceal the amplitude of the displacement that has been wrought. The rule of human actions henceforth derives from individual nature more than from common nature.

In fact, in the lines that follow, Cicero indeed seems to define the propriety—the decorum—of action by its coherence throughout and within an individual life.[104] He compares the conduct of one's life to speaking a language: just as we must employ our maternal tongue, under penalty of making ourselves ridiculous, like those who introduce Greek words into their speech, so we must not introduce any discord in our actions and in all our lives.[105] Internal coherence, fidelity to the particular character of one human life, tends to replace conformity to common human nature and its ends.

Here again, it is tempting to interpret Cicero's statements in a way that dulls the point. But the example immediately provided proves the amplitude of the displacement that has been effected: the example of Cato shows that the difference of individual natures is so powerful ("haec differentia naturarum tantam habet vim") that, in the same circumstances, suicide can be a duty for one but not for another.[106] How then could the example of Cato prove that depending on the character of the agent suicide can be a duty or on the contrary would be judged a crime? Cicero emphasizes that Cato's companions in the same cause did not commit suicide but surrendered to Caesar, and he adds that perhaps public opinion would have condemned them if they had taken their own lives. Why this double standard? Why admiration for Cato's suicide and possible condemnation for the hypothetical suicide of the other enemies of Caesar? Cicero's reply cannot but appear strange to us, I believe. He says that the others had led less austere lives, but nature had endowed Cato with *incredibilis gravitas* that he had constantly exercised and strengthened. Accordingly, such a man had to die rather than look upon the face of a tyrant.[107] It is truly strange that an act inspired by the most rigorous civic virtue, by the loftiest idea of the public or common thing, has for Cicero its true justification in the extreme particularity of an individual character. Cicero is not keen to generalize the maxim of Cato's deed: he was not among the last handful who fought with Cato, for he had submitted to Caesar, accepting to look upon the face of the tyrant. But how could the rule of an action be strictly individual? What is the political meaning of Cicero's reduction of Cato's civic virtue to his individual character, his proper nature?

I would say that Cato's virtue is exercised according to a political perspective that has become "theoretical," in a political framework that has already disappeared. Since Cato's virtue looked to a political form and a regime, an "ethical substance," that were in the process of decomposing, it could not attain its object and so it comes back to the agent whose extreme, even excessive, particularity it expresses—namely, a virtue that is superior to but that also has no relationship to the actual situation. What seeks to be exemplary civic virtue is enacted as an individual or idiosyncratic performance. Perhaps Cicero dreads having to imitate Cato, but the important fact is that Cato cannot be imitated since the framework of virtuous emulation has disappeared, since in truth Cato's deed is already an imitation of real civic virtue. The dissolution of the "ethical substance" of the republic liberates on the one hand human generality, a human nature abstractly said to be rational or reasonable, and on the other virtues and vices that appear as strictly individual characters.

One can see that the most delicate questions of morality, and even the most difficult questions of ontology (such as the status of individuality) are linked to the question of political form. The human as pure moral agent and the human as pure particularity, pure individuality, two phenomena that appear to us to be given, that is, as determined in themselves or by themselves, are shown to be in fact derivative phenomena, if we judge by the Roman experience. From what do they derive? They derive from the distension and finally from the decomposition of the first political form, the original republic, that we have described in broad strokes. What appears to our understanding to be immediately determined—namely, once again, the separation of the universal moral agent and the particular individual—our political reason discovers to be produced by the scission of a now-lost concrete universal, which is the citizen. In this sense, abstract evidence of the moral agent as well as the individual flows directly from their meager reality, a deficiency that in its turn derives from the distension of the political form.

If these considerations hold any validity, it means that something like a "passage from the Ancients to the Moderns" already took place at Rome at the end of the republic. A republican order grounded in the political government of the common thing gave way to an order that soon became imperial, grounded in the legal protection of particular properties and rights. As Alexandre Kojève says in his commentary on *The Phenomenology of the Spirit*: "The Greek Warrior becomes the Roman Bourgeois, who ceases to be Citizen in the pagan sense of the word. The State then has the 'right' (= the understandable possibility) of ignoring him. The non-warrior pseudo-citizens, who are interested only in their private property (Particularity) and ignore the Universal, are at the mercy of the professional soldiers and their leader (the Emperor). This leader, the Despot, will also himself consider the State as his *private property* (and that of his family)."[108]

Of course, the Roman bourgeois at the mercy of the emperor remains at a great distance from the French or English bourgeois who freely elects his representatives. But they have enough in common, and above all the Ciceronian concept of the political order in *De officiis* has enough in common with the liberal concept of the function of the State, to raise the question of the relation between the two "modernities," the two ways of becoming modern, that is, the two ways of becoming an individual.

The Ciceronian Moment

The redefining of the political order wrought by Cicero in *De officiis* seems to confirm our reservations about Leo Strauss's thesis in *On Tyranny*. Caesarism cannot be understood simply as a subdivision of absolute monarchy. The Caesarian moment, which justifiably can be called the Ciceronian moment, redefines the political order in a way that distances us decisively from the ancient civic order, Greek or Roman. The magistrate who "bears the person of the city," whose office is to assign to each his or her rights, and in particular to protect properties—for it is in order to protect their own goods that people assemble in cities—is an unprecedented figure of the political order. One may say that Greek political philosophy has all the tools to conceive this new figure, which is perhaps true even if the notion of *persona civitatis* has no equivalent in Greek, but the main point is that in the Greek experience the political order is always the order of a given concrete community, the active operation of a common thing, and cannot be the object of a functional definition such as the one proposed by Cicero.

The Ciceronian moment is not limited to the period we are considering, the last years of Cicero's life. It is only provisionally and imperfectly closed by the inauguration of the empire. As the passage from Kojève cited above suggests, the imperial regime privatizes the prince no less than the subjects. Whatever its historical success, which stems perhaps above all from the civic energies it still harbors, an inner weakness affects the Roman imperial form. It is far from satisfying the aspiration awakened by the original experience of the city. In this sense, what I call the Ciceronian moment endures and stretches until European political life finally produces its specific political form, the nation-state. The Ciceronian moment is characterized by an undetermined concrete political form; what defines it, one could say, is the indefinite character of the concrete political form and the need to formulate a rule of common life in the absence of this form. In this sense, what we call the Renaissance is the culmination of the Ciceronian moment and prepares its denouement.

Montaigne is without doubt one of the most interesting authors in this context. Leaving aside what Montaigne says of Cicero himself in chapter 40 of book 1 of the *Essays,* "Considerations on Cicero," I will attempt to go right to the question that joins the beginning to the end of the very long Ciceronian moment. It is contained in what Cicero says about Cato.

As we have seen, Cicero presents the suicide of Cato as an example of an act that finds its justification in the *incredibilis gravitas* of the person, that is, in his *propria natura.* As I have said, the rule of action tends for Cicero to reside no longer in human nature and its universal traits but in individual nature and its particular traits. Now, this is a thesis taken up and deployed through the *Essays* by Montaigne, who moreover makes explicit reference to the passage in Cicero we have read. It is the thesis of the "ruling pattern": "Just consider the evidence of this in our own experience. There is no one who, if he listens to himself, does not discover in himself a pattern all his own, a ruling pattern, which struggles against education and against the tempest of the passions that oppose it. For my part, I do not feel much sudden agitation; I am nearly always in place, like heavy and inert bodies. If I am not at home, I am always very near it."[109]

Cato, who was then for Cicero the example of a prodigiously characterized individual nature, plays a great role in the *Essays.* The case of Cato greatly preoccupies Montaigne: "He was truly a model chosen by nature to show how far human virtue and constancy could go."[110] In a sense, Cato represents for Montaigne the contrary or opposite of what he represents for Cicero, general or generic virtue in place of individual character. Cato is *virtue itself.* Thus it is by examining Cato in particular that Montaigne brings to light and formulates the problem of virtue, with its admirable character but also its ambiguities. I limit myself to what is essential for our purpose.

Montaigne leaves nothing to doubt about the intrinsically admirable character of Cato's virtue. Cato is even the example he opposes to the vicious evaluations of "most of the wits of [his] time using their ingenuity to obscure the glory of the beautiful and noble actions of antiquity, giving them some vile interpretation and conjuring up vain occasions and causes for them."[111] But some aspects of Cato's virtue give rise to his perplexity or his reservations. Compared to Socrates, who "makes his soul move with a natural and common motion," Cato has "a pace strained far above the ordinary; . . . we feel that he is always mounted on his high horse."[112] More important for us is the gap between Cato and his contemporaries, between his action and the circumstances of his action: "The virtue of Cato was vigorous beyond the measure of his time; and for a man who took a hand in governing others, a man dedicated to the public service, it might be said that his was a righteousness, if not unrighteousness, at least vain and out of season."[113] The virtue of Cato, as admirable as it is, and in the measure precisely that it is so superior to the state of the mores of his time, appears, at best, "vain" and anachronistic—"out of season"—at worst, "unrighteous," for what is a civic virtue that, by excess of justice, is not in a position to effectively remedy the injustices that afflict the city?[114] In our language, in any case in "existentialist" language, one would say that there is in Cato's virtue a hint of "inauthenticity." Cato sacrifices himself for a public thing *that no longer exists*. This is very *beautiful*—and that is why the poets praise Cato[115]—but up to what point is it just?

A parenthetical remark. Montaigne's reservations have to do with Cato's virtue, that is, with virtue par excellence, moral virtue as such. Doesn't pure moral virtue, detached from every particular political community, from every concrete political good, imply in effect a kind of sacrifice to a community, to a public thing, that does not exist? Doesn't the moral agent who obeys the law out of pure respect for the law push to the extreme the approach or the disposition for which Cato provides the type? Indeed, just as Cato's sacrifice aroused the enthusiasm of the poets, the moral law within me and the starry heavens above me fill the heart, according to Kant, with ever new and increasing admiration and awe.[116] The moral law thus understood is very beautiful, even sublime, but up to what point is this law just, since it is strictly separated from the good of every concrete community? This question is so legitimate that Kant himself is obliged to postulate our belonging to an intelligible realm where we can hope that virtue will be accompanied by happiness. If Cato sacrificed himself for a republic that had ceased to exist, in obeying the law the moral agent, according to Kant, sacrifices himself to a republic that does not yet exist for him, but that will exist after his death, he hopes, either in the other world, or in this world, since history obeys a law of progress.

Let us return to Montaigne. Before seeing more precisely how he confronts what I have called the Ciceronian moment, it should be noted that he himself sets up the parallel between the contemporary situation and the time of Cicero and Caesar: "Good does not necessarily succeed evil; another evil may succeed it, and a worse one, as happened to Caesar's slayers, who cast the Republic into such a state that they had reason to repent of having meddled with it. To many others, right down to our own times, the same thing has happened. The French, my contemporaries, could tell you a thing or two about it."[117] Montaigne does not limit himself here to comparing two periods of history marked by great disorders and to recalling that those who undertake to better the situation sometimes only make it worse. He looks to a strange phenomenon, which has in it something essentially obscure, but whose terrifying and wondrous power he manages to suggest. After saying that "the present moral state of [his] country" pushed him away from home and incited him to travel, and after emphasizing that "through the long license of these civil wars" he and his neighbors had "grown old . . . in so riotous a form of government, that in truth it is a marvel that it can subsist," he adds, "In fine, I see from our example that human society holds and is knit together at any cost whatever. Whatever position you set men in, they pile up and arrange themselves by moving and crowding together just as ill-matched objects, put in a bag without order, find of themselves a way to unite and fall into place together, often better than they could have been arranged by art."[118] Such is Montaigne's social physics: a necessity joining people together is at work that renders the contrast they like to make between order and disorder in large part vain. Montaigne writes not long after:

Necessity reconciles men and brings them together. This accidental link afterward takes the form of laws; for there have been some as savage as any human opinion can produce, which have nevertheless maintained their bodily health and long life as well as those of Plato and Aristotle could do. And indeed all those imaginary artificial descriptions of a government prove ridiculous and unfit to put into practice. These great, lengthy altercations about the best form of society and the rules most suitable to bind us, are altercations fit only for the exercise of our minds.[119]

This part of the chapter "Of Vanity" is in sum the counterpart of chapter 15 of *The Prince*.[120] It contains the most radical and so to speak the most troubling critique of Greek political philosophy that is oriented on the question of the regime, that is, ultimately, the best regime.

If this is the foundation of human order, it has very important consequences for the possibilities open to the virtuous person. By reason of the indetermination or distension of the political form, by reason of the weakly determining character of the political regime, virtue is largely deprived of the framework in which it finds meaning and where it is exercised. How is one to act well if there is not a place to act, more precisely if the framework and atmosphere of action are not "conductors," if the primordial disorder of human society deprives virtue of the light in which it could appear? It is not our concern to search for Montaigne's replies to this question. I would like only to note that the question, posed in this way, helps to clarify the ambivalence of Montaigne's recommendation that very naturally gives rise to perplexity: on the one hand, "to confine the appurtenances of our life,"[121] to "unbind [oneself] on all sides"; on the other, to forge friendship: "And our free will has no product more properly its own than affection and friendship."[122] Breaking all the bonds of "voluntary bondage" of family or State in order to forge the bond of friendship, a bond of "voluntary liberty," is the approach Montaigne follows and encourages. There is the harshness, even the ferocity of the break; and there is enthusiasm for the friend. These traits are rendered clear and coherent if we keep in view the "type" exemplified by Cato. On the one hand, freedom is based on the resolute disposition to sacrifice one's life: "Premeditation of death is premeditation of freedom. He who has learned how to die has unlearned how to be a slave. Knowing how to die frees us from all subjection and constraint."[123] On the other hand, friendship as the product of "voluntary liberty" implies an association that separates and isolates itself from the broader society and in which the two members hold one another in the confidence of perfect conspirators. In short, in the disorder that is at the base of human order, moral light is provided by this kind of individual or private republic that is the person prepared to die, and virtue finds its fulfillment in a friendship that resembles a republican conspiracy.

One can see how Montaigne sheds light on the Ciceronian moment. It is impossible to situate the virtues in a political order that is no longer capable of producing them. There is no longer a public space in which *ratio et oratio* could be deployed. Montaigne draws all the consequences of this fact and answers it in the most deliberate, the most ample, and most radical manner. I do not mean by this to suggest that Montaigne's text is determined and so to speak written by the political, religious, and social context. If that were the case, we would have had as many Montaignes as there were authors in that "disjointed" century. Montaigne's uniqueness resides, on the contrary, in the fact that he was able on the one hand to perceive with unequaled sharpness the traits of the present that he was experiencing together with his contemporaries, and on the other hand to elaborate an inseparably literary and political strategy so bold and inventive that he gave rise to a form of speech that had never been heard before and that brought healing where there was nothing but bloody cacophony. How did he accomplish that?

On the one hand, Montaigne radically calls into question *ratio,* the accepted definition of humans as rational and political animals, rational because they are political and political because they are rational. That reason only nurtures the pretentions of religious and political parties, which in their turn foment civil war. Montaigne deploys the best-equipped and most varied rhetorical and analytical arsenal ever mustered against human reason, against the human pretension to a specific difference. On the other hand, in this assault against *ratio,* another kind of *ratio,* entirely new, emerges. *Oratio* becomes resolutely and so speak officially *private,* but by its range and power and variety it equals or even surpasses the most accepted and most prestigious public *oratio.* The private eloquence of the *Essays* rivals the public eloquence of Cicero and supplants it. It is in the chapter titled "A Consideration upon Cicero" that Montaigne expresses in the sharpest and boldest manner the program and ambition of the *Essays.*[124] The *Essays* are the space wherein what Marc Fumaroli calls "the eloquence of the interior forum" is produced and deployed. Montaigne, "not as a grammarian or a poet or a jurist" but "as Michel de Montaigne,"[125] addresses each one of his readers directly and privately, inviting all readers, starting from the essays they are in the course of reading, to produce in their turn "numberless essays."[126] As it spreads, multiplies, and gains strength, this private communication opens a space that must be said to be public, the new space of the well-named "republic of letters." From the midst of the darkest disorder, the *Essays* build a "city in speech" that differs greatly from Plato's city but that will soon spread its humanizing influence among all Europeans seeking to be educated, that is, to be led out of this crumbling society where people "pile up and arrange themselves by moving and crowding together, just as ill-matched objects, put in a bag without order."[127]

What is the principal content of this new education? It precisely excludes and reproves religious and political novelties. Montaigne does not seek the criterion of the true religion or the just political order. We are not made of a sound and solid enough cloth to measure ourselves by such a criterion, which for that reason would be but an invention of our presumption. But if we have no access to a principle of order, of good political or religious government, if there is for us no "best regime," we can nonetheless find a kind of rule in what Montaigne calls the "human condition" or "our natural condition." This is neither a fact, since in reality out of presumption we never stop turning our backs on it and trying to escape it, nor an ideal like ancient virtue to which we would lift our gaze, since on the contrary "the remembrance of our condition" must dissuade us from letting ourselves be carried away by the prestige of any ideal. "Our condition" is a sort of trembling horizon that we must nonetheless not lose sight of, a kind of wobbly plane on which we must nevertheless take our step, while we are almost irresistibly tempted to conceive a clear and grand idea or an unshakable foundation in whose light or on which we would set up the great machines—the "superhuman" machines—that flatter our presumption. Private *oratio*, which is at the same time public thanks to the power of persuasion of the interior forum now capable of eloquence, awakens and arouses the "self-consciousness" of humanity. The proud political or religious institution of our specific difference, of which the ancient city and the Christian church are the two purest or strongest expressions, is replaced by the gradual spread of reflection, of self-irony, of doubt cast on our superiority, of the critique of humanity in the name of humanity, the critique of mores and tendencies of humanity in the name of the human condition.

Let me return to the general thesis I suggested. Between the time of Cicero and that of Montaigne extended a long—a very long—"Ciceronian moment." Through circumstances that changed greatly, the framework of political reflection and even, in a sense, of political action remained essentially immobile. In search of political order our forebears were at once moved and hindered by the tension between the empire and the city, between imperial law—the *corpus juris civilis,* if you wish—and republican virtues, between the privatization of the republic and Cato's sacrifice. This thesis is not very strong on plausibility since it passes over in silence the distinctive phenomenon of those centuries, which is the power or authority of the Church and the diffusion of Christian mores. What is to be gained in making fifteen centuries of Christianity disappear in an indefinitely stretched Ciceronian moment?

It is not a matter of concealing or even underestimating the influence or the effects of Christianity, however imprecise those expressions may be. Besides, one can recognize that around the figure of the "Christian king" there begins to crystallize the political form of the nation that will succeed the empire. But the power or authority of the Church, the ubiquity of Christian rituals, mores, images, and themes, must not conceal from us that Christianity, the Christian doctrine or proposition, plays only a very weak role in political elaboration during those so-called Christian centuries. By political elaboration I understand at the same time political action, the institutional construction, and the discourse that underlies this action or construction in an operational way. Operational discourse is discourse that justifies rationally, in any case in a convincing or persuasive way, doing this rather than that, choosing one alternative over another, preferring one regime to another, and so on. Political philosophy is such an operational discourse, or it can nurture and guide such an operational discourse, if it does not reduce itself to it. Law also, not as a technique but as the principles of law, of a juridical tradition, can produce an operational discourse even though its approach is narrower than that of political philosophy. Political history, with the accounts and analyses that form its content and the maxims that summarize its lessons, is also a source of operational discourses, but they are rarely enough by themselves since they need to be carried out by political philosophy or law. During the centuries we are speaking of, it was ancient political philosophy, law (in particular Roman law), political history (particularly Rome's) that provided the essentials of the protagonists' political arguing points. It was not "Christianity," not Christian theology. The reason for this is simple and compelling: there is no Christian "political theology." Christian discourse, on whatever register, is not politically operational. Neither by reason nor by revealed Word does it permit justifying doing this rather than that, choosing one alternative over another, preferring one regime over another, except by drawing the essentials of its arguments from political philosophy, law, and political history, as indeed the most authoritative theologians have done, such as St. Thomas Aquinas. The "authoritative text" that was most frequently cited in the "Christian centuries" was probably St. Paul's word, "Let every person be subject to the governing authorities" (Romans 13:1). At the same time it is clear that it has no determined political content whatever. Its political meaning depends entirely on the circumstances. Whatever Paul's intention was when he formulated it, this oft-cited word never after had a "formative" political role. Besides, it was easy to cite an equally authoritative word that went in the opposite direction: "We must obey God rather than men" (Acts 5:29). The meaning of this word, too, depends on the circumstances, and it is equally devoid of a "formative" political content. Christian discourse has its own mode and domain of operation and it is effectively discriminating in the community it orders, the Church, which is ontologically separated from political communities even though it is politically mixed with them.

5

ROME AS SEEN BY THE MODERNS

Machiavelli and the Project of a New Rome

How could political thought in the end become operational? How did it escape the mutual paralysis of the empire and the city? That is the whole history of modern political philosophy, at least of the *first* modern political philosophy that sought to produce political order starting from the absence of order. The second—I emphasized this difference at the start of our inquiry—begins from a specifically modern political experience, more precisely a specifically modern experience from which it draws political consequences. The first aims to produce a political instrument that would be universal, that is, one capable of producing order in all circumstances. This instrument, so familiar to us, is the modern State. The second modern political philosophy reflects on a specifically modern experience, which is no longer the absence of order or an extreme disorder as with the first, but on the contrary a new kind of order, for it does not proceed, in any case not directly, from the political institution or the political command, but results from the actions of the members of society themselves, an order that is immanent in what precisely will later be called society and that the second modern political philosophy designates, as we know, by the name of *commerce*. Our interest here is with the first modern political philosophy, but it can be noted that if the two philosophies or expressions of modern philosophy start from opposing experiences—disorder in the first case, order in the second—in neither case do they take their bearings from a positive political experience. At the most, the second starts from an experience that advantageously modifies the conditions of political life and first of all the conditions of government.

Let us then consider the first modern political philosophy, whose three great moments correspond to the works of Machiavelli, Hobbes, and Locke. They were concerned to produce a stable and reasonable political order by means of a new political instrument. Hobbes formulated the purpose of the instrument, identified its wellspring, and described the nature and interplay of its principal parts. Without modifying the ordering of the whole, Locke perfected it, principally by adding a few safety devices. But what did their predecessor Machiavelli do? Without pretending to summarize in these few words the meaning and import of Machiavelli's work, one can say that although it is anachronistic to make him a promoter of the modern State as an institution, Machiavelli in any case sought to create the conditions for the production of the new political instrument, whatever form it had to take, to elaborate the grammar of what I have called the operational discourse and that he himself called the "effectual truth."

Every solidly constituted political order contains an operational discourse that moreover can contain a certain internal diversity. In the case of Athens, historians and philosophers took up and refined the city's own discourse, which was by itself operational. In the case of Rome, as we shall see shortly,[1] Cicero sought, between Cato and Caesar, the routes to a novel republican principate that never existed save on the scrolls of the *Republic*. Modern political philosophy could not start from the opinions of the city since there was no city, or, as I have stated, there were too many cities, each with its opinions and discourse, whether republican, imperial, or Christian. The Moderns' task then was to elaborate a discourse that would, so to speak, produce the order it spoke of—a discourse that in some way imitated the production of any or whatever generic political order since one could not refer to the existing order, which was nothing but disorder. Instead of *starting* from a *particular* or *concrete* political form and political regime such as Plato and especially Aristotle started from the Greek city and democracy, the Moderns had to aim at a *general* political order; that is, they had to proceed to a political founding by identifying what is common to all founding moments—they had to *imitate a founding in general*. This is precisely what Machiavelli did.

Brief as they are, these remarks help us to read once again with some insight chapter 15 of *The Prince* that I cited at the beginning of this work. Machiavelli opposes *truth* to *imagination*: "many have imagined republics and principalities that have never been seen or known to exist in truth."[2] Certainly the "best regime" of Plato or Aristotle, who are the first among the *molti* Machiavelli has in mind here, has never been seen or known in reality. But it was conceived or elaborated—"imagined"—starting from the real regimes that the Greeks saw and knew. What is properly imagined here is the "best," that is, the difference or distance between what is and what is best. Machiavelli renounces "imagining" because what is real does not provide the political order one could seek to make "better." For him it is not a matter of conceiving the best starting from a real political order, but of conceiving . . . what, starting from what? The "effectual truth"? But of what real political order when there is no longer any real political order? A past political order? Rome's, for example? Yes, but how can one "see and know" a past political order when what we know of it is even more what people, and first of all contemporary people, imagined it to be rather than the "effectual truth"? "To go directly to the effectual truth" is to look for the cause of the political order,[3] to "see and know" it before it is transformed by the imagination of people. Once again: how?

Let us briefly consider one of the chapters of the *Discourses on Livy* where Machiavelli's approach can best be understood, chapter 1 of book 3.

As I have emphasized, Machiavelli cannot start from a concrete political order. He must get to political reality starting from the most general statements about "worldly things." He begins as follows: "It is a very true thing that all worldly things have a limit to their life."[4] Then he makes a distinction between simple bodies and mixed bodies and intends to speak especially of the latter, "such as republics and sects." Since he cannot start from the experience of an authoritative concrete political order, Machiavelli starts from the most general statements and proceeds to make successive divisions.[5] This way he leaves nothing out of consideration (things are this *or* that). Such a procedure embraces, or gives the impression of embracing, the whole of reality. In our idiom one would say that this produces a powerful impression of "scientificity."

This impression is reinforced in the following lines, where Machiavelli speaks of "all the beginnings of sects, republics, and kingdoms." He is emphatically exhaustive. Not only does he begin with the beginning ("all the beginnings"), but the most general maxim he brings out is that one must return to the beginning. Why? Because the beginnings have necessarily in them a certain goodness ("in sé qualche bontà"). Machiavelli does not break with traditional ontology that posits that being and goodness are convertible, but he gives it the narrowest interpretation: if a thing begins to be, undergoes a *primo augumento,* there must be in it a certain goodness, to which corresponds for sects and republics a "first reputation." Machiavelli advances an ontology reduced to the minimum, a "thin ontology," so to speak.

Now, how does one return to the beginning in the case of republics? Machiavelli again proceeds by dividing: the return is made "either by extrinsic accident or by intrinsic prudence." An example of an extrinsic accident is a military defeat that forces the overhaul of all institutions ("tutti gli ordini"). An example of intrinsic prudence is "a law" or "a good man." But before specifying what such a law could be or what the action of such a "good man" could be, the effect that an "extrinsic accident" or an "intrinsic prudence" could equally produce needs to be defined. This effect is that people who live together in whatever political order *si riconoschino*— examine themselves. A *battitura estrinseca,* such as an invasion or a defeat for example, compels people to take a good look at themselves, that is, to take stock at once of their situation, of errors made, of reforms to be undertaken, and so on. One could say that it produces political reflexivity.

What kind of law can produce such an effect? Machiavelli's reply is that in Rome it was all the laws "that went against the ambition and the insolence of men." But laws are not enough; they stand in need of people. They need to be implemented, made efficacious, animated "by the virtue of a citizen who rushes spiritedly to execute them against the power of those who transgress them."[6] "Execution" here needs to be taken literally, since Machiavelli next lists a certain number of notable *esecuzioni* that had excellent effects: the deaths of Brutus's sons, the deaths of the decemvirs, that of Melius, the death of Manlius Capitolinus, the death of the son of Manlius Torquatus, and so on.

The other way of bringing republics back to their beginnings is by the simple virtue of a man of such reputation and example that the good desire to imitate him and the bad are ashamed of living a life contrary to his. Machiavelli then mentions the names of Horatius Cocles, Scaevola, Fabricius, the two Decii, Regulus, and "some others." These good examples produced at Rome "almost the same effect" as executions. The last example Machiavelli mentions is that of Cato who, when he found the city in large part corrupted, was not able to make the citizens become better with his example.

Without going further into interpreting this chapter, it can be noted that Machiavelli at times blurs the distinction between "extrinsic accident" and "intrinsic prudence," as when he says that it is necessary that people "often examine themselves either through these extrinsic accidents or through intrinsic ones." What matters is the effect, which is the same or nearly the same—the effect, that is, the political self-knowledge that prevents corruption. The cause of this reflection is obviously, in the case of executions, fear *(paura)*, and in the case of *esempli rari e virtuosi*, admiration, but an admiration that is directed at sacrifice. It would be saying too much to say that such admiration is a mode of fear, but fear is among its components.

We can see in this chapter to what energetic and subtle distillation Machiavelli subjects the Roman experience. Where the ancient philosophers, and also to a great extent the ancient historians, described and analyzed political regimes, diverse regimes that change and succeed one another, Machiavelli looks for something like a spirit, or a wellspring, or a formula of politics beneath the diversity of regimes, as though politics in general, far from being an impoverishment by abstraction of political life diversified according to the regimes, contained on the contrary what is most concrete in the political thing; as though the beginning of a political order, of any order, far from giving way to this developed and concretized order, or from disappearing in it, continued to accompany it, even to be its truth, the truth to which this order must always be brought back.

I have just spoken of politics in general, of the political order in general, and I have attempted to show how Machiavelli had a more general and, in that sense or in our eyes, a more "scientific" approach than did the ancient philosophers. At the same time, he does not offer us many general notions—less this time than the ancient philosophers—but pursues his intent through a medley of historical figures and episodes. He arouses in us a desire for the notion or the concept, or the group of notions or concepts, that would provide an overall account of what he has brought to light. He arouses in us the desire to make explicit the science that is implicit or hidden in *The Prince* and *The Discourses*.

Let us attempt to satisfy this desire, at the risk of considerably flattening or dulling Machiavelli's intent, by saying the following. Because people are ambitious and insolent they are disobedient. Thus what we are looking for, the handle that we seek in order to produce order or some order, is a means of producing obedience in all circumstances or any circumstances whatever. To say that he invites us and prepares us to elaborate a *science of obedience* is certainly a simplification of Machiavelli's teaching, but a simplification for which he himself arouses the desire. This science in any case will be elaborated as such by Thomas Hobbes.

Hobbes or the Farewell to the Republic

Machiavelli started from the one who enforces obedience or whose ambition is to enforce obedience, namely the prince. In this sense he preserved and even sharpened the distinction, essential for the Greeks, between the one who commands and the one who is commanded. Hobbes starts from the subject, the one who is forced to obey or whose duty it is to obey, namely the English subject. The English civil war made him acutely aware of the difficulties of obedience:

> For who can be a good subject to monarchy, whose principles are taken from the enemies of monarchy, such as were Cicero, Seneca, Cato, and other politicians of Rome, and Aristotle of Athens, who seldom speak of kings but as of wolves and other ravenous beasts? You may perhaps think a man has need of nothing else to know the duty he owes to his governor, and what right he has to order him, but a good natural wit, but it is otherwise. For it is a science, and built upon sure and clear principles, and to be learned by deep and careful study, or from masters that have deeply studied it.[7]

Starting with the subject instead of starting with the prince entails a decisive simplification. What made Machiavellian science so tempting— what made it at once a scandal and a temptation—at the same time made it imperfect and unwieldy. In particular, it introduced an imprecise but fundamental distinction between princes and others, between those who possess *virtù* and those who lack it. By starting from the subject, by starting from the most general condition, Hobbes does not have to take this division into account. It does not exist for him. He can seriously envisage, he can promise himself, a truly general science, that is, one that is truly scientific.

To start with the subject, the one whose duty it is to obey, is in effect to start from the one who disobeys or is inclined to disobey. If he obeyed willingly, there would be no problem of the political order. Hobbes thus starts from the primordial fact of human disobedience, from what he calls "the dissolute condition of masterless men." Thus he starts from the human *condition,* something that is independent of political circumstances, which lies beneath every political form as well as every political regime but that presents a problem, the solution to which is a new political order.

In bringing out the notion of a natural condition that is apolitical or nonpolitical, Hobbes redefines the meaning of politics. For the Greeks, as I have often emphasized, the natural condition of humans is political. The political problem is in some way coextensive with the human problem. To describe the human world is thus to describe political life as it is deployed in its diversity—in the diversity of its regimes. The task of political philosophy is first of all to *describe* and in no way to *deduce.* On the other hand, by drawing out, by bringing fully to light, a natural condition of humans that no longer has any political character, Hobbes gives politics a novel meaning as a function or instrument.[8] The political order is the solution or the instrument of the solution to the human problem. The political order is no longer problematic for *it is the solution* to the human problem—an obvious, in any case an unequivocal solution once the problem has been properly grasped. Order among humans then derives entirely from the political command. Accordingly it is not the task of the political philosopher to describe political life as it is (that would be to describe the bad solutions) but to deduce or infer the good solution once the problem has been grasped. Instead of describing the diversity of regimes, the political philosopher's task is to arrive at the necessity of the sovereign's unity.

The objection will be raised that the deductive order cannot be rigorously held to, for the problem to which the sovereign is the solution has to be adequately described to begin with. But it is not obvious that

Hobbes's description is the most adequate one. Montaigne had the same experience of civil war as Hobbes. Yet, as we have seen, he gives an altogether different description of the basic human condition, one that obtains over and above the largely illusory diversity of regimes: "In fine, I see from our example that human society holds and is knit together at any cost whatever." Or again: "Necessity reconciles men and brings them together."[9] The picture Montaigne paints seems more true to life. Who has ever seen the "war of each against each" that defines the Hobbesian state of nature? In spite of that, it is the State conceived by Hobbes, Hobbes's solution, that has won out. That it did is no doubt because his is the more adequate description of the problem.

What Montaigne does not see or does not bring out is that the consociation that impresses him so much rests on a principle of dissociation. People get closer because they flee one another. Necessity gathers them, but nature separates them. Discerning the natural condition calls for a science that sees deeper than the surface where good sense stops.[10] It calls for a science that penetrates down to the "small beginnings of motion" that are invisible to the naked eye.[11] The State that is constructed on such a science will touch human beings in that point of truth where they escape the illusory order of badly ordered consociations.

Is it possible to define more precisely the crux of the disagreement between Montaigne and Hobbes?

Human consociation for Montaigne is the voluntary bondage of most humans, tempered, or rather invisibly interrupted, by the voluntary freedom—friendship—of some people. There is no sure way to produce the "remembrance of our condition," the awakening that is fortuitous like the nature, virtues, and experiences of each person (Montaigne proposes a "reformation," like Luther). Hobbes on the contrary thinks that this "self-consciousness" is naturally accessible to everyone who is, so to speak, forced to it by his natural condition. Presumption leads to war, and the miseries of war incite people to renounce this presumption, in any case to renounce acting on this presumption. Everyone, as he experiences the consequences of his disobedience, demands a sovereign capable of beating back the ambition and rebuffing the insolence of everyone, including himself.

The "operational" progress in relation to Montaigne is manifest.[12] Henceforth there is no need to seek refuge in republics of friends or friendly conspiracies in order to escape the effects of human presumption. But one will be able, under the protection of the State, to join circles or clubs in which innocent vanity is given free rein. The division between the voluntary bondage of most and the voluntary freedom of a few gives way to unanimous or in any event general voluntary obedience.

It is not certain that Montaigne would have accepted this solution gladly. Even when it is voluntary, obedience is not freedom. It is not certain that he would have consented to go along with the State, even if in his time he was of the king's party, which he had chosen freely. More profoundly, he would have hesitated to embrace the artifice of the State that in gently threatening us with death terribly limits the scope of our experience, including or starting with our experience of the fear of death— death now holds no other meaning for us than as the ultimate punishment of the State. The sovereign State distorts the conditions of experience by narrowing them. One could say that it puts us under a sort of continuous but low-level tension.

These remarks help us to reread the terms in which Leo Strauss characterizes Hobbes's innovation, by which he founded modern political philosophy: "Hobbes's political philosophy is, therefore, different from Plato's, in that in the latter, exactness means the undistorted reliability of the standards, while in the former, exactness means unconditional applicability, applicability under all circumstances, applicability in the extreme case."[13] Thus concern for the applicability of the criterion distorts the search for the criterion itself by circumscribing it: "Respect for applicability determines the seeking after the norm from the outset."[14] But what does "unconditional applicability" mean? In any case for Hobbes this entails the irresistible purpose of repressing pride or presumption, and thus of generalizing or universalizing rightful self-consciousness— the consciousness of our condition. In short, there would be no criterion if the criterion were not applied. The political artifice—the State—sets the proper perspective on our condition; it sets the plane of equality. The criterion is defined only by the effect of the irresistible power of the State.

By proceeding in this way, does Hobbes renounce, as Strauss reproaches him, the fundamental question of the purpose of the State? Is he content to take a common opinion for granted?[15] In any event, one needs to add that this "peace at any price" incorporates or concretizes a new criterion, which is thus rightful self-consciousness, as the State intimidates "at any price" the first movement of the soul that leads to presumption.

I need to recall here what I said regarding Montaigne. Montaigne does not seek the criterion of the true religion or of the just political order because we are not made of sufficiently sound and solid material to judge us by such a criterion. The "Platonic" criteria are in any event situated too high for us to be able to discern them, not to speak of applying them: we are "the investigator without knowledge, the magistrate without jurisdiction, and all in all the fool of the farce."[16] But in the effort to raise ourselves up to the criteria, we forget our condition. So, says Hobbes, who shares at least Montaigne's anti-Platonic diagnosis, the unconditional duty to recognize this condition must be instituted. Strauss thus seems to me to miss something when he affirms that the quest for applicability determines the search for the norm from the start. That is certainly not false, but the quest and the search take place within the horizon of a norm of a higher rank or of a new type, which is the norm or criterion of self-consciousness. There exists a norm only because the sovereign State realizes it. That it is sovereign means not only that it is capable of maintaining peace in all circumstances but also that it allows people to settle on the plane of their humanity, to abide in their "condition."

The Roman Tragedy according to Montesquieu

Let us return to Rome and to the Ciceronian and Caesarian moment, properly speaking. To do that, let us review very rapidly with the help of Montesquieu the arc of Roman history from its origins up to this moment, or, better, let us attempt to experience its tension.

From the beginning, everything turned Rome and every Roman toward the outside: "Since Rome was a city without commerce, and almost without arts, pillage was the only means individuals had of enriching themselves."[17]

The expulsion of the kings led to the rapid spread of magistracies, which fueled the frenzy of ambition: "Having ousted its kings, Rome established annual consuls, and this too helped it reach its high degree of power. During their lifetime, princes go through periods of ambition, followed by other passions and by idleness itself. But, with the republic having leaders who changed every year and who sought to signalize their magistracy so that they might obtain new ones, ambition did not lose even a moment. They induced the senate to propose war to the people, and showed it new enemies every day."[18]

From the beginning, then, "Rome . . . , within a very small orbit, practiced the virtues which were to be so fatal to the world."[19] From the beginning there also appeared a strong link between "Rome's expansion" and its "liberty."

The liberty of Rome was not without disorders since it rested on the war between patricians and plebeians. But this "class war" did not prevent complicity and collaboration when it came to conquering: "war at once united all interests in Rome. . . . In Rome, governed by laws, the people allowed the senate to direct public affairs."[20] And the senate obeyed "the constant maxim of preferring the preservation of the republic to the prerogatives of any order or of any magistracy whatsoever."[21]

Thus at Rome there were continuity and harmony between individual and collective ambition that were not found elsewhere. This is particularly evident in the triumphs: "To obtain citizens, wives and lands, Romulus and his successors were almost always at war with their neighbors. Amid great rejoicing they returned to the city with spoils of grain and flocks from the conquered peoples. Thus originated the triumphs, which subsequently were the main cause of the greatness this city attained."[22]

So much for the tonic note of Rome's history. The point of inflection that is of particular interest to us, as I have already pointed out, is the moment of the "Social War," when the city had to go beyond its own limits, so to speak, when it spread to the point where internal and external mix. This is how Montesquieu describes that moment:

> If the greatness of the empire ruined the republic, the greatness of the city ruined it no less.
>
> Rome had subjugated the whole world with the help of the peoples of Italy to whom it had at different times given various privileges. At first most of these peoples did not care very much about the right of Roman citizenship. . . . But when this right meant universal sovereignty, and a man was nothing in the world if he was not a Roman citizen and everything if he was, the peoples of Italy resolved to perish or become Romans. Unable to succeed by their intrigues and entreaties, they took the path of

arms. . . . Forced to fight against those who were, so to speak, the hands with which it enslaved the world, Rome was lost. It was going to be reduced to its walls; it therefore accorded the coveted right of citizenship to the allies who had not yet ceased being loyal, and gradually to all.[23]

The consequences of this transformation were enormous and ruinous; they augured "the ruin of Rome":

After this, Rome was no longer a city whose people had but a single spirit, a single love of liberty, a single hatred of tyranny. . . . Once the peoples of Italy became its citizens, each city brought to Rome its genius, its particular interests, and its dependence on some great protector. *The distracted city no longer formed a complete whole.* And since citizens were such only by a kind of fiction, since they no longer had the same magistrates, the same walls, the same gods, the same temples, and the same graves, they no longer saw Rome with the same eyes, no longer had the same love of country, and Roman sentiments were no more.[24]

This new situation determined the character of the wars associated with the names of Marius and Sulla: "Over and above the jealousy, ambition, and cruelty of the two leaders, every Roman was filled with frenzy. New citizens and old no longer regarded each other as members of the same republic, and they fought a war which—due to its peculiar character—was civil and foreign at the same time."[25]

In this distended and torn city, the laws of political optics changed, not only because the composition of the civic body was modified, but also because its relation to its rulers underwent a profound transformation. Previously, the citizens had seen in the magistrate, even in the consul who led his triumph, mainly the republic. From now on, they saw only the leader, with a passion that was attached to his personality or particularity. Montesquieu writes:

The laws of Rome had wisely divided public power among a large number of magistracies, which supported, checked, and tempered each other. Since they all had only limited power, every citizen was qualified for them, and the people—seeing many persons pass before them one after the other— did not grow accustomed to any in particular. But in these times the system of the republic changed. Through the people the most powerful men gave themselves extraordinary commissions—which destroyed the authority of the people and magistrates, and placed all great matters in the hand of one man, or a few.[26]

"Excessive preferences" were now "given to a citizen"; the "admiration of the people" ended up "focusing" on "one citizen alone."

This eminent citizen was no longer a magistrate even if he collected magistracies; and the citizens were no longer for him fellow citizens. With respect to the city of Rome he easily adopted the dispositions and the conduct of an enemy: "The Sulla who entered Rome was no different from the Sulla who entered Athens: he applied the same law of nations";[27] "the same fright that Hannibal awakened in Rome after the battle of Cannae was spread by Caesar when he crossed the Rubicon."[28]

To summarize this analysis, one could say that the expansion of the city led to the inevitable ruin of the republic: the elements that the city integrated, that it held together and set in their place within its landscape—or, better, its body—separate, became external and foreign to one another, to such a point that the citizens were henceforth treated by their leaders, or rather their masters, as they themselves had treated their conquered enemies. The decisive articulation was no longer between the city and its enemies but between the new master and his subjects, against whom he waged war or whom he spared at his will. The situation called for a new regime at the same time as a new political form. The city had lost its form, its natural form. A new form was awaited.

Internal and external mixed. The general held a commission from the city, but being far away and for a long time with his army, he became a power by himself, no longer a magistrate but a prince and so to speak a god.[29] He embodied the power of the city that, now that it was corrupted, had passed into him: "No authority is more absolute than that of a prince who succeeds a republic, for he finds himself with all the power of the people, who had not been able to impose limitations on themselves."[30] This remark confirms that Strauss's thesis on Caesarism misses something important. His definition of it as a regime—an absolute monarchy—though in itself unquestionable, leaves entirely aside not only the fact that, as we have seen, this monarchy succeeds a republic, but also that, in its original and complete version, it results from the change from one political form into another, that it constitutes itself by inheriting the energies of the older form that can no longer govern itself.

The enormity of the transformation makes it such that Caesar's undertaking cannot be reproved with much conviction: someone has to devote himself to bringing to term the transformation that is taking place by finally giving an indisputable master to this political form that needs a master in order to be.

Yet, curiously, Montesquieu both affirms the necessary end of the republic and condemns "the crime of Caesar."[31] If it was necessary that someone put an end to the republic, Caesar cannot be a very great criminal for doing so. In any case Montesquieu writes: "Finally, the republic was crushed. And we must not blame it on the ambition of certain individuals; we must blame it on man—a being whose greed for power keeps increasing the more he has of it, and who desires all only because he already possesses much. If Caesar and Pompey had thought like Cato, others would have thought like Caesar and Pompey; and the republic, destined to perish, would have been dragged to the precipice by another hand."[32]

Not only was there something necessary in Caesar's crime, but Caesar's assassination—the punishment of his crime—takes on a necessary character too:

> It was quite difficult for Caesar to defend his life. Most of the conspirators were of his own party, or had been heaped with benefits by him. . . . The more their fortune improved, the more they began to partake of the common misfortune. . . .
>
> Moreover, there was a certain law of nations—an opinion held in all the republics of Greece and Italy—according to which the assassin of someone who had usurped sovereign power was regarded as a virtuous man. Especially in Rome, after the expulsion of the kings, the law was precise, and its precedents established. The republic put arms in the hand of every citizen, made him a magistrate for the moment, and recognized him as its defender.[33]

Yes, but the two necessities or near necessities—the fall of the republic and the assassination of Caesar—do not go well together; they are not easily compatible: if the republican law was so "precise," the republican precedents so "established," it is hard to understand how the republic was so "destined to perish."

Our perplexity does not stop there. Immediately after justifying the murder of Caesar, Montesquieu explains that it had no effect, and that that too was necessary: "So impossible was it for the republic to be reestablished that something entirely unprecedented happened: the tyrant was no more, but there was no liberty either. For the causes that had destroyed the republic still remained."[34] If such was the case, how can one approve of the murder of a tyrant—and of a tyrant that did not lack "moderation"—when the murder has no effect against tyranny? It seems that Montesquieu wants both to emphasize the necessary character of the historical process—the ruin of the republic—and to preserve the republican moral accent.

We cannot stop there. Chapter 12—"The Condition of Rome after Caesar's Death"—begins by affirming the necessity I have just mentioned, but goes on in an altogether different direction: Montesquieu now wants to establish that things could have gone otherwise after the death of Caesar. He insists on the faults of the conspirators. On those of Cicero, whose "vanity" Octavius manipulated. On those of Brutus and Cassius: "Brutus and Cassius killed themselves with inexcusable precipitation, and we cannot read this chapter in their lives without pitying the republic which was thus abandoned."[35] If the republic was in this way abandoned, it means that it still existed. The most surprising statement concerns Cato: "I believe that if Cato had preserved himself for the republic, he would have given a completely different turn to events."[36] After two chapters that have heavily emphasized the necessary or inevitable character of the historical process, Montesquieu countenances very seriously that Cato, the very man whose death in common opinion testifies unquestionably to the end of all republican hopes—if Cato despaired of the republic, how could there still be hope?—could not have saved the republic if he had not taken his life, if he had "preserved" himself for it. Montesquieu not only goes against common opinion, but contradicts what he affirmed so categorically in the preceding chapter: "If Caesar and Pompey had thought like Cato, others would have thought like Caesar and Pompey; and the republic, destined to perish, would have been dragged to the precipice by another hand."[37]

In any case, the uncertainty with regard to the respective roles of necessity and freedom, or possibility, in the final period of the republic leads us to a yet more troubling question since it bears on republican virtue itself. It is this virtue itself, it seems, that caused the final defeat of the republic by inciting Brutus and Cassius to kill themselves "with inexcusable precipitation." But perhaps Brutus and Cassius lacked perfect virtue; perhaps they sinned by excess or by defect? This explanation would not hold for Cato, the embodiment of perfect virtue not only for the republican tradition but also for Montesquieu himself, as he makes clear in a parallel between Cicero and Cato. Yet, as we have seen, Montesquieu believes that "if Cato had preserved himself for the republic, he would have given a completely different turn to events." In taking his life, he did not "preserve himself for the republic," he abandoned it. In short, he deserted it. In the same sentence where he asserts that Cato would have been able to save the dying republic, Montesquieu declares him a deserter. In sum he reproaches him with preferring himself to the republic. Yet one senses that Montesquieu holds nothing against Cato. He explores the ambiguities of republican virtue, which is the cause of Rome's greatness as well as of the final defeat of the republican party.

These passages of the *Considerations,* along with some others, in general hold the reader's attention for the theoretical innovation they are said to contain, namely, the sketch of a theory of historical causality. Henceforth the historian's aim will no longer be to depict exemplary actions but to explain necessary processes. Yet, if we read the texts more closely, as we have just attempted to do, we observe that this theoretical innovation, which is no doubt real, is very closely tied to a new perplexity regarding republican virtue. The history of Rome becomes more necessary in the measure that Roman virtue becomes more problematic. The way we understand history depends on the way we understand Cato's virtue. We need to revisit the enigma or the aporia of Cato, as it appears in the *Considerations.*

Roman virtue appears there as precipitation. By precipitating themselves toward virtuous action, the republican leaders precipitated the republic toward its ruin. The necessity at work here is less that of a process in general than that of a tragedy, in truth a twofold tragedy: "Brutus and Cassius killed themselves with inexcusable precipitation, and we cannot read this chapter in their lives without pitying the republic which was thus abandoned. Cato had killed himself at the end of the tragedy; these began it, in a sense, by their death."[38]

At this point, Montesquieu stops to reflect on "this practice of committing suicide that was so common among the Romans." But, before reading these reflections, it is good to take into account a few lines that Montesquieu has excised from the ending of chapter 12. In the manuscript and in some copies of the first edition of 1734, one reads the following: "It is certain that men have become less free, less courageous, less disposed to great enterprises than they were when, by means of this power which one assumed, one could at any moment escape from every other power."[39] At the demand of the censors these two passages were suppressed before binding was completed. One could say that the censors, whose sole concern was with the religious and moral orthodoxy of the point, nonetheless rendered Montesquieu a literary service. Indeed the tone of the suppressed passage strikes a piercing contrast with the rest of the discussion. The passage expresses with manly assurance what I will call republican orthodoxy: the moral tenor—liberty, courage, greatness—of the life of the ancient Greeks and Romans was superior to that of the Christian Moderns, because the Ancients could deploy all their manly virtues without those being hampered or subverted by a religion hostile to force. Yet, the rest of what Montesquieu develops at the end of chapter 12 is of an altogether different tone. It is marked by a very troubling ambiguity:

> Several reasons can be given for this practice of committing suicide that was so common among the Romans: the advances of the Stoic sect, which encouraged it; the establishment of triumphs and slavery, which made many great men think that they must not survive a defeat; the advantage those accused of some crime gained by bringing death upon themselves, rather than submitting to a judgment whereby their memory would be tarnished and their property confiscated; a kind of point of honor, more reasonable, perhaps, than that which today leads us to slaughter our friend for a gesture or word; finally, a great opportunity for heroism, each man putting an end to the part he played in the world wherever he wished.[40]

Montesquieu, who knew French, could not ignore that to speak of a "great opportunity for heroism [une grande commodité pour l'héroïsme]" was to introduce a doubt. What is an opportune, or convenient, heroism ("un héroïsme commode")?

In case we still had any hesitation, Montesquieu delivers us of it in the next paragraph. Speaking not only of the "facility" but even of the "great facility" of Roman suicide, he explains in what it consists: "We could add to these a great facility in executing the deed. When the soul is completely occupied with the action it is about to perform, with the motive determining it, with the peril it is going to avoid, it does not really see death, for passion makes us feel but never see."[41] Roman virtue, the virtue of heroes, now appears as the effect of blind passion, a blindness that makes executing the action "a great facility." What has happened to the virtue of the republic?

One cannot suspect that Montesquieu improvised here. In the following paragraph that concludes the chapter he seeks the ultimate explanation of the strange phenomenon of opportune suicide or facile heroism in the intimate nature and paradoxical functioning of self-love: "Self-love, the love of our own preservation, is transformed in so many ways, and acts by such contrary principles, that it leads us to sacrifice our being for the love of our being. And such is the value we set on ourselves that we consent to cease living because of a natural and obscure instinct that makes us love ourselves more than our very life."[42] One can see that the Roman tragedy, when its wellspring is explained, comes close to resembling a comedy where love of self becomes its own enemy, where the hero kills himself because he loves himself too much, where the public motives of the action result from private motives of which the agent is unaware. Is it tragic if Cato, to say nothing of Brutus and Cassius, in dying for the republic prefers himself to the republic? Or is it not rather comic? In any case Montesquieu's pity is not for the hero, but for the republic itself: "we cannot read this chapter in [Brutus's and Cassius's] lives without pitying the republic which was thus abandoned."[43]

Montesquieu pities the republic. The republic, not Cato and even less Brutus or Cassius, is the true tragic hero. Roman history is a tragedy, or more precisely, according to Montesquieu, it is the succession of two tragedies, one that ends with the death of Cato and another that begins, "in a sense," with the deaths of Brutus and Cassius. Between the ending of the first and the beginning of the second stand the triumph and assassination of Julius Caesar. Caesar's fate is not tragic, since his crime deserved this punishment. And he evades tragedy in another way since he finally evades death itself by becoming immortal and transforming his own name into a common name.

Rome is the true tragic hero. The same could not be said of Athens or Sparta, even though the Peloponnesian War disclosed the "tragic fate" contained in Athens's boldness. Wherein resides the tragedy that makes Rome what it is?

One must always come back to the distended or torn city. Rome came out of itself and went beyond, far beyond its natural limits, every city's natural limits. It nearly perished in this effort and trial—that was the first tragedy. It did not perish but it changed form. The corrupted city transformed itself into an empire that would perish in worse corruptions, and that was the second tragedy.

The two tragedies make but one sole tragedy, for the two forms that followed one another are very closely linked. The continuity from republic to empire is in part superficial or decorative, as when Augustus ostentatiously preserved republican forms. But it is also real and substantial. In a sense, imperial tyranny results from the breadth and thoroughness of republican power, the power the republic exercised over itself, since the "office of emperors . . . was a collection of all the Roman magistracies."[44] I have already cited Montesquieu's most significant passage on this matter: "No authority is more absolute than that of a prince who succeeds a republic, for he finds himself with all the power of the people, who had not been able to impose limitations on themselves."[45] Even at its worst, the empire resembled a republic more than a monarchy: "What was called the Roman empire, in this century, was a kind of irregular republic, much like the aristocracy of Algeria, where the army, which has sovereign power, makes and unmakes a magistrate called the dey. And perhaps it is a rather general rule that military government is, in certain respects, republican rather than monarchical."[46]

The "republican" continuity from city to empire resides first of all in the fact that the Romans never ceased to be disposed to die willingly. In this sense, the greatness and the misery of Rome have the same cause or wellspring in the disdain of death. Christianity will attack this disdain of death by forbidding killing, above all killing oneself. Whatever their efforts to regain Roman liberty, courage, and greatness, the Europeans never succeeded in recovering Roman sentiments. The most profound or most brilliant thoughts, like to the most violent actions, were equally powerless. What prevented us, no, what prevents us from being Romans once again?

6

CICERO'S INQUIRY

We are wondering about the singularity of Rome, about the unique development that led from city to empire. Montesquieu has just made us aware to what extent this metamorphosis remains not only a political but also a moral, human mystery. This feeling of something puzzling or enigmatic is not the result of historical distance. What was happening to them was to the Romans themselves an enigma that they sought to elucidate with more intellectual rigor and zeal than we are wont to grant them. We can measure that if we take seriously the inquiry of the most intelligent among them, whom the Moderns treat with a condescension that is unjust and that above all deprives them of a very illuminating access to the Roman experience. We have already met him. I mean, of course, to speak of Cicero.

Cicero's Mediation

Cicero, as we know, systematically and so to speak officially introduced Greek philosophy to Rome by making it acceptable to the Romans.[1] His role of mediator excludes any true philosophic originality, and Cicero, in spite of his legendary vanity, makes no such claim.[2] This does not exclude, as we have seen, that in order to take into account Roman circumstances Cicero was led to rework the teaching that came from the Greeks, at times substantially.[3] But that is not what interests us here.

It is precisely the absence of originality in his philosophy that interests us, one could say, since that is what constitutes the originality of his position. He is the one who seeks to shed light from elsewhere on an experience that has not yielded its own clarity. Concretely it is through imitations of Platonic dialogues, or perhaps lost Aristotelian dialogues,[4] that he seeks to grasp the meaning of the Roman political experience. The *De oratore* echoes the *Gorgias* and the *Phaedrus,* as do, of course, the *De republica* and *De legibus,* Plato's *Republic* and *Laws.* The first two dialogues—the third seems to have been left unfinished—are assumed each to take place in a political context that is definite and moreover dramatic: the *De oratore* in 91 B.C., just before the outbreak of the Social War; the *De republica* in 129 B.C., during a political crisis, while Scipio was leading the efforts of the conservatives against the agrarian law instituted by his cousin Tiberius Gracchus, when he was tribune of the people four years earlier. In the disorders that followed this legislation, Gracchus had been assassinated by a crowd led by another relative of Scipio, Scipio Nasica. Gracchus's tribunate was regarded by Cicero and most of his contemporaries as the start of the degradation of Roman political life that would only get worse until the civil war. The dialogue presents Scipio as the only citizen capable of correcting and mending the situation, but it takes place only a few days before the historical Scipio died abruptly and mysteriously.

Let us then read the *Republic,* or what remains of it. The dialogue properly speaking begins in a charming way with an exchange between Scipio and his nephew Tubero, who wants to talk about the great news that has come to the Senate today regarding the second sun.[5] What explains this phenomenon? Instead of attempting to reply, Scipio suggests that these questions are not really to his liking—unlike his friend Panaetius, who "makes such definite statements about things the nature of which we can scarcely guess, that he seems to see them with his eyes or even touch them with his hands."[6] Scipio prefers the attitude of Socrates, who abandoned inquiries into nature as beyond the reach of human reason or as having nothing to do with human life. Tubero challenges this interpretation of Socrates's approach and there follows a learned exchange about Socrates and Plato. We can leave aside the details of the dialogue, but this exchange introduces one of the leitmotifs of the work— already announced in the prologue by Cicero himself—which is the relative place or worth of the theoretical or philosophical life and the practical or political life. Cicero knows how to build up suspense regarding his position, since Scipio, who has just said that these scientific questions do not interest him, will soon tell how he discussed them with his friend Rutilius beneath the walls of Numantius.

To begin the discussion, Philus, who in book 3 will defend the positions of the Skeptic Academy, recalls the Stoic conception of the relation between the city and the world: our dwelling place *(domus)* is not the one bounded by our walls, but the whole universe that the gods have given us as a home and a country to be shared with them.[7] It is not certain that these statements should be taken literally, but by their mere beauty they open us to the question of the place of the city, of the human world, within the whole and thus of the relation between political preoccupations and detached inquiries. One aspect of these questions concerns the relation between knowledge acquired through these detached inquiries and the life of those who are wholly taken up with their practical concerns, who live wholly *within* the city—in short, ordinary citizens, the "people." To what extent can, and should, this detached knowledge be applied to the improvement of ordinary life, people's lives? In our language we would say that certain participants in the dialogue are clearly partisans of the Enlightenment. Scipio gives two examples of enlightened generals—one Roman and the other Greek—calming the fears of their soldiers troubled by extraordinary astronomical phenomena. They calm their soldiers by calmly explaining the phenomenon. In the case of Galus, the Roman general, it was an eclipse of the moon; for the Greek, who was none other than Pericles, it was an eclipse of the sun. Pericles explained, it is said, what he himself had learned from Anaxagoras, whose lectures he had attended *(cujus auditor fuerat)* and thus, in explaining the phenomenon rationally, freed the people *(populus)* from fear.[8] Pericles thus shed rational light on the causes of the darkening by making himself the mediator between the detached science of Anaxagoras and the concerned and fearful soldiers. It is hard to find a more striking example of "enlightened politics."

One cannot help but remark that the Roman army was frightened by an eclipse of the moon, the Greek army by an eclipse of the sun. What more elegant way to suggest that, as the moon receives its light from the sun, the Romans received their light from the Greeks?[9]

To live by the light of the Greeks means for the Romans to take advantage of this light, as in the preceding example where the light was entirely salutary, but also perhaps to be subjected to this light, for there

are circumstances where the light may be undesirable or even dangerous. Perhaps the Greek light, which on the one hand has unquestionably
perfected or refined Roman life, has on the other hand deteriorated it or
corrupted it.

In any case this light is so powerful that it enlightened Rome's beginnings themselves since, by calculating from the recent eclipse reported
by Ennius,[10] one arrives at the eclipse of the nones of July that coincided
with the darkening that occurred at the time of the death of Romulus.
Since it was owing to this darkening that Romulus was numbered among
the gods, one can see that this light touched what is most secret and most
sacred in Rome's origins. The difficulty concerns all political bodies that
are exposed to enlightenment: how does one preserve the obscurity that is
favorable to respect for the origins, thus to patriotism, while welcoming
the light that comes from elsewhere, particularly the light coming from
another political body? How does one appease irrational fears *(religio et
metus)* while preserving respect for the laws and love of country that
cannot be said to be simply rational?

Soon Laelius, a learned and wise citizen—he is surnamed *sapiens*—to
whom Scipio defers regarding civil life *(domi)* and whom he has placed
in the middle of the group, will mark his dissatisfaction at the turn the
conversation is taking. He will refuse to let himself be taken by Scipio's
astronomical and scientific enthusiasm. But before considering Laelius's
intervention, we need to look for a moment at a very beautiful development by Scipio that does not immediately concern our subject but that
we cannot pass over without commentary. It is a sort of elevation above
human things that can be read as an argument in favor of the superiority
of the theoretical life over the practical or political life:

> But what element of human affairs should a man think glorious who has
> examined this kingdom of the gods; or long-lived who has learned what
> eternity really is; or glorious who has seen how small the earth is—first the
> whole earth, then that part of it which men inhabit? We are attached to a
> tiny part of it and are unknown to most nations: are we still to hope that
> our name will fly and wander far and wide? The person who is accustomed
> neither to think nor to name as "goods" lands and buildings and cattle and
> huge weights of silver and gold, because the enjoyment of them seems to
> him slight, the use minimal and the ownership uncertain [levis fructus, ex-
> iguus usus, incertus dominatus], and because the vilest men often have

unlimited possessions [immensa possessio]—how fortunate should we think such a man! He alone can truly claim all things as his own, not under the law of the Roman people but under the law of the philosophers; not by civil ownership but by the common law of nature, which forbids anything to belong to anyone except someone who knows how to employ and use it. Such a man thinks of military commands and consulates as necessary things, not as desirable ones, things that must be undertaken for the sake of performing one's duty, not to be sought out for the sake of rewards or glory.[11]

This fine text takes up the Greek oppositions between, on the one hand, apparent goods and real goods, and on the other necessary things and things desirable for themselves, oppositions that here lead to a clear preference for the contemplative over the political life. It is worth noting the appearance of the notion of the law of nature *(lex naturae),* which will have a long and complex future. It is the law that is common to all people, not to one part among them, and that reserves the property, or rather the disposition of things, to the small number of the wise who are capable of using them. These two seemingly opposed traits conspire to deprive this law of nature of any, at least any direct, political or social relevance. Let us recall that in *De officiis,* Cicero will posit as the origin of the institution of cities the desire to protect one's own goods: "The chief purpose in the establishment of *respublicae* and *civitates* was that individual property rights might be secured. For although it was by Nature's guidance that men were drawn together into communities, it was in the hope of safeguarding their possessions [spe custodiae rerum suarum] that they sought the protection of cities."[12] Taking these two passages together, the first from *De republica,* the second from *De officiis,* allows us to measure the complexity or uncertainty that affects the notions of nature and the law of nature in Cicero.[13]

Greek Notions, Roman Things

Let us come to the intervention of Laelius, who has been rubbed the wrong way by Scipio's sublime thoughts and who even swears by Hercules. I said that Laelius was the citizen whose judgment was authoritative and that Scipio placed in the middle of the group. Here is how he reacts to Scipio's lofty astronomical talk. In fact, he does not speak directly to Scipio, but to the young man Tubero:

You are asking Scipio about those things in the sky, while I think that the things before our eyes are more worth asking about. Why, I ask you, is the grandson of Lucius Aemilius Paullus, with an uncle like Scipio here, born into the most noble family and in this glorious commonwealth, asking how two suns could have been seen and not asking why in one commonwealth there are two senates and almost two peoples [cur in una republica duo senatus, et duo paene jam populi sint]? As you see, the death of Tiberius Gracchus and, before that, the whole conduct of his tribunate have divided one people into two parts [divisit populum unum in duas partes].[14]

How important is it that a people saw or thought they saw a second sun when political circumstances are so pressing? Astronomical science, Laelius continues, will not make us better or happier, while it is possible for us to have one senate and one people, and we are in very deep trouble if this is not the case. And Laelius presses his interlocutors to employ their leisure in a way that is useful to the city by asking Scipio to explain what in his view is the best ordering of the city ("optimum statum civitatis").[15]

It is fitting to have the man who is *princeps civitatis* speak on the subject of the republic.[16] To this good-sense argument—everyone speaks best in his element, and one does not ask a shoemaker for recipes—Laelius adds another that indicates that Scipio's competence does not derive only from his exceptional experience: Scipio frequently discussed these questions with Panaetius in the presence of Polybius, perhaps the two Greeks most versed in political things ("duobus Graecis vel peritissimis rerum civilium").[17] It was thus with supremely competent Greeks that Scipio was in the habit of discussing the Greek question par excellence: what is the best political regime?

In his reply to Laelius, Scipio confirms that no subject concerns him more intensely, like an artisan engaged in the supreme art ("in maxima arte"). As for the Greek experts, Scipio confesses his perplexity: he is divided between his familiarity with Greek notions and his attachment to Roman things: "although I am not satisfied with what the greatest and wisest men of Greece have written about this subject, I am also not bold enough to prefer my own opinions to theirs."[18]

After a few methodological considerations, as we would call them, and after having insisted on the natural sociability of human beings,

Scipio attacks the Greek question in Greek fashion, with a catalog of regimes. If every republic, to be durable, must be governed by some deliberation *(consilio quodam),* this *primum consilium* can be attributed to one alone who is thus a king *(rex)* and the *respublica* a kingdom *(regnum);* or to a few chosen individuals, in which case the city is said to be governed by the will of the aristocrats *(optimatium arbitrio);* or, finally, to the people as a whole, and then the city is popular *(popularis).*[19] In Scipio's eyes none of these is the best, but they are acceptable if they reserve that bond *(illud vinculum)* that binds people by making them members of a political body. It seems to me that this kind of statement is not to be found in Aristotle. Aristotle does not isolate the notion of what we call the social bond or civic bond, even if this abstract notion is included in the concrete notion of friendship *(philia).*[20]

However, each one of these tolerable regimes lacks something important: even under a very just and wise king such as Cyrus, the other members of the political body have no part in making either decisions or laws; even if Marseille, a client city of Rome, is governed with justice by its first citizens, the people there are in a condition resembling slavery; and in Athens, after the suppression of the Areopagus, everything was done by the decrees and decisions of the people, such that the city lost some of its order and beauty since there were no longer any distinct degrees of dignity.[21]

In addition to these inevitable and intrinsic flaws, all these tolerably good regimes are susceptible of rapidly sliding toward their corresponding bad regime. Cyrus's kingship can be quickly transformed into the tyranny of Phalaris; the good oligarchic government of Marseille is in this way very close to the tyranny of the Thirty in Athens; and in Athens, the power of the people was transformed into the madness and license of the multitude. At this point the manuscript is interrupted, but it seems that Scipio next evokes how, starting with the democracy that has become the license of the mob, there arises the tyranny of a faction, whether oligarchic or popular, or of one alone.

In more general and more scientific terms, Scipio indicates that accordingly there are remarkable revolutions, and something like cycles of change and alteration in political bodies.[22] It belongs to the wise to know them, but it belongs to a great citizen and almost divine person to foresee the impending revolutions and to keep a firm hand on the helm. There is in this the suggestion of a science of politics and history more confident of its capacities to foresee than probably could be found among the Greeks.

What follows is of greater interest. Other than the three regimes we have considered, there exists a fourth type of republic. This is the one that merits the greatest approval; it results from the combination and mixture of the other three.[23] Mention of the fourth type, the combined or mixed regime, is connected to the evocation of the changes of regime by the word *itaque*. The three pure regimes are subject to frequent alterations: that is why preference must be given to the fourth that, as a combination of the other three, is not susceptible, one can think, to such alterations and thus allows for hope in a long stability.

Let us note in passing that this preoccupation with the changes of regime is an affect which, without being unknown to us, is less present in the consciousness of modern Europeans than in that of the Ancients. One of the causes of this fact is certainly that European life developed within a political form less exposed than the city to abrupt changes of regime, namely the nation. Because of its quantity—territory, population—as well as because of its quality—it shelters many more nonpolitical activities than the city—the nation offers a "viscosity" that slows the rhythm of change. Granted, European nations went through periods of rapid, even brutal change—periods of revolution—but, in the long run, the European nation was much more stable than the Greek city, going from a long monarchical period to a long democratic one. It would be illuminating to consider the political history of Europe with the help of the notion of mixed regime. But what does this notion mean precisely?

The Notion of the Mixed Regime

Let us turn to Polybius, with whom or in whose presence Scipio discussed these questions, and who gave the classic description of the mixed regime.

In book 6 of his *Histories,* which has come down to us in very mutilated form, Polybius first takes up the Aristotelian classification of regimes, at times using different terms to designate them:[24] "Our position, then, should be that there are six kinds of constitution—the three commonly recognized ones I have just mentioned [kingship, aristocracy, and democracy], and three more which are congenital with them: tyranny, oligarchy, and ochlocracy or mob-rule."[25] Then he describes how regimes are transformed one into another, beginning with the government of one alone or monarchy. Sketched in rather broad strokes, the mechanism goes roughly as follows: the simple good regime degenerates into its vicious form, because the new generations, the king's children, for example, take their advantages for granted and give in to their appetites, and thus they provoke the revolt that brings about the new simple regime that will in its turn undergo the same alteration and the same fate. The political dynamic goes from kingship to ochlocracy, which gives rise anew to "a monarchic master."

Polybius draws the following conclusion from his analysis: "This is the cycle of constitutions, the natural way in which systems of government develop, metamorphose, and start all over again. A clear grasp of the theory may not deliver the ability to make infallible predictions about when some constitutional event will happen in the future, but provided one's judgment is not biased by anger or resentment, one will rarely go wrong about what phase of growth or decline a system has reached, or about what transformation it will undergo next."[26]

One can only be struck by the summary and mechanical character of the thought expressed here, when compared to the thought of Plato and Aristotle. This simplified political science nurtures a confidence in our capacity to foresee the political evolution that the original political science of Plato and Aristotle did not justify or even excluded. Is it Polybius's intellectual rigidity that makes him conceive the illusion of sure knowledge of historical evolution, as though his political science were to Plato's and Aristotle's what scientism is to the true scientific spirit, or is it the Roman experience that, unlike the Greek experience, opens the possibility of a science of political history that is in effect capable of foresight? Is it Polybius's inferiority, or is it Rome's superiority? In any case it is in the text of Polybius that for the first time the two ideas of a science of history and of the authority of the present moment or epoch are established together: "Where the Roman constitution is concerned, the theory gives us our best chance of understanding its formation, growth, and prime, and of predicting its future reversal and decline. For, as I said not long ago, the Roman constitution is a superb example of a system whose formation and growth have always been natural, and whose decline will therefore also conform to natural laws. There will be an opportunity later to develop this idea."[27]

Whoever possesses the science of history is in a position to bring it to its term. Doesn't the science of the cycle of regimes, which makes it possible to foresee the succession of simple regimes, in effect lead to the conception of the mixed regime that will put an end to change or at least slow it considerably? At least this is the undertaking that Polybius attributes to Lycurgus:

> Lycurgus understood the inexorability of the natural processes I have been talking about, and realized how precarious every political system is if it is unmixed and uniform. . . . As a precautionary measure, then, the constitution Lycurgus drew up was not simple and uniform. He bundled together all the merits and distinctive characteristics of the best systems of government, in order to prevent any of them growing beyond the point where it would degenerate into its congenital vice. He wanted the potency of each system to be counteracted by the others, so that nowhere would any of them tip the scales or outweigh the others for any length of time. . . . And the upshot was that the constitution so framed by Lycurgus preserved independence in Sparta longer than anywhere else in recorded history. Lycurgus used calculation to predict how the nature of each of these systems of government would dictate its beginning and its outcome; he drew up his constitution without having suffered.[28]

One may not be obliged to take Polybius at his word and to attribute such a penetrating genius to Lycurgus, but one has to recognize that we have here the first clear formulation of the constitutional principle of the balance of powers, of checks and balances.

But what about the Romans? Polybius replies: "But in the Romans' case, even though the result was the same, in that they created the same kind of regime for themselves, this was not at all the outcome of reason, but of many struggles and trials. On every occasion, they drew on the knowledge they had gained from their setbacks to make the best choices, and this enabled them to achieve the same result as Lycurgus, and to make theirs the best system of government in the world today."[29]

Thus it was experience—trial and error, the experimental wisdom of the Romans—that obtained results equal or superior to those produced by the founding genius of the Greeks. Here again, this is a first that Polybius, the rigid Polybius, offers us. For the first time since the elaboration of political science, experience devoid of science appears as learned, in any case as judicious, as science. One could almost say, to give an idea of the impact Rome had on European intellectual life that had begun with Socratic philosophy, that for the first time history, historical knowledge, became, by its grasp of truth, the equal of philosophy.

In any case, according to Polybius, the Roman constitution attained its highest degree of perfection at the time of Hannibal's war. Here is how this constitution appeared in its full maturity: "There were three fundamental building blocks of the Roman constitution—that is, all three of the systems I mentioned above. Each of them was used so equitably and appropriately in the ordering and arrangement of everything that even native Romans were hard put to say for sure whether their constitution was essentially aristocratic, democratic, or monarchic. This is not surprising: the constitution would have appeared monarchic (or a kingship), aristocratic or democratic, depending on whether one focused attention on the powers of the consuls, the powers of the Senate, or the powers of the common people."[30]

After describing more precisely how the different parts of the constitution functioned, Polybius concludes:

> To a considerable extent, then, each of the three components of the Roman constitution can harm or help the other two. This enables the whole made up of all three parts to respond appropriately to every situation that arises, and this is what makes it the best conceivable system of government. For example, when a general threat from abroad forces the three estates to cooperate and collaborate, the state gains extraordinary abilities: first, since everyone competes to devise ways to combat the emergency, and everyone cooperates in their public and private capacities to complete the task at hand, there is no contingency that it is incapable of meeting; second, decisions are made and acted on extremely promptly. This gives the Roman state its characteristic feature: it is irresistible, and achieves every goal it sets itself.[31]

One needs to note in this description the conjunction of two traits that seem contradictory, that in any case are difficult to reconcile: the underlying perfect equilibrium, on the one hand, and the capacity to extract the greatest possible energy on the other.

Such is Polybius's doctrine of the mixed regime that Scipio reiterates or confirms in *De republica* and that will be widely accepted for a very long time in European history. To what extent is this doctrine truly original? Commentators are all the more willing to emphasize what in classical Greek philosophy is close to it or heralds it since Polybius's intellectual capacities are so obviously inferior to those of Plato or Aristotle. Considered as a political philosopher or political scientist, Polybius seems to be no more than an epigone. This is not a false impression. At the same time, one has to see very precisely that Polybius does not say the same thing as his great predecessors. Let us take a look at some pertinent passages in the *Politics* of Aristotle.

In book 2 we read the following: "Now there are certain people who say that the best regime should be a mixture of all the regimes, and who therefore praise that of the Lacedaemonians. Some of them assert it is a mixture of oligarchy, monarchy, and democracy, calling the kingship monarchy, the rule of the senators oligarchy, and saying it is democratically run by virtue of the rule of the overseers, on account of the overseers' being drawn from the people."[32]

One point then is beyond doubt: there is nothing new in Polybius's doctrine of the mixed regime, as the example of the Spartan constitution shows. It goes back at least to Aristotle's contemporaries.[33] But it is not Aristotle's own doctrine.

What does Aristotle say about the Spartan regime? He speaks of it often, and moreover in general quite severely. I will limit myself to what is pertinent to our subject. The Spartan regime, like nearly all regimes, is a mixture or blend or combination, but of what? Of democracy and virtue.[34] Of monarchy's part, nothing is said.

A little further we read: "the defining principle of a good mixture of democracy and oligarchy is that it should be possible for the same polity to be spoken of as either a democracy or an oligarchy. . . . Just this happens in the case of the Lacedaemonian regime."[35] We recall what Polybius wrote, that a Roman citizen could not tell with certainty if the constitution of Rome was in the end aristocratic, democratic, or monarchic. The similarity between the statements brings out their difference: there too, what is absent in Aristotle is the reference to the part of monarchy, which elsewhere, he says, was divided from the start and then reduced.[36]

These indications confirm what we know from elsewhere. For Aristotle, the regime of the cities is indeed a mixture or a blend, but with essentially two elements or components: democracy and oligarchy. We have seen above quite precisely how Aristotle, after deploying the spectrum of five types of kingship, went on to explain that only two were to be considered: on the one hand, Laconian kingship, which is less a kingship than a magistracy of perpetual *strategos* that can exist in all regimes; and on the other, the absolute kingship of the best man or lineage, which is more an academic hypothesis than a real political regime.[37] In short, the only effective kingship belonged to the past, the kingship of heroic times, when the head of a lineage received the kingship as a reward for his benefactions. Montesquieu was not wrong to write, "an awkwardness is clearly seen in Aristotle's treatment of monarchy."[38] But, as we have emphasized, this "awkwardness" was not due to any defect in the philosopher's understanding, but to the very limits of the Greek political experience, or rather to the single limit of this experience: "if the ancients . . . could not achieve a correct idea of monarchy," it was because they did not have a real experience of this regime that for Montesquieu was one and the same with the political form proper to modern Europe. The original political experience of the Greeks was, dare I say, republican through and through.

Is Polybius's mixed regime, which unlike Aristotle's gives monarchy a place at least equal to that of the other two simple regimes in the mix, the index or translation of a monarchical evolution of the Roman experience starting in the second century B.C.? It would be important to answer this question, but it is difficult to do so. Polybius himself would probably answer in the negative, since he sees the same regime in place from the beginning in Sparta. Moreover, one cannot see how, in terms of the way they function, the two Roman consuls have anything more "monarchical" than the two Spartan kings. That said, the range of Roman domination, to which Spartan domination cannot be compared, necessarily puts the military commander in an unprecedented position: he is of course first of all in the service of Rome, but that means that now his views must encompass the entire Mediterranean world.[39] Scipio Aemilianus, the friend and disciple of Polybius, is that *princeps reipublicae* who embodies the implacability of ancient warfare when he destroys Carthage or Numantius, but also, when he converses with his friends, a novel philosophical effort to find one's way in a history that has become universal.

A Roman Philosophy?

Let us come back to the *De republica*. Scipio has just said that the regime that merits the greatest approval is the mixed regime. Laelius answers that he knows well Scipio's opinion on this point that he has often heard him express. In short, he does not want to hear any more about the mixed regime. What interests him is to know which of the three simple regimes Scipio deems the best. At this point there is a lacuna in the manuscript.

The text resumes with Scipio presenting the views of a defender of democracy. Liberty resides, has its *domicilium,* in no other regime except the one in which the people have sovereign power *(summa potestas)*. Nothing is sweeter than liberty, which, if it is not equal, is no longer liberty.[40]

But here is the most interesting aspect of this argument for democracy. Democracy is presented as deriving naturally from the full understanding of the fact that law is the bond of civil society ("civilis societatis vinculum") and that there is or ought to be by law an equal right ("jus legis aequale"). Hence, by what right can a society of citizens be held together, when the status of the citizens is not equal ("cum par non sit condition civium")?[41] Here this understanding of democracy veers from the Greek understanding and experience. It is less political than it is legal or social. It derives from the very fact of human sociability, from the very fact of the civil order and the equality of status it implies.

There are important lacunae in what follows. The argument in favor of aristocracy can be passed over. Laelius asks Scipio once again which of the three simple regimes he prefers. Scipio repeats his preference for the mixed regime. But if he truly had to choose one of the three, it would be monarchy. The text, again, has lacunae. There seems to be mention of the quasi-paternal role of the king. But Scipio quickly restates the difficulty of choosing. Laelius returns to the attack: the rest of the discussion hangs on the answer to this question. Then Scipio says, "Then we should imitate Aratus: in undertaking to speak about great matters he believes that one must begin from Jupiter." The statement leaves Laelius perplexed: "Why Jupiter? How is this subject anything like that poem?" To which Scipio replies, "Only that we should duly take our starting point from him, whom all men, learned and unlearned, agree is the one king of all gods and men."[42] Laelius is ever more perplexed. Scipio's answer is not very clear to me either. He presents an alternative: either the notion of one king only in heaven ("rex unus in caelo") is an invention of the leaders of republics ("a principibus rerumpublicarum"), in which case there is this highly authoritative opinion and all these witnesses to prove that all nations are in agreement on the fact that a king is what is best, to the extent that they believe that all the gods are governed by the will of one alone; or, if these ideas about the gods are errors born of ignorance, one must listen to the masters of learned people who through thorough study of the universe have understood that the entire world is governed by an intelligence (here the manuscript is interrupted). Here is how I understand the passage: either Jupiter is a political invention of the wise in which everyone believes, or Jupiter is an invention of ignorance or superstition, but which has been corrected by the learned who have understood that nature is governed by one principle only. In both hypotheses, the cause of kingship is powerfully reinforced, though by different routes.

In any case, Scipio's treatment of kingship is very different from his arguments concerning aristocracy and democracy, which were political through and through. Here, the argument is clearly metapolitical and takes a cosmological direction when it is interrupted. Something appears that once again leads us away from the Greek experience.

Laelius asks Scipio to come down from these heights and to consider more concrete and proximate realities. Scipio replies obligingly, "But if you like, Laelius, I will give you witnesses who are neither very antiquated nor in any respect barbarians." To which Laelius tells him, "That's the kind I want."[43]

The consideration of kingship is brought back from heaven to earth, and not only to earth but to Rome itself. What does Scipio say, more precisely? Scipio says that Rome has been without a king for less than four hundred years, which is not long for a city; that moreover the first king, Romulus, reigned only six hundred years ago: even he is not very ancient. Scipio is concerned to bring kingship closer to the present. Cicero here does the opposite of Aristotle in the *Politics*, who, as we have recalled, pushed kingship back to the distant origins, to "heroic times."[44] For Scipio, kingship does not belong to a time truly different from the present.

What follows tends to confirm our interpretation. Scipio asks, "Tell me, did Romulus reign over barbarians?" Laelius: "If what the Greeks say is true, that everyone is either a Greek or a barbarian, then I'm afraid that he must have ruled barbarians. But if we use that term of manners rather than languages, then I don't think the Greeks were any less barbarian than the Romans."[45]

Scipio does not want to dwell on this topic, even though he was the one to raise the question. In what concerns us, we are looking not at the nation but at the intellectual development. And Scipio, returning to the starting point of their exchange, concludes as follows: "If men who were both intelligent and fairly recent wanted to have kings, then my witnesses are neither very ancient nor inhuman savages."[46]

The movement of the argument tends then to establish that kingship does not belong, in any case not necessarily, to barbarian times. Scipio, with the help of Laelius, saves, dare I say, the royal regime from the obscurity and barbarism of the distant past, to make it a legitimate element of an enlightened present and future. One cannot help thinking that the two interlocutors—Scipio in any case—endeavor to remove the bad name that had been weighing on kingship for nearly four centuries.

I will deal more quickly with the segment that follows. Laelius asks for arguments rather than witnesses. Scipio refers him to the argument of his inner sense, to what goes on in his soul, or to what he wishes for his soul. Laelius readily recognizes that he desires that his soul should be governed monarchically or royally, that the best part of his soul, the *consilium,* should alone rule over the passions. Scipio then asks why he then hesitates regarding what he must think of the commonwealth. If there is not one authority, there is no longer any authority.[47]

Laelius replies quite sensibly that he would like to know what is the difference between one and several, if the several are just. The argument by analogy between the political order and the order of the soul is reversible: why wouldn't the good of the soul not be that of a just aristocracy of the faculties?

Scipio does not answer the objection. He now appeals to Laelius's familial and social experience. Whether in his country house or his city house, he confides the oversight of his affairs to one supervisor only. And he alone governs the whole of his "household."[48] Why then does he not agree that it is the same in a republic and that the rule of one alone, provided he is just, is best?

It appears that the arguments in favor of kingship tend to bypass the political order, to rest on an analogy, be it cosmological, psychological, or domestic.

Scipio, however, then advances a political argument that bears, naturally enough since he has already spoken of the beginning, on the end of the kingly regime, on the expulsion of Tarquin the Proud. But the argument this time is ambiguous. On the one hand, in effect, Scipio explains the Romans' hatred of kingship by the character of a single man, Tarquin, whose relentless arrogance made the name of king become hated by the people.[49] And at the end of the segment, he concludes that because of the injustice of one of them, that entire form of the commonwealth was destroyed.[50] This particular accident seems to leave intact the general merits of this type of regime. But on the other hand, the insistence placed on the accidental character of the fall of kingship draws attention to the fragility of this regime.[51]

Scipio thus summarizes the results of this section of the inquiry. If in his eyes the kingly regime is preferable by far to the two other simple regimes, the regime that is balanced and compounded from the three primary forms of government ought to be preferred even over kingship.[52] This mixed regime includes equality or impartiality *(aequabilitas)* and stability *(firmitudo)* such that, if at least the principal citizens avoid great vices, it will not be subject to turmoil. There is no reason for revolution when each person is firmly set in his own rank.[53]

The first book ends with Scipio expressing the fear that his speeches, if he continues in this vein, resemble more those of a master who is teaching than of a participant in an inquiry pursued in common. Accordingly he now settles on a terrain where his friends will be his equals: he will deal with the Roman regime as it has been passed on from generation to generation, explaining both what this regime is and that it is the best. He will thus be able to fulfill the task he took on at the start of the conversation, which was to inquire into the best form of government ("de optimo civitatis statu"), and he will do so by referring to the example of our republic ("exemplum nostrae reipublicae") as a touchstone.

Laelius enthusiastically approves of this plan. He praises the unique qualities of Scipio, who would be in the first rank of the best regime if it existed, which is not the case at the time of this meeting, and who better than anyone can give the most useful advice for the future, he who has provided for its future by defeating two terrors that threatened this city.[54]

Thus in book 2 Scipio will deal with "our republic." Taking up an idea often expressed by his teacher Cato, he explains why the regime of Rome ("nostrae civitatis status") is superior to that of all other cities. In other cities, the regime was in general organized by one legislator alone, such as Minos in Crete or Lycurgus in Sparta. But at Rome the republic was shaped not by one person's talent but by that of many citizens, and not in one person's lifetime but over many generations.[55]

If the opposition between Sparta, founded by one alone, and Rome, "constituted" by many *(multi)*, is sharp, the case of Athens seems to be equivocal or intermediary. Scipio mentions a succession of Athenian legislators: Theseus, Draco, Solon, Cleisthenes, then *multi alii,* and finally, when Athens was already beaten and laid low, Demetrius of Phalerum. One has to ask whether Athens is closer to Sparta or to Rome. If one goes by the criterion of the comparison—the number of founders—Athens seems much closer to Rome. At the same time, one cannot avoid the impression that Scipio means to cast Athens on the side of Sparta. Athens underwent many changes and revolutions such that it had many founders, many Lycurguses if you like, but this abundance is a defect. The *multi* of Athens, dare I say, are inferior to one, while the *multi* of Rome are superior to one. The suggestion here is that Athens is a failed Sparta, whereas Rome is superior to Sparta. The Greek cities were always greatly dependent on the virtues, especially the prudence of their leaders, the legislators and reformers. Rome developed according to a wisdom that, to be sure, relied on individual virtues, but that enveloped them, since the city was larger than those virtues.

Rome is exemplary—new and exemplary—in that it shows the limits of individual virtues. According to Scipio's report, Cato explained that there never was a genius so vast that he could miss nothing, nor could all the geniuses brought together in one place at one time foresee all contingencies without the practical experience afforded by the passage of time.[56]

Thus one must ascribe to Cato the Elder one of the first formulations of the theory of spontaneous order and of Hayek's idea that the functioning of the social order rests on an immense amount of information that could not be mastered by any individual or group of individuals, however zealous and capable one might imagine them to be.

Another idea that was destined to have a great future, which is a mode or first form of the preceding one, is the "conservative" idea that there is superior wisdom in experience and longevity, in what has lasted a long time.[57]

Neither Scipio nor Cato nor even Cicero are figures one would willingly associate with a spiritual revolution. Yet, the Greek rapport between humanity and the city is here profoundly modified. With the Greeks, individual citizens, as dependent on the city as they were, were so to speak the equal of the city, since the city in turn depended on them, on their commandment and obedience. This equality will take on spiritual meaning and become paradoxically visible with the figure of Socrates, who deals with Athens as he would an individual interlocutor to whom he would have some reproaches to address. At Rome the mutual dependence between the citizen and the city is loosened and the city becomes definitely greater than the person, with the consequence that the wisdom of the city prevails over that of the best person.

The properly Roman quest for the best regime must thus take an altogether different direction than the Greek quest. Instead of looking ahead and above—to the ideas of the good and the best—it looks first of all behind, in the depth of time, to the origin. Cato had written a historical work titled *Origins*. That is why, Scipio says, that like him he will go back to the origin of the Roman people. He will more easily attain the object in view if he shows the republic as it is born, grows up, and comes of age, and as a strong and well-established body politic, than if he makes up some republic as Socrates does in Plato.[58]

These last words resound like an astonishingly clear anticipation of what Machiavelli will claim for himself in chapter 15 of *The Prince*, which we have often cited: "But since my intent is to write something useful to whoever understands it, it has appeared to me more fitting to go directly to the effectual truth of the thing than to the imagination of it. And many have imagined republics and principalities that have never been seen or known to exist in truth."[59] The critique of Greek philo-

sophical "idealism" was thus developed at Rome, before being radical-
ized to form the basis of modern political philosophy that, as we know,
wants to be "realist."

Is saying this "overinterpreting" a few words that should not have
such a philosophical significance? In any case, a little further, the novelty
of Scipio's philosophical method and the rupture with the Greek approach it implies are underscored. Laelius in effect says, "We see that you
have introduced a new kind of analysis, something to be found nowhere
in the writings of the Greeks."[60] Thus he is criticizing Plato: that great
man, the greatest of all writers, chose his own territory on which to build
a city to suit his own ideas. It may be a noble city, but it is totally alien
to human life and customs.[61] Immediately after, he makes a clear allusion
to Aristotle and his school as those who indeed described the diverse
regimes, but without providing us with a definite model.[62]

One could say that Laelius reproaches Plato with an excess of idealism and Aristotle with an excess of empiricism. The two opposed critiques provide the key to Scipio's approach, which in sum joins the two
methods.[63] By focusing on the exemplary case of the Roman republic,
Scipio makes a synthesis of Platonist idealism and Aristotelian empiricism, and so corrects one by the other. It is the history of the Roman
republic, judiciously told, that must provide the orientation the Greeks
sought in political philosophy.

The Recourse to History

The status of the historical account announced by Scipio is yet far from
being clear. He does not ignore the distinction between historical facts
and legendary stories since, after recalling certain traditions concerning
Romulus, he says: we pass here from legend to historical facts ("a fabu-
lis ad facta").[64] His "history of Rome" will nonetheless be different
enough from what we take these words to mean. It will be a judicious
blend of facts and fables, or fictions. Scipio very deliberately keeps for
himself a little, or much, of Plato's freedom.[65] Cicero's De republica is in
this sense closer to—as the similarity in titles precisely suggests—Plato's
Republic than to the Constitution of Athens, or Aristotle's Politics, or
yet to Thucydides's History.

Let us look at a few points.

Scipio insists on the exceptional foresight Romulus displayed in choosing the site of Rome: on the bank of a river flowing to the sea by a large estuary, in such a way as to benefit from the advantages of the sea all the while avoiding its drawbacks. He understood that maritime sites are not suited to cities that are founded with hopes of duration and empire. Coastal cities are subject to instability and corruption, as the fate of Carthage and Corinth demonstrates. He adds, "What I said about Corinth is probably just as true for Greece as a whole."[66] Scipio pursues a quite insistent polemic against Greek things, a polemic that here reaches so to speak the very being of Greece, which is reproached, dare I say, with lacking being: "And of course the islands are surrounded by water and are virtually floating—along with the institutions and customs of their cities."[67]

The first great political measure of Romulus that Scipio mentions is the rape of the Sabine women.

> In order to strengthen his new city he adopted a new and somewhat crude plan, but one that, in terms of bolstering the resources of his kingdom and people, shows the mark of a great man who looked far into the future: he ordered Sabine girls of good family, who had come to Rome for the first annual celebration of the Consualia in the circus, to be seized, and he placed them in marriages with the most important families. This led the Sabines to wage war against the Romans; and when the battle was indecisive, he made a treaty with Titus Tatius the Sabine king at the urging of the women who had been seized. By that treaty he admitted the Sabines to citizenship and joint religious rituals, and he shared his rule with their king.[68]

Scipio here glosses over the brutality of the procedure as quickly as possible, of which Livy will give a much more complete account.[69] On the other hand, he emphasizes the extraordinary associative energy at work in this decisive episode of Rome's formation. The Sabine women interpose themselves between their fathers and their husbands; the cause of the war becomes the principle of peace. In the sentence that concludes the brief narration of the episode, the three verbs—*adscire, communicare, sociare*—indicate the act of joining together, of putting in common, of associating. For his part, Livy will not conceal the very unequal character of this union.[70]

A last remark on the Sabine episode. It manifests how the private and the public are convertible, more precisely what felicitous political effects derive from certain private affects. It seems that this trait distinguishes Rome from Athens, and perhaps from the Greek cities in general.[71]

After the death of the Sabine king Tatius, all the power fell to Romulus. He then relied much more on the authority and judgment of the fathers ("patrum auctoritas consiliumque").[72] Contrary to Livy, who brings to light Romulus's tyrannical traits,[73] Scipio/Cicero multiplies the indications suggesting that this extraordinary man had little taste for personal power: as soon as he no longer shared power with Tatius, he was quick to share it more with the fathers, the protosenate or informal senate that he assembled. Thus, from the beginning, from its foundations, the Roman regime, which appears to be kingly, tends toward the mixed form. In that sense it is close to the regime of Sparta. Romulus "recognized and approved the same policy that Lycurgus at Sparta had recognized slightly earlier, that states are guided and ruled better under the sole power of a king if the authority of the most responsible citizens is added to the monarch's absolute rule."[74]

Scipio then emphasizes that Romulus is at the origin of the custom of taking the auspices that the Romans have retained to the great advantage of the republic. In addition, he had the plebes divided up under the protection of the leading citizens, a very useful measure, as he was to show later.

The final remark concerns Romulus's penal policy. He maintained order by fixing a fine to be paid in sheep and bulls, not by violence and torments. By underlining the mildness and moderation of the penalties instituted by Romulus, Cicero suggests that even the first Romans were very far from being barbarians and that Rome was, so to speak, born civilized.

I have already mentioned the paragraph that follows and the bizarre argument that Cicero/Scipio laboriously develops.[75] He situates the history of Rome in the chronology of Greece, more precisely in the chronology of the Greek enlightenment, leaving aside entirely the question of knowing whether, in the time of Romulus, it had spread much in Latium. The fact that Homer lived many years before Romulus is enough to guarantee, it seems, that the latter belonged to enlightened times.

The argument concerning the death and deification of Romulus is curiously twisted, or exaggeratedly subtle, unless Cicero deliberately intends to make it contradictory and self-refuting. It comes down to something like this. In an enlightened age, when the taste of barbarian times for fictions had been long lost, the Romans nonetheless gave credence to the testimony of a simple peasant. At the instigation of the fathers, who wanted to repel the odious suspicion that they had caused Romulus to perish, this peasant declared that on the hill now called the Quirinal he had seen Romulus, who told him that he was a god and was called Quirinus. The principal sentence is the following: Romulus's intelligence and virtue were so great that people believed the story told about him by Proclus Julius, a farmer, something that for many generations men had believed about no other mortal.[76] Thus, if I understand the argument well, the fact that in an enlightened age people believed incredible reports about the death of Romulus is proof of his extraordinary merits. In the end the *fabula* reveals the *facta* more than it conceals them.[77]

After the death or disappearance of Romulus, the senate tried to govern the republic by itself without a king. The people did not allow it and in their regret over Romulus they incessantly demanded a king. Then, in their wisdom the *patres* or *principes* conceived a new combination unknown to other nations. They instituted an interregnum.[78] Up to the time the new king was proclaimed, the city was not without a king, and this provisional king did not remain so for long, in order not to feed the desire or acquire the means of keeping power. In fact, the *interrex* "reigned" for only five days, with the senators succeeding one another in the post. The institution of the *interrex* thus allows time to choose a new king. The Roman innovation, if I understand it rightly, is the institution of elective kingship.[79] Not without pride, Cicero emphasizes that at that time this still-new people grasped what had escaped the Spartan Lycurgus, who did not believe that the king should be elected but simply accepted or received provided only that he was of the blood of Hercules. Thus the first Romans, rustic as they were, did not let themselves be impressed by dynastic prestige but sought virtue and wisdom for their kings.

The Roman people were even already so enlightened that, neglecting their own nationals, they welcomed as king, with the approval of the fathers, a man of foreign race.[80] They had a Sabine come from Cures to reign at Rome, since this man, Numa Pompilius, had a great reputation for virtue and wisdom.[81]

Seeing that the Romans, as a consequence of Romulus's institutions, were inflamed with eagerness for war, the new king judged that they were in need of some correction on this score. He divided among them the lands conquered by Romulus and encouraged them to cultivate those lands—a better way than pillage to obtain what they needed. He implanted in them a love of tranquility and peace. Through religious ceremonies he softened spirits that were inflamed with the habit and the desire to wage war. He also established markets, games, and all sorts of gatherings. In short, through all these institutions he restored humanity and mildness in souls that the taste for war had made savage and inhuman.[82]

At this point, Manilius interjects a question: is the story true that King Numa was a disciple of Pythagoras himself, or at least was a Pythagorean? Scipio replies angrily that this whole story is false and is not only an invention but a clumsy and ridiculous one; in truth these lies are intolerable! Why this sudden anger of the noble Scipio? He explains in any case and with scientific precision that Pythagoras came to Italy 140 years after the death of Numa, in the fourth year of the reign of Tarquin the Proud, that is, in the Sixty-Second Olympiad. Manilius is indignant that such a serious error was given credence for so long. He is above all relieved and content: "I can happily accept that we were not educated by foreign and imported learning, but by home-grown domestic virtues."[83] This expression of pride is very understandable, but its underlying thesis is hardly compatible with what Scipio was saying shortly before, about the time of Romulus being an enlightened time coming after Homer and Lycurgus, which presupposes Greek influence as early as Rome's beginnings.

In fact, Scipio corrects his friend immediately but delicately. One must consider the progress of the Roman republic and by what natural development it attained its perfection; then one will see that the Romans knew how to make the institutions borrowed from other places much better than they had been in the place of origin.[84] What Scipio is suggesting then is that the Romans improved what they received from the Greeks, a proof of their *consilium* and their *disciplina,* it being understood, he concedes, that fortune was not against them.

We will quickly touch upon the successor of Numa Pompilius, the warrior king Tullus Hostilius. Nevertheless Tullus achieved something very significant in establishing the law governing declarations of war. He gave to this innovation, which was very just in itself, the religious sanction of the Fetiales ("sanxit feciali religione"), so much that any undeclared war was deemed unjust and impious.[85]

After Tullus Hostilius, we come to Ancus Martius, the son of the daughter of Numa, on whom also the *imperium* was conferred by a *lex curiata*. Once again we have an associative action, this time directed to the Latins: "adscivit eos in civitatem." This king is, so to speak, given short shrift by Cicero, who remarks here that "Roman history is obscure" since, though we know the mother of Ancus, we do not know his father. The insistence on the obscurity of the beginnings of Roman history prepares, if I may say, the sudden surge of light: "At this point, the city first seems to have become more cultivated by a sort of graft of education." The metaphor of grafting gives an idea of the depth of the transformation produced by foreign influence. Another metaphor gives an idea of its sweep and speed: "It was no mere trickle from Greece that flowed into the city, but a full river of education and learning."[86]

This flood of Greek culture had political consequences, and first political causes. The successor of Ancus Martius was in fact the son of a Greek immigrant, Demaratus, thanks to whom the graft would be successful. Demaratus was a rich Corinthian, easily the first citizen of his city by his distinction, authority, and wealth, who, as he could not endure the tyranny of Cypselus, came to settle with great riches at Tarquinii, a prosperous city of Etruria. He was accepted as a citizen there and married a woman of Tarquinii, with whom he had two sons that he educated in all the arts according to Greek methods. One of his sons was granted citizenship at Rome, where, on account of his amiability and learning he became so close to king Ancus that he was thought to have a part in all his plans and to be almost associated in the kingship. Upon the death of Ancus, he was unanimously elected king by the people under the name of Lucius Tarquinius, which he had taken after abandoning his Greek name.

Cicero has told a very edifying story indeed, with the Roman people, who undoubtedly disregarded national preference, unanimously electing as their king an immigrant remarkable for his *humanitas* and *doctrina,* whose father moreover had sought refuge in Italy to escape tyranny. Roman kingship up to this point is nothing like what we call by that name.

It would be interesting to compare Cicero's treatment of Lucius Tarquinius's rise to kingship, which has come down to us incomplete, with that of Livy. One difference, it seems—but perhaps Cicero dealt with this aspect of his career in the lost fragment—is that Livy emphasized the role of the wife of Demaratus's son, Tanaquil, who was of high rank and could not accept that her marriage had made her fall from the rank of her birth. The Etruscans actually disdained her husband on account of his foreign origin. Thus, disdaining the natural love of her country and to see her husband honored, she resolved—it was she who took the initiative—to abandon Tarquinii. One is tempted to say that in analyzing Tanaquil's motives Livy sets up a comparison between the Etruscan city and Rome that irresistibly makes one think of the contrast between the old Europe, prisoner of her history, and the United States of America, where everything is possible. Rome is Tanaquil's America. Among a new people, "where all advancement came swiftly and depended upon ability, there would be opportunities for an active and courageous man."[87]

Another difference, related to the first, is that Livy insists on the episode's "Etruscan component," if I may call it so. He gives his Etruscan name, Lucumo, to the man who will become Lucius Tarquinius, and devotes space to the heavenly signs that Tanaquil knows how to interpret. Cicero on the other hand seems to be careful to erase any trace of Etruscan influence on Rome. One can think that he prefers to emphasize the impact of Greek arts and sciences rather than of Etruscan superstition.

Thus, Lucumo, making wise use of his wealth and talent, as we already know from Cicero, became close to the king, to the point that he shared authority in public and private, civil and military affairs. But how did he succeed the king who in his will named him tutor of his children? First, he sent the children out on a hunting party. Then he plunged into an election campaign in grand style. Tradition has it that he was the first who declared his candidacy for the throne and made a speech to win the votes of the plebeians. As can be imagined, he explained what a good Roman he was, though a foreigner. He was not lying in speaking so. Accordingly he was elected by an overwhelming majority. Literally, by an overwhelming majority the people ordered him to rule.[88]

Let us come back to Cicero. After Tarquin, who had been the first to make a speech to win the votes of the plebeians, came Servius Tullius, who, according to tradition, was the first to reign without being called to the throne by the pople. Born from a slave of Tarquin, and perhaps from the king himself, he received a Greek education of the best kind. Cicero evokes very quickly the not altogether straightforward way Servius Tullius came to the throne. Making believe that Tarquin, whom the sons of Ancus had had killed, was only wounded, Servius declared, with persuasive affability, that he would administer justice on Tarquin's order. Without leaving it up to the senators, once Tarquin was buried he addressed the people and, called to reign, had himself granted *imperium* by a *lex curiata*. Servius Tullius began to reign without the formal approval of the citizens but with their support and consent.[89] There is no doubting that Cicero softens as much as possible the tyrannical aspects of Servius Tullius's rise to power. Is this because, as certain commentators suggest, his disapproval of the way Servius came to the throne is balanced by his approval of the new constitution that is generally attributed to him?[90]

In any case, Servius Tullius is the one who formed the Roman political body by distributing the population into six classes—each in turn divided into "centuries"—according to wealth, in such a way that the voting power was not with the masses but with the rich, a precaution that must always be observed in a commonwealth so that the greatest number do not have the greatest power. Since voting takes place beginning with the wealthiest classes and centuries, a voting majority of the people is normally achieved before the humbler citizens are consulted. In such a census-based regime the multitude is neither excluded from voting, which would be arrogant, nor excessively powerful, which would be dangerous.[91] In this way no one was entirely deprived of the right of suffrage; and those whose vote counted most were those who had the greatest interest in maintaining the state in the best possible condition.[92]

With Tarquin the Proud the revolution was set into motion.

What took place at this decisive moment? There is an element of tragedy here, for Tarquin, tainted by the murder of the best of kings, did not have a clear conscience (or, he was not in his right mind—"integra mente non erat").[93] And as he feared the punishment of his crime, he wanted to be feared. Relying on his victories and his wealth, he reveled in his violence and was incapable of ruling his own mores or the appetites of his relatives. After being raped by Tarquin's elder son, Lucretia took her own life. Thereupon, a man of outstanding talent and virtue,

L. Brutus, threw off from his fellow citizens the unjust yoke of harsh slavery. Although he was a private citizen, he upheld the whole commonwealth; he was the first in the city to show that when it comes to preserving the freedom of citizens no one is a private person.[94] We have already mentioned, regarding the outcome of the episode of the Sabines, the role that private affects played in Rome and how in that city these were in some way convertible into public sentiments and productive of public affects. Perhaps it was this role of "private initiatives" in Roman politics that Cicero alluded to when he evoked, to deal with it later, the admirable trait "of such a character that nothing similar is to be found in any other commonwealth."[95]

Cicero then resumes the discussion of book 1 on the meaning of Tarquin's experience for the kingly regime in general, characterized by the fact that it is a good regime susceptible of becoming the worst through the fault of one individual alone. Cicero emphasizes that the Greeks, unlike the Romans, had two words to distinguish the good king from the bad king, whom they called tyrant.[96] One is tempted to say that he points out here a superiority of the Greeks who employed two different words to designate two things that are indeed very different. I believe, however, that he intends the opposite. The ambiguity of the word *rex* corresponds to the ambiguous character, the fragility, the lability of the regime itself. Since any king can become a tyrant, there is a sort of superior prudence in the Roman refusal to distinguish between king and tyrant, in the invincible distrust of the Romans with regard to the dangerous prestige of the name of king—*nomen regium*.[97]

What follows is striking: "Let there be opposed to this man [this tyrant] another, who is good and wise and knowledgeable about the interests and the reputation of the city, almost a tutor and manager of the commonwealth [quasi tutor et procurator reipublicae]; that, in fact, is the name for whoever is the guide and helmsman of the city. Make sure you recognize this man; he is the one who can protect the city by his wisdom and efforts. And since this concept has not yet been treated in our conversation, and we will often have to consider this type of man in our remaining discussion . . ."[98] The lacuna in the manuscript is particularly regrettable here, for it seems that Cicero was beginning to advance a political proposition. In any event, the argument takes a somewhat surprising turn. Cicero/Scipio has underlined the fragility of monarchic power and the dangers attached to the prestige of the name of king. How can one guarantee that the kingly remedy to kingly tyranny will not be worse than the evil? Make sure you recognize this man. Once again: how? The art of recognizing the *tutor et procurator reipublicae* was probably developed in the following books, but it is clear that there is a tension between the need for distrust regarding kingship as such and the demand for trust in the kingly individual who must correct the wrongdoings of tyranny. If the kingly regime is the regime that so easily transforms itself into its opposite, how can one have trust in the opposite of tyranny?

It is thus impossible to state with precision and confidence just what is the Ciceronian doctrine of the "protector" of the republic. One can think that Cicero himself was such a protector when he repressed Catiline's conspiracy. In that case the figure is impeccably republican. Cicero at the same time gives the figure kingly traits that suggest an outline of the Augustan principate. The thought has for us a metapolitical resonance when Cicero says in sum that through one man alone injustice has come, and through one man alone justice can return.[99] The figure of the protector of the republic is rich with an excess of possibilities, a faithful translation of the indetermination of the Roman political order when human association is still seeking its way in vain among the city, the empire, and, as I have just suggested, the Christian church.

At the end of what I have called the Ciceronian moment, Machiavelli will in a certain measure recover the figure sketched by Cicero and will rethink its possibilities to make it at last operational. Fifteen centuries later, the same inquiry is taken up again or continues, but this time the Roman indetermination will be reversed into an unprecedented determination of political order and action.

Cicero and Machiavelli

We have seen at some length how in chapter 1 of book 3 of the *Discourses on Livy*, Machiavelli explains that a sect or a republic must often be brought back to its beginnings.[100] This is done either by an extrinsic accident or intrinsic prudence. An extrinsic accident could be a military defeat. Such a reversal forces people to reflect on their situation. They also refocus their thinking in the wake of intrinsic accidents that can arise from a law or from a good person who acts by the example he sets and the virtuous deeds he does. In any event, legislative measures need to be made effective by the virtue of a citizen who courageously works to execute them against the power of those who break them. As we know, these *esecuzioni* that Machiavelli recommends are in fact most often death sentences that by their extraordinary character renew fear in the hearts of citizens—because citizens who no longer fear necessarily break the law.

Nothing indicates that Cicero envisaged that the protector of the republic would have recourse to the measures of terror recommended by Machiavelli, even if he himself dealt rather expeditiously with Catiline's accomplices. In any case, he praises Brutus, with whom Machiavelli, who calls him the father of Roman liberty, begins the "narration and discourse" concerning the men who made Rome great. Cicero emphasizes that Brutus was a *privatus*[101]—a private individual—whereas Machiavelli speaks of particular individuals *(uomini particulari)* who made Rome great.[102] Cicero and Machiavelli in effect both emphasize the fundamental political role in Rome—in Machiavelli's terms, the "numerous good effects"—of what we have already called "private initiatives."

In any case, Machiavelli proposes an interesting interpretation of the saving figure limned or outlined by Cicero. He describes this *alter oppositus,* this opposite of the tyrant, who must act contrary to the tyrant, as an individual capable of unleashing terror against potential tyrants and all breakers of the law. He is a strange figure who blends the private and the public, the opposite of tyranny and something resembling tyranny. One has the impression that Machiavelli at last gives a sharp edge to what Cicero had in mind at the moment when the republic was assailed by would-be tyrants; and that, to finally exit the Ciceronian moment, he makes a weapon given a first shape by Cicero himself operational.

We will observe an analogous transformation of the mixed regime that Cicero fears will not be as stable as its law of construction made it seem and whose salutary imbalance Machiavelli will liberate.

Later in book 2, Cicero, all the while evoking through examples how the mixed regime works and what its merits are, brings out the difficulty of maintaining the balance or the good blend: "Nature itself [*natura rerum ipsa*] however, required that, as a result of their having been freed from monarchy, the people should claim rather more rights for themselves. . . . This development was perhaps not completely rational, but the nature of commonwealths often overcomes reason."[103] The proposal has its place in an aristocratic or oligarchic argument, in any case one in favor of the small number of those who are competent and prudent, those who are rational, a quality which, because of their nature or situation, eludes the many. At the same time, taken by itself, it suggests that political life as such is resistant to reason, a resistance deriving from the fact that those who defend their rights are naturally prone to go beyond their rights. That is of course the very justification of the mixed regime—the one that proposed to balance claims against one another—but it is also the cause of its fragility. In endeavoring to make room for everyone's right, everyone is incited to go beyond his right.

Is it possible to avoid this outcome, this "nature of political things" whereby, as Rousseau says roughly, the causes that make political institutions necessary make their abuse inevitable? But isn't giving up the search for balance giving up all concern for justice, isn't it endangering the political thing itself? Machiavelli will look for a way out in a political approach that, instead of averting or combating the imbalance, will accept it, let it be, not to abandon the republic to destruction but to give it a novel dynamism that deliberately embraces the imbalance itself in order to govern the movement that carries it away, to govern it better by going along with it more resolutely.

Machiavelli is the first political author to question whether balance and stability, which make the mixed regime desirable, are really good for republics to pursue. In his eyes the Roman experience shows—and therein lies its uniqueness and its worth—that better effects can be expected from imbalance (a certain imbalance) and instability (a certain instability). He explains his thinking very well in chapter 6 of book 1 of the *Discourses*.

Machiavelli distinguishes two great types of political behavior, the first exemplified by Sparta and Venice, the second by Rome. Sparta and Venice are closed cities whose governments were "steady and closed off" early on. Those who joined the city later—and there were not many, for the city was not hospitable—had in any case no reason or possibility to cause trouble—no reason, for nothing had been taken from them; no possibility, because they were held in check and marginalized. Such a republic is stable, but it is hardly capable of lasting expansion, as precisely the examples of Sparta and Venice show. Accordingly, it would be good for such a city to have a constitution or law that prohibited its expansion. Machiavelli continues: "Without doubt I believe that if the thing could be held balanced in this mode, it would be the true political way of life and the true quiet of a city." One sees that Machiavelli in principle does not question the desirable character of balance and rest. In this sense he does not question here the ancient goals. But he adds immediately, "But since all things of men are in motion and cannot stay steady, they must either rise or fall; and to many things that reason does not bring you, necessity brings you." Necessity in particular can lead to expansion *(ad ampliare)*. If the city has been so ordered as to maintain itself without expanding, then the necessity to expand leads to its ruin. The conclusion: "Therefore, since one cannot, as I believe, balance this thing, nor maintain this middle way exactly, in ordering a republic there is need to think of the more honorable part and to order it so that if indeed necessity brings it to expand, it can conserve what it has seized." It is thus "necessary to follow the Roman order and not that of the other republics."[104]

The necessity of expansion can be triggered by many accidents, but it rests fundamentally on the impossibility of making a rigorous distinction between attack and defense, or of adopting a purely defensive posture: "For if it [a republic] will not molest others, it will be molested, and from being molested will arise the wish and the necessity to acquire."[105] Without being aware of it, people pass from defense to attack and from the necessity to acquire to the wish to acquire. Besides the movement of things, the external accidents that produce the necessity to acquire, there is in addition the internal movement that makes one pass from the necessity to the wish to acquire. One sees why "to follow the Roman order" is the more honorable part: because this is to act in conformity with nature, that is, with the movement of human things; one does not allow oneself to be distracted or thwarted by the desire that appears so reasonable—by the illusion—of rest or quiet. The imaginary republics that chapter 15 of *The Prince* speaks of are immobile republics, arrested at a point of balance where it is impossible to stay, for it is necessary to go up or down. The "effectual truth of the thing" is first or finally the necessary and unending movement of human things, to which one must be in a position to give an adequate response.

To be disposed for movement is to be prepared for empire. And to be prepared for empire is to constitute a numerous and armed people. Now, once a people is so constituted, it is capable of defending its liberty against the oppression of the few. We have here one of Machiavelli's most important theorems, a theorem that links the empire to what can already be called democracy: "If you wish to make a people numerous and armed so as to be able to make a great empire, you make it of such a quality that you cannot then manage it in your mode."[106]

Let us return to where we started, with Cicero's assertion: "Nature itself, however, required that, as a result of their having been freed from monarchy, the people should claim rather more rights for themselves. . . . This development was perhaps not completely rational, but the nature of commonwealths often overcomes reason." In placing the nature of things, and the very nature of republics, at the origin of the people's passions that he does not approve of, Cicero sketches a criticism of the oligarchic order and the mixed regime that he otherwise recommends—a criticism that Machiavelli will bring to its conclusion: instead of deploring the people's excess, one should understand it as a reaction against the desire that animates the great to oppress them. There could not, properly speaking, be excess where there is no golden mean, where the middle way cannot be exactly maintained because one passes from "not enough" to "too much" without being able to stop at the point of inflection or even to discern that point, which probably does not exist—an imaginary middle. Of course, the political agent—the "prince"—will not let himself be carried away by the people's passions but will rely on them to distance himself from the few and in this way create the necessary space to *vivere libero*.

Rest and Motion

These remarks prompt us to return to a question that is closely linked to the very notion of political philosophy, the question of the criteria of politics, or more precisely of political judgment. I have already quoted and commented on the passage in which Leo Strauss summarizes Hobbes's innovation, the principle and mainspring of modern political philosophy as Hobbes deploys it for the first time: "Hobbes's political philosophy is, therefore, different from Plato's, in that in the latter, exactness means the undistorted reliability of the standards, while in the former, exactness means unconditional applicability, applicability under all circumstances, applicability in the extreme case."[107] What does it mean to seek an unconditionally applicable norm? As we have seen, it means seeking a norm that can be produced and made to work with irresistible efficiency. Finally, it means for Hobbes to construct the sovereign who, with his excessive force, is capable of repressing any expression of pride—the excess of any member whatever of the political body.

Machiavelli was not, strictly speaking, looking for a new norm. He takes note instead of the failure or defect of all accepted norms. The movement they pretend to ignore is stronger than they are. The "effectual truth of the thing" is the irrepressible movement of human things. As we have seen, Machiavelli distinguishes in a very striking way the "effectual truth" from true political life ("vero vivere politico") and from the true quiet of a city ("vera quiete d'una città"). Machiavelli thus recognizes up to a certain point the legitimacy—the "truth"—of the ancient norm of the republic aimed at rest, the norm of the mixed regime. He pertinently identifies this ancient norm as a middle way ("via del mezzo"). The problem is that this norm—the balance that is so desirable—prevents us from seeing that human things go up or down but cannot remain at a point of balance, that they are always in movement. Accordingly, one has to change the direction of one's gaze. Instead of looking upward, to the imaginary republic or principality whose rest makes it so pleasant to contemplate, one has to look downward, in any case to focus on the movement itself of human things by resisting the temptation of the ideal, which is the temptation to rest.

What in the end is Machiavelli doing in proposing what he calls the "Roman order" for us to imitate? He sets up motion itself—the possibility and the necessity of motion—as the authority. Paradoxically—contrary to the opinion of "all authors"—motion itself is the norm. But how is this possible? To the contrary, isn't a norm, a criterion, a standard something that is necessarily unchanging and immobile? What could a changing criterion be? Machiavelli's boldness is such that he endeavors by every means precisely to make motion itself appear as the norm, in any case as what should be taken into account above all else. The very radical character of his thinking will prevent his being taken seriously as a philosopher: where are his "ideas"?

Machiavelli allows us to see better what Hobbes accomplished. He elaborated a univocal norm—thus an immobile one—that does not prevent movement. The law of the sovereign simply prevents citizens from hampering one another. The sovereign occupies this immobile seat of power that protects the free movement of the members of society.

The difference between Machiavelli and the ancients is that what for the ancients was the limit of reason—namely, motion that eludes reason—becomes for Machiavelli, and after him for the moderns,[108] the principal fact that a more ambitious or more resolute or daring reason must grasp.

One cannot help noting a connection between this transformation and the one that took place a century later in physics, which abandoned the notions of final cause and proper place and took as its task the discovery of the laws of motion. In the case of Machiavelli, chronology of course prohibits envisaging any influence of the new physics on his politics, as it is possible to do in the case of Hobbes. It must be acknowledged then that it was a political author—Machiavelli—who was the first to place at the center of attention a motion that does not tend toward any rest, a pure motion. This does not mean that the modern scientific revolution flows from the political and moral reform Machiavelli introduced, but it does help us to measure how radical the latter was—how radical, but also how enigmatic its character.

I do not hold the key to the enigma, but I believe one must emphasize the role of the Roman experience, an unfinished and unending experience that is waiting to be interpreted, and to be consciously and deliberately taken up again. Machiavelli aims to incite us to "follow the Roman order," not to reproduce it, but to take it up again, to extend and amplify the novel arrangement that Rome inaugurated in the mobilization of human forces. Rome was the great engine that produced force and motion. The science of Rome is one part—the constitutive and primordial part—of the science of human forces.

Machiavelli's successors will be able to forget Rome, and even turn against it,[109] having elaborated—with what help of the new physics matters little here—a science of life itself as motion. "Life itself is but motion."[110] English psychology will describe human life as an unending race without a goal,[111] or as an unending flight.[112] It will put in the forefront the notions of power and desire of power. The latter confirms but also covers over Machiavelli's analysis of the sliding or tipping from *mantenere* to *acquistare*.[113] The notion of power is of course inseparable from the notion of freedom; power and freedom are the two aspects or expressions of motion. For modern political philosophy and for modern politics in general, freedom is freedom of movement, of human life conceived of as movement, of the human individual understood as a "quantity of motion."

Unlike the free will of tradition, this freedom is not the opposite of necessity. The movement that is to be left free or made free is in sum a necessary movement. The validity of the criterion of freedom is guaranteed by the power of necessity. Since the motion cannot be stopped, it must be left free. Herein lies the ambiguity of contemporary emancipation. Why is it "forbidden to forbid"? Is it because freedom as such is essentially *good*? Or is it because it is actually *impossible* to forbid freedom? The latter argument was employed by Spinoza or Bayle to defend freedom of opinion. Humans have no power over their thoughts; they cannot compel themselves nor therefore be compelled to believe this or that. Freedom of thought rests on the necessity of our thoughts. Paradoxically or ironically, the "intolerance" of illiberal times presupposes our freedom: it presupposes that our thoughts depend on our freely formed dispositions.

How then does our political regime, the heir or rather the product of all these developments, present itself? Our "best regime," our "mixed regime," is now defined not by a stable balance but on the contrary by a capacity for free movement. The hallmark of the classical mixed regime was to tend toward rest; the hallmark of our mixed regime is to be open to movement.

Our mixed regime *does not resemble* a classical mixed regime because the two poles, the two great defining parts of a mixed regime, have become *politically invisible*. There were the few and the many;[114] now there are "citizens in general," that is, "all." What comes to the fore, what is visible, what is politically established, is that all citizens are *equally* free, free to participate in making laws and to assert their independence as they wish.

At the same time, of course, we cannot escape the necessity of setting up a few checkpoints and organizing a certain balance: *checks and balances, distribution* or *separation of powers*. The "powers" in the new regime are very different from the "parts" in the old, even if the principal powers are also two in number. Where there were the few and the many, there are now the executive and the legislative. The new powers do not correspond to the old parts because they are *abstracted* from society.

But is there not a contradiction between the movement our regime wishes to facilitate and the balance, perhaps even the immobility, that will establish itself between powers that "check" each other? Montesquieu writes, "The form of these three powers [the legislative is here divided into two parts] should be rest or inaction. But as they are constrained to move by the necessary motion of things, they will be forced to move in concert."[115] Montesquieu here deflects a considerable objection with affected neglect; with exaggerated ease he solves a very difficult question of political physics. How can there be balance and motion at the same time—the freest and the fastest motion possible? Montesquieu evokes "the necessary motion of things," when his whole intent in *The Spirit of the Laws* is to analyze the complex interplay of institutions and dispositions that makes possible the improbable and prodigious blend of stability and motion that is our modern regime.[116] For him anyway, the necessary motion of things would lead rather to despotism.

If the separation and balance of powers do not lead to immobility, it is not because of the necessary motion of things but because power—the State as the aggregate of powers—is separated from society. The sovereign State is sufficiently stable, fixed, and elevated above society to be able to let members of society be free—laissez-faire, laissez-passer.

Now, it is because of this freedom, through the mediation of this freedom, that the two parts of the classical mixed regime recover their being and interaction in the modern regime—that the few and the many, that class struggle return to the fore. Then the debate on justice naturally joins the line of argument that Aristotle had put forth: "For all agree that the just in distributions must accord with some sort of worth, but what they call worth is not the same; supporters of democracy say it is free citizenship, some supporters of oligarchy say it is wealth, others good birth, while supporters of aristocracy say it is virtue."[117]

The difference with the Greek city is that on the one hand the many can rely on the State to guarantee or increase their part, and on the other the few can take advantage of the freedom to invest and acquire, which is also guaranteed by the State, to become as wealthy, as "unequal," as they want and as they can be.

It is not only the mediation of the State or the separation of the State and civil society that prevents the rich and the poor in our regimes from coming to blows as they did so often in the ancient cities. For a long time Rome was able to survive the ever-renewed imbalance of the mixed regime because territorial expansion allowed the demands of the people to be satisfied, demands that were awakened, as Cicero explained to us, by the fall of the kings. How did *our* mixed regime survive class struggle even after the end of colonial empires that, according to the Leninist or Roman interpretation, offered it a last respite before destroying itself? We know the answer: if our mixed regime does not fall in spite of its permanent imbalance, it is because it does not cease to run after the "growth" that allows the demands of the many to be more or less satisfied without killing or robbing the rich and even allowing the rich to become even richer. Growth is the *race* that prevents our mixed regime from falling.

The exploitation of nature does not liberate us from politics; it does not make us pass from the government of men to the administration of things, as the Saint-Simonians had hoped. It is our regime itself that, in its creative imbalance, obliges us and makes us able to transform nature.

In summarizing what he calls the "system" of the Romans, Montesquieu writes, "they acted as destroyers in order not to appear as conquerors."[118] As for us, not only not to appear as conquerors but not to be conquerors (of other people), we have engaged in a conquest of nature that is more and more destructive. But how can we *demobilize* our forces when their gathering and mobilization are the wellspring of the whole of the modern development, the wellspring of this new Rome that at first was Europe and that is now humanity in motion?

III

EMPIRE, CHURCH, NATION

7

THE CRITIQUE OF PAGANISM

The Political and the Religious

In his *Pensées*, Pascal wrote:

> If we are too young our judgement is impaired, just as it is if we are too old.
>
> Thinking too little about things or thinking too much both make us obstinate and fanatical.
>
> If we look at our work immediately after completing it, we are still too involved; if too long afterwards, we cannot pick up the thread again.
>
> It is like looking at pictures which are too near or too far away. There is just one indivisible point which is the right place.
>
> Others are too near, too far, too high, or too low. In painting the rules of perspective decide it, but how will it be decided when it comes to truth and morality?[1]

But how will it be decided when it comes to truth and morality? When Pascal wrote what we have just read, the city had long before disappeared, and with it the "perspective" on the city, which is also the perspective of the city, that allows human things to be seen as a unified whole, thus with enviable clarity. The lack of perspective, or the uncertainty, the vagueness of perspective that Pascal assesses derives in considerable measure from the fact that the perspective of and on a new city was added to the perspective of and on the visible city, of and on political order properly speaking. The new city, the city of God proposed by Christianity, is invisible, its laws and mores altogether different from those of the visible city and at times opposed to them. Montesquieu describes the change that the Christian religion produced in the ancient city in a way that states the essential in a few words:

> Most of the ancient peoples lived in governments that had virtue for their principle, and when that virtue was in full force, things were done in those governments that we no longer see and that astonish our small souls.
>
> Their education had another advantage over ours; it was never contradicted. In the last year of his life, Epaminondas said, heard, saw, and did the same things as at the time that he was instructed.
>
> Today we receive three different or opposing educations: that of our fathers, that of our schoolmasters, and that of the world. What we are told by the last upsets all the ideas of the first two. This comes partly from the opposition there is for us between the commitments of religion and those of the world, a thing unknown among the ancients.[2]

It is important to keep in mind both Pascal's perplexity and Montesquieu's diagnosis. It is not certain that we have ever really overcome the first, or the causes of the first, since it is not certain that our situation has become fundamentally different from the situation that was the object of Montesquieu's diagnosis. It is not for lack of trying. One could say that at least since the thirteenth century or the start of the fourteenth, since Dante's *Monarchy*, Europe has been in search of the unification of human life in order to overcome the division induced by Christianity. This is not my personal historical interpretation. It is the very theme of European history and in particular the wellspring of the construction of the modern State. Look at Hobbes, who at the same period as Pascal, like him, underlines the difficulty of orienting oneself in the human world and of finding the perspective point from which to see it. But whereas Pascal simply expresses his perplexity, Hobbes identifies a specific illness for which he seeks the remedy: "Temporal and spiritual government, are but two words brought into the world, to make men see double, and mistake their lawful sovereign."[3]

Men see double in the Christian world because they are exposed to a double power. To put an end to this diplopia, the two powers must be reduced to a unity by granting sovereignty to the temporal power, the only one that can properly and legitimately be power. As Rousseau will say, "Of all Christian authors, the philosopher Hobbes is the only one who correctly saw the evil and the remedy, who dared to propose the reunification of the two heads of the eagle, and the complete return to political unity, without which no State or government will ever be well constituted."[4]

In effect, the European political bodies in the end organized themselves in accord with Rousseau's wishes and in conformity with Hobbes's project. The illness finally found its remedy.

However, things are not that simple, as simple as an illness cured or a problem solved. There is no doubt that, precisely in order to solve it, Hobbes tended to simplify the problem by making it simply a problem of power. The duality or division of the human world, which is corrupting or in any case demoralizing, derives from the duality of the temporal and spiritual powers. Suppress the duality, and the unity of the human world or human life is by that very act reestablished. But does the human world lend itself to such geometric or arithmetic handling?

First of all, what kind of unity are we dealing with? It is not the ancient city that is reestablished, nor the unity of the world of Epaminondas. Unlike the Greek unity, which was *given,* here unity is *produced* by an institution that is especially charged to produce it, the sovereign State. To mention just one problem, the production of this new unity gives rise to a new division, between the State and what will be called civil society, by giving this old expression a novel meaning. The Europeans are not done with "seeing double." Once again, they do not know where they are; they are "lost," but in a new way. Marx—the "young" Marx—described this new division in the most acute manner: "Where the political state has attained to its full development, man leads, not only in thought, in consciousness, but in *reality,* in *life,* a double existence—celestial and terrestrial. He lives in the *political* community, where he regards himself as a *communal being,* and in *civil society* where he acts simply as a *private individual.*"[5]

What is particularly interesting for us in Marx's analysis is that he does not limit himself to noting a new division around which modern political life is organized, but he characterizes it in terms that harken back to the previous division: "The political state, in relation to civil society, is just as spiritual as is heaven in relation to earth. It stands in the same opposition to civil society, and overcomes it in the same manner as religion overcomes the narrowness of the profane world; i.e., it has always to acknowledge it again, re-establish it, and allow itself to be dominated by it."[6]

Thus the new division overcomes the previous one by displacing it and, in a certain fashion, repeating it. Yet Marx did not think that the new division was more bearable than the old one. People would not rest until they overcame it by instituting a type of association in which they would take part without division or alienation. One could say that Marx took up what Hobbes had done: where he found division, he wanted to produce unity. He was less fortunate than Hobbes in his conception of the tool that was to produce this unity. Whereas the sovereign State showed itself to be impressively effective in domesticating the spiritual power, the workers' political organization, the Communist Party, did not succeed in uniting the political State and civil society, except in the deceitful and violent form of the totalitarian regime. Whatever Marxism's fate, the fact that our political and social life continues to be organized around this division that Marx characterized in such striking fashion and that does not cease to torment us even if we have given up trying to overcome it, suggests that the old division is not simply an old thing or a thing of the past, but that it is still at work in the deep layers of our political existence.

As I have already suggested, the original problem cannot be reduced simply to a problem of power, even if the principle of the unquestionable effectiveness of modern political solutions resides in an understanding of political life in terms of power. But if the interpretation of political life in terms of power heralds, prepares, and facilitates the solution of political problems by means of a certain power structure—sovereign power, balance, distribution or separation of powers, and so on—this mechanical understanding of the phenomena entails a simplification that needs to be assessed. Montesquieu himself, as we have seen, who of all the modern authors is the one who contributed most to make us conceive political life, in particular the life of free regimes, as a mechanism of powers, in describing the internal division that affects modern or Christian nations never once uses the word "power." He speaks of different or opposing educations, of ideas that upset other ideas, of commitments that contrast with other commitments. All of this is certainly affected by the Hobbesian reworking that gives the monopoly of legitimate power to the secular or profane State, but the political transformation does not abolish the internal division of educations, ideas, and commitments that on the contrary it presupposes. It only aims at preventing or limiting its direct political effects.

The division remains, but each of the soul's two commitments being hampered in its manifestation and soon drained of its vitality, it is hardly recognizable and observers can think that the division introduced by religion belongs to the past. It is important to note that the modern State represses almost equally the two divergent movements of the soul: not only does it severely circumscribe the public expression of religious convictions and affects—religion is henceforth essentially a private thing—but it makes and is organized to make the "ancient freedom," that is, the direct expression of civic commitments, impossible: citizens can act only through their representatives. The modern State thus rests on the repression, in any case the frustration, of the two most powerful human affects: on the one hand the passionate interest in this world as expressed in active participation in the common thing, and on the other the passionate interest in the eternal and the infinite as expressed in the postulation of another world and participation in a community of faith. As I have said, with these two fundamental movements of the soul repressed or frustrated, the soul no longer recognizes itself, and thus observers conclude that we have entered a postcivic as well as a post-Christian era.

Perhaps they are right, since the listlessness of the civic passions as well as the religious affects seems beyond question, in Europe at least. However, it should not be forgotten that in spite of the proliferation of tools of social knowledge, of the ever-increasing refinement of statistical techniques, our societies are very difficult to observe and are perhaps among the most opaque that have ever existed, because of the structure—the political regime—I have pointed out: the expression of certain fundamental affects is systematically repressed or frustrated. Hence, the state of souls, if I can use that expression, is particularly debatable. The most refined tool to describe and analyze the state of souls in a country such as ours was traditionally literature. But literature is equally affected by the timidity and indecision that pervade social life along with personal life. One can only regret the time when literature opened the most direct access to the intimate metabolism of social life and analyzed it in the most incisive fashion.

It still was, or was even especially, the case at the start of the modern regime, when our political bodies took the form they have kept to this day. What I have called the timidity or indecision of souls was then perceived with a clarity we have become incapable of. One can understand that there is an intrinsic difficulty in clearly grasping a phenomenon that is characterized by indecision or vagueness. Chateaubriand described it in an unforgettable way under the name of the "vagueness of the passions."[7] He deals with it in a very short chapter with that title in his *Génie du christianisme,* which originally served to introduce the story titled "*René,*" which is an illustration and deployment of the idea contained in the chapter. Let us set the story aside and stay with the abstract or general description:

> It remains to speak of a state of soul that, it seems to us, has not hitherto been well observed: the state of soul that precedes the development of the passions, when our faculties, young, active, whole but confined, have exercised themselves only on themselves, without aim and without object. The more peoples advance in civilization, the more this state of vagueness of the passions increases; for something very sad then happens: the great number of examples we have before us, the multitude of books that treat of man and his feelings, make one smart without experience. . . . The imagination is rich, abundant, and wonderful; existence is poor, dry, and disenchanted. One dwells with a full heart in an empty world.[8]

Chateaubriand's style is certainly not that of a contemporary sociologist, but it is not hard for us to recognize ourselves in this description that aims at being scientific—Chateaubriand's concern is to "observe" a "state of soul," or at least to connect this description to our own experience. I limit myself to underlining its most striking trait.

The phenomenon under consideration joins the youth of individuals and the old age of civilization; it affects the young individuals of an old civilization. This is perhaps the first time that "youth," in the sense we give to that term today, becomes a determining element or parameter of the collective situation. It is the condition and the affects proper to youth that mark the common life of all, youth understood as maturity of the faculties, but of faculties that have not yet found their object. This includes, of course, as Chateaubriand clearly implies, youth understood as sexual maturity that is not yet engaged in a "lasting relationship," as we say today. This desiring and empty youth is confronted with a multitude of books and examples that saturate its imagination. To the desiring emptiness entailed by youth is added the perplexity induced by the inflation of reference points. One can see that the saturation of the juvenile imagination by the medley of "cultural references" did not wait for the contemporary means of communication to make its effects felt. A desiring and empty heart, an imagination stifled by a multitude of images, perplexity—the effect of all that is paralysis, or rather energy turned on itself: "the heart turns on itself and coils up on itself in a hundred ways, to use forces that it feels are useless to it."[9]

Chateaubriand then notes: "the Ancients hardly knew this secret restlessness, this bitterness of stifled passions that all ferment together: a great political existence, the games of the gymnasium and the parade ground, the affairs of the Forum and the public square, filled their moments and left no place for the troubles of the heart." Chateaubriand thereby strikes the first chord of a tune that Benjamin Constant will orchestrate a short time later and to which he will attach his name. The life of the Ancients, being a life of action in the full sense of the term and including a corresponding happiness, does not know the uncertainties of the life of the Moderns, which is much more a life of "reflection," including and first of all their political life, founded on "representation."

The two other factors that contribute to the state of soul that Chateaubriand endeavors to describe are the participation of men in the "society of women"—"they render our character as men less decided"—and the influence of Christianity. In the case of the latter, it is not a matter of Christianity as Church, the sacramental institution, Christianity in its vigor, but of a sort of refraction of Christianity,[10] an affective refraction in the form of a certain "disgust for the things of life," an "impression of sadness," even a "tinge of misanthropy." These are sentiments that make the souls that experience them "strangers in the midst of men." Chateaubriand concludes the chapter as follows: "Thus we have seen the birth of this culpable melancholy engendered in the midst of passions, when these passions, having no object, consume themselves of their own in a solitary heart."

Are we prey to this "culpable melancholy" Chateaubriand speaks of? The point seems the more excessive in that nothing for us would be truly "culpable."[11] But if, between Chateaubriand and us, souls may have changed color, their "state" remains determined by the same factors, that is, by the absence of the two major "objects" that are a "great political existence" and a religious life devoid of timidity, by their absence or rather their presence in the state of demoralizing traces of possibilities of life that one feels incapable of either embracing or forgetting. Haunted equally by the forum and the cloister, incapable of making civic as well as religious commitments, individuals are morally immobilized by this division that long ago has been overcome politically and that is no longer explicitly painful as it was for Chateaubriand and Constant. Our insensibility, or the dullness of our pain that is mere uneasiness, is what distinguishes us from the "romantics."[12] Where the romantics judged themselves "culpable" for being unable to choose and to act, we claim our unlimited "right" to choose, that is, not to choose. And with a condescension tinged with envy we leave the action to peoples who are still capable of passions.

The intent of this last series of remarks was not to provide a description of our political, moral, or spiritual situation, but only to suggest that if the "remedy" elaborated by Hobbes and recommended by Rousseau has in effect cured the "evil" of the division of the two powers, it has covered over rather than solved the problem that is at the root of the division of the two powers, namely, the division of the two cities.

Until now I have given a partial description of the political arrangement that heals the harm of the division of the two powers by covering over the problem of the division of the two cities. I considered only the unification of the collective body by the sovereign State monopolizing legitimate power—which is in effect the first moment of unity by which it is fitting to begin—leaving aside the second moment, the moment of duality and division, that of the separation between Church and State, the religious and the political. The unity of the sovereign State, plus the separation of Church and State, is for us the complete solution to the problem of the two cities. However, the preceding remarks have made us aware of a difficulty: with the sovereign State severely circumscribing the public expression of religious convictions and affects, the liberty of the Church separated from the State, although a genuine liberty, will be at the same time the liberty of an association subordinated within the

State, or, more concretely, of an association that is independent but intimidated by the State. Hence the notion of separation has in it something misleading, in the measure that the condition of the Church or of
religious association in general is determined by its place in the political
structure: the religious association is in one sense effectively separated
from the State, but in a structure determined by the sovereignty of the
State. In no way do Church and State have the same status.

The regime of separation, with all its advantages, has this drawback
that the nature of the religious association within it is necessarily much
obscured. Attention is focused principally on the individual and his or
her rights, which the secular and neutral State guarantees. The contradictory situation, the "impossible situation" of the Church—independence
and subjection—is not perceived and certainly is not perceived as a problem because it appears to be the logical consequence of the principle that
governs our political order: the goal, the raison d'être of the State, is to
guarantee the rights and liberties of individuals, including the freedom
of opinion that includes religious liberty. The freedom as well as the
subjection of the Church are the twofold consequence of this principle:
Christians are free to be such, but are in no way allowed to impose their
views on others, who are free not to be Christians. All of this goes very
well, but the perspective underlying the structure is that the Church, the
religious association, is a sum of individuals that have such-and-such
opinions. Yet this is the perspective of the State, in any case the doctrine
of the State on the Church and not that of the Church on itself. The
Church considers itself not as an association among others in an all-
encompassing society whose "pluralism" the State guarantees and preserves, but as a complete society that has its principle in itself and whose
goal is infinitely more important than that of any other society—it considers itself the *respublica perfecta* whose independence is not simply
functional but ontological, and that thus could not be subordinated to
any other authority or institution, including the secular State. In this
sense, the subordination of the Church to the sovereign State is an appearance to which the Church consents or is forced to consent, but that
obscures its true nature as a complete society.

It is important to add that the obscuring produced by the sovereign
State does not affect only the Church. It also concerns political society
itself, though in another way. The State makes it too appear as a sum of

individuals whose rights it guarantees. The State is in a sense separated—abstracted—from the nation just as it is separated from the Church. The proof is that a nation that is for the most part Christian can be governed by a State that is scrupulously secular.

The State, which is the great instrument of modern politics because it orders individuals—because it institutes the political order founded on individuals—is also the great obstacle to our understanding of ourselves because it masks or deforms the collective bodies—the "cities"—of which the individuals are members. It interposes itself between us and ourselves; it hampers at the same time that it mediates our relation with the cities we are part of—the Church and the nation.

The Greek city was immediately political. It governed itself directly as this concrete community, without a State or even a government, only magistracies. It was sufficiently *one* by itself to do without and not even to have the idea of *one* State or government.

In the course of European history, the need for explicit and abstract unity—the two characters of the unity of the State—grew ever stronger and more and more determining.[13] The vector of Europe's political history is the victory of the monarchy in the proper sense of the term. But as long as the ancien régime, or "feudalism," lasted, the State did not succeed in detaching or abstracting itself entirely from society.[14]

One has to wait until the French Revolution—let us leave aside the English and American histories—for the perfect political State ("der vollendete politische Staat") Marx speaks of to appear, for the political State to attain its true development ("seine wahre Ausbildung"). It is the new heaven of a new earth. It brings with it a viewpoint that does not coincide with that of any concrete community since it orders individuals and not communities—or it orders communities by ordering individuals. Although criticisms of the State were never lacking, the radical character of this separation and the extent of its consequences were only rarely measured because, in spite of its abstraction, it seemed in the end to merge with a concrete community, that of the nation. Today, with the development of a European political agency, one sees the viewpoint of the State explicitly detaching itself from national viewpoints, in truth from any collective viewpoint whatever. This is such that we can look with envy at the situation of division that motivated the speculative efforts of Hobbes and still in the eighteenth century the indignant tone of

Rousseau. Our condition of perception, dare I say, or of social knowledge is much less favorable. The effort to overcome the first division set in motion new divisions and has become itself a principle of separation that has spread through all aspects of life. The State has mediated all the communities—the Church, the nation, classes, families. The unifier of all of them is at the same time the divider of each one, whose perspective now is divided between its own perspective and the perspective of the State. What makes our life externally more ordered and easier is also what makes our self-knowledge more difficult.

The very complex interplay of divisions, unifications, and redivisions that is proper to Europe and the West was in a decisive way set in motion by the appearance of a human association that is an unprecedented kind of society: the Church. It is important to grasp anew the original nature of this society that, after so many and such profound transformations, is today both unrecognizable and recognizable. We are motivated here by an interest in the political thing, not in religion. We are engaging in an exercise aimed at grasping, in the case of this very particular society that is the Church, the political order independently of the viewpoint of the State—or of the individual viewpoint, which is the same—thus to understand the political or religious association as such or starting from it, and not as a sum of individuals asserting their interests and their opinions.[15]

Yet when we take up a question having in some way to do with religion, where religion is in some way involved, there immediately arises for us, as if it were obvious, the necessary *separation* of politics and religion. The goodness of separation is obvious. It will be said, for example, that the problem with Islam is that it does not separate the political from the religious. It is a practical truth, in the sense that for us a regime that separates the political from the religious is a good regime. It is also a theoretical truth, in the sense that for us politics and religion are "things that are naturally separate."[16]

Let us turn our attention for a moment to this self-evident truth. We have a clear and distinct idea of separation, but the things that are separated are by comparison vague. What is the political? What is the religious? In truth we do not raise the question. We know that it is good to separate them since they are naturally separate. We know that it is good to separate two things whose nature we do not know, or in any case whose nature we are not concerned to know more precisely.

One can see the trap we have carefully constructed and into which we necessarily fall. We do not perceive the mutilated or unbalanced character of our perception, our "intelligence," because it seems to coincide with the movement of reason itself that is to distinguish, and thereby to separate. Reason is, so to speak, contained in the number two: it discerns that two things are distinct or that one implies the other; it distinguishes the effect from the cause, and so on. To distinguish, to separate satisfies the reason and satisfied reason goes no further. The notion of separation satisfies our reason that has no desire to go further. Thus, the idea of the necessary separation of the political and the religious separates our reason from the political as well as the religious: they cannot become for it something that needs to be thought about.

What happens when what is to be thought about, the object we seek to understand, is a politico-religious or theologico-political situation or regime that ignores separation? Since we think starting with separation, the self-evident truth of separation, we will necessarily characterize or define this situation, this regime, by the negation of separation. We will necessarily define it by the *confusion* of the political and the religious. For us, those who ignore separation "confuse . . . things that are naturally separate." They commit an intellectual error that *we* do not commit. The principle of separation thus deploys its force: it fosters the separation between *we* who separate and *they* who confuse—I say in passing, as Péguy emphasized, the principles of modern analytic reason separate us from "all preceding humanities" and, let me add, from all humanities outside the West. This sense of superiority that the increase of separation I have just mentioned instills in us evidently does not incite us to study with much care the situation, the regime that is marked by such "confusion."

We encounter a difficulty, however, if at least we extend the inquiry ever so little. Why would others—the "forebears" and the "foreigners"— confuse things that are *naturally* separate? The self-evident truth of separation prevents us from recognizing the scarcely plausible, in any case the very obscure character of our affirmation. To confuse things that are naturally separate, one has to truly do it on purpose. Why? How? The difficulty comes out in a very striking way in Montesquieu, who is the great thinker of separation, in every sense of the term—analytical as well as institutional. He writes, "only singular institutions thus confuse . . .

things that are naturally separate."[17] The examples he gives in this context are chiefly the Spartans and the Chinese. This is nonetheless a lot of people and, especially, many worlds—very different worlds: the earlier world of the Greek city with the greatest political prestige; the world outside Europe with the greatest antiquity, wealth, and power. To speak simply of "singular institutions" that "confuse things naturally separated" is to employ very thin ropes to lift very heavy loads.

But let us see more precisely how Montesquieu describes these "singular institutions" that "confuse things naturally separate," in particular how he describes the Greek city. We are confronted with two representations or images that could not be more different. On the one hand, as we have seen, there is the education that was "never contradicted" of Epaminondas, who "in the last year of his life said, heard, saw, and did the same things as at the time that he was first instructed."[18] We have here an impression of perfect unity and continuity, of serenity and happiness. On the other hand, there is Montesquieu's description of the action of Lycurgus: "Lycurgus, mixing larceny with the spirit of justice, the harshest slavery with extreme liberty, the most heinous feelings with the greatest moderation, gave stability to his town. He seemed to remove all its resources, arts, commerce, silver, walls: one had ambition there without the expectation of bettering oneself; one had natural feelings but was neither child, husband, nor father; modesty itself was removed from chastity. In these ways, Sparta was led to greatness and glory."[19]

To say that Lycurgus "confuses things naturally separate," or that he confuses "all the virtues" is to say too little: if we lend credence to this picture, it violently holds together things naturally opposed. It is the same phenomenon, but the image of happy unity and continuity that took shape around the name of Epaminondas is replaced by the image of violence, of deliberate contradiction, of monstrosity that surrounds Lycurgus. Not only do the two images not go together, but the contrast between them is glaring. The power of separation acts and imposes itself on the very image of the city that does not separate but confuses: unity and serenity and at the same time violent and screeching contradiction.

If we follow the logic of separation to the end, it leads to a kind of destruction of the object that shatters into incompatible images. How is the inevitability of analytical destruction to be avoided?

Montesquieu's starting point is separation, which is the modern political and scientific order. Whatever is outside this order he defines as confusion or violence. This is to define the object to be studied in a way that puts an end to the inquiry. The clear idea of separation brings us squarely before the obscure thing and leaves us there. This is not how we can understand the Greek city, or any city. We need to proceed otherwise.

The temptation, or the easy way, is to take the opposite route by simply opposing to the analytic approach that both shatters and crushes the object an explicitly and emphatically synthetic approach that affirms its glorious unity. This is the properly "reactionary" temptation, the easy way out. In the case that concerns us, it consists of saying that the city is in no way a confused or violent unity, but on the contrary a "beautiful whole." It is to say the opposite of what analytic reason says—this time the object is beautiful—but it is also to say the same thing: the city is a totality whose elements are "fused." Analytic reason and the protest against analytic reason both say or express the same thing, that the city is resistant to analytic reason. But whereas analytic reason penetrates the city violently to reveal its violence, the "reactionary" protest violently repels analytic reason by opposing to it the untouchable integrity of the city.

The capital point is thus to avoid from the start the violence of analysis. In the case that concerns us, this means to avoid the violence of self-evident separation. We need to start from the city that ignores separation, without considering that this "ignorance" is a defect or that it envelops confusion and violence. This is the only way to avoid being "self-centered." In order to escape the self-evident character of separation, we need to start not from the city where politics and religion are "confused," but from the city that is both political and religious—from the city that is both a political community and a religious community. This is still the ancient city, but considered not as a city that hinders or represses a separation that ought to be there but as a community that is inseparably political and religious. If we begin from the phenomena of the ancient city as an inseparably political and religious community, in which the gods are the gods of the city, we observe that where analytic reason saw the clear idea of separation, we necessarily encounter the obscure notion of community. If what we call politics and religion appear as two aspects of the phenomenon of community, we begin to escape the alternative in which analytic reason confines us—either separation or violent confusion—and we can envisage as equally possible or equally "natural" configurations that the political community and the religious community are not differentiated on the one hand, and on the other that they are separated. The only hypothesis implicated by our approach is the plasticity of our communitarian nature, which seems to be at least a plausible hypothesis.

I will not say any more about the ancient city. I examined it at length in part I. My concern here was to show the limits of what analytic reason can achieve and to open another perspective. It was also of course to posit the ancient city as a type, the type of the political community that is inseparably a religious community, because the gods are the gods of the city.

Here an ambiguity immediately arises. In the case where the two communities are not differentiated, where they are *the same,* is it that the political community is also a religious community, or that the religious community is also a political community? One can say that it comes down to the same thing since in both cases the two are the same. But the identity can be looked at in two distinct ways, and this constitutes a logical or notional difference. Of course, these considerations cannot be separated from the historical experience that gives us real examples of these two logical possibilities. The ancient city—where the gods are the gods *of the city*—is an example of the first type. For the second type—where the religious community is also the political community—there is in reality only one example in the Euro-Mediterranean region before the development of Christianity and Islam: the community of the Jews defined as the people *of God.*

In the Jewish experience the people comes to be as a people, is fashioned as a people, by the loving and provident design—the Providence—of the one God. If, in the Greek experience, the political community is in the foreground and the gods are many (in reality, their number is indefinite), in the Jewish experience, God, as the one and only true God, comes first, and it is as a consequence of this oneness of God that the people, his people, is unique, that is, "chosen" or "elect." It is elected among the "nations."[20] Since it is unique among the nations, it is separated from them by the "hedge of the Torah," the Law that separates this people and demands their separation.

These remarks are extremely summary, but we immediately see what the Christian proposition has in common with the Jewish proposition: the religious association as communion is the product of the initiative of the one true God, the same one true God who seeks to covenant with humans, and in consequence it forms a unique community, distinct from all others and especially from the innumerable political bodies. In this sense or in this measure the Christian communion is made on the Jewish model. The difference is that the Christian communion does not constitute a visibly circumscribed people among the innumerable peoples, but on the contrary tends to embrace all nations—when Paul abandoned the Synagogue to become a Christian he made himself the "apostle of the nations." The Church is indeed visible but it is even more invisible: as Augustine emphasizes, some who are visibly outside and who even persecute the Church will be among the elect and in that sense already belong to it invisibly; some who visibly take part in its sacraments will be among the reprobate and in this sense are already invisibly alienated from it.[21] Behind the visible plurality of the innumerable nations, there is an invisible duality, the duality between people animated by love of self and those who are animated by love of God: "two cities were created by two kinds of love: the earthly city was created by self-love reaching the point of contempt for God, the Heavenly City by the love of God carried as far as contempt of self."[22] Behind the visible plurality of the innumerable nations, there are essentially two cities, the earthly city and the heavenly city, the city of men and the city of God. These cities constitute the subject of Augustine's great treatise.

Augustine's *City of God*

I made rapid mention of what Christianity has in common with the Jewish experience, namely the idea of a close and even intimate covenant between God and his creatures, and how they differ. Whereas the Jewish people is zealous to separate itself from the nations, the Church is zealous to convert them. Now the Christian project, if I may speak of it so, deployed itself in a world where the "nations"—all or nearly all the nations—were already united *politically* in the framework of the Roman Empire, such that the Christian Church, in spite of its indifference or disdain for the "world," found itself very dependent for its missionary action on a specific and even unique, indeed extraordinary, political development that was altogether of this world, which was the establishment of the Roman Empire.

For Augustine, a citizen of the Roman Empire, the question of the worth and meaning of the empire and of the Roman experience more generally is at the heart of *The City of God.* One could say that in this treatise Augustine identifies the meaning of the Christian experience through a permanent comparison with the Roman experience that he simultaneously strives to delineate. The second aspect of his undertaking interests us almost as much as the first for, as we have seen at great length in part II, the question of the meaning of the Roman experience is one of the most difficult of all questions. As I emphasized, we are lacking a "science of Rome" that would have the solid principles and clear contours of the other political sciences at our disposal, which are, to repeat once more, Greek political science—the science of the Greek city and its regime—and modern political science, which is basically the science of the modern State that is the guarantor of human rights. This "science of Rome" would provide an account first of all of the transition from the city to the empire. We have seen well enough in discussing the theses of Leo Strauss that this transition cannot be understood simply as a change of regime.[23] Elaborating such a science was not within Augustine's plan when he embarked on composing *The City of God.* However, for reasons we will shortly consider more precisely, his plan required that he take into account the Roman experience as a whole, from Romulus to the Christian Church.[24] If we take seriously the element of political analysis in it, his undertaking is in part a contribution to this science. Moreover, taken according to its principal objective, this undertaking yields a novel and particularly interesting matter for us, since Augustine describes a human association that is neither a city nor an empire, but one that, animated by a principle of its own, is complete and self-sufficient, which is the Church. In our perspective, we will say that with the description of the city of God Augustine offers us a novel and unique political form that probably neither ancient nor modern political science can adequately grasp.

We are thus incited to consider the Church from a somewhat unusual point of view, which is as a political association—with the adjective used here not in a weak or metaphorical meaning but in a strong and full sense. Immediately, a significant succession of political forms—the "Roman series"—takes shape under our eyes: the city, the empire, the Church. The city is characterized by the intensity of the association, the empire by its extent. The Church for its part seeks to constitute a more intense and more intimate association than the city, and that is yet at the same time more extended than the empire. It is not for us to consider the validity—the truth—of this claim of the Church. The Church is of interest to us as a novel human association, a novel political form. This form is elucidated with the greatest breadth and precision in Augustine's *City of God*.

The occasion that gave rise to the composition of *The City of God* is well known. On August 24, 410, Alaric's Visigoths entered Rome after having long threatened and laid siege to it, and pillaged it for three days before going on to pillage elsewhere. This "fall of Rome" was not a great political event since the emperor Honorius and his administration had several years earlier retired to Ravenna. And the empire survived what was in the end but an episode. However, the symbolic impact was huge within the Roman world, above all paradoxically in those parts further removed from Rome, as the letters of Saint Jerome, who by then had retired to Bethlehem, bear witness. Above all, the event contributed to sharpen and crystallize the debate on the significance, bearing, and consequences of the new times, the *tempora christiana,* for the fate of Rome, the most glorious and complete human association, the human association par excellence. Let us recall that at the beginning of the fourth century Constantine had authorized Christianity in the empire (by the Edict of Milan in 313) and that at the end of the century Theodosius had supported the Church, in Augustine's words, "against the ungodly by just and compassionate legislation."[25] The "fall of Rome" in 410 raised more pointed questions about the political effects of this political victory of Christianity. There were accusations that the newly established religion had disarmed Rome.[26] It was in this context that Augustine embarked on his great work.

To adequately answer the enemies of Christianity, Augustine has to deploy the complete and true meaning of the new religion. He begins by considering the effects of Christianity on the old city, by attempting to show that they are good rather than bad, but he can do that only by accepting the perspective of the old city up to a certain point. He must then, on the other hand, show that the new religion not only introduces modifications in the life and mores of Rome, but that it truly brings about a new city whose principles or wellsprings are radically distinct and different from those of the old Rome. When one reads *The City of God*, especially the first books, one must not lose sight that Augustine is engaged there in the particularly difficult exercise of defending the new city before the tribunal of the old, all the while setting up the tribunal of the new whose laws and principles are very different from those of the old and are even opposed to them. He summons the new city to appear before the tribunal of the old, all the while setting up the new tribunal that judges the old city. Augustine lets us see—on a very large screen, dare I say—the intrinsic and perhaps insurmountable difficulty of any Christian statement about politics.

Here in very brief outline is the plan of *The City of God*:

Books 1–5—refutation of those who believe that worship of the pagan gods is a necessary condition to the prosperity of human affairs and who explain present miseries by the prohibition of this worship

Books 6–10—refutation of those who defend worship of the pagan gods not for the sake of this life but in view of the future life

Books 11–14—the origins of the two cities

Books 15–18—their progress and development

Books 19–22—the ultimate ends of the two cities and the triumph of the heavenly city

It is easy to be unjust toward the first books of *The City of God*. The polemic against the adversaries seems exaggerated, overdone, redundant. Augustine, one is tempted to say, is piling it on. We need, however, to consider the following facts.

Whether we are Christians or not, and even if we are very hostile to Christianity, we do not take paganism seriously. By paganism I mean the pagan religion with its innumerable gods and goddesses. The "neopagans" among us, those who celebrate the solstice and dance around the fire, are really very few in number. The progressivism at the root of the modern representation of history forces us to consider, willy-nilly, that the victory of Christianity over paganism represents a "historical advance," that Christian monotheism is "superior to" polytheism, either because it constitutes the true religion or because it is more rational and prepares from afar the modern emancipation from all religion. Popular and effective paganism holds no interest for us and we are inclined to underestimate the force of its resistance, its "resilience," in Augustine's time. Just because the innumerable petty gods are boring to us does not mean that they were not very important to Augustine's contemporaries. By taking into account their gods at length, even to mock them, Augustine was taking his contemporaries seriously.

We moreover need to make an effort of the imagination, to try to recapture for ourselves the political context. The fall of Rome at the hands of the barbarians was a humiliating defeat for the Romans, accompanied by the misery and violent deeds that ordinarily follow defeats. In this kind of situation, there is always a question that is passionately debated: who is responsible for the defeat? The most diverse arguments are exchanged, with little consideration not only for the truth, but for the most elementary likelihood. The most popular argument, the most persuasive answer to the question of responsibility in the eyes of those who suffer defeat, is often that they have been stabbed in the back. To face up to such a situation, to answer accusations that are sometimes odious or absurd but at times subtle, engages one in a long and complex response, along a gamut of arguments that range from the most brutal, even vulgar, to the most refined. If we take these elements into account, if we take the political context truly seriously, we will be less inclined to find Augustine's polemic tedious or excessive and more disposed to read him carefully.

If one thinks that equating the sack of Rome in 410 to a great defeat exaggerates the significance of the event, one will say simply that with the substitution of Christianity for paganism as the religion of the empire, Rome experienced a very important change of regime. Certain members of the political class, if I may speak of it so, were persuaded that this change produced a weakening and a degradation of the Roman political body. Against them Augustine wanted to show that on the contrary the change brought progress and amelioration. The question then is whether the *tempora christiana* are better than the earlier epochs. The preamble (*praefatio*) is intensely political: Augustine's concern is to *defend* a city—the city of God—against those who "prefer their own gods to the Founder of that city." Augustine emphasizes that the difficulty of his task is "to convince the proud of the power and the excellence of humility." The king and founder of this city ("rex et conditor civitatis hujus") has revealed its meaning and goal in the Scriptures of his people: "God resists the proud but he gives grace to the humble." Now, the earthly city, especially the proudest earthly city, loves to appropriate this goal, this intention, to itself and to boast about it; Rome attributed to itself the special calling to "spare the conquered and beat down the proud." One can grasp the difficulty of the task of persuading the pride of those who ascribe to themselves the mission to tame the proud. The external force and the internal weakness of the earthly city consist in its being dominated by the passion to dominate *(libido dominandi)*.

The debate concerns first of all or especially the cruelties committed during the sack of Rome. Augustine is indignant that some, who escaped death thanks to a new clemency encouraged by Christianity, impute the miseries that struck the city to the same Christianity: "many escaped who now complain of this Christian era, and hold Christ responsible for the disasters which their city endured."[27] These woes are indeed real, but they belong to the custom of war: *mos bellorum, consuetudo bellorum*. There is nothing new in this. What is new is that fierce barbarians, *contrary to the custom of war,* spared a great number of inhabitants of Rome by respecting the immunity of vast sanctuaries consecrated to the name of Christ. That must be ascribed to Christian times. What elsewhere would have been allowed by the law of war was forbidden in these consecrated temples or places.

Augustine wants to establish that the respect of asylums was something entirely without precedent in human history. He bases himself on Roman documentation that he reads with great care. Citing the *Aeneid,* he recalls that the Greeks had no respect whatever for the Trojan temples and altars. This allows him to turn the accusation back on his opponents: the pagan gods were unable to protect Troy. The statue of Minerva itself was captured by the Greeks after they had massacred its guardians. She was adored so that she would watch over the country and its citizens, yet she was powerless to guard even her own guardians.[28] Thus Rome confided its fate to "conquered gods." It is wiser to believe not that Rome would have averted this latest disaster if its gods had not perished before it, but that they would have perished long since if Rome had not done the impossible to preserve them. By citing Virgil, Augustine appeals to the authority of the greatest Latin poet. But what authority can even the greatest poet have to decide a question of fact when everyone knows that poets often lie? Augustine suggests that a story so unfavorable to Rome—the city took "conquered gods" as protector gods—could not have been invented; and so Virgil is to be believed. When they evoke these facts, the Latin poets are not liars, but people of good faith who were constrained by the truth to acknowledge this.[29]

In order to establish the universal character of not respecting asylums in the sacking of cities, Augustine is not content with the testimony of the poets, even though he begins with Virgil and treats him at greatest length, no doubt because the name of Virgil commanded the greatest authority. He also mobilizes the historians, in particular Sallust,[30] but also, without naming him, Livy. The review leaves no doubt in his eyes: if the Roman historians, who give precise accounts of the capture of numerous cities and willingly recall the acts of Roman clemency that could be observed, at no point make any mention of the temples' inviolability, this is because such a respect was entirely unknown at the time since it was contrary to or foreign to the *consuetudo bellorum*. What has just happened at Rome testifies to a new custom (*mos novus*), "something which changed the whole aspect of the scene."[31] This change must be attributed to "Christian times."

The Justification of Providence

Augustine's considerations represent one of the first efforts in a genre filled with difficulties, one to which historians and sociologists, following the theologians or alongside them, will contribute: the examination of the effects of Christianity on the lives of men. As is well known, this examination leads authors to very different and at times opposing conclusions. What interests us here in the first place is the Christian viewpoint. It is natural enough that a Christian author like Augustine judges these effects to be positive and draws attention to the happy modification of the "face of things" brought by Christianity. It should be noted that Augustine is here *responding* to an accusation. This development is a defense rather than an illustration of Christianity. How could a religion that announces and brings about the true good not improve the life of humans? However, at this point a difficulty arises that Augustine's perspective allows us to grasp clearly. The amelioration brought by Christianity could only be indirect, for its intent is not to introduce a new religion into the world in order to improve the world, but to introduce people into a new city in order to sanctify them. The amelioration of human life that we speak of can concern only this zone of uncertain status situated at the interface or intersection of the two cities. And if Christians can legitimately expect to observe indirect positive effects, they will not be surprised at times to notice indirect negative effects: by troubling the vicious functioning of the earthly city through the good it brings, Christianity is susceptible of hindering the good effects that the vicious city can produce. Good and bad effects could at times appear as the two opposite and inseparable aspects of the same phenomenon. For Machiavelli, for example, the softening of mores induced by "our religion" entails a softening of the civic virtues and thus a degradation of the conditions of common life.

Let us come back to the text of Augustine, who by emphasizing the softening of the "custom of war" that is due to Christianity accomplishes the easiest part of his task and now encounters the difficulties implied in the genre he has begun to execute, which is the justification of Providence.[32] He has just severely reprimanded those pagan ingrates who impute the fall of Rome to Christianity when they owe their safety to the same Christianity. But the argument in favor of the religion is immediately transformed into an argument that calls it into question: "why does the divine mercy extend even to the godless and ungrateful?" Augustine replies: "God, in his providence . . . has willed that these temporal goods and temporal evils should befall good and bad alike, so that the good things should not be too eagerly coveted, when it is seen that the wicked also enjoy them, and that the evils should not be discreditably shunned, when it is apparent that the good are often afflicted with them."[33] One could say that if God did not treat the good and the bad equally or nearly equally in what concerns temporal goods and evils, even the good would be incited to desire the first excessively and to fear the second excessively. The argument considerably limits the extent of the visible improvements that Providence can bring to the lot of humans: if God were more visibly just, he would reward the just more visibly and thereby risk corrupting them by making them love those goods excessively that reward justice so visibly and so certainly. It is in treating the good and the bad in the same way concerning temporal goods and evils that God is just or makes justice possible, for it is in the way they receive temporal goods and evils that men become good or bad, just or unjust: "what matters is the nature of the sufferer, not the nature of the suffering."[34] If the world were "more just," the notion of justice would lose its meaning.

The following chapter completes and inflects the argument. The distinction between the just and the unjust—which is at the root of the reproaches against Providence—is maintained, but it is looked at more closely. It is not only that those who lead a most praiseworthy life are not without faults, but more precisely that they refrain from instructing or warning or—as at times they should—from rebuking and correcting those who misbehave.[35] One could say that good people who complain of Providence, or to Providence, are asking it to exercise a justice whose execution falls to them in the first place; they passively complain of the injustice of those whom they ought actively to correct.

Why this passivity, not only of "the weaker brothers in the married state, who have children or look to have them, who are masters of houses and households," but also of "those who have a higher standard of life"?[36] It is rooted in a certain laziness and in the fear of offending people who can do harm by attacking those goods that the just use legitimately and innocently, but with more avidity than is appropriate.[37] Thus, the good and the wicked both are struck not because they live together in evil but because they both love this temporal life,[38] not equally to be sure, but yet with a similar love. Now, the good ought to disdain this life so as to be in a position to reprimand and correct the wicked and thus to gain for them eternal life. Augustine adds this, which is striking: "if [the bad] refused to be partners in this enterprise [ad quam consequendam si nollent esse socii], they ought to be borne with, and loved as Christians should love their enemies [ferrentur et diligerentur inimici] since in this life it is always uncertain whether or not they are likely to experience a change of heart." Augustine's language, one can see, is political: *socii, inimici.* Justice is not simply an individual disposition; it implies participation in an active association that is militant and combative and that ignores immobility as well as neutrality. One must add, however, that Augustine concludes chapter 9 by considering the lot of the individual human soul: as the example of Job shows, affliction is for the good a means to chastise themselves and to know with what intense piety and selflessness they love God.[39]

The two themes Augustine took up here, the softening of mores produced by Christianity on the one hand and the reticence of good Christians to publicly challenge the wicked on the other, will undergo numerous subsequent developments. They condense two great stakes in the discussions concerning Christianity, or, more precisely perhaps, they are two ways of approaching the question of the political and moral effects of Christianity. Here Machiavelli would be the most interesting author to consider, since, as I was recalling, he fused the two themes to produce the most implacable charge against Christianity: it is precisely the softening of mores one credits to Christianity that is the cause of the injustice or immorality—of the victory of the wicked—and that is otherwise lamented.[40]

Machiavelli also ascribes to Christianity a development of an altogether different nature. Speaking of Ferdinand of Aragon, the "Catholic king," and after recalling how he had reconquered the kingdom of Granada from the Moors, he writes: "Besides this, in order to undertake greater enterprises, always making use of religion, he turned to an act of pious cruelty, expelling the Marranos from his kingdom and despoiling it of them; nor could there be an example more wretched and rarer than this."[41] For Machiavelli, "our religion" brought both a new cruelty—a "pious cruelty"—and a new softness, which is in sum worse, since now that men are no longer exposed to the *consuetudo bellorum,* they are no longer forced, or they are less forced, to fight with all their might against enemies who are now inclined to spare them. In this perspective, Christianity offers a bad combination of cruelty and softness, and one looks to the ancient pagans as offering a good combination of harshness and moderation, or clemency.[42] In short, these critics judge Christianity the way Jacques Bainville judged the Treaty of Versailles: too harsh for being soft, too soft for being harsh.

Augustine and the Machiavellian tradition are thus critical of a certain passivity of Christians in the face of the "wicked." But they impute this passivity to different causes: the Machiavellian tradition to resignation to the divine will and respect for the order willed by God,[43] Augustine to a too-great though not necessarily culpable attachment to the goods of this world. The two interpretations are not incompatible. Together they help to delimit a certain defect in self-knowledge to which Christians are exposed, for they can easily interpret their timidity in the face of evil, motivated by too much attachment to "possessions," as piety respectful of the divine order.

The Suicide of Lucretia

Among the woes that followed in the wake of the sack of Rome was of course the fate of the women. Rape was part of the *consuetudo bellorum* and Alaric's troops, despite their new softness, on this score behaved according to custom. Some women preferred to take their own lives than to submit to such outrage. What human heart ("quis humanus affectus") would refuse to pardon such an act that in itself is a crime, a homicide? Conversely, it would be mindless to make accusations against those women who did not want to take their lives, thus refusing to avoid by this crime the crime of another.[44] Thus Augustine does not judge persons. This reserve does not prevent him from then engaging in a detailed analysis—more detailed at times than we would like—of the moral problems involved in the experience of suffering rape. As he himself states, our argument ("nostra disputatio") will have to pursue a very narrow course "between the claims of modesty and reasoned argument (inter pudorem atque rationem)."[45] In order to attain a proper understanding of chastity *(pudicitia),* one has to conquer or overcome modesty or shame *(pudor)* up to a certain point. In fact, the fault or error of women who commit suicide to avoid rape resides in the confusion between *pudicitia* and *pudor.* More precisely, *pudicitia* knows how to distinguish between the soul and the body, the voluntary and involuntary, whereas *pudor* tends to confuse them. The fundamental point is the following: a woman has nothing in her to punish by a voluntary death when, raped without any consent on her part, she is the victim of another's sin.[46]

To develop his analysis, Augustine detaches himself from the drama that has just unfolded and considers, or reconsiders, a famous case, perhaps the most famous case of suicide for the sake of chastity or shame, the case of Lucretia.

Lucretia was traditionally the object of high praise at Rome. She was for the Romans a heroine of chastity. Augustine begins by confirming the accepted evaluation of Lucretia. Is she to be judged adulterous or chaste? Who would find it difficult to answer this question? And he cites "someone [who] puts the truth well in a declamation on this subject: 'They were two persons involved, and only one committed adultery.'"

Then Augustine shows things in an entirely different light. He addresses the laws and judges of Rome. A chaste and innocent woman has been killed. He charges them to pronounce sentence against the guilty party. But the guilty one is this chaste and innocent woman; it is Lucretia herself. Surely, you cannot have her stand before you to punish her, but why praise her? Why praise so emphatically the murderer of a chaste and innocent woman?

Now, Augustine will raise questions that cause *pudor* to blush. He treads where we hesitate to go. Perhaps Lucretia knew something we cannot know? Perhaps she knew she was not innocent, having experienced pleasure in spite of the violence of the act? Herein lies the dilemma: if she consented in some measure to the adultery, why praise her? If she remained chaste, why did she kill herself?[47]

But Augustine does not want to envisage this possibility any further. He abandons it. He willingly recognizes that Lucretia had no part in this crime in which she was but a victim. The question nonetheless returns: Why then did she kill herself? What was the motive of this deed? Augustine answers: "It was due to the weakness of shame, not the high value she set on chastity [non est pudicitiae caritas, sed pudoris infirmitas]." As I pointed out, *pudor* differs from *pudicitia* in that it confuses the soul and the body, the voluntary and the involuntary. It perpetrates this confusion because it sees things from the outside as others see them or rather do not see them, since they are incapable of seeing what goes on in the soul. Lucretia was "a Roman woman, excessively eager for honor."[48] She feared lest her fellow citizens should believe she had some part in the crime. That is why she presented her death to the eyes of men as a witness to her thought since she could not show them the secret of her conscience ("conscientiam demonstrare non potuit").[49] By this deed Lucretia attempted the impossible, to reveal what cannot be revealed, what remains necessarily invisible. This is an impossible undertaking, but an almost irresistible temptation for a woman of honor.

The Christian women who experienced the same violence—Augustine returns to the present circumstances—are still alive, having refused to add a crime to the crimes of others. They are content with the testimony of their conscience ("testimonium conscientiae"). They are innocent before their conscience, and also before God.[50] Excessive concern for human opinion—for "honor"—led a noble woman to make of herself the murderer of a noble woman. Faith in the true God allowed the Christian women to be content with the testimony of their conscience, sparing them the crime of homicide against themselves. Conscience, as it was recognized or brought out, perhaps even produced by Christianity, liberates the human soul from the tyrannical grip of honor and public praise.

This is not the place to examine the notion of conscience, to ask in particular if or to what extent it is specifically, even exclusively, a Christian notion. I would like only to make a remark that is directly linked to our context. There is nothing biased in the Augustinian analysis of the "Lucretia case." It repeats in sum what Livy had Lucretia herself say. Lucretia knew very well how to distinguish between the body and the innocent soul, between the *corpus violatum* and *animus insons,* and, in a striking agreement of the pagan author and the Christian author, has her make of her death the *testis* of her innocence. The inflection or rupture between paganism and Christianity is indeed to be found where Augustine situates it: not in the rigorous distinction between body and soul—the already ancient achievement of Greek philosophy—but in the capacity to act according to this distinction. One could not state the matter more clearly than Lucretia herself does: "as for me I am innocent of fault, but I will take my punishment [ego me etsi peccato absolvo, supplicio non libero]."[51] She adds immediately after: "Never shall Lucretia provide a precedent for unchaste women to escape what they deserve." Honor suicide, which honorable women teach one another, is the only way to render effective a sentiment of innocence that cannot suffice by itself. When Augustine writes that the Christian women who did not follow the example of Lucretia "have the glory of chastity within them, the testimony of their conscience,"[52] we can get the impression that he gives way to a pomposity that distorts rather than reveals the phenomenon he intends to clarify. But his language that is to us declamatory, forging equality between "the glory of chastity" and "the testimony of conscience," between glory and conscience, ought to draw our attention to the significance of the moral transformation that was induced or at least confirmed and solidified by Christianity. If there is a glory of chastity, of the internal awareness of innocence, it is because the interior is now sufficiently real and strong to balance the power and authority of the exterior, of external opinion. The interior has acquired enough being and force not only to "absolve oneself from sin," but also to act according to this awareness and "free oneself of the punishment."

To explore a bit the question of conscience, it will be useful to say a word about the comic reversal of the tragedy of Lucretia that Machiavelli accomplished in his comedy, *Mandragola*, composed in 1518.

Livy's narrative provides the thread of a tragedy of honor: Lucretia kills herself *because* she is innocent. The Christian critique of human honor as developed by Augustine resolves the contradiction of honor and puts an end to tragedy by establishing the power of conscience. In the Machiavellian transformation it is Lucretia herself, in any case a new Lucrezia, who consents, if not to rape, at least to a sexual relation she had at first repelled with horror and indignation, in order to from then on live in accord with her interest and pleasure, to live "free," as we would say today, and no longer according to the rules of ancient honor or of the Christian conscience. The pivot of this transformation is a manipulation of her conscience.[53]

In Machiavelli as in Livy the story begins with a beauty contest, or more precisely a very animated discussion among several young men on the question of where or who is the most beautiful and virtuous woman. The identification, then the sight, of this woman arouse in one of the young men an irrepressible and obsessive desire to obtain her. For Sextus Tarquin as for Callimaco, the problem is the same: Lucretia, or Lucrezia, is married, and she is virtue itself. What is to be done? Tarquin simply has recourse to force.[54] Callimaco, who is perhaps an example of the softening of mores favored by Christianity, intends only to seduce her. Whereas Lucretia is *killed* by the very principle of her virtue—honor—Lucrezia is *corrupted* by hers, which is conscience.

It is not possible here to summarize the intrigue of *Mandragola*. Here is the heart of the matter. It concerns persuading Lucrezia, who is keen to become pregnant, to drink a mandrake potion that is supposed to cure her infertility. The undesirable effect of this potion is that "the man who first has to do with her after she has taken this potion dies within eight days, and all the world can't save him."[55] This argument easily suffices to persuade the old husband to cede his legitimate place to the young lover just this one time, which, one does not doubt, will be but the first of many others.

How did the virtuous Lucrezia let herself be persuaded to act against her conscience? Everyone was involved in the matter, including her mother and her husband. But it was obviously the intervention of her confessor, Frate Timoteo, that was decisive. He alone possessed the authority to persuade her that she could commit adultery in full assurance of her conscience. Here is the decisive passage of his intervention:

> As to the conscience, you have to take this general principle: that where there is a certain good and an uncertain evil, one should never leave that good for fear of that evil. Here is a certain good, that you should become pregnant, will acquire a soul for our Lord. The uncertain evil is that the one who will lie with you after you take the potion may die; but those who don't die are also found. But because the thing is doubtful, it is therefore well that Messer Nicia not run that risk. As to the act, that it might be a sin, this is a fable, because the will is what sins, not the body; and what causes it to be a sin is displeasing your husband—but you please him, taking pleasure in it—but you have no pleasure from it. Besides this, the end has to be looked to in all things; your end is to fill a seat in paradise, to make your husband happy. The Bible says that the daughters of Lot, believing themselves alone in the world, lay with their father; and because their intention was good, they didn't sin.[56]

Machiavelli here has us assist at the corruption of the Christian conscience, which thereby he favors and so to speak teaches. What is the difference between the Christian conscience and the Christian conscience that is corrupted or on the way to corruption?

For the Christian conscience, the testimony of conscience is enough. If she had not succumbed to corruption, Lucrezia would have simply told Frate Timoteo: I see clearly that the action you recommend to me is contrary to the law of God. Speak no more of it to me.

On the road to corruption, the conscience becomes active and calculating. It no longer simply judges the action; it directs the intention. Instead of being the incorruptible *testis,* it becomes itself corrupting in di-
recting the intention so as to authorize actions that are most contrary to
the divine law.

As can be seen, Machiavelli attacks not only the political effects of
Christianity. With the enemy's skill, he goes to the heart of the Christian
operation. Intelligently sacrilegious, he brings about a conscience's corruption by the director of conscience. Machiavelli makes the principle
that for Augustine sums up the moral progress brought about by Christian times into the wellspring of a novel corruption.

The Problem of Cato

In concluding his analysis of the case of Lucretia, Augustine emphasizes
that the prohibition against killing has no exception, "for to kill oneself
is to kill a human being."[57]

Of course, this rule that admits no exception does admit some exceptions. They are of two kinds: when God himself has expressly given the
command to kill, as he did to Abraham, or when the order was given by
legitimate political authorities, the repositories of public power ("personam gerentes publicae potestatis").[58] It seems to me that there is some
uncertainty in Augustine's text that at times seems to include within the
orders of God the political law that commands that criminals be killed
on a par with God's orders directed toward a specific person, and at
other times seems to clearly distinguish the political law and the command of God, bringing out the contrast between the generality of the
former and the specific character of the latter. However that may be, in
both cases, the one who kills is not the one who kills: "one who owes a
duty of obedience to the giver of the command does not himself 'kill.'"[59]

Augustine has to face one last objection: suicide is perhaps never just
or wise, but at least it testifies to a greatness of spirit *(magnitudo animi)*
that is worthy of admiration. Augustine at first seems disposed to make
this concession, but he withdraws it immediately. If one reasons more
closely about the problem, it becomes clear that such an action indicates
rather "weakness in a mind which cannot bear physical oppression, or
the stupid opinion of the mob."[60]

There is one case, however, Augustine goes on to say, where suicide seems to result from greatness of spirit: the case of Theombrotus. After reading Plato's book dealing with the immortality of the soul, Theombrotus, or Cleombrotus, hurled himself from a wall and so passed from this life to a life that he believed to be better. Why is Augustine disposed to speak of greatness of spirit in his case? Because Theombrotus did not intend to flee any misfortune, or any guilt, real or imputed: he was not fleeing any evil. He only wanted to attain a better life; he sought what was better.[61] His choice had the structure so to speak of a good choice, a wise decision. Yet it was not a good choice or a wise decision. Why? Augustine's reply is a bit disappointing in that it is an appeal to human authority: Plato himself was witness that Cleombrotus's act "showed greatness rather than goodness," since "the same intelligence which gave him his vision of the soul's immortality enabled him to decide that this step was not to be taken—was, indeed, to be forbidden."[62]

One senses that Augustine has some difficulty refuting the argument from greatness of spirit, according to which suicide, in certain cases at least, is the sign and the effect of a great spirit. But Cleombrotus is not really the problem: he is an academic case, used or invented to illustrate an argument, to fill a space in the scheme of possible human actions. There is a case that is much more serious in the eyes of a serious Roman, more serious even than the case of Lucretia. What is the most famous suicide in all of Roman history? It is obviously that of Cato, who exemplifies the nobility of republican life, the greatness of republican virtue. The name of Cato, Augustine concedes at the start of his analysis, carries *auctoritas*. Because Cato was held to be a wise and learned man ("vir doctus et probus"),[63] it was thought quite naturally that his deed was worthy of being imitated.

How then does Augustine depreciate, debase, or discredit Cato's glory? He begins by saying rather lamely that Cato's friends, themselves also *docti quidam viri,* strove to dissuade him from such a resolve, esteeming that it was the sign of a weak rather than a strong spirit. But then comes the argument that decides the matter for Augustine. Cato himself advised his son to go on living and to place his hopes in Caesar's kindness: "Why did he counsel such a shameful course, if it was shameful to live under the shadow of Caesar's victory?"[64] Cato would never have commended to his son a conduct that he himself would have judged intrinsically shameful or culpable. What then was the real well-spring of Cato's suicide? Here is how Augustine identifies the motives that determined Cato's action in his last hour: "he loved his son, for whom he hoped and wished for Caesar's pardon, as much as he grudged the praise that Caesar would win by sparing his own life. . . . Perhaps we may put it more gently, and say that Cato would have been embarrassed at receiving Caesar's pardon."[65] According to this interpretation there is nothing republican, no relation with the common good, in the motive of Cato's suicide. It was a supremely personal motive. Whether the accent is on envy of Caesar's glory or shame at owing him life, it is always a rivalry of glory. What Augustine implies is that there is no greatness in such a selfish motive.

We know that Cato's suicide is a sort of touchstone in the moral and political history of Europe. We have already dealt with the evaluation of Cicero, who justifies Cato's conduct by his "proper nature," marked by an *incredibilis gravitas* which made it impossible for Cato "to have to look at the face of a tyrant."[66] Let us briefly compare Cicero's analysis with that of Augustine. It is certainly more favorable to Cato. Cicero follows, dare I say, the party line, the line of the good party, the party of the *boni*: the wellspring of Cato's conduct is to be found in his opposition to a tyrant. Cato must leave a world where he would be forced to look at the *face* of the tyrant. This adds perhaps a more personal color to political opposition. In any case, in comparison with Cicero, Augustine intensifies the face-to-face to the point where it loses its political character: Augustine's Cato does not have before him a tyrant but someone who threatens to spare him, to let him live when he could easily take his life. Surely one can call the power to take or give life tyrannical, but Augustine's accent falls elsewhere. To spare a life that could be taken is glorious, and Cato envies Caesar that glory. Cato cannot stand owing his life to Caesar. He cannot stand this humiliation. The only way to escape this humiliation and to deprive Caesar of the glory of sparing him is to kill himself. By sparing him, Caesar would become his master; by killing himself, he deprives Caesar of his mastery and in that measure he defeats him. He defeats him in the competition for glory. Augustine's interpretation, as I have stated, depoliticizes the confrontation between Cato and Caesar. But in Cicero's interpretation politics was already *in statu evanescendi,* since the justification of Cato's deed resided in his own individual

246 EMPIRE, CHURCH, NATION

nature and not in the common good. If Cato had sacrificed himself for the common good, his deed could have and should have been imitated. But as I have emphasized, there was no longer a common good. All that remained for Cato was to be faithful to himself, to imitate himself by an inimitable deed.

In our earlier analysis of Cicero's evaluation of Cato, we encountered Montaigne, who throughout the *Essays* again and again reflects on the figure of the republican hero. Here I need to comment on a passage that is particularly interesting for us, since Montaigne directly cites the text of Cicero we have just discussed, while criticizing, without naming Augustine, the text of *The City of God* that was our starting point. Here is the heart of Montaigne's development:

> And if his goodness, which made him embrace the public advantage more than his own, did not hold me in check, I should easily fall into this opinion, that he was grateful to fortune for having put his virtue to so beautiful a test and for having favored that brigand in treading underfoot the ancient liberty of his country. I seem to read in that action I know not what rejoicing of his soul, and an emotion of extraordinary pleasure and manly exultation, when it considered the nobility and sublimity of its enterprise: *Deliberata morte ferocior.* This enterprise was not spurred by some hope of glory, as the plebeian and effeminate judgments of some men have judged (for that consideration is too base to touch a heart so noble, so lofty, and so unbending), but was undertaken for the beauty of the very thing in itself, which he, who handled the springs of it, saw much more clearly in its perfection than we can see it.
>
> Philosophy has given me pleasure by judging that so beautiful an action would have been unbecomingly located in any other life than Cato's, and that it belonged to his alone to end thus. Therefore it was according to reason that he ordered his son and the senators who accompanied him to make some other provision for themselves. *Catoni . . . moriendum potius quam tyranni vultus aspiciendus erat.*[67]

Montaigne repeats very precisely the argument and the very words in which Cicero explained why Cato's deed could not be imitated or, as we would say, generalized. He congratulates "philosophy" for this judgment that confirms the very lofty appreciation he himself has of this deed. And this judgment of philosophy, he insists, shows why it was reasonable for Cato to dissuade his son and the senators who accompanied him from following him in death. But Cicero does not speak of Cato's son; he speaks only of "the others who surrendered to Caesar in Africa [ceteri, qui se in Africa Caesari tradiderunt]." We recall that Cato's son is, on the contrary, at the center of Augustine's attention, in the argument by which he means to show that Cato's conduct was obedient to personal and selfish motives, that it cannot be justified by reason. It is very probable that Montaigne intends here to defend Cato's merits against Augustine's critique. This is all the more probable in that a few lines earlier Montaigne had taken to task "the plebeian and effeminate judgments of some men," who explain Cato's conduct by the "hope of glory." Augustine certainly is among those men. One understands better then why Montaigne evokes "philosophy" a bit grandly and how it provides confirmation for his sentiments: Montaigne's judgment is supported by that of "philosophy" and goes against the "plebeian and effeminate judgments" of theology.

Why "plebeian and effeminate judgments"? What is "plebeian and effeminate" in the judgment that explains Cato's suicide by "some hope of glory"? Montaigne adds immediately: "for that consideration is too base to touch a heart so noble, so lofty, and so unbending." And to an action done for glory he opposes an action done "for the beauty of the very thing in itself." This is what "plebeian and effeminate judgments" cannot conceive: an action done for the beauty—the "nobility" and the "loftiness"—of the action itself. Common people and women cannot grasp human motives that rise above utility or self-interest, of which the quest for glory is but one expression. Montaigne silently envelops Augustine and theology in his harsh judgment of the two great categories of human beings that according to "manly" opinion constitute the principal support of religion.

We will not attempt to choose between Augustine's and Montaigne's interpretations. I will however raise one difficulty in Montaigne's, one that he himself moreover acknowledges with a smile. If it is the beauty and the difficulty of the deed that motivate Cato, then concern for the public good necessarily takes a back seat. Cato even finds himself in the thorny position of being "grateful to fortune for having put his virtue to so beautiful a test" by favoring Caesar's undertaking against freedom. If that is the case, one would have to admit that in a corner of his soul Cato was rejoicing over the misfortunes of the country that gave him the occasion to exercise such rare virtue. It seems clear in any case that in Montaigne's eyes the determining motive of Cato's last and greatest deed did not principally concern the country or the common good.

As for Augustine, the judgment he makes of Cato does not exhaust his appreciation of Roman politics or the Roman spirit. Augustine's approach is not reducible to the "demolition of the pagan hero." For there is another Roman hero whose sacrifice was not a suicide though it could appear as such and whom Augustine regards with favor, even with admiration bordering on enthusiasm. That hero was Regulus.

The horrible end of Regulus—his atrocious death freely, deliberately chosen—is proof that the pagan gods do not protect even those who are so scrupulous in their fidelity to their oaths that they not only leave their country but even return to their cruelest enemies.[68] How will the pagan interlocutor to whom Augustine gives voice respond? He switches terrain. He does not defend the gods; he turns to philosophy, or at least he invokes the greatness of the individual spirit. Regulus could be happy, even in the midst of these horrible tortures, thanks to the virtue of his spirit. Yet Augustine refuses to enter the discussion so familiar to the Ancients about the happiness of the wise man.[69] His intention is not to establish the nature of Regulus's virtue.[70] Rather, he suggests that one look for the true virtue that is also capable of ensuring the happiness of the city. Herein appears the contradiction of the pagans. They glory in counting in their ranks a citizen such as Regulus and they fear having a city that resembles him. Why does Augustine say that the pagans fear having a city that resembles Regulus? What would a city that resembles Regulus be? It would be a city whose citizens are not concerned with this life and are ready to leave the city where they were born in obedience to the gods. It would be the city of people who are pilgrims on the earth. That looks very much like the city of the Christians.

Augustine takes up again the figure of Regulus after having considered the suicides of Lucretia and Cato. He declares he "should put Marcus Regulus above Marcus Cato" based on what the Romans themselves say of their two heroes.[71] Instead of killing himself out of pride and jealousy for glory, as did Cato, Regulus preferred to suffer the slavery and torture of his enemies rather than avoid them through death. This he did to obey the gods. Thus the most courageous and illustrious defenders of the earthly country, though they worshipped false gods, were nonetheless not false worshippers and they even kept their oaths very faithfully.[72] Whereas Cato, in spite of the greatness of spirit that might be granted him, remained a prisoner of pagan pride—or pagan vainglory—Regulus is the example of those defenders of the earthly country whose sacrifice and virtues tear down the walls of this prison, or almost tear them down, or would tear them down if that were simply possible. Paganism and Christianity exclude and in a sense oppose one another—as pride and humility exclude and oppose one another. Christianity came to break and to heal pagan pride. This is the axis of *The City of God*. But Regulus is the almost unbelievable figure—unbelievable for the pagans, unbelievable for the Christians—of a paganism on the point of overcoming itself, of an earthly city in process of becoming—but it is impossible—a heavenly city.

The Causes of the Greatness of the Romans

As we have just seen, Augustine is as harsh on Cato as he is generous regarding Regulus. This is his ambivalence, the Christian ambivalence with respect to pagan greatness. We will find confirmation of this divided disposition in Augustine's overall appreciation of the Roman Empire, of what we could call the whole of the Roman phenomenon.

Book 5 is devoted to studying the causes of expansion of the Roman Empire. Augustine inquires: "Let us go on to examine for what moral qualities and for what reason the true God deigned to help the Romans in the extension of their empire; for in his control are all the kingdoms of the earth."[73] The cause of this immense phenomenon resides neither in the caprice of ridiculous or shameful gods nor in blind necessity, but in the free action of humans on the one hand and the Providence of the true God on the other. It is neither chance nor necessity, but human liberty aided by divine Providence. Now, if God aided the Romans, if he deigned to help them, it was because their mores were in some way worthy of this aid. Of course, Augustine does not use the verb "merit" since, according to the theology that he more than anyone else contributed to elaborate, humans could not "merit" divine grace. But it is not properly a question here of divine grace that sanctifies souls but only of the assistance God accords to certain people in their natural capacity, an assistance that, coming from a just God, must obey a law of justice and therefore correspond to a particular merit of the Romans. In any case, Augustine has such little disdain of the achievements of pagan Rome that he declares they were helped by God. But what were these Roman mores, what character in them so motivated the active favor of God? This is what he will examine.

As usual, Augustine's documentation consists of Latin authors. He formulates his thinking through a commentary on Latin authors, in particular Sallust. Yet the term "documentation" is not appropriate here, for he treats these Latin authors as sources not only of information but also of valid and judicious judgments, as authorities. He may complete or extend their judgment, but in the essentials he leaves it to these pagan authors to describe and judge pagan Rome. What then were the Roman mores?

All peoples, with the sole exception of the Jewish people, honored false gods. This then is not proper to the Romans. What was proper to the Romans, according to Sallust, was an extraordinary desire for praise, an extraordinary passion for glory *(cupido gloriae)* that worked wonders. Of course, cupidity as such, including cupidity for glory, if one can use that expression, is a vice rather than a virtue. But among the Romans—and herein lies what is proper to them—this vice became a sort of virtue by its very excess: they suppressed all other desires by the enormity of this one desire.[74] The Romans, in any case the first Romans, were above the weaknesses and vices of most people because they desired glory more than anything else and more than any other people desire it.

How was this love of glory expressed politically? First of all, by a passionate desire to obtain the country's liberty, and then to ensure its domination.[75] Liberty at first, and then domination.

This passage from the desire for liberty to the desire for domination, which seems natural and necessary among the Romans, attracts our attention since for us, as I have noted, liberty and domination are mutually exclusive. A little further, Augustine gives a more precise description of this passage or connection: "The important thing for the men of that time [when the Romans were besieged by the Etruscan allies of Tarquin whom they had expelled] was either to die bravely, or to live in freedom. But when liberty had been won, 'such a passion for glory took hold of them' that liberty alone did not satisfy them—they had to acquire dominion."[76]

It seems that *sola libertas,* once it is acquired, is not enough to quench the passion for glory once it has been lit—lit probably by the very effort to regain liberty. On this point Augustine, no more than the Latin authors he follows, does not seek to state more precisely the exact relation between the passion for liberty and the passion for domination, or the exact nature of each, nor does he ask himself whether both are not rooted in a third passion that would be their common source. In particular it is not clear that the passion for glory is the common source of the two, even if it accompanies both, especially the desire for domination. What Augustine, following the Latin authors, sees deployed at Rome with unique breadth and intensity is the dynamic interplay of the three fundamental political passions that are inseparable from one another, that pass easily from one to another, and that exchange their signs in a way that throws moral judgment into perplexity. It will no doubt be said that the desire for glory is good when it nurtures the passion for liberty, bad when it feeds the passion for domination. But though that statement certainly meets with the approval of the moral person within us, it is missing an essential point, which is the ambiguity of political passion, with the so to speak irresistible passage from the passion for liberty to the passion for domination.[77]

On this point at least, Augustine is not far from Machiavelli, who considers the same Roman experience but with the intention of founding it anew on even more solid bases by enabling the Moderns, when they imitate pagan Rome to overcome the weakening induced by Christian Rome and its critique of pagan Rome, a critique whose great monument is *The City of God.* Where Augustine sees a great (the greatest) political experiment, but one that is completed, finished, and judged—judged by the new city—Machiavelli also sees the greatest political experiment, but one that did not understand adequately or whose possibilities of development the "princes" did not exploit to the fullest. In any case, Machiavelli, like Augustine, unceasingly shows us the ambiguity of republican political passion with its movement that leads necessarily from the love of liberty to the love of domination.

To the liberal tradition that is principally if not exclusively concerned with the rights and rightly understood self-interest of individuals, contemporary political writing likes to oppose a so-called republican tradition often referred to as "civic humanism," whose principal preoccupation would be the common good and civic virtue. Machiavelli is readily described as the one who renewed this republican tradition, giving it a novel edge. It is not possible for me to enter into this kind of writing that is so profuse today. However, Augustine, in helping us to understand the Roman perspective, helps us to measure how far the idea contemporary authors have of the republic is from ancient republicanism. *Our* idea of the republic is an obstacle to understanding the ancient republic; it intrudes between it and us. The erudite historians who painted and enshrined this tradition of "civic humanism" as an axis of our history are the prisoners of contemporary prejudices. The contrast between the two republicanisms can be summarized as follows. Modern republicanism makes a vigorous distinction between private or "selfish" motives and public or "selfless" motives of action, that is, between the motives of the individual and those of the citizen, and of course accords priority to the latter. Ancient republicanism largely ignores this distinction. If we read the Latin historians in particular, we see that the motives we would call "private" invade the space we call "public." There is a very compelling reason for this: the domain of the individual and the private has not yet been identified as a separate domain. All the human motives are at work in the city because the city is the sole locus of action—there is no "civil society" where individuals would "assert their independence as they please," to recall the formula by which Montesquieu characterizes English liberty. This is because all the human motives are constantly at work in the city. It is on account of this extraordinary concentration of all the motives of action that the ancient city represents for subsequent ages the most impressive deployment of human nature or of what I would be tempted to call the *human operation.*

What deceives us is that the ancient hero, the great citizen, prefers his city to his own life. We interpret that as a selfless behavior that sacrifices the individual to the citizen, but it is nothing of the sort since in effect the individual does not exist. The city constitutes the whole domain of the action of the person and the citizen; it is the locus of the deployment and reverberation of his action, where that action receives the only adequate reward, which is the wage of praise. The citizen does not really exist apart from the city or independently of the city, and in any case it is in the city that his life finds its meaning.

What also deceives us, as I have already evoked, is that we do not consider seriously the link between the passion for liberty and the passion for domination. We think they are by nature distinct, that the passion for domination of the Ancients, particularly the Romans, is so to speak an independent characteristic, proper to a particular people or time, to the age of war. Or we think that the passion for domination is a pathological development, a corruption. It is true that the Latin historians themselves, Sallust in particular, mark the moment when, after the destruction of Carthage, Roman life and politics were overcome by cupidity. "Hence the lust for money first, then for power, grew upon them; these were, I may say, the root of all evil."[78] But the corrupt state is not simply the contrary of the sound state. It is also its extension. Is it not the same movement of the spirit that at first has the Romans stand up to the kings, then against the neighbors who threatened young Rome, and later, when Rome no longer had any enemy to fear, became the limitless cupidity for money and domination ("pecuniae et imperi cupido")? This phenomenon is not proper to the ancient city. We curiously pay little attention to the link that is nonetheless so evident between modern democracy and modern imperialism. The two world wars—in which the democracies of the West had to fight at first a Germany that was less democratic indeed than they were and that had imperialist "war aims," and then a Germany that joined the most implacable tyranny with the most disjointed imperialism—largely conceal from us one of the most interesting phenomena of modern European history, what in truth is its axial phenomenon: the rising power of Europe or of the West in the world is of a piece with the rise to power of republican government and then of democracy in European countries and North America. The two greatest modern colonial empires belonged to the first two republics of modern Europe.[79] The movement that leads naturally and as though necessarily from *libertas* to *dominatio* is not unknown to us.

I said that Augustine, no more than the authors he follows, does not make an effort to identify precisely the relation between the desire for liberty and the desire for domination. However, Augustine mentions and comments on a distinction introduced by Sallust between *ambitio* and *avaritia*. In the first period of Rome's history, *ambitio* prevailed over *avaritia* in the heart of the Romans; later, *avaritia* was unleashed.[80] Augustine cites the following sentence of Sallust: "It was, at first, ambition rather than greed that worked on men's hearts; a vice closer to virtue."[81] Sallust's hesitation is noticeable. He explains his thought in the sentence that follows, which Augustine also cites: "The good man and the worthless wretch alike covet glory, honour, and power. But the good man directs his efforts along the right way; the man who lacks the moral qualities works towards his goal by trickery and deceit."[82] The good man and the one who is not good desire the same things: *gloria, honor, imperium.* They differ by their means: one takes the *vera via* of virtue; the other has recourse to every kind of deceit, to "all means." Sallust here takes up in sum the Aristotelian scheme of action. It can be noted that the one who is not *bonus* is said to be *ignavus,* that is to say, weak or lazy; he does not have the strength of spirit to seek what he aims at or desires by sticking to honorable means. There are thus a good or an honorable and virtuous ambition, and a vicious ambition to which another name must be given.

Augustine quotes, paraphrases, or comments on Sallust in a way that suggests approval. He largely confirms the distinction Sallust introduced between ambition and cupidity, which indicates that he acknowledges up to a certain point the validity of pagan moral distinctions. He does not confuse the virtues and vices of the pagans under the rationale that they did not receive the grace of Christian truth. However, he underlines the intrinsic fragility of good ambition itself, due to the fragility, the inconsistency of what it aims at, namely glory, the glory that rests on the unreliable judgment of people, on human opinion that is so fallible: "Virtue is superior to glory, since it is not content with the testimony of men, without the testimony of a man's own conscience."[83] Augustine can then decisively modify Sallust's analysis. Virtue is not to be confused with good ambition that seeks glory through honorable means; it must aim at a more solid goal. Finally: "the only genuine virtue is that which tends to the end where the good of man is, which surpasses any other good."[84]

As I have said, one must not exaggerate the distance or the difference between virtuous Rome and corrupted Rome. What Augustine finds particularly interesting in the testimony of Sallust is that he underlines the ambiguity of the Roman virtues, which is at the same time of course the ambiguity of the Roman vices—as long as these vices have not become entirely vicious in an insatiable *avaritia.* Sallust even indicates that the admirable dispositions of the first Romans were not by themselves sufficient to produce a truly just order. From the beginning the injustices of the stronger provoked the separation or the secession of the plebs, and there were other dissensions. In fact, Sallust as cited by Augustine goes on to say that the Romans only lived in justice and moderation ("aequo et modesto jure") as long as, after the expulsion of the kings, they had Tarquin and his Etruscan allies to fear.[85] After the war against them, disorders set in again, for the patricians subjected the plebs to the yoke of slavery, mistreating them as the kings had done. These disorders came to an end with the Second Punic War "because then once again came the pressure of a serious threat, which checked their restless spirits, and distracted them from these disorders by a more urgent anxiety, and recalled them to domestic concord."[86] Thus, on the word of the Romans themselves, their civic virtues never sufficed, even in the least corrupt times, to ensure a just order: they needed the reinforcement of fear aroused by a very serious threat from the outside. Sallust confirms in the most authoritative manner that no human city can rest on its own virtue.

A final remark on this point. The fact that the ordering of the whole depends on external pressure indicates that no part of the city is simply virtuous, simply just. Augustine notes that in the civil discords, the patricians wanted to dominate, while the plebeians refused to serve.[87] This observation, made into a general principle, will be at the center of the political analysis of the classes Machiavelli will propose: "For in every city these two diverse humors are found, which arises from this: that the people desire neither to be commanded nor oppressed by the great, and the great desire to command and oppress the people."[88]

Augustine will now point out the providential meaning of the Roman adventure—the use that God made of the vicious virtue or virtuous vice of the Romans. After the long-lasting and famous empires of the East,[89] God willed that there would also be an empire of the West, coming later but more illustrious in extent and power. Why and how did this empire arise? "To suppress the grievous evils of many nations, he [God] entrusted this dominion to those men, in preference to all others, who served their country for the sake of honour, praise, and glory, who looked to find that glory in their country's safety above their own and who suppressed greed for money and many other faults in favour of that one fault of theirs, the love of praise."[90] The historical phenomenon Augustine evokes in a few words is certainly grandiose. One can, if one wishes, detect a

Western prejudice in this powerful sketch that shows us the Romans subjugating the Oriental monarchies that were prisoners of the multitude of their vices, because they, the Romans, had only "that one fault," the love of praise. This passion did not make them saints but it rendered them better and less depraved men.[91]

The following chapter opposes the Romans aiming at glory to the Christian apostles who preached the name of Christ in places where it was not only disapproved but was the object of utter detestation.[92] Love of the true God renders one capable of doing more difficult things than those produced by the love of glory that attains its luster of greatness only at the price of subjection to human opinion.

The chapter's last sentence will detain us, since Augustine seems there to *justify* the dispositions and conduct of the Romans. For those Romans, who belonged to the *civitas terrena*, and all of whose duties were contained within that city, "what else was there for them to love save glory? For, through glory, they desired to have a kind of life after death on the lips of those who praised them."[93] The passion for glory is the greatest and in sum the best passion that people who live not eternally but in the succession of birth and death can harbor or nourish.[94] It motivates the most complete dedication to this mortal city and at the same time it points in the direction of a kind of immortality. In this sense, acting for glory is doing the most that is humanly possible—the maximum that those who have not yet been enlightened regarding true immortality can do.

In a striking manner, Augustine presents this glory as an effect of the justice of God. Of course, since this city was essentially mortal, dedication to the city could not receive the reward of eternal life. But God would have deprived the Romans of their just reward, of the reward they merited, if he had not granted them "the earthly glory of an empire which surpassed all others."[95] He granted them this glory. "They have no reason to complain of the justice of God, the supreme and true."[96] Twice Augustine cites St. Matthew: they have received their reward.[97]

Thus the justice of God extends to the life of the pagans. But if this earthly city contains or receives its own justice, it does not have its end in itself but is ordered to the other city. The best of the Romans, Augustine explains, are *exempla* for the Christians: "the citizens of that Eternal City, in the days of their pilgrimage, should fix their eyes steadily and soberly on those examples and observe what love they should have towards the City on high, if the earthly city has received such devotion from her citizens, in their hope of glory in the sight of men."[98]

The Refuge of Romulus and the Church of Christ

With chapter 17 of book 5 comes a sharp change of direction. Without warning, Augustine begins to lower and depreciate glory and more generally the political order itself: "what does it matter under whose rule a man lives, being so soon to die, provided that the rulers do not force him to impious and wicked acts?"[99] The condition or restriction is not negligible, but it changes nothing in the sharp distancing with regard to the whole political life magnetized by glory, animated by the passion for liberty and for domination, the republican political life that Augustine had described in the preceding chapters with a sympathy not devoid of serious reservations, but in the end, it can be said, with an interest and an attentiveness at times bordering on admiration. Now he is making us hear an altogether different tune.

The obsession with glory, Augustine explains, prevented the Romans from seeking to get along with other nations: they held to their triumphs. Is it not the case that if they had gotten along without either victors or vanquished, "the condition of the Romans and that of the other peoples would have been precisely the same?"[100]—above all if they had done right away what was later done very generously and very humanely ("gratissime atque humanissime"), namely "associating in the commonwealth as Roman citizens, all those who belonged to the Roman Empire." The difference between victors and vanquished, the difference of condition, so dear to the Romans, is in the end very little: "Take away national complacency, and what are all men but simply men?"[101]

Here one has to charge Augustine with a certain bad faith. For what is he doing? To the Roman Empire and its wars and glory he opposes the results or effects of the Roman Empire, particularly the peace and gathering or unification of humanity. One could say that Augustine wants the effect without the cause. No one could become *civis Romanus*, a citizen of the Roman Empire, before that empire came into existence. Nothing in the experience of those times suggests that the ancient peoples could be gathered *concorditer*—the way Europe is being unified today. Besides, European unification results from the wisdom acquired at the price of two enormous wars, and it is not certain it will be as solid as the Roman Empire.

One can understand that Augustine corrects his appreciation somewhat after giving considerations that are on the whole very favorable to Rome. One is not surprised that he shows little enthusiasm for triumphs and massacres. But the critique of empire he broaches in chapter 17 is hard to handle, for it would easily lead along a path Augustine would find it repugnant to follow. What he has begun to oppose here to the glorious massacres of the Romans is not the sacrifice of the martyrs he evoked in chapter 14, but the peace and comfort of a society all of whose members share the same condition and know that they share it—a society all of whose members are equal. In chapter 17 Augustine gives a vigorous sketch of what will become the standard critique of glory in the Enlightenment period, which is the critique of glory in the name of security and bourgeois virtues: "As far as I can see, the distinction between victors and vanquished has not the slightest importance for security and for moral standards in which human dignity consists [ad incolumitatem bonosque mores, ipsas certe hominum dignitates]."[102] *Incolumitas* is the state of citizens who enjoy all their rights; it is the *sécurité* so dear to Montesquieu.

To beat down the pride of victors, to make it clear that they do not in fact enjoy a different condition, Augustine raises the following two questions in particular: Are these proud conquerors exempt from the taxes on their lands? Do they have the right to know things forbidden to others? What is there in Augustine's presentation—I was going to say in his staging—that erases and makes void the difference between victors and vanquished so dear to the Romans?[103] Taxes and knowledge. One could say the economy and culture, the two pillars or wellsprings of bourgeois society.

Augustine could not oppose a too-tempting image of a world where there is neither victor nor vanquished, where all are fellow citizens sharing the same civil and intellectual condition, to the Roman Empire motivated by the passion for glory and victory. Such a contrast, instead of turning his readers toward the city of God, inciting them to seek eternal goods, would risk turning them in the opposite direction, and inciting them to seek the goods of this world—to prefer comfort without glory not only to glorious massacres but also to eternal life. Thus he ends the chapter by emphasizing anew the exemplary merits of those Romans who, for the sake of glory, did such great things and suffered such hardships, something that ought to mortify the pride of Christians and incite them to redouble their ardor.

This movement that goes from tempered praise to comparative praise of glory by passing through its harsh critique reveals the complexity or the difficulty of Augustine's approach. The Christians are of necessity critical of pagan glory, but not to the point where they would be tempted to be satisfied with the peace and comfort of earthly life. The human critique of glory, in the name of simply human goods, must be completed, enveloped, overcome by its properly Christian critique—in the name of the complete or supreme good that can only be God himself.

Augustine concludes chapter 17 with a stunning comparison between "the remission of sins, the promise which recruits the citizens for the eternal country" and "that refuge of Romulus, where the offer of impunity for crimes of every kind collected a multitude which was to result in the foundation of the city of Rome."[104] The happy effects of this *impunitas* had already been evoked in book 4: Romulus "took measures to ensure that when they were granted a share in the community after abandoning their former way of life, they would no longer have to think about the punishment to which they were liable, the fear of which had impelled them to greater crimes, so that in the future they should be less aggressive in their attitude to society."[105] The perspective of inclusion in the new city frees the refugees from the crime-inducing fear of punishment. Romulus's asylum heralds the redemptive gathering of the city of God, of which it is a sort of "foreshadowing." Romulus had gathered all sorts of people without, dare I say, asking for their passports, into the city he was founding, fugitive slaves, criminals of every kind, outlaws.[106] It was a sort of sketch, a "shadow" of what God would do with the whole of humanity, who all in all are fugitive slaves—slaves to sin fleeing the law of God—who all are outside the law or deprived of justice as long as they are deprived of the grace of God, as long as they have not entered the city of God. In this sense, and from the beginning, what goes by the name of Rome constitutes the pagan effort, the simply human effort that anticipates and heralds in the clearest manner God's way of acting, if I may use such an expression. Augustine here presents Rome as a sort of transition between paganism and Christianity.[107]

Moreover, Augustine deliberately uses Roman political language to designate Christian realities. In chapter 21 of book 10, for example, as in other places, the martyrs are designated as particularly honorable or illustrious citizens of the city of God. He even adds: "If it were not contrary to the usage of the Church [ecclesiastica loquendi consuetudo], we might call those martyrs our 'heroes.'"[108]

A final remark. We have just seen that Augustine very explicitly compares Romulus's gathering of the crowd of outlaws in the *asylum* that was the beginning of Rome and the remission of sins that gathers citizens for the eternal country.[109] In book 22, chapter 6, there is another interesting parallel between Romulus's foundation and that of Christ. Augustine begins by citing at some length the strange discussion in the *De republica* that we have already described in which Cicero explains regarding the founder of Rome that the proof of Romulus's extraordinary greatness resides in the fact that the Romans believed the fable of his deification at a time when people no longer believed such fables since they were enlightened.[110] Augustine, of course, does not pass up the opportunity to gently tease Cicero, "among the most learned and eloquent of all mankind,"[111] who thinks he can sell us such a muddled explanation. The fact is, according to Augustine, that the fable of the deification of Romulus is clearly a matter of superstition,[112] a superstition that "the community, as we say, drank in . . . with its mother's milk,"[113] a superstition born with the birth of Rome and that in later times no one dared to abandon. Among conquered peoples, it was out of fear of offending the master. As for the Romans themselves, Augustine describes their attitude in a very remarkable expression: Rome had believed it not only out of love of this error but in surrendering to the error of its love.[114] In his eyes, the *superstitio* of the Romans was caused by their natural and legitimate love of their founder.

This generous appreciation of the pagan founding helps Augustine to articulate the specific character of the Christian founding. In the case of the Church the truth comes first: "although Christ is the founder of the eternal heavenly City, that City's belief in Christ as God does not arise from her foundation by him; the truth is that her foundation arises from her belief in Christ as God."[115] Pagan Rome believed that Romulus was a god because it loved him as its founder; Christian Rome—the Church— loves Christ, and that love is its foundation, because it believes that he is

God. From one to the other, the order of human motives is inverted. In the first, there was in the beginning a reason to love Romulus, and naturally people were disposed to believe even something false of the beloved one; in the second, there was in the beginning a reason to believe, and then to love, in true faith, without rashness, not what was false, but what was true.[116]

Digression on Glory

We need to say more about the idea of glory because it is at the center of the Augustinian critique of the earthly city and because it is of very great interest in itself.

Glory, or the passion for glory, is the political passion par excellence. It is accordingly the passion of the person of action par excellence, since political action, or action in the political domain, is action par excellence. Two aspects, or two components of glory can be distinguished.

On the one hand, since action is contingent and fleeting—it disappears while it appears—people desire to give it solidity and a sort of permanence. Glory aims to preserve what is passing. Glory deliberately seeks the impossible. It seeks the immortality of human action, at least of certain actions, precisely those that are glorious.

Only an extraordinary action is worthy of lasting. Extraordinary means an action that is more than human, in which the one acting raises himself, to a certain extent and for a time, above humanity. To do so he must necessarily raise himself above others, lord it over them, to become in short "a god among men."[117]

As one can see, this movement, this disposition, this aspiration, the desire for glory that we are prone to regard as an extravagance or a folly, is as it were embedded in the ontological constitution of human life, or it is a natural response to it, a response to the contingency and the fragility of our actions. In short, it is a response to our mortality.

On the other hand, because it is a movement to "leave man behind," glory, glorious action, necessarily entails being carried away, losing balance, going to excess. It is necessarily or essentially dangerous, as much for the one acting as for those on whom he acts.

More precisely, it entails a sort of internal contradiction. The glorious man wants to be recognized for his intrinsic and substantial superiority:

he wants to be recognized ultimately, as I said, as a god among men. This intrinsic and substantial superiority can only reside in an essential independence with relation to other men. The glorious man demands that other men recognize, confirm, and celebrate his independence. He wants to be absolutely independent of other men, and it is he who needs them the most. At the end of the day, he needs all human beings to declare that he has no need of them. Coriolanus, for example, suffers cruelly from this contradiction. Furiously avid of glory, he cannot bear praise, for praise makes him dependent on those who praise him.[118]

Glory is not an essential element of modern political and moral life as it was of ancient life. Most of the time it is present only in diluted and debased forms, as in the star system, or even perverted forms, as in the "cult of personality." This is because it was the object of a systematic critique from the start of the modern enterprise. One could say that the constitution of the moral perspective that is still ours began with and rests upon a critique of glory—a critique of glory that is clearly distinct from the Christian critique.

I said that the quest for glory is a response to our mortality. The modern perspective also is a response to our mortality. Let us say it in the most prosaic way possible, since the Moderns mean to substitute truthful prose or prosaic truth for lying poetry or the poetic lying of both the Ancients and the Christians: for the Moderns since at least Bacon and Descartes, the proper response to our mortality is not to risk one's life for glory, but to prolong it through medicine. This considerable change of perspective, which to us appears so reasonable and self-evident, contains something mysterious, as I noted in the introduction to this inquiry. Since then we have been able to measure the immense progress of medicine and to observe that it has effectively given us the means to considerably prolong human life, but at the time when the decision was made to prefer life to glory, medicine had no more power to heal us than in the time of Pericles. It is the perspective on our condition that changed *before* we had found the means, including the medical means, to effectively transform this condition—if indeed we have effectively transformed it.

Let us attempt to characterize a bit more precisely this change of perspective. I mentioned the names of Bacon and Descartes. As is well known, Descartes saw in the new science that he helped elaborate the means to render us "as it were masters and possessors of nature." The project of the mastery of nature indeed constitutes a principal component of the modern project. According to many authors, it is one and the same with the modern project that is simply aimed at mastery. A formula of Bacon's, less discussed than Descartes's although it is well known, can help us sharpen our analysis. According to Bacon, the modern instauration seeks to achieve or to produce "the relief of man's estate," the relief of the human condition. I dare say this formula is more interesting than Descartes's, and in any case it states explicitly the only humanly understandable goal of Cartesian mastery.

The relief of the human condition[119]—this formula that is so beautiful and so persuasive nonetheless has something paradoxical in it. There is something paradoxical in making the human condition the object of human action. Why? Because the condition is what conditions; it is the starting point of action. Isn't making the transformation of the conditions of action the goal of action, fashioning a circle or putting oneself in a circle by forgetting the ends of action? The condition is what by definition does not change: humans are mortal. To take the relief of one's condition as one's goal is in short to propose to render humans "less mortal."

In any case, to envisage the human condition in a new way is to envisage human mortality in a new way. As I said, in the ancient order, the pagan order, the order of glory, something beyond death, is aimed at: mortals, precisely because they are mortal, aim at a sort of immortality. For the Moderns, this is not reasonable; it subjects human life to a pressure or traction that is exhausting and in the end vain.

Thomas Hobbes, Bacon's very independent disciple who was also his secretary, sees in glory, whether it appears as pride, vainglory, or concern for reputation, a source of disorder and as it were the knot of the human problem, the knot that needs to be cut. How? By *repressing* the desire for glory. Only the sovereign State is capable of repressing the "children of pride" that people are, and to bring them back so to speak to the level of their condition and thereby to relieve it by making them attach themselves to real and solid goods and no longer to imaginary goods. The State forces them, dare I say, to run on level ground while keeping their eyes set before them instead of trying foolishly and vainly to fly toward the stars. Instead of being troubled by immense and vague aspirations, life becomes a race from one desire that can be satisfied to another that

can be satisfied, a race that ends only at death. Under the State that represses their vain desire for glory, humans can at last behave in keeping
with their mortality.

Is this race from one desire to another that ends in death less vain
than the quest for glory? That's a subject for discussion. What would be
the proper relation to our mortality?

Montaigne spent his life adjusting to death. Well before Bacon, Montaigne was giving us the task of "relieving our miserable human condition" (Bacon probably borrowed the expression from him). Like Hobbes,
he saw the source of our miseries in presumption. Montaigne at times
separates and at times combines the pagan desire for glory and the Christian desire for immortality. In both cases, one "leaves man behind." Man
must be brought back to himself, to the "nothingness" of his mortal condition. How? Hobbes, as we have just recalled, will force man to remain
on the level of his condition by means of the State. Montaigne does not
dispose of this instrument, this artifice, and he does not conceive it. What
does he propose to us? It's a question of how to be a man, simply a man,
a man who "plays the man well and properly," if what is proper to man
is to want to "escape from the man." And for the one who would attain
it, who would attain to remaining so to speak within the limits of humanity, how can he "enjoy his being rightfully" when he must die?

If one does not want to look beyond death to a form of immortality,
if one wants to look at death exclusively as a fact of nature, how does
one relate to it? There are in the end two possible and opposed answers:
to be always thinking of it, and to never think of it, except at the moment of death. In the *Essays* Montaigne continually oscillates from one
to the other, giving to each the most extreme, the most abrupt form. But
at the same time he seeks a middle term between always thinking of
death and never thinking of it, a middle term to which he gives a charming name that becomes for him a technical term, *nonchaloir*: "I want a
man to act, and to prolong the functions of life as long as he can; and I
want death to find me planting my cabbages, but careless of death [*non-
chalant d'elle*] and still more of my unfinished garden."[120]

The ancients did not have the idea of "relieving" the human condition. It was not the object of their action, but rather—precisely—the
condition of their action. They lived, that is, they acted according to the
movement or movements that this condition leads us to, between the de-

scent toward the beast and the ascent toward god or the divine—whence for us their terrifying harshness. They were capable of compassion and clemency and they honored those virtues. Marcellus wept over Syracuse before destroying it. After granting compassion its due, after giving a thought to our "common condition,"[121] he obeyed the *consuetudo bellorum,* the custom of war; he obeyed victory since it is through victory that man makes himself eternal. For Marcellus and the Romans in general there is an immense difference of condition between the victor and the vanquished. The victor is more than human, the vanquished less than human. Victory brings out the two extremes, the two poles that define the human condition and between which human life moves—the two extremities or the two poles that remain implicit or indistinct in the conditions of peace. Compassion or clemency has its place among the pagans; it can inflect action—in the case of Marcellus, it could suspend it for a moment—but it cannot be the wellspring of a new course of action.

The Christian critique of pagan glory has much in common with the modern critique—or inversely. For one as for the other, pagan glory is *vain* glory. But the Christian critique does not draw its support from the solid satisfactions of the mortal body: it invokes and postulates a real immortality. It has a certain sympathy for pagan glory, for it shares with the pagans the sentiment or conviction that the wellspring of human life is a movement toward the divine—a movement that the Christian religion means or claims to lead to its real goal. The Christian critique cannot countenance the brutality of Thomas Hobbes that simplifies things, for though it denounces the prideful error of pagan glory, it acknowledges a certain legitimacy, a certain nobility in the movement of the soul that aspires to glory. Whereas Thomas Hobbes rebuffs a ridiculous vanity, the Christian critique is concerned to reveal a noble error, where the accent can fall either on the nobility of the error or the erroneous character of the noble movement. One finds in Augustine at times one, at times the other accent. We have seen how he deals with the suicides of Lucretia and Cato and the sacrifice of Regulus.

An essential condition of glory, an essential condition for glory to be possible or to hold meaning, is to consider that there are great distances within the human condition, or that it rests on or is constituted by great internal distances. Christianity also recognizes great distances within the human soul. These are partly the same as for the pagans, as is evident in

Augustine's treatment of the case of Lucretia, torn between the glory of chastity and the dishonor of its loss. The difference is that these distances are considered as essentially inaccessible to view from the outside. If the principle of the pagan order is glory—more generally, public praise and blame—the principle of the Christian order, as I emphasized, is conscience. Lucretia's error or weakness, as we saw, was not to be content with the judgment of her conscience.

Glory is at the center of the pagan regime of the imagination. This regime rests on a certain confusion of the visible and the invisible, the soul and the body, a confusion that gives this regime its force at the same time that it foments its aberrations. The most extreme possibilities of the soul want to find a visible expression that would receive public praise or blame—praise that can go as far as deification, blame that can go as far as shameful torture. What holds together the elements of the human world is thus the imagination that renders the invisible visible or that sees the invisible in the visible, that binds the high and the low, animals, humans, and gods. Man is a blurred or uncertain notion between animal and god, a notion that gives rise to opposing images ("divine" or "animal"), or whose indeterminateness is concretized in opposing images, but that are united, superimposed, or melded in the "mythological scene." Because of this flow of the imagination, the mythological scene is easily "obscene," with *eros* forming the link between the animal, the human being, and the god. One could say that the essential modality of this regime, the one that expresses it best, is *metamorphosis*.[122] A mortal woman receiving the embraces of a god who has taken the form of an animal is the most expressive representation of the pagan regime of the imagination.

As critical as he can be, Augustine shows esteem for the pagan order of glory as it is deployed in political life and action. He has altogether different sentiments regarding pagan religion. It is in effect in that religion that in his eyes the intimate vice of this order can be seen most clearly and so to speak conspicuously, the pagan religion, as I previously indicated, that Augustine pursues with unflagging severity.

Popular Religion

Augustine at length and in detail describes Roman religion, the religion of the many, the popular religion of the city, lacerating it with all the resources of indignation, derision, and sarcasm. Personal memories and remorse contribute to be sure to the force of his feeling: "When I was a young man I used to go to sacrilegious shows and entertainments." The popular divinities on the stage in theaters or during certain rites occasioned obscenities impossible to describe. For example, during festivities honoring the mother of the gods, the vilest actors sang before her litter things that would have made their own mothers blush, to say nothing of the mother of the gods.[123]

It is not necessary to follow Augustine as he evokes these indignities. The question of principle is what to think of a religion in which the gods commit deeds that would make most men blush, while, in the order of things, men are expected to blush for their own evil acts before the gods. Pagan religion inverts the natural relation between humans and gods; as a consequence, it corrupts people. It corrupts them quite directly, in that people are then tempted to imitate the gods that are represented doing all sorts of strange things. Augustine cites the example of Terence, an immoral youth who, contemplating a mural depicting Jupiter showering gold upon the lap of Danae, boasts that he is imitating a god, "and what a god to follow."[124] It could moreover be noted in passing that Augustine here raises a question that, in spite of the difference in times, holds great meaning for us—the question of the influence of theatrical shows. He worries about the effects of these stagings of the pagan gods on adolescents in particular, just as we worry about the influence of violent or pornographic films.

The question of theatrical shows is in no way anecdotal. It is moreover not exhausted by a consideration of the effects, good or bad, of this or that show. Theatrical shows are a very serious matter. In the spectacles it applauds, a people represents itself, shows how it relates to the world and how it formulates for itself the human problem. It expresses its self-awareness, with its possible contradictions. In chapter 13 of book 2, Augustine remarks that the Romans, even as they honored the gods who demanded that their wicked deeds and crimes be celebrated on the stage, at the same time barred actors from all civic honors. Therein surely lies a difficulty: "How can it be consistent to deprive theatrical performers of any political standing, and at the same time to admit theatrical performances as an ingredient in divine worship?"[125] The Greeks were more consistent; they thought "themselves right to honour actors because they worship gods who demand theatrical productions." Thus the Greeks and the Romans are engaged in a dispute; there is a dispute among pagans themselves. Let them settle it among themselves, says Augustine rhetorically: let them straighten things out. Rhetorically, for, in effect, Augustine is quite prepared to propose the Christian solution, which is the only satisfactory solution to the dispute among the pagans. He presents the problem and the solution in the form of a syllogism. "The Greek proposition is: 'If such gods are to be worshipped, it follows that such men are to be honoured.' The Romans put in the minor premise: 'But such men are in no way to be honoured.' The Christians draw the conclusion: 'Therefore such gods are in no way to be worshipped.' "[126] Such is the syllogism of the false gods, in the conclusion of which paganism refutes itself. More precisely, Christianity provides the dialectic solution to the contradictions of paganism, the contradictions between the Greek and Roman evaluations of gods and humans as they are manifested in theatrical shows.[127]

A last remark. The pagans contradict themselves because the Romans contradict themselves and so in doing contradict the Greeks. As for the Greeks, they do not contradict themselves; they are consistent—they are brazen but consistent. Thus, Augustine's whole dialectical argument rests on the advantage he gives the Romans, who contradict themselves, over the Greeks, who do not contradict themselves. (A pagan could say simply: the Greeks are right and their position is consistent; the Romans, weak in mind or heart, do not know what they think or they lack the courage to admit it.) In fact, Augustine brings to light a twofold contradiction or incoherence in the Romans, a prideful incoherence and an honorable incoherence. The prideful incoherence is in some way made public by Scipio himself in the *Republic*, who boasts *(gloriatur)* that the Romans do not want their life and reputation exposed to the insolent calumnies of the poets.[128] This is surely an honorable concern for their own dignity, but it is prideful impiety toward their gods. The law protects people, but not the gods. The other incoherence of the Romans is on the contrary honorable. Although they are dominated by a dreadful superstition to the point of honoring gods that required these shameful theatrical shows, they nonetheless are mindful of their dignity and modesty and, unlike the Greeks, keep themselves from honoring the actors who stage such shows.[129] The dishonor they impose on their actors honors the Romans: thus they acknowledge in part or indirectly the indignity and thus the falsity of their religion.

Augustine compares the Greek Plato to the Romans, to the extent that the laws of Rome and the discourses of Plato share the same hostility toward the lying poets. Plato is surely much more consistent than the Romans. He shows the Romans what, with their character, they ought to have done.[130]

In any case, the Romans themselves, at least certain Romans, perceived more or less clearly the limits and the vices of the pagan religion, the religion of the city. But they lacked the strength of mind, or more probably of spirit and heart, to put an end to the city's subjugation to ridiculous and shameful gods.

The Critique of the Pagan Sages

Augustine is thus interested in the "most erudite pontiff" Scaevola, and in general in "the more intelligent and thoughtful" Romans, among them Cicero and above all Varro, a very penetrating mind.[131]

It is reported that the most erudite pontiff Scaevola distinguished three categories, or three kinds of gods: one introduced by the poets, another by the philosophers, the third by the city's leaders.[132] Obviously, the fact that the pagan gods are classified according to the domains or the skills or arts of humans strongly suggests that they are a product or products of human art. But Augustine's critique does not take this direct route. He enters into the thought of Scaevola, who has his own critiques to make of each kind of religion.

The first kind is worthless because many fictions of poets are unworthy of the gods. The second is not suited to cities for it encompasses superfluous things and, above all, things the knowledge of which is harmful to people. What things? For example, the learned teach us that Hercules, Asclepius, Castor, and Pollux are not gods, for they died in conformity with the human condition. Or again, cities do not have true representations of what the gods are because—and here philosophers properly speaking certainly intervene—a true god has no sex, no age, nor defined body parts. These are the philosophic propositions, one could say the philosophic truths, that the most erudite pontiff, as well as Varro himself, does not want the people to know. Thus, these two eminent Romans esteem that it is advantageous for cities to be lied to in the matter of religion. Here of course Christians break with the learned men of paganism. Augustine is indignant toward a religion that does not meet people's natural and legitimate expectation. "What a splendid religion for the weak to flee to for liberation! He asks for the truth which will set him free; and it is believed that it is expedient for him to be deceived."[133]

According to Augustine, according to Christianity, there is a condition common to all human beings: they are all slaves to sin and alienated from truth; they are all equally deprived of liberty as well as truth. This proposition, one could say this diagnosis, breaks with the pagan sentiment of human things. The ancients certainly recognized that there is something common to all people, which is what makes them human, and that is that they are "mortal"[134]—mortal like the animals, but at times splendid like the immortal gods. They are then intermediaries, it must be repeated, between beasts and gods. In this sense, humans constitute the category of beings that has the greatest breadth—greater of course than that of the animals, but in a sense also greater than that of the gods, who are only what they are—and that for this very reason has the greatest instability. That is why the incarnation of paganism, dare I say, is the "hero," who, being neither beast nor god, nonetheless unites, in a dazzling short circuit, the beast and the god.

Greek philosophy in some way stabilizes this disposition of things when Aristotle, according to genus and specific difference, defines man as a political and rational animal. A plane of "human affairs" is thus identified, with the "moral virtues" that are proper to it. But the "heroic" movement is only displaced or "specialized"; the philosophic life properly speaking will be "superior to the human level. For someone will live it not insofar as he is a human being, but insofar as he has some divine element in him. . . . We ought not to follow the makers of proverbs and 'Think human, since you are human,' or 'Think mortal, since you are mortal.' Rather, as far as we can, we ought to be pro-immortal."[135]

This effort is obviously reserved to a very small number. But all people probably, one way or another, experience the desire for immortality, in any case the desire to be joined with the immortals. Since they are political animals, it is fitting to give them gods that encourage them to fulfill their familial and civic duties. They are "false gods," surely, but they meet the needs of people in their cities all the while they give a splendid or terrible image of the world—the Whole—that is beyond the cities.

The pagan ordering that places the many in the realm of nontruth is subverted by Christianity, which affirms at the same time that all people, absolutely all people, including philosophers, share the same condition of misery and error—they are all "slaves to sin"—and that they are all, absolutely all, including the many, capable of truth, and of the highest truth—"capable of the true God." In this way Christianity humbles the proud and elevates the humble.

On its side, modern philosophy rejected classical philosophy's resignation or consent to the radical separation between the few and the many, between the philosopher and the nonphilosopher. It took the Christian stance by identifying a truly universal human condition, common to all without exception, including even philosophers. This is no longer the sinful condition but the condition of nature, the state of nature in which the life of humans is solitary, poor, nasty, brutish, and short; and it proposed a truth accessible to all, including the many, the truth or truths of a new political science and a new science of nature that together were capable of relieving, improving, and finally overcoming, up to a certain point, the human condition of nature.

I spoke of ancient philosophy's resignation or consent to the radical separation between the few and the many, the philosopher and the nonphilosopher. Neither of these two terms is satisfactory. They rather translate the embarrassment of the modern or Christian reader before the ease, even the alacrity, with which the ancient philosophers affirmed that there exists a difference of nature between the philosophers and those who are not philosophers, which is to say the rest of us. At the same time, ancient philosophy itself, in any case ancient political philosophy, included a reforming component that was very limited and timid, or "conservative," if one compares it to the revolutionary boldness of modern philosophy, yet one that was real. Augustine himself evokes what he sees as the embarrassed efforts of Cicero and Varro to reform up to a certain point the religion of the Romans by distinguishing religion from superstition. He cites Cicero at length, but he is rather harsh on this "Academic philosopher . . . who maintains that everything is uncertain, [and who] does not deserve to be treated as an authority in such matters."[136] Cicero certainly distinguishes religion from the superstitions handed down from the ancestors, but he is so intimidated by the tradition of the city (*consuetudo civitatis*) that he believes himself obliged to affirm that "our ancestors" had already separated religion from superstition, something that envelops him in a contradiction from which he cannot extricate himself. Augustine is even less impressed by Cicero's efforts in that "he would not have dared even to mutter, in a popular assembly, the opinions reasonably proclaimed by the eloquent speaker in that philosophical debate."[137]

Augustine shows more respect for Varro, who does not hesitate to admit that "if he had been founding that city at the beginning, he could have consecrated the gods and their names according to the rules of Nature."[138] Indeed, in openly declaring that there are numerous truths about which it is useless for the people to be instructed, and numerous errors that are advantageous for them to take as truths despite their falsity, Varro reveals the whole policy of the so-called learned men whose influence governs cities and peoples.[139] But if one considers his personal thought, it is clear, according to Augustine, that Varro came close to a correct idea of God, whom he considers "the soul which governs the universe by motion and reason."[140] There remained but one step for him to take, which was to understand that since the soul is affected by change, the true God is an immutable nature, the creator of the soul.

In any case, in spite of the efforts of minds like Varro, in the pagan world, the leaders of cities, the "deceivers," are in the end just as much prisoners of error as the "weak" and "deceived." Pagan religion is both proud and humiliating because the recognition that religion is instituted by humans, which is always just beneath the surface and thus at times explicit, is accompanied by the requirement to submit to it as if it came from the gods. Only the grace of Christian humility can break the bewitchment of this two-faced lie that enslaves cities.

As I have already emphasized, Christianity's point of impact is the separation between the few and the many. What Christianity attacks is not social or political inequality but the pertinence of the distinction between the few and the many, the philosopher and the nonphilosopher, with regard to the capacity to attain or receive the truth. Where pagan religion offers obscene theatrical productions and scandalous myths to the many, disavowed with more or less frankness by the best of the few who strive to promote a less corrupting teaching, the Christian religion addresses to all and makes public everywhere the same liberating teaching. Whereas among the pagans the mysteries are shrouded in secrecy and meant for initiates only, the Christian mysteries are offered publicly and even ostensibly to everyone. In Christianity, there is no "secret doctrine."[141] Thus over the philosophers Augustine has the advantage of *parrhesia,* the liberty or boldness of speech of the Christian apostle who offers the same salutary truth to all.[142]

8

THE TWO CITIES

It was necessary to examine with some care the "critique of paganism" that occupies such a great place in *The City of God*. However, it is now time to deal with the principal theme around which Augustine's argument is organized and that gives the whole undertaking its meaning.

Cain and Abel, Prototypes of the Two Cities

How does Augustine describe relations between the two cities?

The point from which to begin is that unlike nations in general among themselves, unlike also what takes place between Israel and the nations, the two cities Augustine deals with are not *visibly* separated. Certainly, the Church is in one sense and in one part visible, but with this important qualification that we have already encountered: on the one hand, among its very enemies are concealed its future citizens, and even among its most sworn enemies lie hidden predestined friends, who as yet do not know it themselves; on the other hand, among those who are joined to the Church by the communion of the sacraments, some will not have a share in the eternal destiny of the saints. This mysterious and troubling mixing of the two cities is admirably summarized in the famous sentence: "In truth, those two cities are interwoven and intermixed in this era, and await separation at the last judgement."[1]

Let us now go much further in the treatise, to the beginning of book 14. There Augustine formulates with great force what could be called the principle of the city of God. God not only willed to unite the human race through the likeness of human nature, he willed to unite people in a tighter and stronger bond *(vinculum)* and even in a bond of parentage *(quadam cognationis necessitudine)* by having all people born of one person only.² The terms Augustine uses make the divine creation narrated in Genesis appear more precisely or specifically as a very broad and radical political foundation since the concern is to establish humans in unity by the bond of peace, beginning with one person. The question of the final goal or raison d'être of creation—why would God, who as necessary and infinite Being is perfectly self-sufficient, produce something other than himself?—has not been answered with any great assurance in the Christian tradition, nor could it be given a sure answer. Augustine here does not answer it, properly speaking, but he suggests that the divine plan be considered as a political foundation, as the foundation of a city characterized by a unity of unprecedented quality and depth.

According to the divine intention, the individual members of the human race were not destined to die.³ How could God intend beings that he created in his likeness to die? Humans experienced death, became "mortals," because the first two human beings merited it by their disobedience. Their fault was so grave that human nature itself suffered deterioration. Consequently, along with human nature, the bondage of sin and the necessity of death were transmitted to the descendants. Moreover, this death, the death of the body, is but the least consequence of the disobedience of the first parents, since, according to Augustine's daunting teaching, a just punishment would also precipitate all people in a "second death," this one an eternal death, if the unmerited grace of God did not save some of them.⁴ Whatever one makes of this teaching, it should be noted that the language employed is political: Augustine speaks not only of disobedience and punishment, but also of bondage *(obligatio peccati)* and liberation.

These notions provide access to the underlying but determining structure of human life, whose variegated surface ordinarily exercises such an irresistible attraction on us. In fact, "although there are many great peoples throughout the world, living under different customs in religion and morality and distinguished by a complex variety of languages, arms, and dress, it is still true that there have come into being only two main divisions, as we may call them, in human society: and we are justified in following the lead of our Scriptures and calling them two cities."⁵ We see how the immense diversity and variety of human things is brought back to a unity, not the all-in-all passive unity of the human race that the Moderns observe when they are moved by the "sentiment of those like oneself" which Tocqueville saw as the affect proper to democratic man,[6] but the active unity or simplicity of a choice that is offered to every human being. It is not enough to observe our common humanity, nor to accomplish "humanitarian" actions that follow naturally from this observation, for what we have in common that is deepest, what in sum we share that is most meaningful, is the necessity for each to *choose* between the two cities. What we have in common that is deepest and most meaningful is not our passions, or our sentiments, but our actions.

Of what more precisely does this choice consist? Let us turn to the final chapter of book 14. There we find the most synthetic and most famous formulation of the difference or contrast, in truth, of the opposition between the two cities. We are told that "two cities were created by two kinds of love: the earthly city was created by self-love reaching the point of contempt for God, the Heavenly City by the love of God carried as far as contempt of self."[7] Augustine goes on to explicate the opposition in these terms:

- One city seeks its glory from men; for the other, God as witness of its conscience is its greatest glory.
- One city is dominated by the passion to dominate; in the other, mutual service is rendered by charity, the rulers by ruling, the subjects by obeying.
- One city, in its masters, loves its own strength; the other says to its God: "I will love you, Lord, my strength."[8]

We will probe more deeply the opposition between the two cities by considering their prototypes as the Bible gives them to us in Cain and Abel.

The biblical account of Cain and Abel is surely of great interest for us. Cain represents the ambivalence of human civilization. He is the first who is said to have cultivated the soil, the first who is said to have become the builder of a city. He was, in short, what we would call a benefactor of humanity and to that extent the first man susceptible of being praised by men. It is he who, properly speaking, begins human history, at least the history of civilization. It is he who puts to best use, in any case to the most active use, the resources he had in hand upon leaving the garden of Eden. At the same time, of course, he represents the violence and murder that come with human civilization.

As for Abel, he was not concerned either to plant or to build. He was a shepherd who pastured small livestock. Whereas Cain, farmer and builder, sought to dwell on the earth and settle it, Abel was, Augustine says, *tanquam peregrinus,* like a stranger—a stranger to the earth, or on the earth.[9]

So Cain killed his brother Abel. The reasons for this murder are not clear. We know only that Cain was very irritated that God looked favorably on Abel and his offering, while he did not look favorably on Cain and his offering. The reasons for the divine preference are not indicated by the biblical text, something that has opened up a vast field for exegetes. What is Augustine's approach? Here is the synthetic statement with which he introduces the discussion: "The first founder of the earthly city was . . . a fratricide; for, overcome by envy [invidentia victus], he slew his own brother, a citizen of the Eternal City, on pilgrimage in this world."[10] Before taking a closer look at the expression "invidentia victus," let us read a bit further.

Augustine emphasizes that this first crime gives us the "archetype" of an action characteristic of the earthly city. One should not then be surprised if, much later, when the city destined to be "the head of the earthly city" was founded,[11] one could see a sort of imago of this first exemplar. Rome was founded the day Remus was killed by his brother Romulus. The two fratricides are, however, very different. More precisely, the two couples of brothers are very different. At Rome, in the Roman imago, the two brothers were equally citizens of the earthly city: "Both sought the glory of establishing the Roman state."[12] But the two brothers together cannot receive as much glory as one or the other would receive if he were alone. To share it is to diminish it. To attain the greatest glory, the glory attached to *tota dominatio,* to the one who rules alone, Romulus killed his brother. "What would have been kept smaller and better by innocence grew through crime into something bigger and worse."[13] The story of Romulus and Remus is certainly deplorable, but, Augustine implies, it is a rather simple story since the rival brothers coveted the same goods.

The story of Cain and Abel is more complex and more interesting. The two brothers did not experience the same desire for earthly goods. It cannot be said that one envied the other out of fear of seeing his power diminished if they shared domination. One of the brothers in effect had no ambition whatever to dominate in the city his brother was founding. But if the two brothers were not rivals, why did Cain kill Abel? Not because he was in conflict with a wicked man like himself, who was liable to diminish his share of earthly goods, but because, being wicked, he envied his brother who was good—he envied him although his brother willingly let him have all the earthly goods he could desire. Augustine speaks of "the diabolical envy that the wicked feel for the good simply because they are good, while they themselves are evil."[14]

It is of course tempting to consider Augustine's explanation as a simple tautology. Cain killed his brother because Cain was a wicked or bad man. In fact, the point of the argument is not Cain's wickedness, but Abel's goodness. Cain hates or envies this goodness. He hates or envies what is the natural object of love. How is this possible? Because he is wicked or bad, of course. But how can one be wicked, if to be wicked means to hate or envy what is good, to hate or envy one who is good?

Augustine explains things roughly in the following way. The character of the good, its natural tendency so to speak, is to be shared. It becomes greater, it becomes better, by being shared. The goodness of Abel would not have been diminished if his brother had rejoiced and shared in the divine favor of Abel. It would even in a certain sense have been augmented by the increase of their friendship; and of course, Cain himself would have become better. The logic of the good, one could say, is as follows: the more it is shared, the more it is possessed. It is the contrary of the logic of appropriation, even though what we desire to appropriate are of course the same good things. Concerning the truly good things, "anyone who refuses to enjoy this possession in partnership will not enjoy it at all."[15] Why would Cain not love the good that it is natural to love? Because he does not want to share; he does not want to *partake*. He does not want to partake in the goodness of his brother. And so he hates his brother whose goodness wants to be shared, something Cain hates above all else: "This is a sin which God particularly rebukes, namely, sulkiness about another's goodness, and a brother's goodness at that."[16]

Thus, the rivalry between Romulus and Remus expresses the division within the earthly city, which is divided against itself. With Cain and Abel the conflict between the two cities comes to light. At the common source of the two divisions or conflicts is the depraved human will, sin. The spirit of Christianity, if I may say, resides in the simultaneous affirmation of the human vocation to a perfect unity and of the divisive power of the human will that people cannot make righteous by their own power.

Christianity and Human Life

We can take as our starting point Augustine's remark, "The human race is, more than any other species, at once social by nature and quarrelsome by perversion."[17] The Christian perspective includes two affirmations that seem contradictory: man is the most social being and at the same time the one most given to discord, the most unsocial being. Augustine links the opposing attributes to two parts or two distinct aspects of the human being: it is man's nature that is social, and it is his vice, that is, his will, that is unsocial or given to discord. We have here a fundamental Christian thesis that Augustine more than anyone else contributed to formulate and sharpen: man's nature is good; his will is bad or inclined to evil. The two theses, or the two parts of the one thesis, far from being contradictory, are of a piece for Augustine. The very definition of a bad will is that it is the perversion of a nature that is good or capable of good. Augustine explains at length how the human will, naturally attracted by the good, can nonetheless choose evil. The bad will does not have its cause in the good nature; it is in some way without cause.[18]

In any case, if the evil will does not have its cause in the good nature, the presence of the evil will in the good nature has its first source in the first sin. The ambivalence of the human being divided between friendship and hostility is rooted on the one hand in the *good nature* of the human soul and on the other in the *fallen condition* of the human being; it is rooted in the "nature vitiated by sin." But the word "ambivalence" is hardly appropriate here since, in fact, it is the will that trumps nature and turns people over to the enmity of the earthly city. This enmity can only be overcome by the radical healing, the complete rectification, of the will—a transformation so profound that only divine grace can bring it about. Indeed, if the human will is evil, humans cannot really will the good without being "informed" by the divine will that wills for them before they themselves begin to will. Thus the struggle between the two cities unfolds at a level of depth that is not accessible to human eyes and that evades the usual instruments of social life—only the special instruments and skill of the Church are able to work at this depth.

A remark: Augustine's analysis is suggestive, illuminating, and possibly convincing for whoever adopts the perspective of the inner person and is sensitive to the "depth of evil." But it hardly helps us to order life in common. Whoever is concerned above all with the visible, effective social order is looking for a more useful statement. Accordingly, the complex Augustinian analysis is energetically simplified by Hobbes. A proposition with four terms—nature, will, sociable, unsociable—is replaced by one with two terms: nature, unsociable. For Hobbes, people's nature separates them more than it unites them; they are naturally unsociable. And if it is their nature that is unsociable, there is no wrong in that, no need to bring in an evil will. The Augustinian knot that joins a sociable nature and an unsociable will and that only the grace of God could untie is cut by the human institution. For Augustine, hatred has to be healed. For Hobbes, it is enough to master hostility. The sovereign State will take care of that. Such is the moral simplification that makes modern political philosophy trenchantly effective. This philosophy, the philosophy of human rights, presupposes human unsociability, a morally neutral unsociability.

Let us come back to Augustine. If indeed discord tends to separate people, it testifies at the same time to their deep unity: they have in common this bad will; they share the same sin. They all descend from the "one man" who separated himself from God. What did this first fault consist of? How was it transmitted to the descendants of the first couple? These questions go to the heart of Christian anthropology.

The great difficulty of this doctrine is obviously that original sin, unlike personal sin, is "contracted" and not committed. It is a state and not an act. People are guilty without yet having committed any personal fault. This seems to overthrow all our ideas of justice. How does Augustine confront this difficulty?[19]

The sin of Adam and Eve was personal. The first two human beings—the *primi parentes*—were thus justly punished with death, having been created to experience no kind of death if they did not sin. From then on all their descendants had to experience this punishment, for from them nothing could be born that was different from them.[20] The doctrine of original sin follows as it were necessarily from the affirmation of human unity as inclusion of the human race in the first man. It constitutes its maximal expression.

If humans are *born* sinners, it is that the *drama* of the fault and the punishment of the fault have become for the descendants of the first couple a *state* or *condition*: the gravity of the fault entailed a sanction that profoundly vitiated or degraded human nature, in such a way that what was only a penalty for the first sinful humans, in the first place death, has become nature for all their descendants.[21] The drama of the crime and punishment of the first couple has become a natural state for their descendants, who are born criminals and mortals.

Augustine is never content with a formulation. He takes up the question again a little later in book 13 by adding a few specifics. To make the thesis clearer or at least less shocking, he distinguishes between individual form and common or "seminal" nature: the form in which we were each to live individually had not yet been created nor distributed among each of us, but the "seminal nature" out of which we would come already existed.[22] From then on, since this nature was corrupted by sin and justly punished, human was to be born from human in an identical condition.

The introduction of the notion of *condition* allows for the resolution, or in any case the attenuation, of a difficulty included in the Augustinian usage of the notion of nature. As we have seen, Augustine unceasingly repeats that human nature, like all natures, is good and that it is the human will that is evil. If it is the human will that is evil, why would a good nature *transmit* an evil will? The reply, as we have also seen, is that nature has been vitiated *(vitiata)*. Thus the will has become nature, and nature has become bad—at least in its exercise if not in its being. Catholic theology will be forever looking for the satisfactory formulation to state both that human nature is essentially good as the work of God and gravely affected by evil as the heir of the wrongdoing of Adam and Eve and its punishment. The term that best seems to allow the two ideas to be held together is not "corruption" but "wound": human nature is "wounded in the natural powers proper to it."[23] In any case, recourse to the notion of *condition* allows for the attenuation of the difficulty by formulating more precisely what is meant. The "corruption of nature" is seen more precisely as the passage from one condition to another, from the condition of "original justice" to the condition in which this justice has been lost—a sinful and mortal condition. Passing from one condition to the other, humanity passes from a regime of human life to another regime, from a just regime to a corrupt regime. I will not say that everything becomes clear, but in our experience, in particular our political experience, we find analogies that illuminate the Genesis narrative.

In sum, what Augustine describes is the contagion of a rebellion or a disobedience.[24] Because it voluntarily abandoned the master whose slave it was, namely God, the soul of our first parents could not retain in its power the slave of which it was the master, namely the body. Then Augustine continues by citing Saint Paul (Galatians 5:17), the flesh began to covet against the spirit and it is with this struggle that we are born.[25]

However, against the Manichees, and to a lesser degree the Platonists,[26] Augustine is careful not to inculpate the "flesh": "For the corruption of the body, which weighs down the soul, is not the cause of the first sin, but its punishment. And it was not the corruptible flesh that made the soul sinful; it was the sinful soul that made the flesh corruptible."[27] Augustine explains that there is a carnal way to inculpate the flesh: "For anyone who exalts the soul as the Supreme Good, and censures the nature of flesh as something evil, is in fact carnal alike in his cult of the soul and in his revulsion from the flesh."[28] The head and source *(caput et origo)* of all vices is the pride that rules over the devil, who is without flesh.[29]

How does Augustine conceive the mechanism of this first sin? He of course follows the Genesis narrative faithfully, all the while explicating or completing it. He presents the serpent as the tool of the devil, something that is not made explicit in the biblical text. The devil thus uses the serpent to speak deceptive words to the woman. It is, Augustine says, the weaker part of the human couple that he attacks first to arrive by degrees at the whole, judging that the man is not easily credulous or capable of letting himself be led into error unless he surrenders to the other's error.[30] In this way, when he came to the point of transgressing the law of God, the man did not let himself be seduced to the point of believing his wife's words to be true, but he obeyed her out of conjugal affection ("sed sociali necessitudine paruisse"). For it is not in vain that the Apostle said: "Adam was not deceived, but the woman was deceived."[31] Eve, in effect, welcomed the serpent's words as true. Adam, however, did not want to separate himself from his wife (literally, from his sole associate) even if that implied being associated with her in sin. He is no less guilty, for he sinned knowingly and deliberately.[32]

The sexual stereotypes—the woman easily tempted by what is pleasing to the eyes and good to eat, the man more thoughtful, more prudent—are at the service of a very sharp analysis of what could be called the mechanism of a collective sin, a common sin. The first sin is not Eve's; neither is it Adam's; nor is it Adam's added to Eve's. It is the sin of Adam and Eve, the sin of the couple considered as a "whole." Eve is seduced and deceived ("seducta et decepta"), and Adam is not, but it is the reflected consent of Adam that seals the common sin. It would be useless to seek to determine who is the "more guilty" of the two.

Politically, this story of the serpent and the apple needs to be taken very seriously. The first couple forms in truth the first city, the first "common thing." What takes place is determined by the structure of what is common. It is the *necessitudo socialis*—the need Eve experiences for Adam's approval on the one hand, to which Adam's indulgence of Eve corresponds on the other, for they would not have sinned if they had been indifferent to one another—that leads both of them not only to two like sins, not to the same sin, but to a common sin. This common sin, with its consequences, becomes the sin of the common thing they form and subsequently the sin of the common thing formed by the lineage of the first couple, the sin of humanity. The first sin, which is the personal and common sin of Adam and Eve, becomes the original sin—a sin not personally committed but "contracted" by their descendants, because the latter necessarily share in the common thing as it took its form in the wake of the first sin. In nontheological terms, if all the possibilities and all the energies of human sociability, or of the human bond, are condensed in the first couple, the crisis induced by their disobedience becomes coextensive with this sociability, in all the developments that sociability will undergo in the course of history. With the fall, humanity, dare I say, finds its character.

Let us come back to the mechanism or drama of the fall. Adam sinned knowingly, as we know. But how is this possible? How, still clear of any fault, of any evil inclination, was he able to commit such a calamitous blunder? Augustine suggests the following answer: before experiencing the divine rigor, he could have been mistaken in believing that his fault was venial.[33] But, Augustine insists, this first sin was extremely grave, as indicated by the fact that it transformed human nature, consigning it to death and the wrenching of the passions. Wherein precisely resides this gravity? It is not that the food Adam and Eve ate was bad or harmful, but that it was forbidden. Or, more precisely, it was bad or harmful only because it was forbidden.[34] Indeed God could not have planted anything bad in paradise. Adam could have touched the tree and eaten of its fruit without committing any fault if God had not formulated the prohibition.[35] If God gave an order, pronounced a prohibition concerning a tree in the garden, it was to elicit obedience, the virtue that is in some way the mother and guardian of all the virtues of the rational creature.[36] It is in effect useful for the rational creature to obey the will of his Creator; it is harmful to follow his own will. Moreover, the divine command was easy to observe—only one kind of food in all the abundance of paradise was forbidden to humans—all the more easy to observe in that in this condition of original justice the will effortlessly mastered desire.[37] In short, Adam and Eve's disobedience was all the more unjust in that observance was the more easy to keep.

Augustine draws a parallel between the disobedience of Adam and the obedience of Abraham: "Abraham's obedience is renowned in story as a great thing, and rightly so, because he was ordered to do an act of enormous difficulty, namely, to kill his own son. By the same token, the disobedience in paradise was all the greater inasmuch as the command was one of no difficulty at all."[38] In both cases, it will be noted, the divine command is completely *arbitrary*. Therein lie the heart and crux, but also the whole difficulty, of Augustine's interpretation. Therein lie the heart and crux, but also the whole difficulty, of Christian and biblical anthropology.

To what extent is Augustine's argument persuasive? To what extent do we find in our psychological and moral experience analogies that make it plausible and meaningful? Rousseau in any event was not persuaded and in his *Letter to Beaumont* he reversed the argument.[39] In a note he wrote in the *Letter*, Rousseau seems to have in mind our passage from Augustine. It begins as follows: "To resist a useless and arbitrary prohibition is a natural inclination, but one that, far from being vicious in itself, conforms with the order of things and the good constitution of man, since he would be incapable of preserving himself if he did not have a very lively love of himself and of the preservation of all his rights just as he has received them from nature."[40] Our two authors agree on one point: the divine command was arbitrary. From this proposition they draw opposite consequences. Whereas for Augustine this command should elicit salutary obedience, for Rousseau it naturally and legitimately elicits rebellion—"to resist." Whereas for Augustine following one's own will is a principle of aberration, for Rousseau love of self and even a "very lively" love of self is necessary to preserve oneself.

Let us continue to read Rousseau. "Someone who could do everything would want only what would be useful to him. But a weak Being, whose power is farther restrained and limited by the law, loses a part of himself, and demands in his heart what is taken away from him. To impute this to him as a crime would be making it a crime for him to be himself and not someone else. It would be simultaneously wanting him to be and not to be." Rousseau's argument could not be more radical. Law in itself signifies a mutilation for the weak being we are: it is a subtraction of "power." It thus elicits a legitimate complaint that comes from the "heart" and that expresses the very being of the one to whom the law is given.

It is Rousseau who best articulates the dispute between the Christian concept and what will be called the modern concept of relationship to the rule and therefore of right conduct: between sinful man and man as holder of natural rights, between the one bidden to be humble and to obey the rule and the one bidden to be proud and to vindicate his rights. Let us try to make the terms of the opposition more precise.

For the two men, for the two human types, relation to oneself is relation to a certain power. Augustine writes concerning the words of the serpent to the woman: "When would the woman have believed this assertion, telling them they had been held back by God from something good and beneficial, if there had not already been in her mind that love of her own independent authority and a certain proud over-confidence in herself, of which she had to be convicted and then humbled by that very temptation?"[41] The sentiment of love of one's own power leads to prideful presumption, which is the beginning of sin *(initium peccati)*. Whence there is need for a rule and for the humiliation contained in the rule. The rule or law humbles, abases, rebuffs, and restores to a more exact sentiment of himself a being who raises himself and puffs himself up through presumption. The man of Rousseau, on the contrary, as we have seen, experiences his power as a force in his weakness: he needs his power—all his power—to live. Yet the law weakens this being who is already weak and feels his weakness, and it makes him feel his weakness even more.

Love of one's own power is a specification of love of self. For Rousseau, "the only passion born with man, namely love of self, is a passion in itself indifferent to good and evil; . . . it becomes good or bad only by accident and depending on the circumstances in which it develops."[42] For Augustine, there could be no love of self that is neutral between good and evil, or indifferent to good and evil. Either love of self is "right," in accord with the rule, or else it is "perverse" because it disobeys the rule. Either it is right or it is wrong. The self does not exist outside a determined relation to the rule, a relation of conformity or on the contrary of disobedience. Either, or: this alternative is the ethical translation of the ontological status of the self, which is the condition of creatureliness. For Rousseau, the self is first of all a relationship to self that is ethically neutral, love of self that is indifferent to good and evil. The self is by itself what it is. Hence law is fundamentally against nature: it seeks to force people to be what they are not, and so it forces them to make believe that they are what they are not.

From this come two opposed conceptions of the lie of human life, the lie that is at the heart of human life. For Rousseau, as we have just seen, the law that tyrannizes a weak being is the root of the lie. For Augustine, not to live according to the rule, in the way for which he was created, is the lie for man.[43]

As we have just seen, Augustine and Rousseau thus represent two opposed ways of understanding human life. For the first, since humans are essentially dependent on their Creator, human life can only find its due order in obedience to the Creator, to his law or his grace. For the second, since the human being can only be understood as a "quantity of life," dare I say, that desires to preserve and enjoy itself, the law, as useful and even necessary as it can be otherwise, always inflicts a mutilation, a subtraction, of life. And if for Rousseau Augustine's exegesis consecrates the tyranny of law over nature and a misunderstanding of our condition of nature, for Augustine Rousseau's philosophy, supposing he could have known it, gives voice to and justifies the revolt of "vitiated nature" against its condition of creature.

We cannot let things stand at that, however. The polarity I have just brought out, however well founded, risks making us neglect a very significant element of the Augustinian perspective on human life. Augustine's relation to law or rule is less univocal than it appears by contrast with Rousseau. When he abandons properly exegetical or theological discourse and simply formulates his perception and evaluation of the social and moral life of men, Augustine is less distant from Rousseau than we would expect: he too has no great confidence in the powers of the rule.

In book 19, where he provides the most synthetic as well as the most dynamic exposition of his understanding of the human world, Augustine lets flow a great gush of eloquence, and as he unfolds the miseries of this life he declares he cannot hold back his tears.[44] The appeal to emotion precedes a quite restrictive and even unfavorable evaluation of the dispositions that master or govern the emotions, namely, the virtues. Pagan philosophy did not overlook the miseries of human life, but they appeared as the occasion or the matter of the virtues rather than as a characteristic or quality of human life that can be considered on its own and, so to speak, apart. By evoking these miseries in a deliberately pathetic manner, Augustine lessens the power of the cardinal or human virtues.

Here is what Augustine writes about virtue in general:

> What of virtue itself, which is not one of the primary gifts, since it supervenes on them later, introduced by teaching? Although it claims the topmost place among human goods, what is its activity in this world but unceasing warfare with vices, and those not external vices but internal, not other people's vices but quite clearly our own, our very own? And this is the particular struggle of that virtue called in Greek *sophrosyne*, which is translated "temperance"—the virtue which bridles the lusts of the flesh to prevent their gaining the consent of the mind and dragging it into every kind of immorality.[45]

Augustine's argument unquestionably distances us from the Greek understanding of virtue as the culmination and fulfillment of human nature and prepares the modern, especially Rousseauian, interpretation, according to which virtue is added to nature as something external. Augustine certainly does not go as far as Rousseau, who, as we have seen, ends up making virtue something that is contrary to nature, but he nonetheless underlines its exteriority in relation to the primary goods of nature *(prima naturae)*, an exteriority whose sign is its fragility. Whereas the Greek philosophers have a tendency to show virtue victorious if not triumphant, the master of the soul's peace, Augustine presents it as engaged in a continual war, a war it is always on the verge of losing. This is the case in particular of temperance, the virtue especially in charge, dare I say, of the war against the weakness of the flesh, a war we cannot win by our own forces and for which we must ask the help of God.

The role of the virtue of prudence and that of justice likewise testify that human life consists of working or struggling *(laborare)* without being able to find rest *(requiescere)*. Augustine devotes his longest discussion to the fourth cardinal virtue, courage. But *fortitudo* here should rather be translated as "strength of soul." Augustine begins by saying that this virtue is the most irrecusable witness of the human miseries that it is constrained to endure with patience. Indeed, what better witness of the miseries of this life can there be than the virtue that bears the miseries of this life? But how does it bear them and does it truly bear them? Augustine has not enough sarcasm for the Stoic sages who have the boldness to assert that miseries are not miseries since they have the strength to bear them or in any case since they can always escape them by taking their own life: "What a life of bliss, that seeks the aid of death to end it!" And again: "Is anyone so blind as to fail to see that if it were a happy life it would not be a life to seek escape from?"[46]

Then, changing tone, now more melancholic than polemical, Augustine meditates on this strange and terrible decision to take one's life, proof of the overwhelming force of the miseries of this life.[47] In this act that in the eyes of the Stoics represents the maximum of the soul's strength, Augustine sees the testimony of its defeat.

From all this it emerges that true virtue, the virtue that does not lie, the virtue that does not make believe it conquers when it is defeated, must, so to speak, integrate the fact that human beings cannot be completely happy in this life. It must then rest on hope in the future life.[48] The philosophers, who believe only what they can see and thus do not want to believe in this happiness that they do not see, devote all their efforts to fabricating for themselves a perfectly imaginary virtue. Human life is so filled with miseries that it is necessarily unable to experience happiness that is both present and effective. Either happiness is hoped for in the future life, or else, if one claims to lay hold of it in the present, it is necessarily imagined or imaginary.

Let us set aside the future life. Augustine agrees with Rousseau that with their laws and virtues, people do not succeed in ordering their lives in a tolerable way. If for one the law is the law of God, if for the other it is the invention of man, for both it hardly affects a human life that is more passive than active, that is, dare I say, more a deployment of weakness than strength.

What Augustine has to say about human justice in book 19 will permit us to go further into this aspect of his thought. In chapter 6 he offers us a reflection that is both subtle and pathetic on judicial torture as emblematic of the miseries of social life. This kind of torture carries a sort of rationality or even necessity: it has to do with revealing the truth that is hidden in the conscience of human beings. But the result is that a man suffers a certain penalty for an uncertain guilt. The judge, Augustine explains, subjects the accused to torture out of fear of condemning an innocent man to death, and the result is often that it is an innocent man who dies under torture. What strikes us here is not the denunciation of judicial torture as such, even if it is particularly vehement and if we associate such vehemence with Voltaire rather than St. Augustine. Rather, what is striking is that Augustine here accuses no one and certainly not the judge, whom he assumes to be wise and well intentioned. But the judge is "in the darkness that attends human society."[49] Human society chains him and forcibly drags him to this office that he would think it criminal to desert.[50] A necessity of the social machine is at work here: "the wise judge does not act in this way through a will to do harm, but because ignorance is unavoidable—and yet the exigencies of human society make judgement also unavoidable."[51] Augustine is at pains, as I have said, not to accuse the judge, and even all in all to excuse him, but at least the judge should be content not to be guilty without pretending also to be happy. Instead of being puffed up with the importance of his social role, let him recognize a misery in this necessity and let him hate it within himself, and if he has some sentiment of piety, let him cry out to God: " 'Deliver me from my necessities!' "[52]

Let us try to identify Augustine's perspective with a little more precision. If we employ the classification of the Ancients, we will say that Augustine's perspective is neither practical nor theoretical. His concern is neither to guide action nor to consider unchanging realities. His concern is rather to arouse a specific disposition, half-practical since it concerns evaluating human behavior and half-theoretical since it is constituted by a "view" of the human condition that does not change. This "intermediate" perspective is made clearer yet upon reading the following chapter, in which Augustine considers the frightening wars by which the Roman Empire was built. It is surprising to note that here the man who was among the first to attempt to formulate a doctrine of just war instead shows reticence about the idea. It can be said that the wise man will only engage in just wars, but it is the injustice of the enemy that requires him to wage this just war: "this injustice is assuredly to be deplored by a human being, since it is the injustice of human beings, even though no necessity for war should arise from it."[53] Augustine's perspective is obviously not that of practical or political life with its urgencies—to defeat an unjust enemy; neither is it that of the theoretical life, for example that of Thucydides striving to identify the human wellsprings of the phenomenon of war. It is then an intermediary perspective that could be called affective or pathetic, since it has to do with forming, dare I say, a sorrowful disposition in the face of human miseries. It is a disposition that incites us to desire to enter into the city of God, but it is not certain that it helps us much to orient ourselves in the cities of people.

The City of God and the People of God

I just mentioned the city of God and the cities of people. There is a human gathering, a people that does not belong to the cities, the nations, and yet is not the city of God. I mean of course the people of God, the Jewish people.

Augustine compares the legislator of the Hebrews to the legislator of the Spartans. The comparison of Moses and Lycurgus follows upon discussions of miracles and more generally of the fact that the invisible God willingly manifests himself in a visible form. The pagan legislators claimed to receive from the gods, or from divine beings, the inspiration for the laws they decreed. Augustine notes on this score how Lycurgus invoked Jupiter or Apollo.[54] The case of Numa and the nymph Egeria comes to mind.[55] They needed of course to be believed. On the contrary, in the case of Moses, Augustine explains, the divine intervention was visible and even striking to the eyes of all.

As we have already seen in the context of the discussion between Augustine and the pagan sages such as Cicero or Varro,[56] the true God does not distinguish between the few and the many. Since the law had to be proclaimed by the angels in a terrifying manner *(terribiliter)* not to one man only or to a small number of sages, but to an entire nation and to an immense people,[57] great things took place on the mountain in the sight of this people. Certainly the law was given through the mediation of one man alone, but in the presence of the multitude that witnessed the redoubtable and frightening things that were taking place.[58] The difference between Moses and the pagan legislators is that Moses appeared to the eyes of all and in a way one would dare to call spectacular as the simple instrument of the all-powerful God, whereas Lycurgus, Numa, or Romulus manifested in their way of proceeding those uncertain traits, that lack of clarity and sincerity, that are characteristic of pagan things, in any case of the pagan religion.

At the beginning of the following chapter, Augustine compares the human race to an individual: "There is a process of education, through the epochs of a people's history, as through the successive stages of a man's life." In any event this applies to what concerns the people of God.[59] The human race is like an individual who progresses inasmuch as one considers the people of God, or inasmuch as one considers the human race in light of the development of the people of God. There is no history of the education of the human race, one could say, except in the measure that there is a sacred history, that is, a history of the holy people. This education consists of rising from temporal and visible things to the knowledge—to the grasp—of eternal and invisible things. In this education of humanity, the chosen people play a decisive role for the following reason: "But even at the time when visible rewards were promised by divine revelation, man was commanded to worship one God, lest, even for the sake of the earthly benefits of this transient life, man should subject his mind to any being other than the Creator and Master of his soul."[60] In this way the chosen people were the intermediary, in some way the hinge between the two worlds, the bridge leading from temporal and visible things to eternal and invisible things.

Of course, in Augustine's eyes for the education of humanity, which is the revelation of truth, to be complete there must be a decisive detachment from the mixture of the temporal and eternal characteristic of the condition of the Jewish people. The final education of humanity requires that the revelation of the truth become a truly universal way *(universalis via)* that does not belong as such to a particular nation but has been granted by God to all nations to be common to them.[61] It belongs to the divine mercy to embrace the entire human race. Accordingly, "the Law and the Word of God did not stay in Sion and Jerusalem but went out from there so that it might spread through the whole world."[62]

The fact remains that this *universalis via* was at first especially proclaimed to the Hebrew people, whose political community was in a manner consecrated to prophesy and announce the city of God that was to be gathered out of all nations.[63] In Augustine's eyes, the coming of Christ introduced a perpetual division among the Jews between those "who attach themselves to Christ and continue steadfastly in his fellowship" and those "who persist in their hostility to Christ to the end of this life."[64] Henceforth the old covenant *(vetus testamentum)* from Mount Sinai that bears children destined for slavery is of no value except insofar as it bears witness to the new covenant.[65] Augustine goes on to say, "Otherwise, as long as 'Moses is read,' a veil [velamen] is laid on their hearts; on the other hand, whenever anyone passes over from that people to Christ, the veil will be taken away [auferetur velamen]."[66] The passage from the old to the new covenant is of a piece with the displacement of the *intentio* that turns away from material bliss and now attaches itself to spiritual bliss.[67]

Pascal will rework this notion of the "veil": "The veil which is drawn over these books for the Jews is also there for bad Christians, and for all who do not hate themselves."[68] He will take up the Pauline elements Augustine had already put to use, but his interpretation of the relation of the old and new covenants will be less "triumphalist" than the latter's. In this context the most significant passage is probably the following: "The Jewish religion, then, was formed on the pattern of the Messianic truth, and the Messianic truth was recognized [from] the Jewish religion, which prefigured it. Among the Jews the truth was only figurative; in heaven it is revealed. In the Church it is concealed and recognized by its relationship to the [figure]. The figure was drawn from the truth. And the truth was recognized from the figure."[69]

Christians cannot leave behind "the religion of the Jews" as if it no longer had any pertinence for them. Pascal begins, or titles, a lengthy fragment thus: "To show that true Jews and true Christians have only one religion."[70] The truth is indeed present in the Church but it is "concealed." It appears as truth, it is "recognized," only if it is placed in relation to the "religion of the Jews." Then it is "recognized from the figure." The truth of the Church is discovered only after and in the measure that it is recognized as the truth pointed to by the figure of Israel. Israel and the Church *together* constitute the structure of the revelation of the truth. In one sense the Church does not cease to *need* Israel as its most proper *proof.*[71]

Christianity, the Jewish Law, and Greek Philosophy

Let us return to Augustine and more precisely to book 10. It is in large part devoted to an at once sympathetic and critical examination of "the Platonist Porphyry." We cannot enter into this examination. I would like to make only one remark. After advancing the propositions that I cited above on the role of the Jews in the history of salvation, Augustine has this to say on the way Christianity resolves the perplexities of Porphyry the Platonist: "This is the way which purifies the whole man and prepares his mortal being for immortality, in all the elements which constitute a man. We have not to seek one purification for that element which Porphyry calls the 'intellectual' soul, another for the 'spiritual,' and yet another for the body itself. It was to avoid such quests that our Purifier and Saviour, the true Purifier and the all-powerful Saviour, took upon himself the man in his entirety."[72]

One can see that there is a sort of parallelism between the role of the Jewish people and that of Greek philosophy or wisdom in the development of the history of salvation. The formation of the Jewish people, like the elaboration of philosophy, both mark a decisive qualitative progress of the "self-awareness" of humanity. This progress in both cases comes at the price of a separation or rupture within humanity: the separation or rupture between the people of God and the "nations" and the separation or rupture between the philosopher or wise man and the "vulgar," the latter deriving from the separation and even the rupture between the soul and the body that is the condition and achievement of philosophy. One could say that Jewish election and Greek philosophy break the course of humanity to raise its level. Neither the progress nor the rupture should be underestimated. In the perspective drawn by Augustine, one can say that Christianity preserves or confirms the advances achieved by these two ruptures while it overcomes them by restoring human unity on a higher plane through the mediation of the God-man. Augustine's presentation makes Christianity appear as the resolution of the most profound and fruitful fractures of human unity, the Jewish and the Greek.

However, if the triangle is turned over, if Christianity is looked at starting from the Jewish law and Greek philosophy, the landscape changes considerably. To look at Christianity starting from the Jewish law and Greek philosophy is what Leo Strauss in particular does. Christianity then appears as a "synthesis" of the Jewish law and Greek philosophy. But a synthesis has this defect that it tends to weaken or blur what is most proper, most sharp, most "interesting" in each of the two elements. By synthesizing the Jewish law and Greek philosophy, Christianity on the one hand blunts the cutting edge of the divine Law that as such commands all actions and regulates life in all its aspects, and on the other hand circumscribes the freedom and in the end changes the meaning of philosophic inquiry that it puts in the service of dogma. Christianity then appears as the tempting but disappointing mixture of a law that does not truly command and a philosophy that does not truly seek. Accordingly, for Strauss the Christian combines in one being two human dispositions that are contradictory in their primary wellspring and that consequently can only constrain and hinder one another.

What would Augustine reply? He would probably counter Strauss with the symmetrical reproach. Strauss confirms and even accentuates the separations and ruptures: the separation between philosophy and the law, between the philosopher and other people who live under the law, between the Jews and the nations, with the Jewish law being the Law par excellence. He certainly has good reasons for this: if the Jewish law, like Greek philosophy, is obliged to accept and even affirm a deep and so to speak ontological separation among humans, this separation is not made out of a liking for separation but out of an intransigent love of the human good. Besides, the Jewish law is not specific to the Jews: it is the best law for humans.[73] And, of course, philosophy leads those who are capable of it to the most ample human good. Extending the law, like disseminating philosophy, would thus be to dilute one as well as the other. Let us grant all that to Strauss. But why would the immense majority of humanity not know the Law of the true God or in any case be excluded from its benefits? This is the mystery of election. And how could the greatest human good—wisdom—evade nearly all people? This is the mystery of the few who are wise or of the rarity of the "philosopher's nature." To reject the Christian synthesis is to accept two "separations" against which something in the human being can only protest. That would be at least one possible answer to Strauss's critique.

Moreover, it could be said in addition that Christianity is not so "synthetic" as that. The doctrine that extends the same law or rather the same rights to all and that "makes philosophy popular" is the philosophy of the Enlightenment, or, if one wishes, of the "religion of humanity." Christianity in a certain measure preserves the two ruptures that we are considering: Christian "universality," as I have already emphasized, does not cease to explicitly join itself to Jewish "particularity." And the Christian promise could not be formulated without the prior philosophic discovery, the Platonic discovery, of the soul in its radical distinction from the body. This is such that if we take modern democracy into consideration, Christianity instead of being simply a "synthesis" is in the position of a "middle term" between the Jewish and Greek "separations" on the one hand and the unification or "maximum synthesis" of the Moderns on the other. However summary they may be, these remarks introduce the question that underlies our perplexity here, the question of the universal.[74]

The Question of the Universal

The preceding considerations on the Jewish law, Greek philosophy, Christianity, and democracy help us to pose in a more precise and concrete way the question of the universal. These four great moments of the history of humanity, which also constitute the four great spiritual determinations of Western humanity, not only form a chronological succession but also mark the major stages on the gradient of increasing universality that sums up for us the only possible meaning of human history. What is intelligible for us is the general or universal. History appears as intelligible to the extent that within it progress toward the universal is taking place. At least that is the conviction that has dominated the Western mind since the eighteenth century.

There is indeed a tension between the general notion of progress—progress is "progressive"—and the fact that each of these four moments constitute as many ruptures or innovations. Must we think that the latest innovation—democracy—"preserves and surpasses" the gains of the first three? It would be very satisfying to be able to embrace with assurance such a view, which could be readily labeled "Hegelian." But Leo Strauss has alerted us to the risks of "synthesis." On the other hand, to choose one of the four moments for itself, to stop there as if the harbor of the human adventure had at last been arrived at, would take away the desire—and first of all the reason—to consider this historical succession in itself as worthy of our interest. How are we to proceed?

Let us first note the rather undetermined character of the notion of generality or universality when it is reduced to itself. It can certainly be said that any progress of humanity, any progress of civilization, entails a progress of generality, the passage from a certain particularity to a certain generality. In the Greek world as in the Roman world and the Christian world, a decisive progress was accomplished by the passage from the familial or feudal order to the civic or national order. But this extension, or generalization or equalization, entails a substantial transformation of the primitive elements, a substantial transformation that reveals or produces a new element. In the case of the Greek city, this new element is the common *(koïnon)*; in the case of Rome, it is the public thing *(res publica)*; in the case of the European nation, it is the *public* in its different declensions: public interest, public opinion, public space. Stated otherwise, every progress in generality requires a new human association as the framework of a novel human operation. In the cases that we have just considered, the new association is the city, or the nation; the operation is "self-government." Progress in generality or in universality is but one aspect of a substantial transformation—the "quantitative" aspect of a "qualitative" transformation. Moreover, this entails some uncertainty in the evaluation of "progress." A modern nation whose regime is "republican" or "democratic" is incomparably more "general" or "universal" than an ancient city, since all its nationals are also citizens. But since, precisely as a consequence of the great number of citizens, the regime of modern democracy is necessarily representative, the operation that is proper to the modern political form is very different from the operation proper to the ancient political form. The modern nation-state is unquestionably more "general" or more "universal" than the ancient city; it is not evident that its "self-government" is better, more complete, more accomplished, more in keeping with what the word "democracy" necessarily leads one to understand.

Besides, there is uncertainty regarding the extension, the "level of generality" that the ancient city exhibits, especially the Greek city and in a unique way Athens. Its civic body is relatively restricted, but the landscape changes if in its operation we include philosophy, which was born there: the citizens are not numerous, but one of them—Socrates—is a citizen of the world. Over the political operation the philosophic operation emerges and detaches itself from it. There too the progress in generality or universality accomplished by philosophy—the progress that is the "greatest progress" in the measure that the philosopher as philosopher breaks all ties to a particular political body, even to his own family—is inseparable from its own proper operation, which is the "theoretical life." In revealing the "theoretical life" as a human possibility, the philosopher separates himself from other men at the very moment when he otherwise defines man in his universality as a "political animal" and "rational animal."

The necessary link between the progress of the universal on the one hand and on the other the production of a new association that is the framework and the means of a new operation is not less visible, even if it is less evident, in the case of Israel. The election of Israel in no way signifies a surfeit of particularity or particularism. The regime of particularity is the pagan regime of civic or "national" divinities—the "gods of the cities" or of "the nations." If the pagan city is let down by its god, it will replace it or in any case will seek help from the gods of neighboring cities, especially if these cities are victorious. This is forbidden to Israel: its God is a jealous god. To go to the heart of the matter: its God is the only God, the one who created humans, who liberated his people[75] and gave them the most just Law.[76] The election of Israel is not the intensification,

298 EMPIRE, CHURCH, NATION

or the "maximum," of the old pagan particularity or of human particularity in general. It is the effort to appropriate in the closest possible way a novel notion of divinity; I was going to say the full notion of God as infinitely powerful and perfectly benevolent—the pagan gods are neither one nor the other. As Deuteronomy emphasizes and the Psalms deploy, the Creator, infinitely exalted above every creature, is at the same time the being that is "closest" to humans, to all and to each. Israel discovers and operates the overwhelming nearness of the most distant. This discovery and this operation rigorously separate Israel from the "nations."

As for Christianity, I will not come back to the question whether the Christian Church assimilates while it surpasses the two Jewish and Greek ruptures, or whether on the contrary it offers only a bland synthesis. What is in any case certain is that it too brings a new association or communion, the Church itself, as a real universal community, the framework and instrument of a new operation: charity. What is also certain is that the new Christian unity—the progress in universality that Christianity represents in our eyes—is accompanied by a new separation that in turn redoubles itself: the essentially invisible separation between the city of God and the earthly city that is confusedly and very imperfectly refracted in the separation between the visible Church and non-Christians. In effect, the great Catholic unity will appear more and more as a division or as a factor of division: the *respublica christiana,* or Christendom, is in the end but a modest part of the human world and within itself is divided or fragmented into confessions that are hostile to one another or that in any case could not be said to be united by charity. The modern political movement—including in this term modern political philosophy and the transformation of public spirit and of the political and social affects it arouses or accompanies—can be understood as an effort to overcome the Christian separation, to bring about a universality that is at last truly and effectively universal.

In any case we cannot avoid asking the following question: what for us Moderns is the association, the framework, and instrument of what operation, in which the earlier divisions of humanity are overcome? The answer that comes naturally to mind is obviously that this association is humanity itself, which is more universal than the universal Church. But what does the human association or humanity as an association mean? Whom does it encompass? Everybody, of course. But what does everybody mean? Everybody living? But by what right are those who are dead cut off from humanity? By what right are the unborn cut off from humanity? And of the living, are not most in effect invisible to us? In short, humanity as universal association is in one sense just as invisible as the invisible Church. We do not know how to determine the form and the limits of this association. Whence of course the vast career open to the makers of humanity, to those who believe themselves capable of determining who truly belongs to humanity and thus who is outside the pale of humanity. For example, some were saying not long ago that humanity is those who are yet to be born and that as for the present it is the proletarians and the allies of the proletariat. With the hindsight of experience we are struck by the arbitrariness of ideological definitions of humanity. But to many they appeared plausible and obvious, and they even aroused their enthusiasm. The undetermined character of the notion of humanity is an invitation to put forth an arbitrary, ideological determination of humanity.

If we are uncertain about the very existence of a community of humanity or of humanity as a community it is that we do not know the answer to this question: what would be the *proper operation* of this universal community? If there is a universal human community or association, it is the framework and instrument of some action; it "does" something. The city is the framework and instrument of a specific action—chiefly "self-government." The Church is the framework and the instrument of a specific action—the "life of charity," "sanctification." But what about humanity? Well, in spite of what Dante advances with so much assurance,[77] it is difficult to conceive what this operation would be; and thus it is difficult to maintain that humanity constitutes an effective political community.

These remarks help us to account for the way philosophies of history beginning in the eighteenth century were deployed as though they were self-evident and necessary. The operation of humanity as a whole that must be postulated and situated somewhere was supposed to come to sight in the movement of history that, through stages the philosophers of history conceive in different ways, leads to a goal on which all or nearly all of them agree: the unification of humanity. There is history in the modern sense of the term only because a movement toward the unification of humanity is observed or postulated. But it could be said that the philosophies of history run aground when reaching the harbor. For, if the moving principle of history is the effort to attain unity—this is intelligible, and there are strong enough arguments to maintain it—what happens once we have achieved the unity of humanity, that is, once we have reached the end of history? What then does humanity do? This is where the philosophers of history do not know what to say, or they utter childish nonsense. But if united humanity has nothing to do, then it does not exist or it no longer exists. Or again, if the final state of humanity cannot be truly thought because it is impossible to say what human activity would consist of, the understanding of human history as a process oriented toward unity and universality is itself cast into doubt.

There is, however, one philosopher who tried to answer the question we are raising of what is and first of all whether there is an operation proper to humanity considered in its entirety or as a whole without giving in to the temptation of positing an end to history, or if he did it, it is an end that does not end. That philosopher is Immanuel Kant. Because he does not posit an end to history, Kant cannot categorically affirm that humanity is advancing through necessary stages toward a sure future. But he can identify the signs of progress, more precisely the signs of a moral disposition and destination of humanity. The proper operation of humanity, according to Kant, is to fulfill its moral destination.

As we have seen, the gathering of humanity for a common operation is hindered by the two highest and most universal expressions of humanity: philosophy and revealed religion. By positing the "theoretical life" as the superior goal of humanity, philosophy rends the fabric, dare I say, of common humanity whose life is essentially "practical." Revealed religion, whether Jewish or Christian, also ruptures human unity, but in an altogether different way by separating the Jewish people from the "nations" or by separating the two cities and believers from nonbelievers.

Thus, to achieve a rigorously universal or universalizing definition of the moral destination of humanity, to be able to legitimately consider humanity as a gathering engaged in a common operation, Kant must reform philosophy at the same time as religion. At the same time that he brings religion back within the limits of reason alone in such a way that it no longer separates people by dogmas they cannot understand,[78] he moralizes philosophy so that from a prideful knowledge that separates the learned person or scholar from other persons,[79] it becomes a moral activity subjected to the criterion of the "total destination of man." In the "Architectonic of Pure Reason," Kant distinguishes between the "scholastic" concept of philosophy, according to which philosophy aims only at the "logical" perfection of knowledge, and the "cosmic" conception of philosophy, according to which philosophy is the science of the relation that all knowledge has to the essential ends of human reason:[80] "This ultimate end [of reason] is the destination of man, and the philosophy which relates to it is termed Moral Philosophy. The superior position occupied by moral philosophy, above all other spheres for the operations of reason, sufficiently indicates the reason why the ancients always included the idea—and in an especial manner—of Moralist in that of Philosopher."[81]

In this way Kant succeeds in mending—I do not dare say patching—the moral fabric of humanity that was doubly rent, by prideful philosophy and by dogmatic religion.

There remains one difficulty. The signs of the progress of humanity are equivocal. More precisely, if one can observe the signs of a progress toward peace, freedom, and the rule of law, toward a "republican constitution" of the States, one must inquire into the wellspring of this movement. Is it the result of an increasingly clever organization of the "self-seeking inclinations" of humans,[82] or of a moral conversion by which "morally practical reason pronounces in us its irresistible *veto: there is to be no war?*"[83]

In this way at the same time he arrives at the moral unification of humanity and in order to arrive at it, Kant opens up a division at the heart of the human makeup; in any event he emphasizes and sharpens a division between the self-seeking inclinations and respect for the moral law. This division not only affects the individual members of the human species, it calls into question the very meaning of the movement of humanity taken as a whole or according to its total destination. Is humanity going toward an ever more clever "devilishness," or is it an increasingly moral species, more and more moved by respect for the moral law? It is that much more difficult to eliminate this uncertainty since the visible effects of the two opposed dispositions resemble one another so much.

In the final analysis, the Kantian scheme ends up imitating or repeating the Augustinian scheme. For Kant also we are confronted with an inextricable mix of the two cities, the one animated by the "self-seeking inclinations," the other by respect for moral law, the city of God here giving way to the kingdom of ends:

> The concept of every rational being as one who must regard himself as giving universal law through all the maxims of his will, so as to appraise himself and his actions from this point of view, leads to a very fruitful concept dependent upon it, namely that *of a kingdom of ends*.
>
> By a *kingdom* I understand a systematic union of various rational beings through common laws. Now since laws determine ends in terms of their universal validity, if we abstract from the personal differences of rational beings as well as from all the content of their private ends we shall be able to think of a whole of all ends in systematic connection (a whole both of rational beings as ends in themselves and of the ends of his own that each may set himself), that is, a kingdom of ends, which is possible in accordance with the above principles.[84]

It might be feared that Kant's chisel is not enough to give the kingdom of ends the determined character it essentially lacks. Respect for the moral law and the resolve to consider every reasonable being always as an end and never simply as a means do not provide the principle of a common operation capable of giving life to humanity taken as a whole.

We have charted the sequence of forms—of some principal forms—of human association while emphasizing in each instance that the association under consideration exists only as the framework and instrument of an operation that is proper to it. We have assumed that the passage from one form to another was not fortuitous but motivated by the defects or shortcomings of the preceding form. More precisely: since the operation that associates also separates, the succeeding form strives to overcome this separation. In this sense we have confirmed the common opinion that the development of humanity is intelligible as the progress of generality or universality, but with this important complement or corrective: universality, whatever its tenor or its form, rests on a universalizing *operation*. It is on this point that the form that is in appearance the most universal, and conceived to be such, is also the most disappointing: it is difficult, as I have just said, to state precisely in what the operation that gives life to the kingdom of ends consists exactly.

The difficulties presented by the Jewish law, Greek philosophy, and the Christian Church are real indeed, but they cannot be resolved or overcome by throwing oneself into the universalism of a humanity that would be by itself its own proper form. The Jewish law that separates the chosen people from the "nations," Greek philosophy that separates the "philosopher's nature" from the rest of humanity, the Christian Church that separates the city of God and the earthly city, each one of these three great determinations of the human has more substance and coherence than the apparently clearer idea of human generality or universality.

The *question* of the universal is indeed in one sense *the* most pertinent and encompassing question, but it is not resolved at the end of history. If history had an immanent end that gives it meaning, it would have reached it long ago. To tell the truth, if history had an immanent end, how could it ever have begun? Nothing is stronger than the end, and human history would have begun by the end. Indeed, that is what has happened. The end that does not cease giving the beginning again and makes it possible to begin again unceasingly is nature, human nature. The only possible principle—the only possible cause—of the movement of human history is man himself, who strives to order his humanity by governing himself.

9

THE STAKES OF MEDIATION

At the end of chapter 8 we considered the four great "versions of the universal" that are Jewish law, Greek philosophy, the Christian Church, and humanity understood according to the modern perspective. Now, if these are all so many replies to the question of the universal, one could also say that they are so many replies to the question of God. In both cases it is a matter of reaching, so to speak, the limit of what can be thought, the largest or highest thought. The close solidarity between the two questions is obvious in the case of Jewish law and the Christian Church. It also quickly shows itself in the case of Greek philosophy that, as we will shortly see more precisely, is an effort to attain the right idea, the "rational" idea of the godhead or the divine. As for humanity understood in the modern perspective, it has left behind the Jewish, Christian, and Greek or philosophic notions of the divine in order, now that it has expelled the "highest" idea, to embrace the simply "largest" idea, which is the idea of humanity itself. In the modern notion of humanity, not only is the divine present by its absence, but humanity thus understood is the framework of a religion of which it is also the object, the "religion of humanity."

Taking into account the road we have traveled to this point, the most enlightening way to enter into the question of the link between the universal and the divine, between humanity and divinity, is to consider how Augustine treats the philosophical approach, especially the Platonist approach to the question of God.

Plato Christianus

Augustine shows great respect for the "learned Varro" when, as a philosopher or in the manner of the philosophers, he inquires into the true nature of things and of the gods in particular—even if he reproaches him for his timidity in the face of the *consuetudo civitatis*. This respect and sympathy for philosophy is transformed into admiration and enthusiasm in book 8 when he considers the philosophy of Plato. Plato's philosophy is so close to the Christian truth that Augustine is led to believe that Plato became acquainted—through an interpreter—with the Sacred Scriptures during his stay in Egypt.[1] The Platonist philosophers sought God in the right direction and arrived at the right conclusion that he made all beings and that he could not have been made by any.[2] The tone Augustine employs to treat of Platonist philosophy is altogether different from the one he had adopted in speaking of pagan religion. He gives us the feeling of passing from darkness to light or that the world is at last set right.

As we know, for Augustine there are two great facts that break the monotony of the darkness, dare I say, two decisive ruptures by which humanity disposes itself, makes itself capable of accepting Christian truth. On the one hand is the Jewish people: "the Hebrew people was gathered and united in a kind of community designed to perform this sacred function of revelation,"[3] the *mysterium* or *sacramentum* that is the covenant for eternal life between God and humans; and on the other, Greek philosophy, at least Platonist philosophy.

Yet despite this decisive progress in the knowledge of the true God, the Platonists held that sacrifice had to be offered to a multitude of gods.[4] Not only did a decisive philosophic progress not lead to a corresponding religious progress, but the religion of the Platonists is striking in its derangement. For Augustine it was now no longer a question of criticizing pagan religion in general, nor of celebrating the particular merits of Platonist philosophy. It was a question of analyzing this unique phenomenon of the pagan religion interpreted or transformed by Platonist philosophy, a mixture that is in some way the final state of pagan religion, the state that is the most intellectually refined and at the same time the most corrupt, and the backdrop against which the Christian religion emerges and in contrast to which it yields its meaning most directly.

Augustine congratulates Plato for recommending that the poets be expelled from the city.[5] For both, what the poets say of the gods is unworthy of the gods. The principal point on which Augustine and Plato are joined is that "all gods are good."[6]

Let us pause a moment with Plato's own text, to which Augustine did not have access.

In book 2 of the *Republic,* when Socrates and his companions are outlining the elements of the best possible education for the guardians of the city and after emphasizing the role of music and gymnastics, they turn their attention to the stories children are told. These stories derive from the poems of Hesiod and Homer and the other poets who "composed false tales for human beings."[7] The greatest falsity is the one that bears on the most important beings, "the gods and the heroes."[8] What matters first of all is to correct what is said about the gods and to elaborate models for speaking about the gods ("oï tupoï peri theologias").[9] *Theologia* here means what is said about the gods, speech about the gods. The term belongs to the language of philosophy and not to that of religion. *Theologia* is not "theology" as divine science or learned discourse about the gods; it is the *way of speaking about the gods* in the city.

How does one speak about the gods? According to what "type"? The first thing that must be said is that "the god is really good."[10] "Then, [Socrates goes on to say,] the god, since he's good, wouldn't be the cause of everything, as the many say, but the cause of a few things for human beings and not responsible for most. For the things that are good for us are far fewer than those that are bad; and of the good things, no one else must be said to be the cause; of the bad things, some other causes must be sought and not the god."[11] And after Adeimantus exclaims, "I give my vote to you in support of this law . . . and it pleases me," Socrates declares, "Now, then, . . . this would be one of the laws and models concerning the gods, according to which those who produce speeches will have to do their speaking and those who produce poems will have to do their making: the god is not the cause of all things, but of the good."[12]

The second law would concern the fact that the gods do not change form. In effect, a thing is that much better the less it changes. Now the god and what pertains to the god is the best possible in every respect. Thus, every god simply remains in the form proper to it.[13] The second law and model is this: "the god is altogether simple and true in deed and speech, and he doesn't himself change or deceive others by illusions, speeches, or the sending of signs either in waking or dreaming."[14]

Had he known Plato's text itself, Augustine would no doubt have been confirmed in his appreciation of Plato's extraordinary merit. But an attentive reading would have made him see that Plato's intention here is not to propose the dogmas of true religion or to elaborate the propositions of true philosophy. He is concerned to educate the guardians of the city through good laws and principles, and perhaps also to begin to orient those who have a philosophic nature in the direction of the *idea* that does not change. The concern is to reform the religion of the city—in Varro's language, the *theologia civilis*—while providing directions leading to the *mundus* for those who are capable of leaving the city—in Varro's language, those who seek freedom in the *theologia naturalis*.

However this may be, the Platonist reform produced effects that were assuredly far removed from Plato's purpose and intentions. Plato's "reformed theology" has its meaning, as I have just pointed out, in the framework and for the needs of the virtuous city. What does it become when circumstances detach it from the civic framework? When the rapport with the gods is not principally organized by the needs—whether structural or circumstantial—of the closed city but must be formulated in the open space of the Greco-Roman Empire? What happens to the divine when its framework of expression is transformed and expanded to the dimensions of the "world"? Such a transformation profoundly modifies human life; it modifies the life of the gods no less. This is indeed the context in which Augustine's critique has its target and meaning: the pagan religion with reference to which the Christian religion discloses its proper character most clearly is not the pagan religion of the cities in its original spontaneity; I might say, it is the religion of the cities that have undergone two important and related transformations, the intellectual transformation produced by Platonism and the political transformation produced by the passage from city to empire. The two transformations are connected, since they involve two ruptures in the closedness of the city, the perspective or horizon of philosophy as well as that of empire being humanity as a whole or the "world."[15]

What then becomes of the religion reformed by Plato when it is detached from its civic framework? The Platonism that is at work here is obviously very simplified, but it retains what is at the heart of Plato's re-form: "all gods are good" and "gods never mix with men."[16] What religion will the Platonists be able to elaborate and recommend on this basis?

The problem to be resolved can be formulated as follows: how can humans enter into relation with gods that are surely good but who have nothing to do with humans? It is a problem of *mediation*. Through what mediator or mediators can humans enter into relation with gods that are so conceived?

The paradox of this politically unmoored Platonism, this "depoliti-cized" Platonism, is that, through a process whose shameful character Augustine unflaggingly denounces at the same time he emphasizes its strange logical or even ontological necessity, the only mediators that can be envisaged under these conditions are the *demons*.

Structurally the Platonists, or the so-called platonists, obey the same necessity as Plato himself, as it shows up in the dialogue of Socrates and Diotima:

> "What would Eros then be?" I said. "A mortal?"
> "Hardly that."
> "Well, what then?"
> "Just as before," she said, "between mortal and immortal."
> "What is that, Diotima?"
> "A great daemon, Socrates, for everything daemonic is between god and mortal."
> "With what kind of power?" I said.
> "Interpreting and ferrying to gods things from human beings and to hu-man beings things from gods: the requests and sacrifices of human beings, the orders and exchanges-for-sacrifices of gods; for it is in the middle of both and fills up the interval so that the whole itself has been bound to-gether by it. Through this proceeds all divination and the art of the priests who deal with sacrifices, initiatory rituals, incantations, and every kind of soothsaying and magic. A god does not mingle with a human being; but through this occurs the whole intercourse and conversation of gods with human beings."[17]

But the "platonists" inflect or "concretize" the understanding of the "daemon" in such a way that Augustine will have no difficulty in conclud-ing that it is indeed a "bad angel."

In this way the Platonist reform, in identifying the right idea of the true God or coming close to it, induced a religion that adores the demons, with all the absurd or sordid magical practices this adoration entailed.

Augustine explores these consequences at some length by considering the work of Apuleius.[18] The most interesting point for us is that a shocking and quite absurd religion in sum logically derives from the necessities of the most exactly and scrupulously conceived mediation. Since the gods live in their splendid isolation, it is the intermediaries between gods and humans, the demons, that necessarily become the object of human adoration. Now, who or what are they? Their nature is obviously determined by their intermediate character. Thus they combine human and divine attributes. They are according to "species, animal; soul, subject to passions; mind, rational; body, composed of air; life-span, eternal."[19] The main point is that the demons share human passions. Thus the religion of Apuleius consists in honoring or adoring beings that one would not want to resemble. It is all in all the contrary of a religion; it is more precisely contrary to the virtue of religion that consists in imitating what one adores, or venerates: "It is nothing but folly, nothing but pitiable aberration, to humble yourself before a being whom you would hate to resemble in the conduct of your life and to worship one whom you refuse to imitate. For surely the supremely important thing in religion is to model oneself on the object of one's worship."[20]

While they distance the gods from men and thus form an idea of the gods that is more worthy of their true nature, the Platonists nevertheless fall into a perverse religion, the adoration of demons, because they do not attain a satisfactory solution to the problem of mediation; they do not determine the true mediator. Augustine exhausts the combinations of demonic mediation, of the possible associations or mixtures of human and divine attributes. The good demons could not be mediators, for being good and eternal and thus blessed, they are much closer to the gods than to humans. The effective mediator, the one that is so to speak situated at equal distance from humans and gods, the one who displays the most equal mixture of human and divine attributes, is indeed the bad demon, since it is at the same time both miserable—a human attribute—and eternal—a divine attribute.[21]

There could of course be another possibility. There could be another equal mixture, the one that a blessed mortal would display.[22] Can a mortal be blessed? That is a great question among humans.[23] Some, considering their condition *humilius,* have denied that humans can be capable of happiness *(beatitudo)* as long as they lead a mortal life. Others, carried away by presumption, have dared to say that mortals, if they possessed wisdom *(sapientiae compotes),* could be blessed. The words he uses indicate that Augustine is not among those who hold the latter opinion. Nonetheless in the following lines he treats of it with understanding, even with respect. He emphasizes its coherence. The wise person, the philosopher, can appear as the mediator between the unhappy mortals and blessed immortals.[24]

However, it is much more believable and probable that all humans, as long as they are mortal, are necessarily also unhappy.[25] Thus, the mediation between humans and gods cannot be assured either by the good demons, or by the bad demons, or by the wise men. Whatever way one conceives it, whatever way human and divine attributes are associated in it, an intermediary being cannot be an effective mediator. If mediation cannot be ensured by an intermediary being, where is it to be sought? It must be sought in a being that, instead of being an intermediary, is at the same time one and the other extreme: "we must look for a mediator who is not only human but also divine."[26] The man-God is thus the mediator we seek.

Augustine adds the following precisions: "And yet he is not the Mediator in that he is the Word; for the Word, being pre-eminently immortal and blessed, is far removed from wretched mortals. He is the Mediator in that he is man." We do not have to look for other mediators to raise us by degrees to divinity since the blessed God who is the giver of blessedness "became partaker of our human nature and thus offered us a short cut to participation in his own divine nature." And it is in the form of a servant ("in forma servi") that he effects his mediation.[27]

Augustine defends the credibility of the union of the two natures in the person of Christ by underlining that the union of soul and body that constitutes the human being is even more incredible.[28]

Incarnation and Mediation

Thus, in depoliticized or imperial paganism, mediation is "demonic," the demon being understood as the "erotic" dynamism of the human soul highlighted by Plato or, more and more, as a distinct spiritual substance. In Christianity the mediation is that of Christ, who is man and God, and the Church is mediating as "the body of Christ." In the modern order of human rights, so-called subjective rights, it seems there is no longer any mediation. Since the mediator is an intermediary between humans and gods or the divine and that the divine or relationship with the divine is no longer publicly acknowledged in our regimes—it is a private matter, *Privatsache*—one does not see where to look among us for the mediator or mediation. But if that is true, then an essential element of the human world, in any event an element that was essential during the two preceding waves of our history—the pagan and the Christian—has disappeared for us. It is or it would be a singular phenomenon. The matter merits reflection.

How is one to come to terms with the question of the fate of mediation in European history? The decisive moment, the one that offers the most to think about, is certainly the Reformation. The Reformation rejected the mediation of the Church as a separate and visible institution. Instead of being saved by partaking in the sacraments of the Church, instead of being saved by being part of the Church, the believer instructed by Luther is saved by faith in the Word of God, by faith alone *(sola fide)*, faith produced in the soul by grace alone *(sola gratia)*. "Nor was Christ sent into the world for any other ministry except that of the Word. Moreover, the entire spiritual estate—all the apostles, bishops, and priests—has been called and instituted only for the ministry of the Word, even though it is otherwise today."[29]

The Old Testament, says Luther, is filled with commandments or laws of God that prescribe all sorts of good works, but that does not suffice for those works to be done, for the laws or commandments do not give any power for that. They are set down for one thing only: so that humans might see in them that they are powerless to do good and that they might learn to despair of themselves and seek help elsewhere. Once people are altogether humbled, annihilated in their own eyes, finding nothing in themselves that could justify them, they can hear the other Word, the Word of the New Testament, the commitment and the divine promise to grant every grace, every justice, every peace, and every liberty to the believer in Christ. Thus the promises of God give what the commandments require and fulfill what they ordain, such that everything, commandment and fulfillment, belongs to God alone.[30]

The Church as a separate spiritual society was mediating by virtue of its very separateness. Once the mediating separateness of the Church is abolished, only the preaching of the Word puts sinful humans in contact with the grace of Christ the mediator:

> Rather ought Christ to be preached to the end that faith in him may be established that he may not only be Christ, but be Christ for you and me, and that what is said of him and is denoted in his name may be effectual in us. Such faith is produced and preserved in us by preaching why Christ came, what he brought and bestowed, what benefit it is to us to accept him. This is done when that Christian liberty which he bestows is rightly taught and we are told in what way we Christians are all kings and priests and therefore lords of all [aller Dinge mächtig] and may firmly believe that whatever we have done is pleasing and acceptable in the sight of God, as I have already said.
>
> What man is there whose heart, upon hearing these things, will not re-joice to its depth, and when receiving such comfort will not grow tender so that he will love Christ as he never could by means of any laws or works? Who would have the power to harm or frighten such a heart? If the knowl-edge of sin or the fear of death should break in upon it, it is ready to hope in the Lord. It does not grow afraid when it hears tidings of evil. It is not disturbed when it sees its enemies. This is so because it believes that the righteousness of Christ is its own and that its sin is not its own, but Christ's, and that sin is swallowed up by the righteousness of Christ.[31]

Thus, for Luther the mediation of Christ, without the instrument or complement of ecclesial mediation, is accomplished by the gratuitous encounter between the justice of Christ and the injustice of the sinner, an encounter in which the two poles exchange their traits—justice against sin—while remaining what they are—the one just, the other sinful. In the Catholic ordering, one was a more or less good citizen of the city of God, that is, one was more just to the extent that one was less a sinner and that grace *really* transformed nature; in the Lutheran ordering, the Christian is always *simultaneously* a just person and sinner ("simul jus-tus et peccator").[32] To the extent that grace remains extrinsic, one could say that it shows itself incapable of effectively transforming nature and that thus the mediation of Christ encounters a limit. It is perhaps for that reason that certain expressions of Luther make of the believer him-self a second Christ, so to speak: "A believer is once and for all raised above all things and yet subjected to all things; thus he is like a twofold being and like Christ possesses two natures that are joined in him."[33]

It was necessary to go into Luther's doctrine a little in order to have an opportunity to evaluate the significance of the Reformation in what I have called the fate of mediation in European history. One agrees in general that the crisis of the Reformation is not only of course the moment of the rupture of Catholic *unity* but also the moment of the rupture of the great Catholic *mediation*—the mediation between reason and faith, nature and grace, this world and the next, and also paganism and Christianity. The rupture of Catholic mediation is thought to have decisively contributed to the emergence of a novel figure full of promise that will be neither pagan nor Christian and that will be called by the name of the individual. Moreover, the thesis is adopted just as well by those who judge this new figure of humanity severely, such as Auguste Comte, as by those, much more numerous, who consider this development as a progression or as progress itself. Among all the authors one could consider, Marcel Gauchet is certainly for us one of the most interesting on account of the way he treats this question of mediation.

I will start with a sentence from *The Disenchantment of the World*: "The Reformation brought the beginnings of an appropriate awareness of divine otherness and its consequences, whereby whole sections of social practice were informed and wrought by the dynamics of terrestrial appropriation demanded by a separated god."[34] This sentence implicitly contains the central thesis of the book on the role of Christianity regarding the appearance, establishment, and legitimation of an autonomous human order. What interests us more particularly here are the first words of the sentence and what they imply.

For Marcel Gauchet, Protestantism is in sum the truth of Christianity since it comes close to the fitting consciousness of divine otherness that will produce or permit the emancipation and legitimation of an autonomous human order. We could say that in Gauchet's view the Reformation took a step comparable to that of Socrates in book 2 of the *Republic* that we have discussed. Both cases are concerned with bringing to light a more exact and worthier idea of the god. And in both cases, to achieve a more just idea of the divine is to distance the divine from humans. For Plato, the god has little or nothing at all to do with humans. For Luther, grace, although salvific, remains outside the sinner. However one evaluates it, Gauchet's view draws its legitimacy and the clarity of its interior wellspring from the Platonist or simply philosophic question: "Quid sit deus?"

As we saw in going from Plato to Augustine through the "Platonists," a more fitting idea of the divine gave greater urgency to the question of mediation. As the divine otherness was more clearly recognized, the question of mediation came to the fore more forcefully. In the case of the religion of the city, the very needs of the city in some way constitute the mediation: the gods need to be rendered favorable through sacrifices and other rites. The question of "what the gods truly are" and first of all "whether the gods exist" has no room, so to speak, to emerge. The Greeks neither believe nor disbelieve their myths. Once the city has lost the strength to refer to itself the movement toward the divine, that movement becomes detached from the city, and evades it. The movement is attracted to a more just idea of the divine, resulting from both Plato's philosophic elaboration and the imperial expansion of the framework of common life. It is then that paganism encounters the urgent necessity and absolute impossibility of conceiving a suitable mediation. As we have seen, it is not by discovering a novel intermediary but by making known the one who joins the two poles—the man-God—that Christianity, according to Augustine, proposes the suitable mediation.

What is striking in Gauchet's approach is his devaluation of mediation. Far from being complementary to the search for an ever more fitting awareness of the divine, mediation is in his eyes an obstacle to that search. One can attain a fitting awareness of the otherness of the divine only by renouncing any and all mediation. This thesis is perfectly defensible; it is the thesis of philosophy itself. For philosophy, God is so perfect that he would not concern himself with humans, and humans can approach God only through the "divine" activity of thinking. But no religion can correspond to such an idea of the divine, unless one insists on speaking of a "religion of the philosopher." The religious person expects something of God, whether it be healing from an illness or eternal life, while the philosopher neither hopes for nor fears anything. For him, philosophic activity itself is mediating. The philosopher himself can be called a mediator: he turns people's minds in the right direction.

Unlike philosophy, religion necessarily seeks the most efficacious mediation possible between believer and god, whether that god be conceived in a crude or most exact way. Religion seeks to be as close as possible to the god, to the point of uniting with the god. It seems to me then that Marcel Gauchet gives a very questionable interpretation of the dogma of the incarnation. Gauchet regards the incarnation—which is the mediation that is at the heart of Christianity or that is rather Christianity itself—not as a mediation but on the contrary as the testimony of a definitive separation between the human and the divine:

> The Christian dogma of the *Incarnation* was . . . living testimony, at the heart of faith, of the irretrievable split between the two self-substantiating orders of reality. When God adopted a human form, he emerged as wholly other, so different and remote that without the assistance of revelation he would have remained unknown to humans. . . . Through their mystical union in Christ, the human and the divine were differentiated, as the hierarchical intermixture of the earthly abode and the kingdom of heaven broke down into its basic constituents. . . . Henceforth there would be an inexhaustible sustaining mystery at the heart of the belief system, namely, the mystery of separation and otherness condensed into the figure of the Saviour.[35]

I would like to briefly comment on this impressive text.

If every rapprochement of two elements is equal to their prior distance, if then it can be said that the intimacy of the union achieved by the incarnation corresponds to the infinite distance that Christianity and before it Judaism acknowledges between the creator and his creature, it remains that the intent of the incarnation is to suppress the distance, not to deepen it, to produce unity or union, not separation. The god of the Christians and the god of the Jews are the same God, characterized by the same "otherness" that makes itself known from the first verse of Genesis onward. The reason for the incarnation according to the Christian view is that it is able to accomplish what Jewish law cannot do, which is to really unite the creature to the creator. In Augustine's terms, the law does not give what it commands but grace gives what the law commands. One sign worth noting that Christianity's specific contribution is the union and not the separation, the nearness of the divine and not its infinite otherness, is that the incarnation was blasphemy for the Jews and folly for the Greeks:

Blasphemy: "'I adjure you by the living God, tell us if you are the Christ, the Son of God.' Jesus said to him, 'You have said so.' . . . Then the high priest tore his robes, and said, 'He has uttered blasphemy. Why do we still need witnesses? You have now heard his blasphemy.' "[36]

Folly: "For Jews demand signs and Greeks seek wisdom, but we preach Christ crucified, a stumbling block to Jews and folly to Gentiles, but to those who are called, both Jews and Greeks, Christ is the power of God and the wisdom of God."[37]

Blasphemy is to declare oneself Son of God. The crucifixion is a scandal, for the Jews would not believe in a Messiah so humiliated in this way. The imputation of blasphemy and the sentiment of scandal are the responses to the insufferable *proximity* of the divine. The Greeks for their part cannot conceive that a god would abandon his divine condition to share in the human condition. As Augustine emphasizes in addressing Porphyry, in a passage I have already cited, the philosophers disdain Christ "on account of the body which he received from a woman, and because of the shame of the cross."[38]

The notion of otherness does not provide the solution to the problem it points to. Given that the search for a more just and more worthy idea of the divine necessarily entails for both the philosopher and the religious person a moving away of the divine, an increase in its "otherness" if one likes, a radical alternative soon presents itself: either the divine radically separates itself from humans and settles in its divine condition to enjoy it without any concern for humans, as do the gods of Epicurus or earlier the god of Aristotle; or the divine, separated by its greatness, nonetheless turns toward humans and crosses the abyss that separates them from him to fulfill his "philanthropic" design, which is the meaning of the Christian incarnation. The point of Christianity is not to propose a God pure of all human contamination—Greek philosophy had already done that—but to announce that this God is the friend of humans to the point of assuming their condition.

It is impossible to present the "appropriate awareness of the divine otherness" as a late development since it is from the first moment at the heart of the drama of the Christian's act of faith: the believer must believe this unbelievable thing, that the infinite being abased himself and confined himself to the point of taking on the "form of a servant." From the beginning theology affirmed at the same time as the divine philanthropy the perfect self-sufficiency of the creator God, whom nothing obliged to create nor to become incarnate. Cur deus homo? What is man, Lord, that you should care for him? The first branch of the alternative remains present in the mind and even the soul of the one who has chosen the second: what nurtures his pious gratitude is precisely the fact that the being that has no need of him turns toward him. The two branches of the alternative are thus joined as the two moments of the relation to the divine: awareness of its greatness, gratitude for its benevolence.

It seems to me that the reformers' insistence on predestination, far from indicating a more exact or lively awareness of divine otherness, results from a confusion of the two moments: the indifference of the God who owes humans nothing penetrates in some way the benevolence of the one who made a covenant with them. And humans force themselves to believe in a God who does not love them.[39]

The preceding remarks suffice, I believe, to suggest that the notion of otherness is far too abstract to adequately describe the phenomenon we are seeking to identify. It is a scientific notion that was elaborated much later. Now, the religious experience has for a long time produced a specific notion that envelops or encompasses what the notion of otherness wishes to designate. This is the notion of divine holiness. God is the Holy One. That says indeed that God is the "wholly other," at the same time that it brings the human back to the condition of sinner. Now, not only does the notion of the holiness of God not wait for the Reformation to appear, it is identified even before Christianity since it is at the heart of Judaism. The Psalms, the prayers common to Jews and Christians, speak of the overwhelming nearness of the Holy One and the sinner. I do not know where one would find a more striking or more lively expression of both the divine otherness and the divine nearness.

Thus, if the situation of religion requires that the holiness and nearness of God be joined, the search for the right mediation does not seem contrary to the recognition of divine otherness. It is not an insult to divine otherness, as Marcel Gauchet seems to say in a passage remarkable for its suppressed violence. Speaking of the Church's effort to set itself up as mediator between God and humanity, he writes this: "Any claim by the Church to interpose itself between ultimate otherness and extreme inwardness becomes an absurd hoax, any communitarian bridge thrown across the abyss toward heaven seems an idolatrous misunderstanding of transcendence. To institutionalize communication with the invisible, enabling the faithful to bask continually in the proper interpretation of the Law, guided by inspired pastors, is to clearly ignore our distance from the divine. Ecclesial mediation was thus built on something that cast doubt on the very possibility of mediation."[40]

It is not for the Church a matter of interposing itself but of linking these two directions of being, one opening the soul to the Immense, the other turning it toward its own fragility. It is simply a matter of attaining the right relation between humans and the divinity. This right relation calls for an internal disposition but also perhaps an external institution. Why would a certain organization of humans between them—a certain Church, or a certain "people" in the case of the Jewish people—not be the best means of ordering the relation between humans and God? If humans produce and receive human goods within the framework and by means of a city, why would they not receive the good that is God and even cooperate in God's action, in a special and distinct city, the people of God, the city of God, or the Church? However unsatisfactory or disappointing the mediating institution may be—Yahweh is forever reprimanding and even chastising his people—it is the "bridge over the abyss" without which the Immense and the lowly would flee one another indefinitely.

I am thus not convinced by the thesis that holds that the wellspring of Christian and Western development resides in the "progress of awareness" of the divine otherness that culminates in Protestantism before actualizing its full potential in the world of autonomy that is now our world. The two most acute and incompatible expressions of the awareness of divine otherness are to be found in the philosophy of Plato and his followers on the one hand and in the Psalms on the other. What Christianity brought is mediation, not distance. It is impossible to make the "great modern transformation" come out of a development within the Christian religion when the progress of the awareness in question is older than Christianity itself. One has to search in another direction.

The Mediating Nation

There is one point on which everyone is in agreement. Luther wants to put an end to the mediation of the Church or to the Church as a mediating community. That is the point to which we must always return and from which we must begin anew.

What happens when the entire ecclesiastical state ("der ganze geistliche Stand") is set aside, when it loses its mediating function? The spiritual ministry is appropriated by every Christian in what is called the "universal priesthood." All Christians now share in the priestly dignity; there is no difference among them other than the one born of the *Beruf,* a notion that was produced in the world, if I can put it that way, by the Lutheran translation of the Bible.[41] The notion of *Beruf* unites and in some way fuses the religious sense of the divine calling or vocation and the secular meaning of office, function, or profession. In the course of the development of the reformed societies, especially the Calvinist, this notion will endow the secular professions with a religious quality. It is the notion that provides the broadest base of Max Weber's thesis on the role of Calvinism in the formation of the spirit of capitalism.

The developments studied by Weber do not concern the Lutheran reform as such. In Luther's Germany the combined notions of universal priesthood and *Beruf* brought about a dramatic increase in the legitimacy of secular power. Pierre Mesnard has summarized in a sort of syllogism the irresistible mechanism at work in this:

1. The civil authority has an ordinary share in the universal priesthood.
2. The civil authority is sovereign over the body of Christendom or the gathering of Christians.
3. The civil authority has a preponderant share in the universal priesthood.[42]

The gathering of Christians is relieved of the burden of ecclesiastical order only to fall under the hand of Lutheran princes. What begins with Luther is the replacement of the Christian Church with the German nation, the Christian German nation.

The reformed ordering can only be held together by the mediation of the nation.

The abolition of ecclesial mediation does not put an end to the play of mediation. To be sure, the translation of the Bible into German makes it possible to institute subjective freedom, as Hegel will explain, but this freedom arises and can subsist only in a political community that is *immediately* Christian.[43] The nation is the mediator between the subjective freedom of the Christian and the sovereign grace of God. The God that the Church now seemed too impure or too incompetent to communicate, the nation brought in its still-innocent hands. The subjectivation of Christianity was inseparable from its nationalization. One could say that in absorbing the Church the nation appropriated its mediating function. There is always a need for mediation.

Brief as they are, these remarks oblige us to revisit the theologico-political history of Europe as it is commonly recounted or explained. There is one point on which there is general and rightful agreement and which is not directly affected by what we have just said: the religious divisions provided the most powerful and the most specific reason for the erection of the modern State. The modern State was at first sovereign or absolute so that it had the strength and the right to rise above religious opinions, or at least to decide which would be accepted by the State. Later it transformed this sovereignty into neutrality or it interpreted this sovereignty as neutrality, with the State now wishing to be neutral regarding the religious opinions or convictions of its citizens. In certain European nations the movement of "neutralization" or secularization has barely been completed. This movement that was borne by the sovereign State that was at first absolute and later liberal without question constitutes one of the principal vectors of European history.

The Reformation, or the transformations of which it was both the effect and the cause, namely the subjectivization and nationalization of the Christian Church, came before all this. If the absolute State played a decisive instrumental role in the nationalization of the Christian Church or of Christianity, the spiritual principle of this nationalization manifested itself well before the erection of the State. The nationalization of Christianity came before the construction of the absolute State. The latter was an effect before it became a cause of the former.

It was with the Reformation and its aftermath that the European nations took their form or that the European nation took its specific form. Each nation was obliged to make a radical choice among the Christian confessions, and this choice decisively contributed to define that nation ever after. The nation's choice was more absolute than the will of the absolute prince. Kings fulfilled the wishes of their nations more than they commanded their nations to keep or to change their religion, as the histories of both France and England testify, though with opposite re-sults.[44] This is one of the most mysterious but most determining facts—I believe it is a fact—of our history.

Keeping this in mind will help to make the thesis of the neutralization through the State more precise; the neutralizing State is not an intrinsi-cally neutral State since it is originally the State of a nation that has made its religious choice. What at the end of the process will appear as a neutral State is rather a State that has progressively relinquished its original par-tiality such that the separation between the State and the Church is the term of a story that began with the confusion between nation and religion. The neutral or liberal State is the State of a nation that at first adopted one or another of the Christian confessions. One of the most important po-litical questions facing us is whether this origin has kept a part of its power, that is, whether this original determination still remains determi-nant to some degree today.

I said that with the Reformation the various European nations each took their form or that the European nation took its specific or typical form. The Catholic nations, those that remained Catholic and chose to remain so, are obviously included in these propositions. At the same time, because the nationalization of Christianity produced a deeper transformation in Protestant nations, because they took hold of them-selves or chose themselves with more vigor after they broke with Rome, those nations, at least the Calvinist or predominantly Calvinist nations, achieved more quickly, more vigorously, and more completely the type of the modern European nation than the contemporary Catholic na-tions. The political, economic, and moral elements constitutive of a mod-ern nation—which is more completely a nation—were more quickly, more vigorously, and more completely grasped or produced in Protestant than in Catholic nations. This difference has been reduced considerably, but it has not yet been entirely eliminated in Europe today.

Even though the Low Countries may claim the title, it is generally ac-knowledged that England was the first modern nation, the nation whose politics, economy, and mores provided the standard of what modern politics, economy, and mores would be. But when we say that, the eye of our mind is fixated on the word and the notion of modern and we place the various components of collective life on the scale of the modern. There is nothing wrong with that, but if instead of focusing on the adjective "modern" we focused on the substantive "nation," we would grasp a capital fact of our political history. It is not a matter of ascribing to the nation the occult power of producing all the great things that England was the first to produce, but of pointing out that in being the first modern nation, the first complete nation without the mediation of the empire or the Church, England was the first to lay hold of all the possibilities contained in this political form. The English advance drew its first impulse from the political and religious turmoil that culminated in the Civil War and Cromwell's Protectorate. It was deployed in the arc of conquest that stretched from Naseby (1645) to Waterloo. Afterward, what is referred to as the English ascendancy was but the continuation by inertia of the advantage taken at the start, the difference in energy between England and the other nations decreasing more or less quickly depending on the individual nation but disappearing completely with regard to France and above all Germany at the end of the nineteenth century at the latest. Speaking of the English, Montesquieu writes: "This is the people of the world who have best known how to take advantage of each of these three great things at the same time: religion, commerce, and liberty."[45] By mentioning *three* great things, he necessarily draws our attention to the various components of English superiority. The most important, however, resides in the adverbial phrase "at the same time." What allowed the English to take advantage of these three great things was for them to be the first to dispose of the synthesizing political form that is the nation, the first to liberate the nation of all that hindered it. It was in the sea element, the *free* element, that the nation experienced and exercised its new freedom. One could say, using naval language, that with the England of the Navigation Act of 1651 the modern nation *casts off*.[46]

In order to be complete on the subject of England's advance and not to leave aside a less pleasant aspect, one should add that it was in England that the nationalism of the modern nation was deployed for the first time in all its terrible force, and it was Cromwell, at the height of the founding shock, who voiced it with a violence that will not be surpassed but only vulgarized in the later history of the European nations.[47]

This is not the place to engage in a history of the European nation, even in the form of a very rapid sketch. Nonetheless a word needs to be said about its second transformation or second birth. Nearly three centuries after the shock of the Reformation, Europe experienced the shock of the French Revolution. The parallel between these two great movements is a commonplace of historical reflection. In both cases, a political and spiritual movement was born in a country of Europe, was transformed into a pan-European movement, and in the end had a "nationalizing" effect. In both cases the nations of Europe were, so to speak, activated in their role of frameworks of reference par excellence of common life.

Beyond this parallelism, the examination reveals a deeper analogy. In both cases a movement of subjectivization coincides with a movement of nationalization. At the time of the Reformation the declaration of Christian liberty was inseparable from the national appropriation of Christianity, of the inscription of Christian life in the national framework. At the time of the French Revolution, the Declaration of the Rights of Man or the rights of conscience was inseparable from the inscription of the whole of human life in the framework of a nation that declared itself sovereign. With the Civil Constitution of the clergy, France was the first Catholic country to choose for itself in breaking with Rome, but it was no longer in the name of an appropriation of Christianity. What was appropriated this time? What did the nation mediate this time? The nation was a mediation of humanity.

What had happened? In the framework of the Christian nation, the State had progressively relinquished its confessional partiality; it had manifested and recognized more and more clearly a plane of humanity, of humanity simply—the plane where people are free and equal in their rights. If the nationalization of religion produced an increase in national energies, it was at the same time the cause of permanent difficulties within each nation. A way had to be found to radically neutralize confessional differences, to cut the principle of the confessional disagreements at the root. Ultimately that meant positing and declaring that the reference point of human association, of substantial human association, was no longer the Christian association in any of its definitions, which were all in all accidental. The substantial human association was humanity itself.

Humanity without Mediation

Why should one define the new nation that is no longer confessional as a mediation of humanity? Does this pompous abstraction enlighten us?

Would it not be enough to say simply that the nation is a certain constituency of humanity or that the nation is the result of a certain division or distribution of humanity? I believe however that a notion of this type is indispensable for grasping the meaning of this political form that is so difficult to define. Without that, we are the plaything of the polarity between the universal and the particular and either one simply pushes the nation to the side of particularity, or one distinguishes among the nations according to a scale determined by this polarity, with some being more universalist and others more particularistic. In any event, one loses sight of the dynamic solidarity that exists between the two poles.

What does it mean to speak of a dynamic solidarity? The specificity of the modern nation *is not* to be particularistic: all human associations—political bodies, regions, cities, towns, families—are particularistic. The specificity of the modern nation is that it understands and produces its particularity—let us keep this term despite misunderstandings—as the effect or result of a universal human operation. The "principle of the nationality" is a universal principle, namely the principle of self-determination, the democratic principle of government of oneself by oneself. In this sense, the "German concept" of the nation, which is so explicitly particularistic, is no less universalistic than the "French concept," which is so explicitly universalistic. For one as for the other, *now that the French Revolution has identified humanity as the horizon or reference point,* what matters is to institute, concretize, and actualize this humanity. Rousseau addressed Humanity. Fichte, in the *Discourses to the German Nation,* was intent on speaking only to Germans and for Germans. This does not prevent Fichte's philosophy in these *Discourses* from looking like an imitation of Rousseau's. Fichte lets us see *humanity* taking its most finished form by taking the *German* form. This is something altogether different from the love of particularity, from partiality to "local folks." Every modern European nation casts itself as the human operation par excellence. The European nation has chosen its confessional definition. To help appreciate the revealing continuity of the two types of national form, I would willingly say that every modern nation is a confession or a proposition of humanity.

One can observe that the trajectory of the modern European nation—if we suppose that its period of vitality ends with the Second World War—is appreciably shorter than that of the Christian nation. While the Christian nation's trajectory ends with the revolutionary founding of the modern nation, the modern nation's trajectory ends in the self-destruction of Europe.

The modern nation, whether democratic or on the path of democratization, seems more fragile than the Christian nation. At the start, in the prodigious period at the joining of the two trajectories, the period of the wars of Revolution and Empire, the period of German idealism, the mediation of humanity seemed much more powerful, much more promising, than the mediation of the Church because it seemed more universal. In reality it very quickly showed itself to be much more fragile. As early as the second half of the nineteenth century, the signs of serious political corruption appeared. These signs were for a time covered over by the progress of democracy in most European countries—democracy in the form of representative government and equality of conditions, and also of civilization attentive to the general needs of people. How does one explain this inner fragility of the powerful nations that emerged from the shock of revolution and its aftermath?

As we have pointed out, the rivalry or enmity among Christian nations was no less intense than the one that roused, might I say, the modern nations beginning in 1792. At the same time the enmity of the modern nations produced more profound and destructive effects both visibly and invisibly. In effect, in deploying their rivalry the modern European nations thought of themselves more and more as different, unequal, and perhaps incompatible expressions of Humanity. Whereas the national appropriation of Christianity, after going through troubles and disasters, in the end took on a stable form with the confessional mark of the Christian nation, the national appropriation of humanity under conditions of rivalry and enmity was easily carried away in a process of radicalization. In effect, the assertion of particularity was now unlimited, not because of national particularity itself, which is what it is, but because it drew its energy from the uncircumscribed and unlimited universal of humanity. Unlike the Christian universal that has form and content, the "simply human" universal was devoid of form and opened up the empty space of unlimited possibility.

The Christian nations, even if they were ordinarily moved by the sentiment of the difference of confession, kept a common Christian denominator, however tenuous and passive it usually was.[48] Above all, perhaps, the reference to humanity was available to them as a resource that was not yet mediatized and thematized. It was implicit. However little use was made of it, it was in reserve. And it would be mobilized more and more to remedy the religious divisions whose poison was still at work. The reference to humanity was the more salutary in that it was corrective and not exclusive. On the contrary, once humanity became the most legitimate and even the only legitimate reference point and once the nation mediated it, the modern nations had no more resource to draw from. They had no reserve to share among them when they were carried away by an ever more radical self-assertion.

To be sure, we are here in the realm of what is not certain and cannot be verified. These questions are very difficult. It seems to me that the common interpretations of nationalism as the hypertrophy or pathology of national particularism are very insufficient, for they ignore the source of this energy whose particularistic affirmation is but an expression or perhaps only an aftereffect. The destructive obstinacy of the nations engaged in the First World War manifested the internal rigidity of political bodies that as early as the last quarter of the nineteenth century seemed to have lost their freedom of movement.[49] But if war revealed the fragility or weakness—many today would say the failure—of the nation as mediator of humanity, at the same time it revealed the fragility or weakness of mediatized humanity or of humanity as the source of mediation.

Humanity did not regain its legitimacy and authority until after the second and worse disaster as an aftereffect of the crimes against humanity. But the humanity that came to light as the victim of the ultimate crime no longer had any of the inspiring political force that revolutionary humanity had. It is not a resource for effective political mediation or concretization. The United Nations is nothing of the sort.

Is it possible to imagine a third renewal, by means of a new mediation? What would be this novel principle of mediation, coming after the Church and humanity? It is not apparent to what resource of mediation we could have recourse, after humanity, if our analysis is valid, has so to speak been exhausted in producing the democratic nation. Today common European opinion indeed considers humanity as the only available resource and reference point now that the nations are exhausted. But this humanity, as I have just pointed out, is devoid of political significance; it does not constitute an effective political resource. It is at most the framework of reference of a "fellow feeling" on which it is impossible to base any political construction. It concerns an *immediate* humanity, indifferently encompassing "all people" and "everyone," that offers no resource whatever for mediation. Today among Europeans humanity is the reference point that can be immediately opposed to every effective political undertaking or action. Whereas the humanity that moved the people of 1789 to act was inspiring and capable of nurturing the vastest ambitions, the humanity in whose name the rule is decreed today can only protect what is and prohibit what could be.

NOTES

Introduction: The Dynamic of the West

1. Niccolò Machiavelli, *The Prince,* 2nd ed., trans. Harvey C. Mansfield (Chicago: University of Chicago Press, 1998), 61.

1. What Science for the City?

1. See chapter 3 of this volume.

2. Jean Baechler distinguishes "three Greeces": that of the city, that of the tribes, and that of the tribal monarchies. See "Les origines de la démocratie grecque," *Archives européennes de sociologie* 21 (1980).

3. Aristotle, *The Politics,* trans. Carnes Lord (Chicago: University of Chicago Press, 1984), 1327b23–33, 208.

4. We will later have to consider the very interesting case of the political science developed in Rome.

5. See Thomas Hobbes, *Leviathan,* ed. Michael Oakeshott (New York: Collier, 1962), chapter 46: "Plato that was the best philosopher of the Greeks, forbad entrance into his school, to all that were not already in some measure geometricians." See also Leo Strauss, *The Political Philosophy of Hobbes: Its Basis and Its Genesis* (Chicago: University of Chicago Press, 1963 [1936]), 139ff.

6. Montesquieu, *The Spirit of the Laws,* trans. Anne M. Cohler, Basia Carolyn Miller, and Harold Samuel Stone (Cambridge: Cambridge University Press, 1989). Montesquieu, as is well known, distinguishes among republic, monarchy, and despotism. The republic is the natural regime of the city, monarchy that of the nation, despotism that of the empire.

7. Aristotle, *Nicomachean Ethics,* trans. Joe Sachs (Newburyport, MA: Focus, 2002), 1126b12, 73–74.

2. The Poetic Birth of the City

1. Aristotle, *Poetics,* trans. Gerald F. Else (Ann Arbor: University of Michigan Press, 1970). Aristotle notes that the imitation of men of great worth entails a deliberate embellishment (1454b8–14).

2. Plato, *Republic,* trans. Allan Bloom (New York: Basic Books, 1968).

3. See Plato's affectionate and ironic evocation in book 10 of the *Republic,* 606e–607a.

4. "The poets invented a hundred different theologies." Blaise Pascal, *Pensées,* rev. ed., trans. A. J. Krailsheimer (Harmondsworth: Penguin, 1995), no. 281, 90.

5. Herodotus, *The History,* trans. David Grene (Chicago: University of Chicago Press, 1987), 2.53, 154–155.

6. Eric Voegelin, *Order and History,* vol. 2, *The World of the Polis* (Baton Rouge: University of Louisiana Press, 1957), 72.

7. One can set aside here Circe's transformation of Odysseus's companions into pigs in book 10 of the *Odyssey.*

8. *Brotos* can become substantive to the point that Homer at times says *brotos thnètos,* a redundant expression of our mortality that could almost be translated as "a mortal condemned to die." Thus when Alcinous asks if he would not be a god, Odysseus replies in these terms: "Cross that thought from your mind. I'm nothing like the immortal gods who rule the skies, either in build or breeding. I'm just a mortal man." Homer, *Odyssey,* trans. Robert Fagles (New York: Viking, 1996), 7.210, 186.

9. Simone Weil, *The Iliad or the Poem of Force,* trans. Mary McCarthy (Wallingford, PA: Pendle Hill, 1956), 3.

10. In fact, the elders are quick to take back what they say. See 3.156–160 (Fagles 183–184): "who on earth could blame them? Ah, no wonder the men of Troy and Argives under arms have suffered years of agony all for her, for such a woman. Beauty, terrible beauty! A deathless goddess—so she strikes our eyes, ravishing as she is, let her go home in the long ships and not be left behind . . . for us and our children down the years an irresistible sorrow." Homer, *The Iliad,* trans. Robert Fagles (New York: Viking, 1990), 133.

11. Jean-Jacques Rousseau, *Discourse on the Origins and Foundation of Inequality among Men,* in *The First and Second Discourses,* trans. Roger D. and Judith R. Masters (New York: St. Martin's, 1969), 81.

12. See Seth Benardete, *The Argument of the Action: Essays on Greek Poetry and Philosophy* (Chicago: University of Chicago Press, 2000), 56.

13. Achilles has discovered the limits of heroism, but he is incapable of transforming this awareness into a new form of life or way of living. Once the delay granted Priam for Hector's funeral is past, he will immediately start to kill

anew, to be a hero, until his coming death. (One can note that his great speech in book 9 in answer to the embassy of Odysseus, Ajax, and Phoenix shows a new concern for what is just and witnesses to a new desire, temptation, or wish to retire from the heroic life and to reenter private life, so to speak.)

14. Thucydides, *History of the Peloponnesian War*, trans. Rex Warner (New York: Penguin, 1986), 2.61, 148.

15. Leo Strauss, *The City and Man* (Chicago: University of Chicago Press, 1977), 194.

16. When he succumbs to Hector's blows, Patroclus is wearing the armor of Achilles.

17. See Weil, *The Iliad or the Poem of Force*, 34: "The Gospels are the last marvellous expression of the Greek genius, as the *Iliad* was the first."

18. We indignantly reject the use of the epithet "barbarian" to qualify a contemporary people, custom, or mores, but we use it without much scruple when it comes to the past, especially the distant past. This is of course a gross contradiction, since if the judgment of barbarism or primitivism is unacceptable, it is so for the past no less than the present.

19. Benjamin Constant, "The Spirit of Conquest and Usurpation and Their Relation to European Civilization," in *Political Writings*, trans. Biancamaria Fontana (Cambridge: Cambridge University Press, 1988), part 1, ch. 2, 53.

20. See Christian Meier, *La Naissance du politique* (Paris: Gallimard, 1995), 68 in particular.

21. If the Greek city had no idea of the peacemaking role of the One—of monarchy or the State—it did have the arbitrating role of the legislator. Solon interposed between the few and the many. He fought for "both sides against the other." Aristotle, *The Constitution of Athens*, in *Aristotle and Xenophon on Democracy and Oligarchy*, trans. J. M. Moore (Berkeley: University of California Press, 1986), 5.2, 150.

22. See chapter 3 of this volume.

23. "[The virtue of] justice is a thing belonging to the city. For adjudication is an arrangement of the political partnership, and adjudication is judgment as to what is just." Aristotle, *The Politics*, trans. Carnes Lord (Chicago: University of Chicago Press, 1985), 1253a37–39, 38. See also Aristotle, *Nicomachean Ethics*, trans. Joe Sachs (Newburyport, MA: Focus, 2002), 1134a26 and 1160a13.

24. "With the customary forbearance of the democracy, the people had allowed the friends of the tyrants to continue to live in Athens." Aristotle, *The Constitution of Athens*, 22.4, 165.

25. "Hence expertise in war will also be in some sense a natural form of acquisitive expertise; for one part of it is expertise in hunting, which should be used with a view both to beasts and to those human beings who are naturally suited to be ruled but unwilling—this sort of war being by nature just." Aristotle,

Politics, 1256b23–26, 45. In this passage, Aristotle accedes to a certain extent and "in a sense" to Constant's thesis on war: there is a kind of war that is essentially "acquisitive," which is hunting, whether for wild animals or for human beings that are "naturally fit to be ruled."

26. Recall the well-known oracle pronounced by Carl Schmitt: "Souverän ist, wer über den Ausnahmezustand entscheidet." This raises the question whether the sovereign is the one who *determines* the exceptional situation or the one who is *able* to face and master it.

27. The Greek text preserves a wonderful political ambiguity by using the verb *dechesthaï,* ordinarily translated as "receive": Odysseus receives the scepter from the hands of Agamemnon, but does Agamemnon give the scepter or does Odysseus seize it? The answer no doubt lies between the two. As Fagles translates, Odysseus "coming face-to-face with Atrides Agamemnon, he relieved him of his fathers' royal scepter" (*Iliad,* 2.186).

28. Addressing the few, Odysseus qualifies Zeus as *metièta* (endowed with prudence); addressing the many, he makes the son of Chronos *agkulomèteô* (crafty-minded). The contrast between the two "theologies" could not be more marked.

29. Regarding Odysseus's "name," see Benardete, *The Argument of the Action,* 28–29.

30. Ibid., 29.

3. The Civic Operation

1. The famous chapter 6 of book 1 of Rousseau's *Social Contract* opens with a particularly sophisticated—a particularly "modern"—statement of the modern problematic and ends with a particularly radical formulation of the ancient problematic.

2. See Aristotle, *The Politics,* trans. Carnes Lord (Chicago: University of Chicago Press, 1985), 1282b22–23.

3. One would not consider as a political, or even prepolitical, unit the independent individual that the contract theories place at the center of their arrangement: his independence is the *program* of modern politics; it is never simply "real."

4. Giambattista Vico, *The New Science,* trans. Thomas Goddard Bergin and Max Harold Fisch (Ithaca, NY: Cornell University Press, 1968), par. 547, 192. See Homer, *Odyssey,* trans. Robert Fagles (New York: Viking, 1996), 9.125–128.

5. Immediately preceding the passage Vico cites, we read that "They have no meeting place for council, no laws either." Homer, *Odyssey,* 9.125, 215.

6. Vico, *The New Science,* par. 516, 176.

7. See ibid., par. 1098, 420. Moreover, the savage independence of the Cyclopes who massacred those who penetrated their caves contributed to the "guarding of the confines," thus putting a stop to "the infamous promiscuity of things in the bestial state." Ibid., par. 982, 363.

8. Ibid., par. 561, 200.

9. Ibid., par. 982, 363.

10. Ibid., par. 629, 235.

11. Ibid., par. 583, 210.

12. Ibid., par. 584, 210.

13. Ibid., par. 38, 23–24.

14. Pierre Manent, *The City of Man,* trans. Marc A. LePain (Princeton, NJ: Princeton University Press, 1998), 22–23.

15. Montesquieu, *The Spirit of the Laws,* trans. Anne M. Cohler, Basia Carolyn Miller, and Harold Samuel Stone (Cambridge: Cambridge University Press, 1989), 5.2, 42–43.

16. "My weight is my love." Augustine, *Confessions,* trans. Maria Boulding (New York: Random House, 1998), 13.9, 310.

17. Jean-Jacques Rousseau, *Discourse on Political Economy,* in *The Basic Political Writings,* trans. Donald A. Cress (Indianapolis: Hackett, 1987), 119.

18. Ibid., 121.

19. Ibid., 124–125.

20. Besides, the public law in force in Europe had less and less room for the few. All shared the same political condition of being subjects of the monarch.

21. Jean-Jacques Rousseau, *Discourse on the Origins and Foundation of Inequality among Men,* in *The First and Second Discourses,* trans. Roger D. Masters and Judith R. Masters (New York: St. Martin's, 1969), 157.

22. Ibid.

23. The phrase "at last" is repeated twice.

24. Aristotle, *Politics,* 1253a14–15, 37.

25. See Hobbes, *Leviathan,* ed. Michael Oakeshott (New York: Collier, 1962), ch. 13.

26. Rousseau, *Discourse on the Origins and Foundation of Inequality,* 158.

27. Ibid., 162.

28. Ibid., 102.

29. Ibid., 158.

30. Ibid.

31. Ibid., 158–159.

32. Ibid.

33. See Rousseau, *Emile,* trans. Allan Bloom (New York: Basic Books, 1979), book 4, 236n: "the universal spirit of the laws of every country is always to favor the strong against the weak and those who have against those who have

not. This difficulty is inevitable; and it is without exception." See also Rousseau, *The Social Contract,* trans. Judith R. Masters (New York: St. Martin's, 1978), 1.9, 58n: "In fact, laws are always useful to those who have possessions and harmful to those who have nothing. It follows from this that the social state is only advantageous to men insofar as they all have something and none of them has anything superfluous."

34. Rousseau, *Discourse on the Origins and Foundation of Inequality,* 172.

35. Ibid., 159.

36. Ibid., 87. Rousseau is here addressing especially the patrician magistrates.

37. Ibid., 174.

38. See Aristotle, *Politics,* 1280b5, 1281a7.

39. Ibid., 1280a21–22, 98.

40. Ibid., 1280a34–35, 98.

41. Ibid., 1280a33–34 and 1281a2–3.

42. Montesquieu, *The Spirit of the Laws,* 11.5, 156.

43. Aristotle, *Politics,* 1281a1–2, 99 (modified).

44. Or beauty, since the Greek word *kalon* connotes beauty as well as nobility.

45. Ibid.

4. Rome and the Greeks

1. *The Federalist Papers* presented the brand new Constitution of the United States to the voters of New York to incite them to ratify it. See Alexander Hamilton, John Jay, and James Madison, *The Federalist Papers* (New York: Penguin, 1987).

2. Ibid., no. 9.

3. Ibid., no. 10.

4. Ibid.

5. Ibid., no. 6.

6. Plato, *Republic,* trans. Allan Bloom (New York: Basic Books, 1968), 422e, 100.

7. Aristotle, *Constitution of Athens,* in *Aristotle's Constitution of Athens and Related Texts,* trans. Kurt von Fritz and Ernst Kapp (New York: Hafner Library of Classics, 1974), 2.2–3, 69.

8. Ibid.

9. Ibid., 5.2, 72.

10. Ibid., 5.3, 73.

11. Ibid., 6.3, 73.

12. Ibid., 9.1–2, 77.

13. Plato examines the psychology of the tyrannical man at the beginning of book 9 of the *Republic*. At the end of the preceding book he described the genesis of the tyrant: "It's plain, therefore, . . . that when a tyrant grows naturally, he sprouts from a root of leadership and from nowhere else" (565d1–2). And he asks himself, "What is the beginning of the transformation from leader to tyrant?" What is of interest to us here is the political chronology. The tyranny Plato speaks of comes after democracy—it is the last phase of a liberation of the irrational desires, a liberation that signifies the most complete slavery of the soul for the agent. The tyranny studied by Aristotle in the case of Pisistratus comes before democracy. With souls that are still "restrained," the tyrant is much less tyrannical than he will be later, even if certain techniques characteristic of tyranny are already in place (such as the formation of the tyrant's personal guard).

14. Ibid., 568b7–8, 247.

15. Sophocles, *Oedipus the King*, in *The Three Theban Plays*, trans. Robert Fagles (New York: Penguin, 1984), 873, 209.

16. Aristotle, *Constitution of Athens*, 16.2, 83.

17. See ibid., 16.7, 84.

18. Ibid., 16.9, 85.

19. Ibid., 16.3–4, 84.

20. Ibid., 24.1–2, 94.

21. See ibid., 28.1, 98.

22. Ibid., 28.2, 98.

23. In *Parallel Lives,* Plutarch makes Valerius Publicola the counterpart of Solon: "Solon, though he actually knew of Pisistratus's ambition, yet was not able to suppress it, but had to yield to usurpation in its infancy; whereas Publicola utterly subverted and dissolved a potent monarchy, strongly settled by long continuance; uniting thus to virtues equal to those, and purposes identical with those of Solon, the good fortune and the power that alone could make them effective." Plutarch, *The Lives of the Noble Grecians and Romans,* trans. John Dryden, rev. Arthur Hugh Clough (New York: Modern Library, 1932), 132. The parallel here is obviously forced. The tyrant Pisistratus hardly resembles the tyrant Tarquin. Indeed, he is closer to Solon than to Tarquin. Admittedly, Solon and Publicola have in common that they are leaders of the people and enemies of the tyrants. But Publicola is more courageous or heroic than moderate. Solon's impartial arbitration is foreign to him. At the end of the parallel, Plutarch himself underlines the difference between their respective attitudes toward tyrants.

24. See chapter 1 of this volume.

25. In his treatise *On the Fortune or Virtue of Alexander* (392b), Plutarch congratulates Alexander for having treated the barbarians as equals of the Greeks, against the advice of Aristotle. Aristotle would probably have replied that it was

equality in bondage, given that Alexander demanded "prostration" from the Greeks as well as the barbarians.

26. See Leo Strauss, *On Tyranny* (Ithaca, NY: Cornell University Press, 1968), 190. See also *Faith and Political Philosophy: The Correspondence between Leo Strauss and Eric Voegelin: 1934–1964,* trans. and ed. Peter Emberley and Barry Cooper (Columbia: University of Missouri Press, 2004).

27. Strauss, *On Tyranny,* 191.

28. Ibid.

29. Strauss probably alludes to *De tyranno* (1400). See Thierry Sol, *Fallait-il tuer César? L'argumentation politique de Dante à Machiavel* (Paris: Dalloz-Sirey, 2005), 314ff.

30. See Sol, *Fallait-il tuer César?,* 314: "Salutati's principal argument in the treatise is that Caesar was not a tyrant neither *ex defectu tituli* nor *ex parte exercitii;* it is for this reason that his murder was a crime, the more serious in that his power was then adapted to the situation of the Roman empire."

31. Strauss, *On Tyranny,* 191.

32. Ibid.

33. Ibid.

34. Ibid.

35. Ibid., 192.

36. Ibid.

37. Ibid.

38. Ibid., 192–193.

39. See Aristotle, *The Politics,* trans. Carnes Lord (Chicago: University of Chicago Press, 1985), 1279a22–b10.

40. See ibid., 1284b35–1285b33.

41. Ibid., 1285a19–22, 109.

42. See ibid., 1285a31–32.

43. See ibid., 1285b5.

44. See ibid., 1285b29–30.

45. See ibid., 1286a1–5.

46. See ibid., 1288a15–17 and 1284b25–34.

47. See ibid., 1287b20–22.

48. See ibid., 1288a29.

49. See ibid., 1284b30–31.

50. See ibid., 1286a10–11.

51. See ibid., 1286a16–17.

52. Aristotle says later: "One who asks law to rule, therefore, is held to be asking god and intellect alone to rule, while one asks man adds the beast. Desire is a thing of this sort; and spiritedness perverts rulers and the best men. Hence law is intellect without appetite." Ibid., 1287a28–32, 114.

53. See ibid., 1287a23–25.

54. Ibid., 1287a25–27, 114. These are the terms of the oath taken by Athenian juries.

55. Ibid., 1286a26–28, 111.

56. See ibid., 1286a29–31.

57. The modern democratic argumentation appeals to the *will* of the people—its goodness—rather than its judgment.

58. Aristotle, *Politics,* 1287b29–35, 112.

59. "They selected kings on account of their benefactions, something that is the work of good men." Ibid., 1286b10–11, 112.

60. Ibid., 1286b11–13, 112.

61. See ibid., 1286b14–20.

62. Ibid., 1286b20–22, 112.

63. In book 5, Aristotle studies the "changes" that lead from one regime to another, and thus the best way to preserve each regime, including tyranny. Strauss says at once that the Ancients displayed extreme modesty, and that no phenomenon identified by Machiavelli was unknown to them. So be it, but one must add that Aristotle in any case showed no particular modesty in the face of "political necessities."

64. "Kingships no longer arise today; if monarchies do arise, they tend to be tyrannies. This is because kingship is a voluntary sort of rule, with authority over relatively great matters, but [today] there are many persons who are similar, with none of them so outstanding as to match the extent and the claim of the office. So on this account [people] do not voluntarily endure it; and if someone should rule through deceit or force, this is already held to be a sort of tyranny." Aristotle, *Politics,* 1313a3–10, 173.

65. See ibid., 1297b24–25.

66. "The political men of Greece who lived under popular government recognized no other force to sustain it than virtue." Montesquieu, *The Spirit of the Laws,* trans. Anne M. Cohler, Basia Carolyn Miller, and Harold Samuel Stone (Cambridge: Cambridge University Press, 2010), 3.3, 22.

67. More precisely, they are separated from this chapter by only a short chapter titled, "The Monarchies That We Know" (117).

68. Montesquieu refers to Plutarch, *The Life of Theseus,* and to Thucydides, book 1.

69. Aristotle, *Nicomachean Ethics,* trans. Joe Sachs (Newburyport, MA: Focus, 2002), 1161b8–10, 158.

70. Ibid., 1159b12–13, 154.

71. Aristotle distinguishes between ordinary demagoguery aimed at the crowd and demagoguery aimed at the group of the oligarchs itself (See *Politics,* 1305b23–27).

72. Aristotle, *Nicomachean Ethics*, 1158b33–35, 152.

73. Ibid., 1158b35–36, 152.

74. Ibid., 1159a5–10, 152–153.

75. Cicero says that the city still obeys him more humbly than ever, though he is dead. See *De officiis*, trans. Walter Miller, Loeb Classical Library (Cambridge, MA: Harvard University Press, 1975), 2.7, 191. "Civitas ac paret cum maxime mortuo."

76. See Shakespeare, *Julius Caesar*, act I, sc. 2, ll. 135–137: "He doth bestride the narrow world like a Colossus, and we petty men walk under his huge legs."

77. Cicero, *De officiis*, 2.1–2, 169–171.

78. See Aristotle, *Politics*, 1.1.

79. Cicero, *De officiis*, 1.17, 59.

80. Ibid., 61.

81. Ibid., 57.

82. Ibid., 59.

83. Ibid., 1.16, 52–54.

84. Ibid., 1.17, 55.

85. Ibid., 1.41, 153.

86. For a positive appreciation of Roman openness to what is foreign in opposition to Greek rejection of the barbarians, see Claudia Moatti, *La Raison de Rome: Naissance de l'esprit critique à la fin de la République* (Paris: Seuil, 1997).

87. See Montesquieu, *The Spirit of the Laws*, 24.10.

88. See the article by D. Alland in *Dictionnaire de philosophie politique*, ed. P. Raynaud and S. Rials (Paris: PUF, 1996).

89. International law would then be a major subdivision of the law of nations so conceived.

90. According to Chrysippus, supported by Cicero, "such is the nature of man that the relation between the individual human being and the whole human species constitutes a kind of civil law [ea natura esset hominis, ut ei cum genere humano quasi civile jus intercederet]." See Cicero, *De finibus bonorum et malorum*, trans. R. Rackham (Cambridge, MA: Harvard University Press, 1961), 3.67, 287.

91. "Romulus . . . set to building his city. . . . First, they dug a round trench about that which is now the Comitium, or Court of Assembly, and into it solemnly threw the first-fruits of all things either good by custom or necessary by nature; lastly, every man taking a small piece of earth of the country from whence he came, they all threw in promiscuously together. This trench they call, as they do the heavens, Mundus; making which their centre, they described the city in a circle round it. . . . With this line they described the wall, and called it, by a contraction, *pomoerium*, that is, *postmurum* after or beside the wall." Plutarch, "Romulus," in *The Lives of the Noble Grecians and Romans*, 31.

92. This is the "noble lie" Socrates recommends in the *Republic*, 414d.

93. Plutarch, "Romulus," 29–30. See also: "But at first, not by removal, or increase of an existing city, but by foundation of a new one, [Romulus] obtained himself lands, a country, a kingdom, wives, children and relations. And, in so doing, he killed or destroyed nobody, but benefited those that wanted houses and homes and were willing to be of a society and becomes citizens." Plutarch, "The Comparison of Romulus with Theseus," in *The Lives of the Noble Grecians and Romans*, 48.

94. Livy, *The History of Rome,* trans. Aubrey de Selincourt (London: Penguin, 2002), 1.8, 40.

95. See Cicero, *De republica, On the Commonwealth and the Laws,* ed. James E. G. Zetzel (Cambridge: Cambridge University Press, 1999), 2.10.

96. Romulus, Cicero emphasizes, is much later than Homer. See *De republica,* 2.10. See chapter 6 of this volume.

97. Ibid., 2.1, 33.

98. Cicero, *De officiis,* 1.34, 127.

99. Ibid., 2.21, 249.

100. Ibid., 1.30, 109.

101. Ibid.

102. Ibid., 1.31, 113.

103. Ibid.

104. Ibid., 113–115.

105. Ibid., 115.

106. Ibid.

107. Ibid.

108. Alexandre Kojève, *Introduction à la lecture de Hegel* (Paris: Gallimard, 1947), 116. Quote trans. Marc LePain.

109. Montaigne, "Of Repentance," in *Essays*, in *The Complete Works*, trans. Donald M. Frame (New York: Alfred A. Knopf, 2003), 3.2, 746.

110. Ibid., "Of Cato the Younger," 1.37, 207.

111. Ibid., 206.

112. Ibid., "Of Physiognomy," 3.12, 965.

113. Ibid., "Of Vanity," 3.9, 922.

114. Montaigne writes a few lines above: "Is it wrong of him not to do what it is impossible for him to do?" Ibid., 921.

115. See ibid., 1.37, 207.

116. See Kant, *Critique of Practical Reason,* trans. Lewis White Beck (New York: Liberal Arts Press, 1956), 166.

117. Montaigne, "Of Vanity," in *Essays*, 3.9, 889.

118. Ibid., 886–887.

119. Ibid., 887.

120. See chapter 5 of this volume.

121. Montaigne, "Of the Education of Children," in *Essays,* 1.26, 142.

122. Ibid., "Of Friendship," 1.28, 166.

123. Ibid., "That to Philosophize Is to Learn to Die," 1.20, 73.

124. Ibid., 1.40.

125. Ibid., 3.2, 741.

126. Ibid., 1.40, 224.

127. Ibid., "Of Vanity," 3.9, 887.

5. Rome as Seen by the Moderns

1. See chapter 6 of this volume.

2. Niccolò Machiavelli, *The Prince,* 2nd ed., trans. Harvey C. Mansfield (Chicago: University of Chicago Press, 1998), ch. 15, 61.

3. Ibid.

4. Niccolò Machiavelli, *Discourses on Livy,* trans. Harvey C. Mansfield and Nathan Tarcov (Chicago: University of Chicago Press, 1996), 209.

5. See also the beginning of chapter 1 of *The Prince.*

6. Machiavelli, *Discourses on Livy,* 210.

7. Thomas Hobbes, *Behemoth, or the Long Parliament,* bk. 4, ed. Ferdinand Tönnies (Chicago: University of Chicago Press, 1990), 158–159.

8. There were seeds of that in Cicero, as we have seen in chapter 4.

9. Michel de Montaigne, "Of Vanity," in *Essays,* 3.9, in *The Complete Works,* trans. Donald M. Frame (New York: Alfred A. Knopf, 2003), 887.

10. See Hobbes, *Behemoth,* 158–159.

11. Thomas Hobbes, *Leviathan,* ed. Michael Oakeshott (New York: Collier, 1962), 47.

12. I have already mentioned the progress in relation to Machiavelli. Where there was need to make good use of "extrinsic and intrinsic accidents," there will now be an instrument whose effects are foreseeable, an instrument that can be counted on.

13. Leo Strauss, *The Political Philosophy of Hobbes: Its Basis and Its Genesis* (Chicago: University of Chicago Press, 1966 [1952]), 151.

14. Ibid., 150.

15. "The aim of the State is for him as a matter of course peace, i.e., peace at any price." Ibid., 152.

16. Montaigne, "Of Vanity," in *Essays,* 3.9, 932.

17. Montesquieu, *Considerations on the Causes of the Greatness of the Romans and Their Decline,* trans. David Lowenthal (Ithaca, NY: Cornell University Press, 1968), 27.

18. Ibid., 26–27.

19. Ibid., 29.

20. Ibid., 45.
21. Ibid., 85.
22. Ibid., 24.
23. Ibid., 92.
24. Ibid., 92–93, emphasis mine.
25. Ibid., 101.
26. Ibid.
27. Ibid., 136.
28. Ibid., 106.
29. See Shakespeare, *Julius Caesar*, Act I, Scene 2, ll. 115–116, 135ff.
30. Montesquieu, *Considerations*, 138.
31. Ibid., 111.
32. Ibid., 107–108.
33. Ibid., 109–110.
34. Ibid., 113.
35. Ibid., 117.
36. Ibid., 116.
37. Ibid., 108.
38. Cato did not "abandon" the republic, but he did not "preserve" himself for it.
39. Montesquieu, *Considerations*, 118. A note added the following: "If Charles I, if James II had lived in a religion that allowed them to kill themselves, they would not have had to experience, the one such a death, the other such a life."
40. Ibid., 117.
41. Ibid.
42. Ibid., 117–118.
43. Ibid., 117.
44. Ibid., 146.
45. Ibid., 138.
46. Ibid., 152.

6. Cicero's Inquiry

1. Lucretius is the other capital author who, in another register, presents the doctrine of Epicurus in Latin verse.
2. "My philosophy is not very different from that of the Peripatetics." Cicero, *De officiis*, trans. Walter Miller, Loeb Classical Library (Cambridge, MA: Harvard University Press, 1975), 1.2, 191; "I have followed [Panaetius] in the main—but with slight modifications." Ibid., 3.2, 7, 277.
3. See chapter 5 of this volume.

4. In any case, these were the first dialogues to be written in Latin.

5. See Cicero, *De republica, On the Commonwealth and the Laws,* ed. James E. G. Zetzel (Cambridge: Cambridge University Press, 1999), 1.10. The parhelion is an atmospheric phenomenon caused by the refraction of solar rays by suspended ice crystals in the upper regions of the atmosphere. The phenomenon, which appeared in 129 B.C., was retrospectively taken as announcing the death of Scipio.

6. Ibid., p. 8.

7. Ibid., 1.19, 10.

8. Ibid., 1.25, 12.

9. More directly, Philus recounts how Galus learned astronomy with the help of a sphere constructed by Archimedes himself.

10. It is not clear to me that this is the same eclipse that frightened Pericles's soldiers.

11. Ibid., 1.26–27, 13.

12. Cicero, *De officiis,* 2.21, 249. See chapter 5 of this volume.

13. The two specifications of the law of nature are not simply opposed as the most particular and the most common: they are also complementary in that the one concerns what is subpolitical and the other what is metapolitical.

14. Cicero, *De republica,* 1.31, 15.

15. Ibid., 1.33, 16.

16. *Princeps civitatis:* Zetzel's edition translates this phrase as "leader of the commonwealth"; I suggest "first citizen." It can be noted that Cicero gives Pericles principal status: "Pericles princeps consilii publici fuit" (*De oratore,* trans. E.W. Sutton, Cambridge: Harvard University Press, 1.216, 152). *Princeps senatus:* the first inscribed on the list of the senate by the censors, he is the first to give his opinion. *Princeps,* beginning with Augustus, designates the emperor, since Augustus, under the title of prince of the senate, concentrated all the power in his own hands.

17. Cicero, *De republica,* 1.34, 16.

18. Ibid., 1.36, 16.

19. Ibid., 1.42, 19.

20. Aristotle employs the term *desmos* (bond) only in a physiological context, in the sense of ligament or "ligature." It is not used in the *Politics,* and only once in the *Nicomachean Ethics* (1131a 8), with the ordinary meaning of "imprisonment." It is employed much more frequently by Plato, but most of the time with the ordinary meaning of "shackles." In the *Statesman,* Plato mentions *anthrôpinous desmous* (310a 7), the "human bonds" among which marriages have pride of place. In the *Protagoras* are mentioned *desmoï philias* (322c 3), the "bonds of friendship." In the *Laws,* one reads about *desmoï pasès politeïas* (793b 4), the bonds attendant on every political regime, to designate ancestral customs

or unwritten laws. It seems to me that Aristotle is among all political authors the most reticent about using so abstract or general a term: in his eyes, *philia*, a concrete notion, is moreover specified according to the regime. One may see in Locke's very general formula—the "bonds of civil society"—an expression of "modern abstraction."

21. Cicero, *De republica*, 1.43, 19.

22. Ibid., 1.45, 20.

23. Ibid., 1.35, 20.

24. It does not seem that he had direct access to the text of Aristotle.

25. Polybius, *The Histories*, trans. Robin Waterfield (Oxford: Oxford University Press, 2010), 6.4, 373.

26. Ibid., 6.9, 378.

27. Ibid.

28. Ibid., 6.10, 378–379.

29. Ibid., 379.

30. Ibid., 6.11, 380.

31. Ibid., Bk. 6.18, 384.

32. Aristotle, *The Politics*, trans. Carnes Lord (Chicago: University of Chicago Press, 1985), 1265b33–40, 66.

33. Even if the context is the discussion of Plato's *Laws*, he is not the one in view there. It is indeed true that in book 3 of the *Laws* the Athenian stranger, speaking to his Spartan interlocutor, shows the constitution of Sparta as produced starting with kingship, which was soon divided, then limited by the equal power of the elders, which in turn was limited by the power of the ephors, an institution akin to a power accorded by lot (691d–692d). This extremely stylized presentation cannot be taken as a description or an analysis of the Spartan regime.

34. See Aristotle, *Politics*, 1293b17–18.

35. Ibid., 1294b14–19, 131–132.

36. See ibid., 1313a25–30.

37. See chapter 4 of this volume.

38. Montesquieu, *The Spirit of the Laws*, trans. Anne M. Cohler, Basia Carolyn Miller, and Harold Samuel Stone (Cambridge: Cambridge University Press, 1989), 11.9, 168.

39. Polybius, *Histories*, 6.50, 407: "But if one has greater ambitions than that—if one thinks that it is a finer and nobler thing to be a world-class leader, with an extensive dominion and empire, the centre and focal point of everyone's world—then one must admit that the Spartan constitution is deficient, and that the Roman constitution is superior and more dynamic."

40. In book 8 of the *Republic*, Plato underscores the extreme pleasantness of democratic life. Democracy is "a sweet regime, without rulers and many-colored"

(558c). Plato, *The Republic,* trans. Allan Bloom (New York: Basic Books, 1968), 236.

41. See Cicero, *De republica,* 1.49, 21.

42. Ibid., 1.55–56, 24.

43. Ibid., 1.58, 25.

44. Laelius adds that Romulus lived at a time when Greece was already beginning to age.

45. Cicero, *De republica,* 1.58, 25.

46. Ibid.

47. Ibid., p. 26.

48. Ibid., 1.61, 27.

49. Ibid., 1.62, 27.

50. Ibid., 1.64, 28.

51. Not long after, Scipio says that regarding kingly power, the first alteration and the one whose effect is the most certain ("prima et certissima mutatio") occurs when the king begins to be unjust; then this regime is straightaway dealt a fatal blow; it is a tyrant that rules, and it is the worst of regimes, even as it is the closest to the best ("deterrimum genus, et finitimum optimo").

52. Cicero, *De republica,* 1.69, 31.

53. Ibid.

54. Ibid., 1.71, 32.

55. Ibid., 2.2, 33.

56. Ibid.

57. The insistence here on Roman duration goes against the earlier effort to join the present time and the time of the kings. Such are the ambivalence and the commodity of the authority of history: time is shortened or lengthened at will.

58. Cicero, *De republica,* 2.3, 34.

59. Niccolò Machiavelli, *The Prince,* 2nd ed., trans. Harvey C. Mansfield (Chicago: University of Chicago Press, 1998), 61.

60. Cicero, *De republica,* 2.21, 39.

61. Ibid.

62. Ibid., 2.22, 39.

63. Laelius congratulates Scipio because his speech does not wander but remains attached to one republic only. There is something common to Platonist idealism and Aristotelian empiricism: a freedom of inquiry that can appear to be wandering ("oratio vagans"). Plato's conception rises above real regimes, whereas Aristotle's inquiry goes freely and indefinitely from one to the other. Scipio's approach is attached to, fixed on, a real object. It conforms, so to speak, to the initiative of the object, to its strength and authority. Rome brings down to earth, nails to the ground, the otherwise "ascending" Platonist conception and attaches to itself, "fixes" the otherwise "wandering" Aristotelian inquiry. See ibid., 2.22, 39.

64. See ibid., 2.4, 34.

65. Scipio "Platonizes" when it suits him: "you ascribe," Laelius says, "to Romulus' deliberate planning all the features of the site of the city which were actually the result of chance or necessity." Ibid., 2.11, 39.

66. Ibid., 2.8, 35.

67. Ibid.

68. Ibid., 2.12–13, 36–37.

69. See Livy, *The History of Rome*, trans. Aubrey de Selincourt (London: Penguin, 2002), 1.9.

70. "The two states were united under a single government, with Rome as the seat of power [Regnum consociant: imperium omne conferunt Romam]." Livy, *History of Rome*, 1.13, 46.

71. See Montesquieu, *The Spirit of the Laws*, 11.15, and 12.21.

72. Cicero, *De republica*, 2.14, 37.

73. See Livy, *The History of Rome*, 1.14–15. Romulus perhaps was not sincere in sharing power; he pleased the people more than the fathers; he was the favorite of the soldiers, and he had a personal guard not only in time of war but also in peacetime.

74. Cicero, *De republica*, 2.15, 37. If Romulus legislated as Lycurgus had done at Sparta not long before, this would confirm that Rome from the beginning was playing in the same league, dare I say, as the best-governed Greek cities.

75. See chapter 4 of this volume.

76. Cicero, *De republica*, 2.20, 39.

77. Rousseau gives this idea a splendid formulation: "This is what has always forced the fathers of nations to have recourse to the intervention of heaven and to attribute their own wisdom to the Gods; so that the peoples, subjected to the laws of the State as to those of nature, and recognizing the same power in the formation of man and of the City, might obey with freedom and bear with docility the yoke of public felicity. It is this sublime reason, which rises above the grasp of common men, whose decisions the legislator places in the mouth of the immortals in order to convince by divine authority those who cannot be moved by human prudence. But it is not every man who can make the Gods speak or be believed when he declares himself their interpreter. The legislator's great soul is the true miracle that should prove his mission." Jean-Jacques Rousseau, *On the Social Contract*, trans. Judith R. Masters (New York: St. Martin's, 1978), 2.7, 69–70.

78. See Cicero, *De republica*, 2.12. Livy gives a quite different analysis of the episode. He will not evoke any attempt of the *patres* to do without a king. In spite of their disagreements, all wanted a monarchic regime, for no one had yet tasted the sweetness of liberty—"in variis voluntatibus regnari tamen omnes volebant, libertatis dulcedine nondum experta" (Livy, *History of Rome*, 1.17).

79. Numa, like Tullus Hostilius and Ancus Martius after him, is not content to be elected: he has himself granted *imperium* by a *lex curiata*. These kings of Rome were very republican.

80. "Praetermissis suis civibus, regem alienigenam, patribus auctoribus, sibi ipse populus adscivit." Cicero, *De republica*, 2.25, 40. The repetition of the verb *adscire* emphasizes the associative and assimilating power of Rome in its very youth.

81. According to Plutarch, Numa, who was the son-in-law of Titus Tatius, was called to reign because it was agreed that a Sabine king would succeed a Roman and vice versa.

82. Cicero and Livy present Numa's religious policy in somewhat different ways. Cicero emphasizes the multiplication of rites that were constraining but that cost little, while Livy insists on the substitution of the fear of the enemy with the fear of the gods: the absence of any external dangers ran the risk of unsettling spirits that the fear of the enemy and military discipline had until then contained; therefore before all else he wanted to instill in souls a sentiment—the fear of the gods—all-powerful on a crowd that was ignorant and still rude at the time. See Livy, *History of Rome*, 1.19. However, in chapter 21, Livy nuances his description in a less Machiavellian sense. Under Numa, the fear of the gods became a fervent and even obsessive piety in Rome, to the point that respect for oaths replaced the extreme fear of legal punishment as the principle of government (see ibid., 1.21). And lo and behold, neighboring peoples, who until then saw in Rome less a city than a camp, settled among them to trouble the general peace and were brought to venerate Rome, to the point of considering an attack against a nation wholly devoted to the cult of the gods as a sacrilege (see ibid., 1.21). The refuge of thieves has become the holy nation.

83. Cicero, *De republica*, 2.29, 41.

84. Ibid., 2.30, 42.

85. Ibid., 2.31, 42. Livy ascribes the institution of the Fetiales to the successor of Tullus Hostilius, Ancus Martius. The college of Fetiales was composed of twenty members. The procedure called for sending a mission composed of priests (under their leader, the *pater patratus*) to the country in question to demand reparation for wrongdoings. The potential adversary had thirty-three days to think over the demand. In the event there was no reply, another mission was sent to ascertain the unjust character of this attitude. Then the senate—from the fifth century onward, the people—decided on war. In order to declare it, the Fetiales went to the enemy border where the *pater patratus* threw a bloodied spear. See D. Alland and S. Rials, eds., *Dictionnaire de la culture juridique* (Paris: Presses Universitaires de France, 2003), 771.

86. Cicero, *De republica*, 2.34, 43.

87. "In novo populo, ubi onmis repentina atque ex virtute nobilitas sit, futurum locus forti ac strenuo viro." Livy, *History of Rome*, 1.34, 73.

88. Ibid., 1.35, 74.

89. Cicero, *De republica*, 2.38, 44.

90. Livy's description of the episode is very different. He gives Tanaquil in this too a decisive role and devotes a good deal of space to the "signs" dear to the Etruscans. His conclusion emphasizes, or in any case brings out, the tyrannical aspect of the accession: Servius, supported by a solid guard, was the first to become king without being chosen by the people and with the sole consent of the senate (*History of Rome*, 1.41). Cicero and Livy are diametrically opposed on one point: the first maintains that Servius did not consult the senators, whereas the second holds that he had the support of the senate.

91. See Cicero, *De republica*, 2.22, 45.

92. Livy's analysis and evaluation of Servius Tullius's census-based regime seem very close to those of Cicero. For the historian, Servius is in the eyes of posterity the founder of every difference in the city and of the orders thanks to which a difference was established between the various degrees of dignity and wealth (Livy, *History of Rome*, 1.42). Livy writes further: "Manhood suffrage with equal rights for all, which had obtained ever since the days of Romulus, was abolished and replaced by a sliding scale. This had the effect of giving every man nominally a vote, while leaving all power actually in the hands of the knights and the First Class" (ibid., 1.43, 83).

93. Again here, Livy assigns the primary role to the wife, this time the wife of Tarquin, Tullia, who is the daughter of Servius Tullius; and he notes the "tragic" character of the episode. See ibid., 1.46–47.

94. Cicero, *De republica*, 2.46, 47.

95. Ibid., 2.42, 46.

96. There is a difference in accent, it seems to me, between Cicero and Plato in their description of the tyrant. Whereas Plato insists on the disorder of the soul, the limitless character of the tyrant's desires, Cicero instead insists on the rupture of all human bonds on the part of the tyrant, who wishes to have no bond of shared law, no link of human nature with his fellow citizens or indeed with the whole human race. Ibid., 2.48, 48.

97. In the mixed regimes of Lycurgus and Romulus, "the force, power, and name of king stands out and dominates." Ibid., 2.50, 48.

98. Ibid., 2.51, 49.

99. "Therefore as sin came into the world through one man and death through sin, and so death spread to all men because all men sinned . . . then as one man's trespass led to condemnation for all men, so one man's act of righteousness leads to acquittal and life for all men. For as by one man's disobedience many were made sinners, so by one man's obedience many will be made righteous." Romans 5:12–19, Revised Standard Version.

100. See chapter 5 of this volume.

101. On the contrary, Livy states that at the time of the crisis precipitated by the rape of Lucretia, Brutus occupied an important magistracy since he was the Tribune of Knights, that is, the head of the king's personal guard (*History of Rome*, 1.59). Livy is probably closer to the historical truth, which is not Cicero's primary interest, as we have previously noted. At the beginning of book 2, Livy makes a rigorous distinction between Tarquin and his predecessors. He adds: "It cannot be doubted that Brutus, who made for himself so great a name by the expulsion of Tarquin, would have done his country the greatest disservice, had he yielded too soon to his passion for liberty and forced the abdication of any of the previous kings [si libertatis immaturae cupidine priorum regum alicui regnum extorsisset]. One has but to think of what the populace was like in those early days—a rabble of vagrants, mostly runaways and refugees—and to ask what would have happened if they had suddenly found themselves protected from all authority by inviolable sanctuary, and enjoying complete freedom of action, if not full political rights. In such circumstances, unrestrained by the power of the throne, they would, no doubt, have set sail on the stormy sea of democratic politics, swayed by the gusts of popular eloquence and quarrelling for power with the governing class of a city which did not even belong to them [in aliena urbe], before any real sense of community had had time to grow. That sense—the only true patriotism—comes slowly and springs from the heart [animos eorum consociasset]: it is founded upon respect for the family and love of the soil [pignera conjugum ac liberorum caritasque ipsius soli]." Cicero, too, like Livy, places the blame on Tarquin alone, whose reign is the pivotal point of Roman history. But Cicero emphasizes the intrinsic or essential fragility of kingship, which is prey to the "vice of one alone," whereas Livy traces a history of liberty, or more precisely he distinguishes the prehistory of liberty from its history. The first kings effected a first association, which could not be called either free or not free. Then the excesses of the tyrant-king gave rise by way of reaction to liberty, properly speaking. More precisely:

a. Fear of the early kings civilizes or humanizes people who naturally seek impunity.
b. The tyrant-king and his associates in their turn seek impunity while the members of society in the end accept a certain order. Brutus expels the king and punishes the wrongdoers, first of all his sons themselves. Liberty, at first founded on forging filial ties—*pignera liberorum*—(stage a), is confirmed by the sacrifice of those same ties.
c. What then is republican liberty? It is the ever-possible or ever-threatening punishment of the second or civilized impunity.

102. What is proper to Rome are the private political initiatives, the *privatus* that saves liberty, unlike Athens, which is characterized by the initiative of the

leader of the people and his role as *arbitrator*. In Rome there is no leader of the people who is at the same time leader of the city. It is the Senate, or the principal senators, that governs and sets the tone of the government. But individual initiative (for example, Cato's against Scipio) is necessary to activate and empower the citizens' suspicion regarding a citizen who gets too influential. It matters little whether the suspicion has any foundation: it has its good effects.

103. Cicero, *De republica*, 2.57, 51. The *natura rerum* is the *natura rerum-publicarum* evoked a little further, but it is also the "nature of things" in the broad sense, the "nature of nature" so to speak, "physics," for people as well as things are carried by their own motion, and people are so often beyond the point where it would be fitting to stop.

104. Niccolò Machiavelli, *Discourses on Livy*, trans. Harvey C. Mansfield and Nathan Tarcov (Chicago: University of Chicago Press, 1998), 1.6, 23.

105. Ibid., 2.19, 173.

106. Ibid., 1.6, 21–22.

107. Leo Strauss, *The Political Philosophy of Hobbes: Its Basis and Its Genesis* (Chicago: University of Chicago Press, 1966 [1952]), 151. See chapter 5 of this volume.

108. Montesquieu, *The Spirit of the Laws*, 11.8, 167–168: "it is remarkable that the corruption of the government of a conquering people should have formed the best kind of government men have been able to devise."

109. See Thomas Hobbes, *Behemoth, or the Long Parliament*, ed. Ferdinand Tönnies (Chicago: University of Chicago Press, 1990), bk. 4, 158–159.

110. Thomas Hobbes, *Leviathan*, ed. Michael Oakeshott (New York: Collier, 1962), 55.

111. See Thomas Hobbes, *Elements of Law*, ed. Ferdinand Tönnies (New York: Barnes & Noble, 1969) part I, ch. 9, par. 21, 47.

112. "Desire is always moved by evil, to fly it." John Locke, *An Essay concerning Human Understanding* (New York: Dover, 1959), 2.21, par. 73, I, 367.

113. "He cannot assure the power and means to live well, which he hath present, without the acquisition of more." Hobbes, *Leviathan*, ch. 11. See also Montesquieu: "But, due to a malady eternal in man, the plebeians, who had obtained tribunes to defend themselves, used them for attacking." *Considerations*, ch. 8, 84.

114. Karl Marx, *On the Jewish Question* (1844): "Is not private property ideally abolished when the non-owner comes to legislate for the owner of property? The property qualification is the last political form in which private property is recognized." *The Marx-Engels Reader*, ed. Robert C. Tucker (New York: Norton, 1972), 31.

115. Montesquieu, *The Spirit of the Laws*, 11.6, 164.

116. The extraordinarily fast movement of American life rests on the extraordinary stability of the American Constitution.

117. Aristotle, *Nicomachean Ethics,* trans. Terence Irwin (Indianapolis: Hackett, 1999), 5.6, 1131a25–29, 71.

118. Montesquieu, *The Spirit of the Laws,* 21.12, 380.

7. The Critique of Paganism

1. Blaise Pascal, *Pensées,* rev. ed., trans. A. J. Krailsheimer (Harmondsworth: Penguin, 1995), no. 21, 5–6.

2. Montesquieu, *The Spirit of the Laws,* trans. Anne M. Cohler, Basia Carolyn Miller, and Harold Samuel Stone (Cambridge: Cambridge University Press, 1989), 4.4, 35.

3. Thomas Hobbes, *Leviathan,* ed. Michael Oakeshott (New York: Collier Books), 340.

4. Jean-Jacques Rousseau, *On the Social Contract,* trans. Judith R. Masters (New York: St. Martin's, 1978), 4.4, 127.

5. Karl Marx, *On the Jewish Question,* in *The Marx-Engels Reader,* ed. Robert C. Tucker (New York: W. W. Norton, 1972), 32.

6. Ibid.

7. "This discovery of the Vagueness of the Passions from which all of modern literature derives." Charles Du Bos, *Approximations* (Paris: Fayard, [1922] 1965), 412.

8. François-René de Chateaubriand, *Génie de christianisme,* (Paris: Calmann-Lévy, 1868) part II, book 3, chapter 9, 291. Quote trans. Marc A. LePain.

9. Ibid.

10. Christianity is no longer present in itself, in its vigor, but in its weakness, reduced to the shadow that it casts on the life of humans.

11. One of the injunctions most often heard among us is "Don't feel guilty!"

12. By their "poetry," their "style," the romantics seek to reenchant a world they painfully experience as disenchanted. We do not believe this reenchantment is possible. We are disappointed or discouraged romantics.

13. This results from the irreversible disappearance of the concrete unity of the city. We have seen in part II how Cicero, in *De republica,* is in search of a kingly figure—a *princeps*—capable of restoring civic order.

14. One could say that the end of kingship, which is always concrete, was a necessary condition for the establishment of monarchy.

15. In this sense, we are being faithful to sociology's original inspiration.

16. Montesquieu, *The Spirit of the Laws,* 19.21, 321.

17. Ibid.

18. Ibid., 4.4, 35.

19. Ibid., 4.6, 36–37.

20. See Exodus 15:13–18 and 19:2–8.

21. Most probably Augustine has Paul in mind first of all.

22. Augustine, *The City of God*, trans. Henry Bettenson (Harmondsworth: Penguin, 1972), 14.28, 593.

23. See chapter 4 of this volume.

24. I immediately add that Augustine did not understand the Christian Church as being "Roman," since his intention on the contrary was to rigorously distinguish and even to separate ontologically the Christian Church from every human association.

25. Augustine, *City of God*, 5.26, 223. See the list of increasingly harsh measures against pagan worship in the introduction to *La cité de Dieu*, in *Oeuvres de saint Augustin*, vol. 33 (Tournoi: Desclée de Brouwer, 1959), 176–178.

26. For a few examples, see *La cité de Dieu*, 17–18.

27. Augustine, *City of God*, 1.1, 6.

28. Ibid., 1.2, 8.

29. See ibid., 1.3, 9.

30. See ibid., 1.5, 11.

31. Ibid., 1.7, 12.

32. The advent of "Christian times" is obviously a particularly explicit manifestation of Providence.

33. Augustine, *City of God*, 1.8, 13.

34. Ibid., 14.

35. See ibid., 1.9, 15–16.

36. Ibid., 16.

37. See ibid.

38. See ibid.

39. See ibid.

40. See Niccolò Machiavelli, *Discourses on Livy*, trans. Harvey C. Mansfield and Nathan Tarcov (Chicago: University of Chicago Press, 1998), 2.2, 2, and 3.1, 4; and Niccolò Machiavelli, *The Art of War*, in *The Chief Works and Others*, vol. 2, trans. Allan Gilbert (Durham: Duke University Press, 1965) bk. 2, 623–624.

41. Niccolò Machiavelli, *The Prince*, 2nd ed., trans. Harvey C. Mansfield (Chicago: University of Chicago Press, 1998), 88.

42. The republican tradition readily links this contrast to the sexual stereotype by opposing the "feminine" combination of cruelty and softness to the "virile" combination of harshness and moderation.

43. A respect recommended by the Letter to the Romans 13:1–7: "Let every person be subject to the governing authorities. For there is no authority except from God, and those that exist have been instituted by God. Therefore he who resists the authorities resists what God has appointed, and those who resist will incur judgment." Revised Standard Version.

44. See Augustine, *City of God,* 1.17, 26–27.

45. Ibid., 26.

46. See ibid., 1.18, *in fine.,* 28.

47. See ibid., 1.19, 29–30.

48. Ibid., 30.

49. See ibid.

50. Ibid.

51. Livy, *The History of Rome,* trans. Aubrey de Selincourt (London: Penguin, 2002), 1.58, 102.

52. Augustine, *City of God,* 1.19, 30.

53. See Niccolò Machiavelli, *Mandragola,* trans. Mera J. Flaumenhaft (Long Grove, IL: Waveland Press, 1981).

54. This is not entirely exact. Lucretia resists the threat of death heroically, but when Sextus adds the threat of dishonor to that of death, she surrenders without consenting.

55. Machiavelli, *Mandragola,* act II, scene 6, 25.

56. Ibid., act III, scene 11, 35–36.

57. Augustine, *City of God,* 1.20, 32. Augustine states more precisely that this prohibition against killing concerns only the human race, despite the fact that "some people have tried to extend its scope to wild and domestic animals." This error, this madness of the Manicheans, is to be rejected. The prohibition against killing does not include animals, not to speak of plants, "since they have no rational association with us, not having been endowed with reason as we are [quia nulla nobis ratione sociantur, quam non eis datum est nobiscum habere communem]."

58. Ibid., 1.21, 32.

59. Ibid. Machiavelli will take up this same point with a very different intention: "And although one should not reason about Moses, as he was a mere executor of things that had been ordered for him by God." *The Prince,* ch. 6, 24.

60. Augustine, *City of God,* 1.22, 33.

61. "But also men sometimes desire death in the hope of a greater good. 'I desire,' says Saint Paul, 'to be dissolved, to be with Jesus Christ.' And 'Who will deliver me from these bonds?' Cleombrotus of Ambracia, having read Plato's *Phaedo,* gained such an appetite for the life to come that, without any other reason, he went and threw himself into the sea. Whence it appears how improperly we call 'despair' that voluntary dissolution to which we are often borne by the ardor of hope, and often by a tranquil and deliberate inclination of our judgment." Michel de Montaigne, "A Custom of the Island of Cea," in *Essays,* 2.3, in *The Complete Works,* trans. Donald M. Frame (New York: Alfred A. Knopf, 2003), 316.

62. Augustine, *City of God,* 1.22, 33. If Plato had deemed Cleombrotus's action wise, Augustine says, a bit heavy-handedly, that he would have been the first to take it.

63. See ibid., 1.23, 34.

64. Ibid.

65. Ibid.

66. See chapter 4 of this volume.

67. Montaigne, "Of Cruelty," in *Essays*, 2.11, 374–375. Montaigne cites Cicero's sentence in full in Latin, in which he reads the judgment of "philosophy."

68. See Augustine, *City of God*, 1.15, 24.

69. How can one say that Regulus was happy in suffering torture? But how can one say that he was unhappy when he had chosen to die in this way?

70. See Augustine, *City of God*, 1.15, 25.

71. Ibid., 1.24, 35.

72. See ibid.

73. Ibid., 5.12, 196.

74. See ibid, 197.

75. See ibid.

76. Ibid., 198.

77. I have previously cited Montesquieu: "But, due to a malady eternal in man, the plebeians, who had obtained tribunes to defend themselves, used them for attacking." *Considerations on the Causes of the Greatness of the Romans and Their Decline*, trans. David Lowenthal (Ithaca, NY: Cornell University Press, 1968), 84.

78. Sallust, *The War with Catiline*, 10. 3, in *Sallust*, trans. J. C. Rolfe (Cambridge, MA: Harvard University Press, 1960), 19.

79. Montesquieu already spoke of England as a republic that "hides under the form of monarchy" (*The Spirit of the Laws*, 5.19, 70). But I am forgetting, as it is always forgotten, the federated republic of Holland, which also fashioned for itself a fine empire.

80. Sallust—Augustine does not cite him on this point—ascribes this upheaval to the capture of Rome by Sylla's army, an army that Sylla had allowed to grow corrupt in Asia (*The War with Catiline*, 11.5). It seems that Sallust distinguishes three stages: (1) up to the destruction of Carthage, *labor et justitia*; (2) between the destruction of Carthage and the victory of Sylla, *ambitio* prevails over *avaritia*; and (3) after the victory of Sylla, *avaritia* unleashed.

81. Augustine, *City of God*, 5.12, 199.

82. Ibid.

83. Ibid.

84. Ibid., 200.

85. See ibid.

86. Ibid.

87. Augustine had already concluded chapter 17 of book 2 with the following words: "I am sick of recalling the many acts of revolting injustice which have disturbed the city's history; the powerful classes did their best to subjugate

the lower orders, and the lower orders resisted—the leaders of each side moti-vated more by ambition for victory than any ideas of equity and morality." Augustine, *City of God,* 2.17, 67.

88. Machiavelli, *The Prince,* ch. 9, 39. See also *Discourses on Livy,* 1.4.

89. It could be said that empire was the typical political form of Asia.

90. Augustine, *City of God,* 5.13, 202.

91. See ibid.

92. See ibid., 5.14, 203.

93. Ibid., 204.

94. See ibid.

95. Ibid., 5.15, 204.

96. Ibid., 205.

97. Matthew 6:2 (concerning the hypocrites who tout their almsgiving in the synagogues and in the streets).

98. Augustine, *City of God,* 5.16, 205.

99. Ibid., 5.17, 205.

100. Ibid., 206.

101. Ibid.

102. Ibid. (modified).

103. One can speak of a staging to the extent that Augustine constructs, on the basis of real elements, a "situation of the Roman world" that is rather for-eign to the Roman experience: the Romans showed neither taste nor particular skill for commerce or science.

104. Augustine, *City of God,* 5.17, 207.

105. Ibid., 4.5, 140.

106. "Asylum aperit. Eo ex finitimis populis turba omnis, sine discrimine liber an servus esset, avida novarum rerum perfugit." Livy, *History of Rome,* 1.8.

107. In an obviously altogether different perspective, this is the thesis the anti-Christian Enlightenment will take up: "The Papacy is no other than the ghost of the deceased Roman empire, sitting crowned upon the grave thereof." Hobbes, *Leviathan,* ch. 47. Christians and anti-Christians in any case join in pointing out that Rome evades conventional political classifications. When Montesquieu emphasizes that "Rome was really neither a monarchy nor a re-public, but the head of a body formed by all the peoples of the world" (*Consid-erations,* ch. 6, 75), he echoes what Augustine wrote, speaking of Rome as "the capital of the earthly city of which we are speaking, and which was to rule over so many peoples [quae fuerat hujus terrenae civitatis, de qua loquimur, caput futura et tam multis gentibus regnatura]"—*City of God,* 15.5, 600). It should be noted that at the moment he is writing Augustine does not consider the Ro-man Empire as a thing of the past: "The Roman empire has been shaken rather

than transformed, and that happened to it at other periods, before the preaching of Christ's name; and it recovered. There is no need to despair of its recovery at this present time. Who knows what is God's will in this matter?" (*City of God*, 4.7, 143).

108. Augustine, *City of God*, 10.21, 401.

109. See ibid., 5.17, 207.

110. See chapter 6 of this volume.

111. Augustine, *City of God*, 22.6, 1030.

112. Elsewhere, in ibid., 3.15, Augustine acknowledges that this is also probably Cicero's true opinion.

113. Ibid., 22.6, 1030.

114. See ibid.

115. Ibid.

116. See ibid.

117. As I have pointed out, this is the transformation that provides the starting point of the action in Shakespeare's *Julius Caesar*.

118. With disdain he spurns "acclamations hyperbolical" and "praises sauced with lies." Shakespeare, *Coriolanus*, act I, scene 9, ll. 50–52.

119. As the enterprise progressed, Bacon's relief became Adam Smith's improvement. As confidence increased, we went from "relief" to "improvement."

120. Montaigne, *Essays*, 1.20, 74. "That to philosophize is to learn to die."

121. See Augustine, *City of God*, 1.6, 12.

122. See chapter 2 of this volume.

123. Augustine, *City of God*, 2.4, 51.

124. Ibid., 2.7, 55.

125. Ibid., 2.13, 62.

126. Ibid.

127. Just as Socrates and his companions examine justice first of all in the city that provides a greater support with greater letters (*Republic* 368d–e), theatrical productions, according to Augustine, reveal the interior of the city's soul. They explicate more clearly than anything else the opinion that orients and guides the city. Rousseau also accords to theatrical productions a great power of political and moral revelation, and examines with care the political and moral meaning of the theater, the variations of its content and the status of actors, among the Greeks, the Romans, and the Moderns. See Jean-Jacques Rousseau, *Letter to d'Alembert*, trans. Allan Bloom (Ithaca, NY: Cornell University Press, 1968), 75–92.

128. See Augustine, *City of God*, 2.12, 60.

129. See ibid., 2.13, 62.

130. See ibid., 2.14, 63–64. For the very great esteem Augustine shows for Plato, see chapter 6 of this volume.

131. See ibid., 4.27–32.

132. See ibid., 4.27.

133. Ibid., 169.

134. See chapter 2 of this volume.

135. Aristotle, *Nicomachean Ethics,* trans. Terence Irwin (Indianapolis: Hackett, 1999), 10.7, 1177b27–35, 164.

136. Augustine, *City of God,* 4.30, 172–173.

137. Ibid., 174.

138. Ibid., 4.31, 174.

139. See ibid., 174–175.

140. Ibid., 175.

141. Paganism cannot do without such a doctrine: "velut secretior eorum doctrina" (ibid., 2.15).

142. The apostle's truthfulness is opposed to the esotericism of the philosopher. There cannot be a Christian esotericism. There indeed was a *disciplina arcani*—a phrase coined in the seventeenth century by the French Calvinist Jean Daillé—in the early centuries of the Christian church. But the discipline of the arcana has nothing to do with philosophic esotericism. It concerns a sort of "duty of discretion" that a preacher must observe with respect to catechumens—the nonbaptized—regarding certain sacraments, especially the Eucharist. In a context of misunderstanding and hostility and when the lack of any sacrificial practice deprives Christianity of the name of *religio,* the specific character of the Eucharistic sacrifice needs to be protected from ignorant or malevolent interpretation. The *disciplina arcani* will disappear with the public recognition of Christianity, the general practice of infant baptism, and the disappearance of the institution of the catechumenate. On all these points see Michel-Yves Perrin, "Arcana mysteria," in *Religionen: Die religiöse Erfahrung,* ed. M. Riedl and T. Schabert (Eranos: Königshausen und Neumann, 2008), 119–141.

8. The Two Cities

1. "Perplexae quippe sunt istae duae civitates in hoc saeculo invicemque permixtae, donec ultimo judicio dirimantur." Augustine, *City of God,* trans. Henry Bettenson (Harmondsworth: Penguin, 1972), 1.35, 46.

2. See ibid., 14.1.

3. See ibid.

4. See ibid.

5. Ibid., 547.

6. As we have seen, in certain contexts Augustine can express sentiments that are close to ours: "Tolle jactantiam, et omnes homines quid sunt nisi homines?" Ibid., 5.17, 206. See chapter 4 of this volume.

7. Augustine, *City of God,* 14.28, 593.

8. See ibid.

9. See ibid., 15.1.

10. Ibid., 15.5, 600.

11. See chapter 4 above.

12. Augustine, *City of God,* 15.5, 600.

13. Ibid.

14. Ibid., 601.

15. Ibid.

16. Ibid., 15.7, 604.

17. Ibid., 12.28, 508.

18. "For if nature is the cause of the evil will, can we help saying that evil is derived from good, and that good is the cause of evil? This must be so, if the evil will derives from a nature which is good. But how can this be? How can a nature which is good, however changeable, before it has an evil will, be the cause of any evil, the cause, that is, of that evil will itself? The truth is that one should not try to find an efficient cause for a wrong choice. It is not a matter of efficiency, but of deficiency; the evil will itself is not effective but defective." Ibid., 12.6–7, 479. See chapters 6–9 as a whole.

19. Pascal got himself out of this difficulty brilliantly: "Original sin is folly in the eyes of men, but it is put forward as such. You should therefore not reproach me for the unreasonable nature of this doctrine, because I put it forward as being unreasonable. But this folly is wiser than all men's wisdom. . . . For without it, what are we to say man is? His whole state depends on this imperceptible point. How could he have become aware of it through his reason, seeing that it is something contrary to reason and that his reason, far from discovering it by its own methods, draws away when presented with it?" Blaise Pascal, *Pensées,* rev. ed., trans. A. J. Krailsheimer (Harmondsworth: Penguin, 1995), no. 695, 219.

20. See Augustine, *City of God,* 13.3.

21. See ibid.

22. See ibid., 13.14.

23. *Catechism of the Catholic Church* (Mahwah, NJ: Paulist Press, 1994), no. 405, 102.

24. See Augustine, *City of God,* 13.13.

25. See ibid.

26. See ibid, 14.5.

27. Ibid., 14.3, 551.

28. Ibid., 14.5, 554.

29. See ibid., 14.3, 551.

30. See ibid., 14.11.

31. 1 Timothy 2:14, Revised Standard Version.

32. See Augustine, *City of God*, 14.11.

33. See ibid.

34. See ibid.

35. See Augustine, *The Literal Meaning of Genesis*, in *On Genesis*, trans. Edmund Hill (Hyde Park, NY: New City Press, 2002), 8.29.

36. See Augustine, *City of God*, 14.12.

37. See ibid.

38. Ibid., 14.15, 575.

39. Christophe de Beaumont, archbishop of Paris and Augustinian theologian, had issued a decree against the recently published *Émile*.

40. Jean-Jacques Rousseau, *Letter to Beaumont*, in *The Collected Writings of Rousseau*, Vol. 9, trans. Christopher Kelly and Judith R. Bush (Hanover, NH: Dartmouth, 2001), 31.

41. Augustine, *The Literal Meaning of Genesis*, 11.39, 451.

42. Jean-Jacques Rousseau, *Letter to Beaumont*, 28.

43. See Augustine, *City of God*, 14.4.

44. See ibid.

45. Ibid., 853–854.

46. Ibid., 855.

47. See ibid.

48. See ibid.

49. Ibid., 19.6, 860.

50. See ibid.

51. Ibid., 860.

52. Ibid., 861.

53. Ibid., 19.7, 862.

54. See ibid., 10.13.

55. See Livy, *History of Rome*, trans. Aubrey de Selincourt (London: Penguin, 2002), 1.19: "[Numa] simulat sibi cum dea Egeria congressus nocturnos esse."

56. See chapter 4 of this volume.

57. See Augustine, *City of God*, 10.13.

58. See ibid.; and Deuteronomy 4:9–14.

59. Augustine, *City of God*, 10.14, 392.

60. Ibid.

61. See ibid., 10.32.

62. Ibid., 423.

63. See ibid.

64. Ibid., 17.7, 733.

65. See Galatians 4:24.

66. Augustine, *City of God*, 17.7, 733. Augustine here cites 2 Corinthians 3:15–16. Paul himself was echoing Exodus 34:33–35. From the old to the new

covenant, the meaning of the "veil" is inverted, according to Paul. Moses used the veil to keep the children of Israel from fixing their gaze on a face that was destined to pass. Now, "whenever Moses is read," the veil laid on the heart keeps the face of the Savior from being recognized.

67. See ibid.

68. Pascal, *Pensées*, no. 475, 152.

69. Ibid., no. 826, 250.

70. Ibid., no. 453, 144.

71. Allow me to refer on this subject to my article, "L'Israël de Pascal," in *Port-Royal et le peuple d'Israël, Chroniques de Port-Royal* 53 (2004): 129–136.

72. Augustine, *City of God*, 10.32, 424.

73. See Deuteronomy 4:5–8.

74. As we take leave of Augustine, here is a last citation that is not without contemporary resonance. At the very end of book 10, Augustine contrasts the eternal damnation of the society of the impious ("societatis impiorum aeterna damnatio") and the eternal reign of the most glorious city of God ("regnum aeternum gloriosissimae civitatis Dei"). See *City of God*, 10.32. Thus, the damned still form a society, but only the saved constitute a city.

75. See Deuteronomy 4:32–39.

76. See Deuteronomy 4:5–8.

77. Dante, *Monarchy*, trans. Prue Shaw (Cambridge: Cambridge University Press, 1996), 1.3–4, 6–7: "There is therefore some activity specific to humanity as a whole, for which the whole human race in all its vast number of individual beings is designed. . . . It is thus clear that the highest potentiality of mankind is his intellectual potentiality or faculty. . . . And since that potentiality cannot be fully actualized all at once in any one individual or in any one of the particular social groupings enumerated above, there must needs be a vast number of individual people in the human race, through whom the whole of this potentiality can be actualized."

78. See Immanuel Kant, *Religion within the Limits of Reason Alone*, trans. Theodore M. Greene and Hoyt H. Hudson (New York: Harper and Row, 1960), bk. 4, part 2, ch. 4, 175–176.

79. See Immanuel Kant, "Remarks in the *Observations on the Feeling of the Beautiful and Sublime* (1764–65)," in *Observations on the Feeling of the Beautiful and Sublime and Other Writings,* trans. Patrick Frierson (Cambridge: Cambridge University Press, 2011), 96.

80. Kant's term for what necessarily interests everyone is "cosmic concept."

81. Immanuel Kant, *Critique of Pure Reason,* trans. J. M. D. Meiklejohn (New York: E. P. Dutton, 1959), 475.

82. "The problem of establishing a state, no matter how hard it may sound, is *soluble* even for a nation of devils (if only they have understanding)."

Immanuel Kant, *Toward Perpetual Peace,* in *Practical Philosophy,* trans. Mary J. Gregor (Cambridge: Cambridge University Press, 1996), 335.

83. Immanuel Kant, "Doctrine of Right," in *The Metaphysics of Morals,* part 2, Conclusion, in *Practical Philosophy,* 491.

84. Immanuel Kant, *Groundwork of the Metaphysics of Morals,* part 2, in *Practical Philosophy,* 83.

9. The Stakes of Mediation

1. See Augustine, *City of God,* trans. Henry Bettenson (Harmondsworth: Penguin, 1972), 8.10–11.

2. See ibid., 8.6.

3. Ibid., 7.32, 293.

4. See ibid., 8.12.

5. See ibid., 8.13; he had already done so in 2.14. See Plato, *Republic,* trans. Allan Bloom (New York: Basic Books, 1968), 398a.

6. Ibid., 316.

7. Plato, *Republic,* 377d5–6, 55.

8. See ibid., 377e6–7.

9. See ibid., 379a5–6.

10. Ibid., 379b1, 56.

11. Ibid., 379c, 57.

12. Ibid., 380c, 58.

13. See ibid., 381b4–c9.

14. Ibid., 382e9–11, 61. Mobility on the contrary is a bad sign, dare I say. Sophocles had characterized the Sphinx as *poïkilôdos*—whose songs are deceitful and changing (*Oedipus the King,* 130). Continual change, instability of form, or absence of form will be the sign of the devil for Augustine. He will apply to Satan what Virgil says of Proteus: "formas se vertit in omnes" (*City of God,* 10.10, citing *Georgics,* 4.411).

15. Plutarch will hail Alexander as the one who implements philosophy and extends its benefits to all peoples. See *On the Fortune or Virtue of Alexander,* 327e-329c.

16. Augustine, *City of God,* 8.13, 316, and 8.18, 324. The second maxim is not exactly present in the passages of the *Republic* we have considered, even if in saying that "the things that are good for us are far fewer than those that are bad" (379c), Plato tends to restrict considerably the good god's sphere of activity. But as such it is found in the *Symposium* (203a2), a text to which Augustine apparently had access through the intermediary of Apuleius and that we cite hereafter.

17. Plato, *Symposium,* in *The Dialogues of Plato,* trans. Seth Benardete (New York: Bantam, 1986), 202d–203a, 264–265.

18. See Augustine, *City of God*, 8.16–22, 9.6, 9.8.

19. Ibid., 8.16, 321.

20. Ibid., 8.17, 324.

21. See ibid., 9.13.

22. See ibid.

23. See ibid., 9.14.

24. The demonic power of the philosopher is set forth in a particularly dramatic fashion in the portrait Alcibiades draws of Socrates (see *Symposium*, 215a4–222b). In a more sober but no less explicit way, Aristotle emphasizes the divine or divinizing character of philosophic activity: it is the most self-sufficient activity. The just man, the temperate man, the courageous man are in need of other men to exercise their virtues. But not the *sophos* who, though he may possibly associate advantageously with collaborators, is nevertheless *autarkestatos*. Happiness moreover is taken to reside in leisure. Political and warrior activities, though they prevail by their nobility and grandeur ("kalleï kaï megestheï"), are nonetheless alien to leisure and do not have their end in themselves. The activity of the intellect, on the contrary, has no other end but itself and includes a specific pleasure that heightens the activity. This is Aristotle's conclusion, which we have already cited: "So if the intellect is something divine as compared with a human being, the life that is in accord with the intellect is divine as compared with a human life. But one should not follow those who advise us to think human thoughts, since we are human, and mortal thoughts, since we are mortal, but as far as possible one ought to be immortal *(athanatizeïn)*. Aristotle, *Nicomachean Ethics*, trans. Joe Sachs (Newburyport, MA: Focus, 2002), 10.7, 1177b30–35, 193.

25. See Augustine, *City of God*, 9.15.

26. Ibid., 359.

27. Ibid., 361. It is precisely this "servile" or "humiliating" mediation that the Greeks, including or especially the Platonist philosophers, are loath to acknowledge. Augustine addresses Porphyry in these terms: "you despise him [Christ] on account of the body which he received from a woman, and because of the shame of the cross" (ibid., 10.28, 413).

28. "That the body is united with the soul, so that man may be entire and complete, is a fact we recognize on the evidence of our own nature. If it had not been a fact of familiar experience, we should certainly have found it even more incredible; for it should be easier for faith to accept the union of spirit with spirit . . . than that of a body with an incorporeal entity" (ibid., 10.29, 415).

29. Martin Luther, *On Christian Liberty*, trans. W. A. Lambert (Minneapolis: Fortress Press, 2003), 6–7.

30. See ibid., 13.

31. Ibid., 31–32.

32. With Luther, grace remains outside or extraneous to the sinner that it justifies. The grace of Christ is a mantle that we take hold of to "cover all our blemishes." The difference between Lutheran justification, which includes certainty about the personal salvation of the believer, on the one hand, and Catholic sanctification, which entails the real transformation of the believer, on the other, was formulated in a particularly clear way by Bossuet: "Justification is grace that in remitting our sins at the same time renders us agreeable to God. It was until then believed that what produced this effect had in truth to come from God, but finally had to be in us; and that in order to be justified, that is, from being a sinner to be made just, one has to have justice within oneself; just as in order to be learned and virtuous, one had to have knowledge and virtue within oneself. But Luther did not follow such a simple idea. He wanted that what justifies us and makes us agreeable to God should be nothing in us; but that we should be justified because God imputed to us the justice of Jesus Christ, as if it had been our own, and because in effect we could appropriate it to ourselves by faith. But the secret of this justifying faith yet had something very peculiar: it did not consist in believing in the Savior in general, in his mysteries and promises; but in believing very certainly, each in his heart, that all our sins were forgiven. One was justified, Luther said without ceasing, once one believed with certitude he was justified; and the certitude he demanded was not only the moral certitude that, founded on reasonable motives, excluded agitation and anxiety, but an absolute certitude, an infallible certitude where the sinner had to believe he was justified with the same faith with which he believed that Jesus Christ came into the world." Jacques-Bénigne Bossuet, *Histoire des variations des Églises protestantes,* in *Oeuvres de Bossuet,* vol. 4 (Paris: Firmin Didot, 1852), 9. Quote trans. Marc LePain.

33. Cited in Pierre Mesnard, *L'Essor de la philosophie politique au XVIe siècle* (Paris: Vrin, 1969), 186.

34. Marcel Gauchet, *The Disenchantment of the World,* trans. Oscar Burge (Princeton, NJ: Princeton University Press, 1997), 91.

35. Ibid., 77.

36. Matthew 26:63–65, Revised Standard Version.

37. 1 Corinthians 1:22–24, Revised Standard Version.

38. Augustine, *City of God,* 10.28, 413.

39. See the articles of the Westminster Confession (1647) cited by Max Weber, *The Protestant Ethic and the Spirit of Capitalism,* trans. Talcott Parsons (London: Routledge, 1992), 57–58.

40. Gauchet, *The Disenchantment of the World,* 137.

41. See Weber, *The Protestant Ethic,* 39–40.

42. See Mesnard, *L'Essor de la philosophie politique au XVIe siècle,* 196.

43. The activities of secular life now assume an immediately religious meaning and value. See article 16 of the Augsburg Confession (1530): "Mean-

while it (the Gospel) does not dissolve the ties of civil or domestic economy, but strongly enjoins us to maintain them as ordinances of God and in such ordinances to exercise charity, each according to his calling [ein jeder nach seinem Beruf]." And also article 26: "he (the Christian) did chastise his body, not to deserve by that discipline remission of sin, but to have his body in bondage and apt to spiritual things, and to do his calling [einem nach seinem Beruf]." Cited by Weber, *The Protestant Ethic,* 157–158n2.

44. In spite of appearances, the development I seek to define goes directly against the principle put in place at the Diet of Augsburg in 1555: "cujus regio ejus religio." This principle, which fell under the law of the empire and which assured religious peace in Germany for half a century, held that every territory was to have only one confession, that of the prince, while the right of subjects to emigrate was recognized. The application of this principle parceled out the empire just as it prohibited the production of one or several national forms.

45. Montesquieu, *The Spirit of the Laws,* trans. Anne M. Cohler, Basia Carolyn Miller, and Harold Samuel Stone (Cambridge: Cambridge University Press, 1989), 20.7, 343.

46. The Navigation Act of 1651 limited the Dutch fleet's access to English ports.

47. See Cromwell's speech of September 17, 1656, cited by Carl Schmitt, *The Concept of the Political,* trans. George Schwab (Chicago: University of Chicago Press, 2007), 67–68.

48. The play of the "European balance of power" made it such that nations of the same confession were enemies while nations of different confessions were allies. This limited the development of enmity.

49. The destructive obstinacy of the nations, but also the ineptness of the empires. It is an unintelligent injustice to ascribe the sole or principal responsibility for the Great War to the nation form as such when the share of responsibility of the other political form, the empire, was so important. The actors were more "rational" in the measure that they were more completely "national" (and not "imperial").

INDEX

Abel, 276–279

Abraham, 284

Achaeans: emotions expressed by, 38–39; silence of, 38–39; collective action capacity of, 39; in defense, 39; representation of, 41–42; as Greek cities' mother, 42; Agamemnon's plan regarding, 59–60

Achilles, 41–42, 43–47, 57–59

Actions: city enabling, 4; word's disparity with, 7–10; Christianity rendering uncertain motives of, 8; Europeans joining words to, 9; political speech severed from, 11; as necessary, 12; of Greeks, 39–40; noble, 97, 98; for beauty, 246, 247–248

Actors, 267–269

Adam, 280–286

Admiration: as fear component, 156; citizens focused on by, 163–164

Aeneid (Virgil), 233–234

Affliction, 237

Agamemnon, 39, 56–62

Alaric, 230

Alba, 136–137

Alexander the Great, 113–114

Alternation, 10–11

Ancient civic ordering, 66–67

Ancient political science. *See* Greek political science

Animal: divine joined to, 35; reason joining, 35; human as, 134–135, 148–149

Apolitical experience, 23

Apollo, 56–57

Apology (Plato), 46

"Architectonic of Pure Reason" (Kant), 301–302

Aristides, 111

Aristotle, 19–21, 24, 29–30, 52, 64–65, 95–100, 108–112, 119–129, 178, 183–184, 208

Aron, Raymond, 55

Assassination: of Caesar, 165–166, 169–170; of Gracchus, 173

Astronomy, 176–177

Asylums, 233–234

Athens: politicization of, 52–53; Sparta's differences with, 52–53; war in, 52–53; Founding Fathers on, 106–107, 108; Hamilton on, 106–107, 108; Rome and, 106–114; reforms introduced to, 108–109; revolt in, 108–109; tyranny in, 109–112; Golden Age of, 110; as city, 112–113; as autochthonous, 136, 137; Scipio on, 189

Augustine, 228–241, 243–246, 248–261, 267–273, 274–292, 293–295, 304–307, 308–310